THE BASQUE INS

THE
BASQUE
INSURGENTS

ETA, 1952–1980

ROBERT P. CLARK

THE UNIVERSITY OF WISCONSIN PRESS

Published 1984

The University of Wisconsin Press
114 North Murray Street
Madison, Wisconsin 53715

The University of Wisconsin Press, Ltd.
1 Gower Street
London WC1E 6HA, England

First printing

Printed in the United States of America

For LC CIP information see the colophon

ISBN 0-299-09650-5

This book is dedicated to my wife,
for once again showing me the way

Contents

Illustrations

Tables

Preface

In the following pages, I attempt to describe, analyze, and interpret one of the most perplexing of all contemporary European insurgent movements, Euzkadi ta Askatasuna (ETA), which has been fighting for more than twenty years for the independence of the Basque provinces of Spain and France. Before I begin, however, it is important for the reader to know how I came to write this study, how I performed some of the research, and what values (and biases) are reflected in it.

The origins of this book, like those of any book, are complex and distant. My interest in the subject began in 1964 and 1965, when as a doctoral student in Caracas, Venezuela, I married the daughter of an exiled Basque nationalist political and literary man. For several years after my graduation I put aside my academic career while I served in the United States Army. I served one of those years in Vietnam, where I began to sense something of the complexity of violent insurgencies launched against incomparably stronger enemies. Upon my return to the United States and to the life of a college professor, I worked around the edges of this issue, first as an instructor at Texas A & M University, where many of the ROTC cadets wanted my views on the Vietnam experience, and then for six years at the University of Tennessee at Chattanooga, where a valued colleague, Dr. Fouad Moughrabi, helped me to a better understanding of the Palestinian struggle. In 1973, while Spain and the Basques still lived under the Franco regime, my family and I spent a summer in the Basque provinces, during which I gathered much information about the underground. I returned from that stay convinced that there was much about the Basque struggle that needed to be related and explained to an American public largely ignorant of developments there. The first stage in that project was the publication of my more general work, *The Basques: The Franco Years and Beyond*, by the University of Nevada Press in 1979. Of necessity, my treatment of ETA in that book was superficial, restricted primarily to the relating of several key events in the history of the organization but with little in the way of analysis or interpretation. The present volume is intended as a sequel to that earlier work, one which will enable me to deal in detail with subject matter that I had to skim over before.

As I have presented parts of this study to audiences before I had completed the entire manuscript, I have been faced with a recurring question involving the sources of my data. I am asked where the information comes from, how much of it is "secret" or from otherwise exotic sources, and whether or not I have revealed some sort of classified information. I regret to say that, disappointing as it may be to the reader, nearly all of what he or she will read here has been gleaned from the simple reading of newspapers, magazines, and a number of secondary sources. For the historical chapters, I use key secondary works as well as the principal newspaper in the Basque region, *Deia* of Bilbao, which I have read on an almost daily basis since it began publishing in mid-1977. The analytical chapters are based on several sets of data regarding hundreds of ETA events and hundreds of ETA members, all of which have been derived from public sources. It is true that in 1973 I obtained interviews with several ETA members, but from those interviews I have used only their very personal observations about life in the organization.

As far as timing is concerned, I decided at the outset to terminate my narrative and analysis with the end of the year 1980 and to avoid trying to make the book as up to date as possible. Authors of contemporary works always face the dilemma of how to incorporate material on events that have taken place after their manuscripts were completed but before they have emerged as books. In this case, realizing that it would be impossible to do this, I have elected to end my description with the events of 1980 and to restrict my analysis to data gathered through that year. Certainly there were a number of important developments in Basque and Spanish politics that affected ETA during 1981 and 1982: the visit of King Juan Carlos to the Basque region; the death of an *etarra* under torture by the police; the assassination by ETA of an engineer at the Lemóniz nuclear plant; the attempt by members of the Guardia Civil and the Spanish army to overthrow the government; the decision to deploy regular army troops in the Basque country to suppress ETA; the announced ceasefire by ETA(p-m); the temporary lull in ETA killings; the split of ETA(p-m) into two factions; and many others. I am convinced, however, that nothing has happened to change my general interpretation of ETA and its insurgent effort. Discussion of events after 1980 will have to be left to another project.

I conclude this prefatory remark with some observations on the values I hold and how they come through in this study. First of all, as I tried to make clear in *The Basques*, I see no reason why regional autonomy for the Basques is inconsistent with economic prosperity for Spain, and indeed, I believe that Spain would probably be better off with vigorous regional governments, at least in the Basque and Catalan regions, to assist in the difficult tasks of managing a complex industrial society. More to the point, however, I believe that Basques (and all residents of the Basque provinces) should have the right to determine for themselves the form of government under which they want to live, and that since this is one of mankind's most precious rights it is one that certainly may be defended with force if need be. I therefore have no doubt that ETA's resort to violence in the 1960s and 1970s was justified, given the suppressive nature of the Franco regime.

The central normative question, however, is whether or not the change in regime after Franco's death was sufficient to erode the moral justification for ETA's use of violence. Did the Spanish government change sufficiently after 1975 to make ETA an inappropriate tool for securing and defending Basque rights? As the readers of *The Basques* know, I originally answered that question in the affirmative, and I argued in that book that by 1978 ETA had outlived its historical usefulness. I am now not so sure about that. Certainly the transition to a constitutional democracy in Spain was a change to be welcomed by democrats around the world. As far as Basques are concerned, however, not a lot has changed since Franco's days. The regional government has been given little to work with in the way of resources and powers. The machinery of police state suppression was put back into place in the Basque region almost as soon as it was removed, although candor requires we recognize that it was done only under some severe provocation by ETA. But at the level of the individual citizen in the small towns of Guipúzcoa and Vizcaya, the presence of the Spanish state remains almost as oppressive and irritating as it was in 1975. Perhaps the transition to an all-Basque police force for the region will help correct some of that, but more time will have to pass before we can make such a judgment. In short, while I might have believed in 1978 that ETA was no longer either needed or justified in what it was doing to disrupt Basque and Spanish society, by the time of this writing, in 1982, the issue has become much more ambiguous.

So, too, has the question of whether ETA is a terrorist organization. I adhere pretty much to the definition of terrorism as an act designed to influence behavior (by an individual or by a government) by inducing in that person or government a state of fear or terror. Thus I do not see "terrorist" organizations but rather organizations that may use terrorism as a strategy from time to time. World powers, of course, use terrorism all the time to deter their opponents from launching a war against them; police states do likewise to cow their citizens into a state of submission. Insurgent organizations like ETA may also use terrorism, in which case their targets and tactics will be directed at inducing a state of fear or panic among some specific population, either rank-and-file citizens or law-enforcement authorities. As I spell out in detail in chapter 5, ETA has, in my opinion, used what some might call terrorist tactics sparingly, perhaps fewer than half a dozen times in its entire history. The record will show that ETA has not killed innocent bystanders indiscriminately but rather has kept its use of violence restrained and under control. It is for this reason that I choose not to refer to ETA as a terrorist organization. In saying this, however, I want also to make clear that I do not support or defend the use of violence to achieve one's goals. I have seen firsthand the effects of political violence on three continents, and I do not need to be convinced that violence brutalizes the agent as well as the victim. But the definition of an organization as terrorist is as much an empirical question as it is a normative one; and my objective in this book is to examine the historical record to see what it says about the actual behavior of ETA as an insurgent group, regardless of the epithets that may be used to describe it.

In the end, of course, we do not stand much of a chance of being able to damp down the fires of violence in the Basque country until we come to a better understanding of how and why ETA keeps the struggle alive. After all, thousands of ETA members have suffered, and scores have died, in the struggle, with little to show for all their agony. After more than twenty years of intermittent war in the Basque region, we are obligated to ask how ETA keeps alive its commitment to such a far-off ideal, when to do so is so costly. I address this question at the end of this book, but only after considerable description and analysis. For to understand such a phenomenon, one must not hurl accusation and counter-accusation, or engage in stereotyping and labeling. Understanding requires the mustering of evidence and the objective weighing and analysis of that evidence. In approaching the issue in this way, I have chosen to deal with ETA not as a group of lunatics or evil criminals but as young men not very different from many of the readers of this book—young men who have been subjected to an unusual set of pressures that lead them to live a life of violence and hazard. As I wrote this book, and as you read it, we should all try to keep in mind that, confronted with the same pressures, many of us might have followed the same path ETA has chosen. After you finish the book, I think you will agree with me that we are truly fortunate that we have never been put to such a test.

Acknowledgments

No book is ever the product of a single mind, least of all this one. I wish to acknowledge and express my gratitude for the support and assistance of a number of persons and offices, none of whom, of course, is responsible for what is to come:

to the University of Chattanooga Foundation of the University of Tennessee at Chattanooga, for financial support for my trip to the Basque provinces in 1973;

to the Center for Research and Advanced Study of George Mason University, for financial support for my trip to the Basque provinces in 1978 and 1979 and for a research grant that enabled me to spend most of the summer of 1981 working on the data bases that I use in the analytical chapters of the book;

to Stanley Payne of the University of Wisconsin, for his early encouragement of my work;

to William Douglass of the Basque Studies Center at the University of Nevada, Reno, for his strong support of my various projects over the past several years;

to Chris Hewitt, of the University of Maryland–Baltimore County; Charles Foster, of the Atlantic Council; Martin Arostegui, of Risks International; William Farrell, of the Department of Defense; Brian Weinstein, of Howard University; and Peter Merkl, of the University of California, Santa Barbara; all read parts of the original manuscript and gave me valuable suggestions for them;

to Richard Gunther of Ohio State University, for generously sharing with me his data on political disorders in Spain in 1978 and 1979;

to Virginia Berry of George Mason University's Word Processing Center, for typing the manuscript several times;

to my wife and children, who for several years have allowed ETA to absorb so much of my time, energy, and attention, when I should have been paying more attention to them;

and finally, to the dozens of Basques of all political persuasions who welcomed me into their homes and shared with me the special joys and agonies of life in a daily struggle for liberation. I would like nothing more than to list them all here, but I will not, for several reasons. In the case of the members of ETA who consented to be interviewed, I do not even know their names. For the rest, not only would the list run to several pages, but I would not want to suggest that any of them support my interpretation of ETA, which is certainly not the case. To them, I can only say that I have done the best I could to portray ETA accurately and objectively to my English-speaking audience. For now, until I have the opportunity to thank them in person, the book itself will have to suffice as my way of saying that without them I could not have written a single line.

Robert P. Clark

Burke, Virginia
January 1, 1983

A Note on Style

The distinctive Basque language, Euskera, is well known as one of the principal sources of Basque ethnonationalist self-awareness. Perhaps because the use of Euskera has been so directly linked to political expressions of Basque nationalism, or perhaps because of the Franco regime's attempts to suppress the language, the correct use of words, proper names, and spellings in Euskera is frequently debated among Basques with varying degrees of commitment to traditional nationalism. Since there are several possible approaches to using Basque proper names in a work of this sort, a brief note on style seems in order.

First, with regard to place names, nearly every town and city in the Basque provinces has two names, one in Spanish and one in Euskera. Some of these are fairly similar, enough so that they are almost interchangeable, as, for example, Bilbao (Spanish) and Bilbo (Euskera). However, many others are completely different, as, for instance, San Sebastián (Spanish) and Donosti (Euskera), Vitoria (Spanish) and Gasteiz (Euskera), or Pamplona (Spanish) and Iruña (Euskera). In this book I use the Spanish place names, principally because they are much better known to my English-speaking audience.

Second, there is usually much inconsistency in the writing of the proper names of people. One source of confusion is orthographic. In traditional Euskera usage *b* is used instead of the Spanish *v*, *tx* instead of *ch*, *k* instead of *c*; and many words begin with an unaccompanied *i* instead of adding an *h* (as in writing the Basque word for *to die* as *il* instead of *hil*). Thus, for example, a Basque family name written orthographically in Spanish is Echave, while in Euskera it becomes Etxabe. The Basque surname Etxeberria becomes with Spanish orthography Echeverria.

The second source of confusion lies in the controversy over the given names with which an infant is baptized in the Basque region. Most given names in Spanish have a related but distinct Basque equivalent: Juan (in Spanish) is matched by Jon (in Basque); María (in Spanish), by Miren (in Basque); Ignacio (in Spanish), by Iñaki (in Basque). Basques have struggled for generations for the right to give to their newborn the names appropriate to their language. Until the turn of the century, the Catholic church refused to permit them to use names in Euskera for baptism on the grounds that the language was a "pagan" tongue. After that barrier was eliminated, both Spanish and

French government policies prohibited names in Euskera as symptomatic of ethnic separatism. Today, so far as I am aware, Basques in both France and Spain enjoy the right to name their children as they please, but this freedom is relatively new, and many older Basques still carry Spanish names. On the other hand, in the context of renewed Basque ethnonationalist pride after 1975, it is regarded by many parents as a sign of commitment to the politics of Basque nationalism that one give Basque names to offspring.

As a consequence of all this confusion, one frequently finds contradictory references to proper names. Depending on the source, for example, the name of the former ETA leader may be written (in Euskera) Jon Etxabe, (in Spanish) Juan Echave, or (in mistaken mixed form) Juan Etxabe. Obviously, the correct way to write a person's name is the way he or she prefers that it be written. In some cases, as when an individual has written something that carries his name, I can ascertain what that preference might be. In other cases, the vast majority, I can only guess. Therefore, for purposes of consistency, I will always use the Basque name and orthography whenever I do not know a person's preference.

Finally, I should mention my treatment of the *nom de guerre* used by most members of ETA. At one time or another, most *etarras* have used such names either to disguise their identity or as a label that has special meaning within the organization. In some cases, such as that of José Luis Alvarez Enparanza, the nickname became so well known that in fact more people know him by that name (Txillardegi) than by his real name. In most instances, I have written these code names after the family names and enclosed them within quotation marks. If the code name has become the equivalent of a real name and is used alone, it will be written here without quotation marks, however. This usage is somewhat analogous to that of Ernesto Guevara, who upon joining the Cuban Revolution, dropped Ernesto and made Che his real name as an act of joining his new identity to that of the Revolution.

PART ONE

THE HISTORICAL
RECORD

CHAPTER ONE

The Origins of ETA

The year 1980 ended in the Basque country in a painfully familiar manner: with violence, bloodshed, and death.

On the evening of December 11 at about 8:30, two young men entered a bar in the industrial town of Eibar in Guipúzcoa province and shot to death a twenty-eight-year-old police inspector named José Javier Moreno Castro. Apparently Sr. Moreno had been the target of death threats for some time before the attack and had expressed to friends fear for his life. Although he was not Basque himself and had lived in Eibar only about a year and a half, he had a Basque girlfriend, a native of Eibar, who was with him in the bar the night he was shot. The girl, hysterical and covered with her boyfriend's blood, had to be helped from the bar by friends. One day later, in a telephone call to the offices of the Bilbao newspaper *Deia*, a person claiming to be from the Basque insurgent organization Euzkadi ta Askatasuna (militar) claimed responsibility for the attack.[1]

Less than two weeks later, at about 7:15 on the morning of December 30 in the French Basque city of Biarritz, a twenty-nine-year-old member of ETA named José Martín Sagardía Zaldúa was blown up with a 2-kilogram charge of plastic explosive set to detonate when he started his automobile. Like Moreno, Sagardía died in the company of his girlfriend, who was heard by witnesses to scream (in Basque) "Nere gizona il dute!" (literally, "They have killed my man!"). Sagardía was a native of the small Basque town of Usúrbil, in Guipúzcoa, but since 1974 he had lived in France where he had gone to escape arrest by Spanish police. Those responsible for the attack were not known and may never be. There was considerable speculation, however, that Sagardía was killed by the network of Spanish secret police agents and former members of the French Secret Army, the OAS, who allegedly had already killed at least six ETA members or former members in the Basque region of France.[2]

The Moreno and Sagardía killings were the latest in a series of violent attacks that reaches back to 1968, when the first Basque member of ETA and the first Spanish police inspector fell in separate assaults. From 1968 through the end of 1980, more than 450 people died and many hundreds were wounded in one of Europe's most violent struggles. Since the mid-1970s, ETA has ranked along with the Italian Red Brigades and the Irish Republican Army as one of the foremost threats to the stability of Western European governments.

Yet despite the prominence of ETA in Spanish politics over the last several decades and despite the threat that the organization has posed to the future of the Spanish experiment in democracy, ETA remains relatively unknown. A number of highly respected studies of insurgent organizations, some of them encyclopedic in their treatment of other groups, barely mention ETA, and then only in the same paragraphs with the IRA (a group with which ETA shares a number of characteristics).[3] There exists to my knowledge no study of ETA written in English and available to the general public. Much of what has been written in Spanish about the group is polemical. The current press, especially in the United States, is superficial in its treatment of the organization.

This study is an attempt to fill some of these gaps and to achieve several other objectives as well. In one respect, it is an extension of my earlier study of contemporary Basque nationalism,[4] permitting me the luxury of examining in greater detail the highly unusual blend of revolutionary socialism, armed struggle, and Basque ethnicity that characterizes ETA. It is also a statement of how the Basque case exemplifies insurgent ethnic nationalism in modern industrial countries. Finally, I hope with this study to illustrate the distortions and limitations that stem from the unthinking labeling of all insurgent groups as terrorist despite obvious differences in strategies and tactics. And if I may be allowed a personal note, having seen myself the effects of insurgent violence in Asia and Latin America as well as in the Basque country, I hope that this book contributes to hastening the arrival of that day that must eventually come when young men like Moreno and Sagardía no longer die violently, and young women no longer grieve for them.

Ethnic Nationalism and Insurgent Violence in Industrial Society

In spite of its essential unity as a species, the human race has discovered an amazing number of criteria for dividing itself into countless subspecies. Some of these social fault lines are territorial, while others emerge from the unequal distribution of wealth. The Basque case is an example of still another such line: ethnicity.

Ethnic ties bind a person to others by means of subjective identification, not through classification by outsiders.[5] When a sizable number of people feel bound together affectively by shared clusters of values or beliefs, we say that they form an ethnic group. The value or belief clusters that hold such a group together can be based on many different group attributes, including race (those characteristics that are genetically encoded), religion, tribal affiliation, and language. Not infrequently, a number of these characteristics coincide, in which case the lines separating group from group are made even deeper and wider.

Ethnicity finds its expression through institutions created by the group to advance and defend the values its members share, as well as to try to persuade others to accept, or at least tolerate, those values. In many instances, these institutions suffice to give the group adequate protection or self-confidence; but in some cases, such institutional self-protection is not enough, and the ethnic issue is injected into the political system for resolution. Ethnicity, then, becomes ethnic nationalism when an ethnic group begins to perceive itself as a nation, or as a nationality, which deserves and needs its own political institutions for self-protection and self-advancement. At the extreme, such ethnic nationalism leads to demands for the group's own sovereign state.

In the premodern world, before, let us say the Industrial Revolution, ethnic nationalism was not a political issue.[6] A very large number of what we would now call ethnic groups existed, certainly many more than exist today, but it did not occur to them to demand their own political institutions. Because legitimate political power did not emerge from any sort of popular will, it made little difference if the rulers, and their values and institutions, were alien to the ruled. Since the eighteenth-century political revolutions in France and America and the industrial revolution in England, of course, matters have changed radically. For the last two hundred years, one of the most impelling forces in human affairs has been the notion that a group of people has the inherent right to be governed by rulers with the same values as their subjects, to include, among other things, language and religion. When we consider that there are very few cases in today's world in which the boundaries of a single homogeneous ethnic group coincide exactly with those of a sovereign state (Japan, Haiti, and Portugal are probably the only ones of any size), it is obvious that ethnic nationalism has yet to exhaust its potential for mobilizing large numbers of people in political struggle.

One of the reasons why ethnic nationalism is such an explosive force today is that it is a difficult issue for modern political systems to process. There is considerable debate over whether ethnic ties are "real," exist in the empirical sense, or are only "imagined," exist only in the minds of the group members. In either case, ethnicity is nonrational and nonempirical, a state of being that is completely subjective. What matters in ethnic politics is not the empirical reality of a person's condition (per capita income, for example), but what a person feels about that condition. In the language of psychology, affect is much more important than cognition. Since ethnicity depends so much on affective ties, the importance of an ethnic identity is not intrinsic to the group but instead depends upon importance attributed to it by the members (or opponents) of the group. For many people, group identity or loyalty remains unimportant until it is made important by an attack against the group by outsiders. Modern political systems deal relatively easily with issues that have an empirical base, such as the distribution of income or food or houses. When subjective and affective issues like ethnic claims are being dealt with, however, modern politics finds it extremely difficult to satisfy the contending parties, since what is being demanded cannot be easily accommodated within the rational-logical framework of modern technocracies. This aspect of the issues takes on added importance in a case like that of the Basques and the Catalans, who apparently enjoy a higher material standard of living than many other Iberian peoples against whose rule they protest. We would all do well, however, to heed the words of José Ortega y Gasset in his book *Invertebrate Spain*, written before the Spanish Civil War:

> There are few things so indicative of the present state of affairs as the contention of Basques and Catalans that they are peoples "oppressed" by the rest of Spain. The privileged place which they enjoy is so evident as to make this complaint seem grotesque. But anyone more interested in understanding men than in judging them will do well to note that this feeling is sincere. It is all a matter of relativity. A man condemned to live with a woman he does not love will find her caresses as irritating as the rub of chains.[7]

Until relatively recently, most scholars assumed that the combined pressures of industrialization, modernization, and political development (a term frequently taken to be synonymous with centralization of power) would inevitably force a shift in human allegiances away from traditional, ascriptive criteria like ethnicity and toward more modern, achievement-oriented classifications like occupation, social class, and political party.[8] In certain cases, these transformations have seemed to occur almost voluntarily, undertaken by people under the pressures of educational systems, the mass media, and changing social conventions. In other instances, the changes have occurred under the coercion of a modernizing elite that has grown impatient with the obstacles to development represented by premodern allegiances. In either case, there is usually presumed to be considerable tension in industrializing states between ethnic nations, whose existence antedates the industrialization effort, and a modernizing elite that views the ethnic groups as opposed to state-centered modernization. These modernizers frequently try to resolve this tension by destroying the ancient ethnic ties and replacing them with more functional and rational associations, such as class or profession. Not surprisingly, the response to such efforts from the ethnic groups affected is resistance, at times passive and at other times quite violent.

Given our biases about the relative merit of democracy and other political arrangements, it comes as something of a surprise to note the high level of political violence, disorder, and upheaval that have marked the industrial democracies of Western Europe and North America since the 1960s. Why these states should be the scene of so much violence is an important question that cannot be explored here. But the evidence cannot be ignored: the industrial democracies are as vulnerable to the politics of internal war as are the unstable states of the Third World, and probably more so than the dictatorships of the communist world.

Violence, like other kinds of political action, has diverse origins and takes diverse forms. Much of the violence in Western Europe and North America in the last twenty years or so has a class or economic origin; but the most common cause of organized insurgent attacks on the state is ethnic nationalism.[9] Spain since Franco's death shares with many other democracies the unwanted distinction of being the scene of insurgent ethnic forces. In Northern Ireland, sectarian violence has claimed more than 2,200 lives between 1968 and 1982. Elsewhere in Europe and North America, ethnic nationalist groups, while less disruptive, have nevertheless registered their discontent through low-level violence—in Great Britain (the Welsh), France (the Bretons and the Corsicans), Italy (the South Tyroleans), Canada (the Quebecois), and the United States (the Black Panthers, the American Indian Movement).

Whether or not these movements are terrorist or employ terrorism in their struggle is an empirical question. Like so many other such questions, the search for an answer begins with an appropriate definition. Social scientists and security analysts have labored mightily to produce such a definition of terrorism; but the more they labor, the more distance they put between themselves and the people they try to study. I have no desire to contribute still another definition, especially since from my perspective there already exists a perfectly reasonable one, supplied by analyst Brian Jenkins:

> The threat of violence, individual acts of violence, or a campaign of violence designed primarily to instill fear—to terrorize—may be called terrorism. Terrorism is violence for effect: not only, and sometimes not at all, for the effect on the actual victims of the terrorists. In fact, the victim may be totally unrelated to the terrorists' cause. Terrorism is violence aimed at the people watching. Fear is the intended effect, not the by-product, of terrorism. That, at least, distinguishes terrorist tactics from mugging and other forms of violent crime that may terrify but are not terrorism.[10]

The analysis of a complex phenomenon like insurgent violence in the service of ethnic nationalism may begin with accurate definition, but it can proceed only through the amassing and weighing of evidence. It is to this end that the remainder of this book will be devoted. There is no question that the Basque struggle exemplifies ethnic nationalism in modern industrial society and that ETA exemplifies the use of armed assault to further ethnic nationalist aims. One of the objectives of the book is to describe this struggle and to analyze its diverse but discernible patterns. There *is* question as to the degree to which ETA matches the definition of a terrorist group; I hope that by the book's final pages, the reader will be better equipped to make an assessment on that score as well.

The Basques: An Overview

Euzkadi, the name given to their homeland by contemporary Basque nationalists, stretches inland from the eastern end of the Bay of Biscay, following roughly the lines of two intersecting mountain chains, the Pyrenees and the Cantabrian[11] (see map 1.1). Since 1512, when the present boundary between Spain and France became permanent, the Basque country has been divided by an international frontier, a line that follows, approximately, the crest of the Pyrenees and the Bidasoa River as it empties into the Bay. Together, the Basque provinces of Spain and France occupy about 20,600 square kilometers, about the area of the state of New Jersey. The French provinces of Labourd, Basse Navarre, and Soule cover about 3,000 square kilometers; thus about 85 percent of Basque land falls on the Spanish side of the boundary.

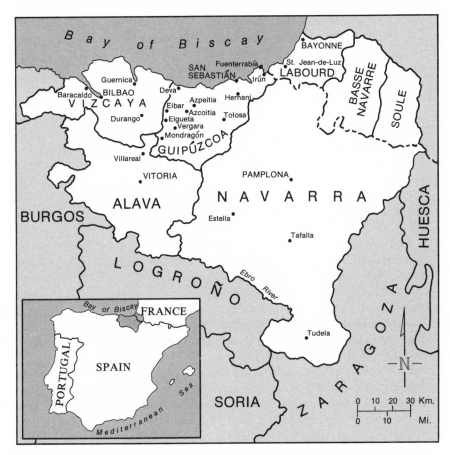

Map 1.1.   The Basque Region.

The setting of Euzkadi, a mixture of coastline, mountains, and plains, has played a central role in shaping Basque social, economic, and political life. To the north of the mountains, on the narrow littoral of the Bay of Biscay, a combination of topography and climate produced an adventurous and daring maritime culture that has given us some of the world's premier explorers. In ancient times, this land was protected by the Cantabrian range on its southern flank. The southern plains, rolling gently southward from the mountains toward the Ebro River, fostered the growth of a cattle and farming culture, one that looked inward to itself and to Spain rather than outward to a world of commerce and exploration. For as long as the Basques have existed as a people, this geographical division has broken the region into two more or less distinct subregions with a vastly different relation to the rest of Spain. To this day, the differences persist and intrude sharply into the political calculations of both Basques and Spaniards. In contemporary political and ethnic terms, the geographic separation manifests itself most clearly in the ambiguous role of the province of Navarra in Basque affairs.

The Basque region of Spain is made up of four provinces: Vizcaya and Guipúzcoa, situated on the coastline and the north slope of the Cantabrian Mountains; and Navarra and Alava, on the south slope of the mountains where the land flows into the Ebro River valley. The region as a whole contains about 17,600 square kilometers, about 3.5 percent of Spain's entire territory. Navarra accounts for more than half of this area, about 10,400 square kilometers. Alava is next largest, with about 3,000 square kilometers. Guipúzcoa and Vizcaya are almost identical in size, with about 2,000 square kilometers each.

In 1976, about 2.7 million people made their homes in the Basque provinces of Spain. This population, which amounted to about 7 percent of the population of Spain, was distributed in a highly unequal manner. The densely populated coastal provinces accounted for more than 70 percent of the total Basque population (Vizcaya, 45 percent, or about 1.2 million; Guipúzcoa, about 26 percent, or about .7 million). The much more sparsely populated interior provinces contained only about three-quarters of a million people combined (Alava, 11 percent of the total, about 245,000; Navarra, 18 percent of the total, nearly 500,000). Of the 500 or so independent townships in these four provinces, only five contain more than 100,000 people, but these five hold more than 40 percent of the total population. At the other end of the spectrum, more than 70 percent of the townships contain fewer than 2,000 people each, but combined they make up only about 8 percent of the total. The significance of midsize towns or cities is relatively slight. Consequently, much of Basque politics has turned on the struggle between the rural areas and small towns on the one hand and the major provincial capital cities of Bilbao (Vizcaya), San Sebastián (Guipúzcoa), Vitoria (Alava), and Pamplona (Navarra) on the other.[12]

By no means are all these persons ethnic Basques. Since the 1950s, about 20,000 to 25,000 Spaniards have migrated each year to the Basque region from other parts of Spain, so that in the middle 1970s only about 65 percent of the population of the Basque provinces was indigenous. Since the great majority of these migrants changed their homes in search of jobs in the relatively more prosperous Basque cities, their arrival has had a differential impact on various segments of Basque society. For one thing, the migrants tend to be largely working class and young adult. For another, they are more heavily concentrated in the provinces where industrialization has more to

offer the job-seeker. In Navarra, where industrialization has proceeded the most slowly, about 80 percent of the population is native-
born. In Alava, Vizcaya, and Guipúzcoa, in contrast, the percentage of
native-born actually drops to about 60 percent. Not surprisingly, non-
Basque Spaniards tend to cluster in working class suburbs of the major
industrial cities, the most significant of which are those on the west
bank of the Nervion River in the largest Basque city, Bilbao. By de-
sign or by accident, non-Basque and Basque workers have regarded
each other with considerable animosity since the former began to
arrive around the turn of the century to work in Basque industry. To
this day, the two groups live in separate neighborhoods for the most
part, have different unions to represent them in labor conflicts, vote
for different political parties, and even, to some degree, speak different languages.[13] It is estimated that as much as 45 percent of the
working class population of the region is non-Basque, and in some
cities or some industries non-Basque workers may constitute a majority.

There are in principle a few genetic characteristics that set Basques
apart from others, such as blood type or the incidence of the Rh-
negative factor in the blood, but these indicators are too diffuse to be
of much importance in establishing the ethnic boundaries of the region. (Although in an earlier time, before medical advances dealt with
the problem, the high incidence of Rh-negative factor was a serious
obstacle to the marriage of Basque women to non-Basque men with
Rh positive blood.) The Basque language, Euskera, on the other hand,
is so complex and so little spoken that it has come to be the most
significant distinguishing feature of Basque ethnicity. Use of the language is highly uneven throughout the region. According to a study
done in the early 1970s, slightly less than 20 percent of the region's
population can speak Euskera, although that percentage increases to
nearly 30 if one considers only the indigenous population.[14] Use of
Euskera tends to be highly concentrated in Guipúzcoa (about 44 percent of the total population, 68 percent of the indigenous population)
and Vizcaya (13 and 22 percent, respectively), with relatively few
Euskera-speakers in Navarra and Alava. Nearly 92 percent of all Euskera-speakers live in either Guipúzcoa or Vizcaya. In 1977, about 9
percent of the school-age children in the region attended *ikastolas*,
schools where all instruction is in Euskera. About 60 percent of the
enrollment was in Guipúzcoa, about 20 percent in Vizcaya, and the
remainder divided equally between Alava and Navarra.[15] Use of Euskera tends to be highly correlated with political preference. In the
four post-Franco elections held in the Basque provinces between
1977 and 1980, the party that has symbolized Basque nationalism

since the turn of the century, the Basque Nationalist Party (Partido Nacionalista Vasco, or PNV) won between 35 and 43 percent of the vote in voting districts where use of Euskera was above the average. In those districts (outside Navarra) where the language is little used, the PNV share of the vote was seven to twelve percentage points less.[16] Perhaps because the use of Euskera is so strongly associated with Basque ethnicity, the Basques' freedom to use and teach the language has been a major source of friction with Madrid for several generations. Overt Spanish policies to discourage use of the language date from the late decades of the nineteenth century. The Franco era was marked by its ferocious repression, and for many years, until 1967, it was against the law to teach the language in schools. Since the advent of Spain's new constitution and the restoration of parliamentary democracy, the role of the regional languages, of which Euskera is the most complex and unusual, is now protected, although the degree to which Madrid will aid in its teaching and propagation (as in public support for ikastolas or Basque-language television programs) remained in doubt in the early 1980s.

Several recent surveys give us a rather clear picture of the extent of Basque ethnic consciousness as opposed to a feeling of Spanish nationalism in the Basque region. A 1975 study of Spanish regions by sociologist Salustiano del Campo and his associates found that in the Basque provinces (defined to exclude Navarra) about 32 percent of the respondents felt their first loyalty to be to their region, compared with about 41 percent who reported their first loyalty to be to Spain.[17] A much more recent survey done in 1979 by American political scientist Richard Gunther reports that when asked to define themselves as members of a particular national group, 34 percent of the respondents of the Basque provinces (again excluding Navarra) described themselves as Basque exclusively, and another 10 percent said more Basque than Spanish. Only 24 percent described themselves as Spanish, and another 3 percent as more Spanish than Basque.[18] The political expression of Basque ethnicity shows somewhat similar levels of ethnonationalism among Basque voters. If we consider as a whole the vote cast for all ethnic Basque parties, combining the vote for the moderate PNV with that for the more intransigent Basque socialist parties, we see that the percentage has climbed steadily upward, from about 35 percent in the 1977 parliamentary elections, to 44 percent in the 1979 parliamentary elections, to 55 percent in the 1979 municipal council elections, to more than 63 percent in the 1980 elections for the newly created autonomous Basque parliament.[19]

The Basque culture is one of Europe's truly ancient cultures.[20] Cave paintings and other remnants of the civilization suggest that industrial growth would influence the shape of Basque nationalist politics. Somewhat the same kind of development took place after World War II, during what many people called the "Spanish economic miracle."

Spain in the 1940s was still an underdeveloped country, with a per capita gross national product of less than $500 and a work force that was still 60 percent agricultural. Added to this backwardness were the destruction of the country during the Civil War and the economic stresses caused by World War II and its aftermath. Whether General Franco actually wanted large-scale industrial development or not, and the evidence is cloudy on this point, the fact remains that Spain desperately needed to industrialize in order to regain its stature in the world and to maintain the Franco government in power at home.

Franco's problem, however, was that he headed a complex coalition of interests, individuals, and institutions that agreed upon little except their fear of the alternative should Franco not prevail in his effort to restore order and national unity. By no means were the coalition partners in accord as to the need for industrial development. Some, like the moderate technocrats of the Catholic lay order Opus Dei, advocated a neoliberal capitalist bourgeois reform of the country's archaic economy to open it up to the fresh winds of liberalism and competition. Others, however, like the landed aristocracy from southern Spain, opposed economic development and the social changes that it would bring.

Franco's solution to this dilemma was to guide Spain through a series of economic and social changes that had the effect of modernizing the country's industry while leaving intact much of the traditional, precapitalist structure of agrarian Spain. During the 1950s, the Spanish economy grew at the rate of 3.5 percent per year. During the 1960s, manufacturing grew at three times that rate. In the 1960s, Spain had the fastest growing economy in Europe, second only to Japan among the industrialized countries outside the Soviet bloc. By 1978, Spain had a per capita GNP of $3,470 and an annual growth rate of about 5 percent. Between 1960 and 1978 the share of GNP in agriculture declined from 21 to 9 percent, a sure sign of industrial growth. Yet, even into the 1970s, only 3.5 percent of all farm owners held 61 percent of all farm land, a figure more nearly resembling El Salvador or Brazil than West Germany or Great Britain.

In one respect, General Franco was remarkably lucky. There were several sources of financial support and foreign exchange that he could tap outside Spain. One such source was the European and American tourists who flocked to Spain each year, bringing with them more than $10 billion in foreign currency from 1961 to 1970. Another was the overseas remittances from Spanish workers who had migrated to Germany, Switzerland, and France in search of jobs, and who sent home regularly their (in Spanish terms) bountiful pay checks. From 1960 to 1970, these remittances totaled more than $3.2 billion. A third source was the United States government, which sent millions of dollars in economic and military aid to Spain in return for the use of air and naval bases on Spanish soil.

These foreign sources of assistance would not have been enough to support Spanish industrialization, however, had it not been for Franco's industrial strategy. In brief, Franco sought to shift the burden of development onto the two major sectors of Spanish society that were not represented in his governing coalition: the country's industrial proletariat and the already industrialized Basque and Catalan regions. The effect was to place a double burden on the Basque working class, a burden as both workers and Basques.

The specifics of Spain's industrial development strategy were simple, even if, to Basque workers, they were contradictory in their effects. The first half of the strategy was to increase industrial production in those areas that already had an industrial base. Workers from poor regions were attracted to the industrial provinces by the lure of newly created jobs, solving thereby the dual problems of insufficient labor in the north and restive unemployed agricultural laborers in the south. The second half of the strategy called for skewing public investment toward the poor regions to increase their industrial potential, even if to do so meant denying public investment resources to the Basques and Catalans. Public investment in social infrastructure (schools, hospitals, roads, housing, parks, and so forth) and in industrial parks would spur growth in formerly poor regions, and southern workers would stay home to find jobs locally.

The effects of this dual policy were disastrous for Basque workers. On the one hand, Basque industry was pushed for increased production, and thousands of Spanish workers were attracted into the Basque region to compete with Basques for scarce employment. At the same time, the Basques were denied the resources needed to deal with the ills of industrial growth: pollution (both air and water), cramped housing, urban decay, congested transportation facilities, inadequate schools and hospitals, and many others.

The results of Spanish industrial policy in the Basque provinces have been decidedly negative. Since the late 1970s, the Basque region has been wracked by political upheaval, capital flight, high unemployment, a considerable degree of civil disorder, and a decline in economic growth.[26] From 1975 to 1977, Guipúzcoa ranked forty-eighth among the fifty Spanish provinces in rate of growth of per capita income and by 1979 had dropped from third to sixth place (out of fifty provinces) in per capita income itself. Vizcaya was fiftieth among the fifty provinces in rate of growth, and had slipped by 1979 from its customary first place to ninth place in per capita income. Alava and Navarra, relatively untouched by political disorder, had rather good economic fortune. Unemployment was another serious problem facing the Basque economy. From a base of almost full employment (an unemployment rate of 0.5 percent in 1960, 1 percent in 1973), the number out of work began to climb sharply after Franco's death to reach 5 percent in 1977, 11.2 percent in 1978, and 17 percent in 1979. The estimated rate was 14.8 percent as of March 31, 1980, compared with an unofficial rate of about 10 percent in Spain generally. Again, Guipúzcoa (with a rate of 18.6 percent in late 1979) and Vizcaya (17.2 percent) were the provinces hardest hit by the economic crisis.

Through the first several years of the 1980s, the economic crisis continued unabated in the Basque provinces.[27] In 1978 and 1979, the gross domestic product of the Basque provinces had dropped 4.5 percent annually; in 1980 and 1981, the decline slowed somewhat, to only 2 percent each year. Thus in only four years the Basque economy had declined some 13 percent. In 1980, steel consumption dropped 5 percent, the use of electric energy in industry 3.2 percent, cement consumption 18 percent, and new housing construction 8.5 percent. Despite an inflation rate between 15 and 16 percent each year, unemployment continued to rise dramatically. In its year-end report for 1980, the Bilbao Chamber of Commerce said that the year had been the worst in memory for Vizcaya's economy. Unemployment rose 36 percent during the year in Vizcaya, and persons out of work were added to the rolls at the rate of more than 1,000 per month. The Basque government estimated the number out of work in the three provinces under their jurisdiction (Alava, Guipúzcoa, and Vizcaya) at some 200,000, or about 22 percent of the economically active population. The official Spanish government figures for 1980 were bad enough, at 11 percent, but that figure rose during 1981 to nearly 17 percent. The Basque government's economic office estimated that between 1976 and 1981 the region had lost some 110,000 jobs. The consequence was a decline in the Basque population, as people left the area looking for employment. In 1980 alone, an estimated 10,000 persons moved away from the Basque region in search of work, a dramatic reversal of the trend of ten years earlier, when 20,000 to 25,000 migrated annually to the region from other parts of Spain.

According to the Spanish government's census figures, during the five-year period from 1975 to 1980, Vizcaya and Guipúzcoa provinces together lost 71,000 of their population.

The consequence of all this was the radicalization of the Basque working class. This was an entirely new phenomenon in Basque and Spanish politics, and the traditional political organizations found themselves unable to respond to the challenge. The PNV continued to focus its attention on political and cultural matters. Because of their exclusively class focus, Spanish socialists and communists were unable to deal with the ethnic demands of Basque workers. Not surprisingly, then, there emerged an entirely new movement, one centered on revolutionary socialism blended with intransigent Basque ethnicity.

The Roots of ETA: 1939–59

The decade or so following the surrender of Basque forces and the flight to exile of the Basque government in the summer of 1937 was a cruel and terrible time for the Basques. Yet for a while, until the early 1950s, many Basques continued to hope for, and believe in, the prompt demise of the Franco regime and a restoration of the Republic and of an autonomous Basque government. When these hopes were dashed in 1951, frustration and despair replaced hope and anticipation in the minds of many Basques, especially the youth of the region. It was in this context that ETA was born, and it is this setting that must be understood if one is to appreciate how and why ETA came to be.

When the bulk of the Basque military forces surrendered in neighboring Santander province and the Basque government fled into exile (first to Barcelona and subsequently to Paris) in August 1937, there was no "Basque Resistance" to speak of, only the shattered remnants of the Basque Nationalist Party and fragments of several labor unions still operating in the region. Within ten years, however, the basic elements of a resistance organization were in place. The Basque government was installed in Paris. The Basque Nationalist Party had rebuilt and was operating in the anti-Franco underground. The Basque and non-Basque labor unions were gradually restoring their networks of contacts within the working sectors of Basque society.

The Basque Resistance (the informal title for what was officially called the Junta de Resistencia, the Resistance Committee—the group charged with coordinating all underground activities in the Basque region of Spain) was forged from a number of different elements.[28]

walkout in Barcelona. By April, strike fever had spread to the Basque country.

For the Resistance Committee, the unrest was both an opportunity and a challenge. The discontent of the workers on economic grounds offered an excellent chance to express political opposition as well, and the committee immediately took steps to halt all economic activity in Vizcaya and Guipúzcoa. Internally, however, the committee was split by dissent from the unions' representatives, who complained that the workers were always the ones asked to demonstrate for Basque political causes and that the professional and bourgeois classes remained on the sidelines as onlookers. Nevertheless the strike calls went forth, setting April 23 as the day to begin. On that day, about a quarter of a million workers representing nearly all the labor force of Vizcaya and Guipúzcoa began a work stoppage designed to last two days. Again, government repression was harsh. Then, to the surprise of the Resistance Committee, the strike spread spontaneously to Alava and Navarra. In Pamplona, 35,000 workers walked off their jobs. Housewives marched in protest over food prices, and police resorted to armed force to put down the demonstrations. But as in 1947, other regions of Spain failed to rise in support of the Basques and Catalans. The Resistance Committee did not follow up on the emotional atmosphere created by the strike, and the Basque president, José Antonio Aguirre, issued a call from Paris asking the workers to return to their jobs. Gradually the strike fever subsided and the Basque provinces became quiet again. It would be the last mass expression of political discontent for many years.

The 1951 Bilbao strike was the final act of the Resistance Committee. The repression imposed from Madrid was so intense that the network of clandestine cells within Spain was left in ruins. Increasingly, after 1951, leadership roles in the Resistance passed into the hands of much younger and less experienced Basques, young men who had enthusiasm for the cause but lacked the organizational experience and personal contacts of the older Civil War generation. In addition, the Western democracies completely withdrew their aid to the Basque government and to the Spanish Republicans in exile in Mexico. For more than five years, President Aguirre and the Basque government had depended heavily on assurances from the United States, France, and Great Britain that they would pressure Franco so hard that his regime would either liberalize or fall. In an effort to cooperate with the Western powers, the Basque government expelled the communist members from its cabinet of councilors and disbanded groups of guerrilla fighters who were being trained on the French side of the Pyrenees to be sent into Spain to assist the Resistance Committee. Nevertheless, as the 1940s wore on and turned into the 1950s and the Cold War heated up in Korea and Greece, the United States lost interest in fighting Franco and in supporting his opponents. Other Western leaders agreed. In July 1951, American Admiral Forrest P. Sherman, Chief of Naval Operations, arrived in Madrid to begin negotiations that would lead to the U.S.-Spain bases agreement. On July 26, Secretary of State Dean Acheson released a credit of $100 million to shore up the Spanish economy. The other Western powers followed suit. In Paris, the French government expelled the Basque government-in-exile from its magnificent building on Avenue Marceau and turned the building over to the Spanish Embassy for its use. Without the support of any outside power and with its Spanish network virtually destroyed by pressure from Madrid, the Basque government quietly withdrew the institutional apparatus of the Resistance, and the heroic phase of the post–Civil War period had come to an end. It was a hard pill to swallow for many young people in the Basque country.[30]

In the immediate postwar period, there were several attempts to mobilize the youth of the Basque country and to turn their restiveness toward organized political action. In December 1945, the Basque Nationalist Party launched a renovated version of its pre–Civil War youth wing, known as Euzko Gaztedi (Basque Youth) or by its initials EG. A decade later, in 1956, key elements of EG carried the organization across the border into Spain to establish the group clandestinely as a part of the Resistance, and it became known as Euzko Gaztedi del Interior, or EGI, for short. Throughout the Franco years and even up to this writing, EG (or EGI, as one prefers) has remained the principal link between the Basque Nationalist Party and the youth of the region.[31]

Euzko Gaztedi was not the only sign of the emergence of Basque youth in the late 1940s. A much more direct forerunner of ETA was the group known as Euzko Ikasle Alkartasuna (EIA), or Society of Basque Students. This organization was of an international nature and had its headquarters in Leiden, The Netherlands. While in theory it was apolitical, in practice its members in the Basque country tended to be sympathetic to the cause of Basque nationalism if not actually independence. The group held its first meeting in the Basque country in September 1947, in a jai alai court in the French town of St.-Jean-de-Luz. In addition to passing resolutions of support for the actions of their members in Spain to preserve Basque language and culture, they also elected an executive committee to manage the affairs of the organization in the Basque region of France. This step led almost inevitably to the transfer of propaganda and literary activities to the

Spanish side of the border. The group began to publish and distribute clandestine magazines and journals throughout Vizcaya and Guipúzcoa, most of them were written in Basque. The young people who directed the effort were not experienced in the ways of a clandestine resistance group, however, and in 1950, following a breach in their security, virtually the entire leadership of the organization were arrested and sent either to prison or into exile. Some from this group later formed the nucleus of ETA. Their failure to survive in the underground had taught them a valuable lesson about the imperatives of resistance activity. As one of them, José Luis Alvarez Enparanza, put it later, "The ease with which we were arrested and the consequences of that roundup—the almost total destruction of the organization—called to our attention what it meant to act clandestinely, and it made it clear to us that serious and continuous work required that we improve our security standards, an idea that would have important consequences in the future."[32]

In 1952, a small group of young men began to meet in Bilbao to discuss politics and to improve their understanding of contemporary affairs.[33] They came from Vizcaya and Guipúzcoa and were the offspring of rather well-to-do Basque nationalist families. They had been brought together by their university studies at Deusto University in Bilbao, by their common experiences (several of them had been involved in the organizing activities mentioned in the previous paragraph), and by their frustration at the passiveness of the PNV in the struggle against Franco. There were in these early days no more than six or seven in the group. Four of them were destined to become leaders in ETA: José Manuel Aguirre, José María Benito del Valle, Julen Madariaga, and José Luis Alvarez Enparanza "Txillardegi." As a part of their self-instruction, they prepared mimeographed copies of essays and discussion papers that they passed from member to member. These papers soon became regularized as a newsletter, to which they gave the title (in Basque) *Ekin*, which means approximately "to do" or "to make." From this newsletter the group soon began to be called Ekin. (At least one writer suggests that the idea for the name came from Editorial Ekin, the name of a Buenos Aires publishing company that had specialized in Basque nationalist books for many years.)[34]

From the very beginning, the Ekin study group disagreed with the PNV on two important matters: the use of Euskera and the link between the return of the Republic and the restoration of Basque autonomy.[35] Ekin advocated making Euskera the sole official language of a new independent Basque republic, a position the PNV thought incredibly utopian, given the scant use of the language even in ethnic Basque areas, not to speak of areas, like western Vizcaya, where the language had disappeared. The two groups also disagreed over the timing of the separation of Euzkadi from Spain. The PNV claimed that it had assurances from all the important parties of the Republic for the automatic restoration of the 1936 Statute of Autonomy as soon as Franco had been overthrown and the Republic restored. In return, the PNV agreed not to seek any further separation from Spain. Ekin disagreed sharply with this idea on the grounds that the Basques had never received any concessions from Madrid without fighting for them and that the PNV deal would prove to be a betrayal of Basque interests. Even in these early days, it was clear that the Ekin youth stood for the creation of a Basque state that would be more intransigent and more demanding than any envisioned by the PNV and that Ekin wanted this state to come into being regardless of what transpired in Madrid.

For more than a year Ekin worked in strict secrecy. The group remained tiny and self-contained. Then during the 1952–53 school year at Deusto, the founders began to recruit new members. In their recruiting, they attracted two new groups of members, some of whom lived in Guipúzcoa. In 1953, Ekin opened new contacts with EGI cells, particularly in Guipúzcoa, that led to Ekin-PNV discussions about the possibility of merging the organizations. (It should be noted that at this point, although Ekin did not necessarily agree with the PNV approach on policy issues, it still held the older leaders in great respect for their role in the struggle over the past two generations. Personal animosity did not appear until some years later.)

For four years, until 1956, Ekin maintained its independent status. Talks were held with PNV and EGI leaders, who held to their original position that Ekin should dissolve and have its members (whose number was steadily increasing) join EGI in a show of unity and respect for tradition. Finally, in 1956, the leaders of Ekin conceded the point and fused the organization with EGI. Ekin officially ceased to exist.

The marriage of convenience was strained from the very beginning. In 1957, three former Ekin members traveled to Paris for the group's first meeting with Basque government officials, including Vice President Jesús María de Leizaola. The meeting was a catastrophe from the point of view of the youths, who saw in Leizaola a dreamy idealist who confided too much in the Spanish democratic parties.[36] That same year, Ekin members now working through EGI wrote a strongly worded negative letter to the governing body of the PNV in Guipúzcoa, the Gipuzko Buru Batzar, accusing the PNV in Guipúzcoa of refusing to aid EGI and of being lethargic. When the PNV demanded to know the names of the authors of the letter, EGI refused to reveal them.[37]

By early 1958, the strains were beyond the ability of EGI to resolve. In the spring, the PNV leadership of Vizcaya formally requested the expulsion of Benito del Valle from the organization and official apologies from EGI of Vizcaya for criticisms they had made of the party. These demands were denied by the former Ekin leaders, and several of them, including Txillardegi, went once more to Paris, this time to see President Aguirre for a solution to the impasse. Although the president appeared willing to compromise, the old guard faction of the party in Vizcaya demanded that the youths accept the authority of the PNV before they could be reinstated. From that point onward through 1958 there were two EGI organizations: one made up of Ekin and a number of EGI militants who had decided to leave the PNV, and the other of EGI members who had chosen to remain within the party.

The division of EGI into two rival organizations lasted only about one year. On July 31, 1959, a new organization came into existence: Euzkadi ta Askatasuna, or Euzkadi and Freedom. In a short time its initials, ETA, began to appear spray-painted on walls in the larger Basque cities. In a few more years, ETA would have a major impact on Basque and Spanish politics. Observers inclined to look for symbolism saw much in the choice of a date for the founding of the new organization. July 31, 1959, was the sixty-fourth anniversary of the founding of the Basque Nationalist Party by Sabino de Arana y Goiri.

CHAPTER TWO

The Ideological Struggle within ETA: 1959–70

For more than the first decade of its life, ETA's overriding organizational problem involved a fierce struggle among the proponents of three relatively distinct sets of ideological principles. To the outsider, the struggle often seemed mired in complex rhetorical argument over obscure points of marxist or ethnic theory. Dozens of pamphlets and books addressed the issues. Heated debate was carried on at all levels, from the assembly down to the village cell. The objective of the struggle was effective control of ETA and the consequent legitimacy conveyed by its name, which carried considerable symbolic weight. ETA was not just another Basque nationalist organization. After the mid-1960s, it was perceived by many young Basques as the only real alternative to the Basque Nationalist Party, the PNV. Moreover, in the tense environment of the anti-Franco underground, clandestine groups could not enjoy the luxury of pluralism. The ideological tenets that drove ETA had to be sharply focused and uncompromising if they were to mobilize young Basques and maintain their morale over long periods of hardship. None of the protagonists in the ideological debate could afford to admit that the fine points over which they were arguing were unimportant. Each debate had to be treated as an ultimate battle. For these reasons, the ideological struggles (in the plural, for there were in fact several that overlapped one another in both time and personalities) came to define the identity and indeed the very reason for ETA's existence.*

ETA and Ideology: The Issues and Their Origins

ETA's ideological debates focused on a set of polarized issues around which groups of ETA members rallied according to their personal, cultural, and class affinities. The links and relations among

---

*The reader will find the lists of ETA members, political terms and organizations, and events in the history of ETA contained in the appendices a useful reference in the review of ETA history that follows.

these issues defy easy description. Some had to do with strategic or tactical choices, while others focused on ultimate philosophical or even metaphysical concepts such as the relationship among race, language, and ethnicity. Some issues were relatively new and emerged through the 1960s as the debates took form; others were conflicts of long standing that had sharply divided Basques from one another as long ago as the nineteenth century. These issues overlapped one another, and only occasionally did the dividing lines formed on one issue carry over to coincide with those stimulated by others. The ETA membership was fragmented into many competing factions by these issues, and eventually the organization would be split into several new subgroups by their force. In sum, the issues shared relatively few common features: they defined the enemy; they described the nature of the threat emanating from that enemy; and they prescribed the correct tactics and strategies to be followed to meet that threat and defeat the enemy.[1]

In addition to the debates carried on in countless meetings of ETA leaders and ordinary members, the ideological struggles were conducted in print. First of all, there were pamphlets, books, journal and newspaper articles, and speeches appearing at irregular intervals, sometimes with the organization's seal of approval, at other times simply as one person's opinion on an important matter. (See table 2.1 for a description of the key documents in this set.) In addition to these, there were the regular publications of ETA and of the groups that split off from the parent organization through the course of the decade. From the beginning, ETA published a journal or magazine called *Zutik* (meaning, approximately, "on our feet" or "standing"), which came out periodically through the decade. Several versions of the magazine were published, including one that contained extra notes or news items and another that was published from ETA's branch office in Caracas. Counting all of its various versions, perhaps as many as two hundred or more separate editions of *Zutik* appeared between 1960 and 1967. The pages of the journal were used to express the ideas and opinions of factions within ETA, and control of the magazine came to be highly prized in the infighting that went on over the years. The various factions of ETA became so accustomed to using the journal for their debates that when they split off from the parent organization they usually established a counterpart journal to keep up the flow of words and ideas.

A number of major issues that dominated the ETA debate had been important to Basque nationalists since the turn of the century. From the earliest years of their movement, Basque nationalists had argued with one another over three key questions: intransigence versus coop-

Table 2.1 *Principal Documents in the Ideological Development of ETA in the 1960s*

DATE	TITLE	AUTHOR	SOURCES AND COMMENTS
October 1961	Untitled speech to Basque community in Paris	José Luis Alvarez Enparanza "Txillardegi"	Beltza, *El nacionalismo vasco en el exilio, 1937–60* (San Sebastián: Editorial Txertoa, 1977), pp. 151–58. Expression of unrest of Basque youth. Called for creation of patriotic front.
May 1962	*Principios de ETA*	First Assembly	*Documentos* (San Sebastián: Hordago, 1979), 1:525–28; Beltza, pp. 96–99. First complete statement of ETA's ideological principles.
1962–63	*Vasconia: Estudio dialéctico de una nacionalidad*	Federico Krutwig (a) Fernando Sarrailh de Ihartza	Issued in two editions: Buenos Aires: Ediciones Norbait, 1963; San Sebastián: Ediciones Vascas, 1979. See also *Documentos*, 3:75–112; Beltza, p. 93; Gurutz Jáuregui Bereciartu, *Ideología y estrategia política de ETA: Análisis de su evolución entre 1959 y 1968* (Madrid: Siglo Veintiuno, 1981), 215–25. First statement of third-world position and of principles of revolutionary war.
January 1964	*Manifiesto de ETA al pueblo vasco*	ETA Executive Committee	*Documentos*, 3:199–202; José Mari Garmendia, *Historia de ETA*, 2 vols. (San Sebastián: L. Haranburu, 1979), 1:283–87. First open call to people to join struggle.
1963–64	*La insurrección en Euskadi*	Third Assembly	*Documentos*, 3:129–50; Jáuregui, pp. 225–37. Document first used as ETA training manual, later adopted as policy by Third Assembly. Sets forth basic principles for conduct of guerrilla struggle.

1964–65	*Carta abierta de ETA a los intelectuales vascos*	Drafted by Third Assembly, published 1964, approved 1965 by Fourth Assembly	*Documentos*, 3:507–18; Garmendia, 1:151–61, 287–303; Jáuregui, 253–63. Defined ETA as "a revolutionary Basque movement for national liberation."
1965	*Bases teóricas de la guerra revolucionaria*	José Luis Zalbide, approved by Fourth Assembly	Garmendia, 1:168–79. ETA statement on principles of guerrilla warfare.
1965–66	*Informes políticos a la dirección de ETA*	Txillardegi	*Documentos*, 4:423–29; Garmendia, 1:201–7, 334–50. Response from Txillardegi to attempt by Iturrioz to take over the organization.
1965	*La cuestión vasca* and *El nacionalismo revolucionario*	Two separate works, both written by Federico Krutwig	Garmendia, 1:207–15; Jáuregui, chap. 13. Works presented to the Fifth Assembly to support the "internal colonialism" thesis.
1966	*Ideología oficial de ETA*	Approved by Fifth Assembly	*Documentos*, 5:173–89; Garmendia, 2:187–91. Official version of resolutions approved by Fifth Assembly. ETA is defined as "a Basque socialist movement for national liberation."
1968	*Hacia una estrategia revolucionaria vasca*	José Luis Zalbide (a) K. de Zunbeltz	*Documentos*, 8:116–69; Jáuregui, pp. 417–18 and elsewhere. Placed Basque struggle in category of wars against imperialism.

eration with Madrid; "going it alone" versus joining with others for political purposes; and independence versus autonomy. The PNV adopted the moderate position on these issues. Thus they argued for cooperation with the Spanish government and for joining with like-minded Spanish political parties (especially those of a Christian Democratic orientation) for pragmatic purposes. The PNV also argued that regional autonomy within a broader Spanish political framework was the greatest degree of separation Basques could realistically hope to attain. To advocate something more extreme not only was utopian but actually did a disservice to Basques and Spaniards by forcing them into postures of antagonism and hostility over something that was impossible to achieve. Other Basque political groups of the time, such as Aberri and Jagi-Jagi, advocated the most intransigent of the three positions. They argued that, first, conciliation and cooperation would only encourage Spain to oppress the Basques even more, and that only by being intransigent could they achieve any concessions from Madrid; second, that since no Spanish party could ever be trusted to be sympathetic to Basque demands, there was no point in entering into any sort of alliance with them—such alliances would end inevitably in betrayal of the Basque cause; and finally, that independence and not autonomy should be the long-term objective of Basque nationalists. Even if it were true that real independence was impossible to attain, these groups claimed, only by demanding independence could they force Madrid to concede limited gains through some sort of regional autonomy arrangement. Since the Spanish government would grant only half of what the Basques asked for, the Basques should demand twice as much as they really thought they could obtain.[2]

Much of the ETA debate had been heard before in Basque nationalist circles, but there was a new element that involved the clash between ethnicity and class. Broken down into its constituent parts, this new issue involved four key subissues: (a) ethnicity versus class as an organizing principle for the revolution; (b) nationalism versus socialism as a guiding ideology; (c) the conduct of the struggle based solely on ethnic Basques versus integrating non-Basque immigrants in the conflict; and (d) the use of "direct action" or "activism" (euphemisms for insurgent violence) versus nonviolent organizing among the masses of industrial workers. Factions within ETA mixed these issues together in myriad formulas and in ways that at times defied logic. At the risk of oversimplification, we can identify three separate strands in the debates.

The earliest ideological theme to appear in ETA's pronouncements put greatest emphasis on the ethnic or cultural aspect of the struggle for Basque freedom. The advocates of this approach, of whom the best known was José Luis Alvarez Enparanza "Txillardegi," held that language was the principal or even the sole valid definition of a nation. The Basques were defined as unique by their ethnicity, which in turn was a product of their language. Were Euskera to disappear, the Basques would disappear as a nation. The only way to save Euskera and the Basque nation was to establish a sovereign state based on the Basque language and dedicated to its preservation and propagation. In the short run, this approach suggested that ETA should support a Basque national front composed of all ethnic Basque political groups regardless of their social class. Cooperation with groups outside Euzkadi was unnecessary and undesirable and probably would damage the movement severely. The only aspect of the linguistic approach that dealt with class at all was its advocacy of humanistic socialism, to give each social class the benefits of Basque culture (especially, but not exclusively, in Euskera). The adherents of this ideology were called, variously, "ethnolinguists," "culturalists," or "nationalist workers."

In sharp contrast to the linguists were those who argued that social class was more important than ethnicity in the struggle to free the Basque people. According to this point of view, very much influenced by marxist writings of the European New Left of the early 1960s, what mattered most to the Basques was the liberation of their working class in company with that of workers in all parts of Spain. Basque workers were as oppressed by the Basque industrial oligarchy as they were by the industrial oligarchies of Spain, Britain, and the United States. Just because an industrialist had a Basque family name and spoke Euskera did not make him an ally of Basque workers. On the contrary, he was an even more dangerous enemy because his threat to the workers would be covered over by his Basque ethnicity (what Marxists would call "a clouded consciousness"). True liberation of the Basque working class could occur only in alliance with Spanish workers, who would struggle against their class oppressors at the same time. The most notable advocate of this approach was Paco Iturrioz, who headed ETA's Political Office during the mid 1960s. The group generally paid little attention to the Basque language and culture, and instead tried to organize people in the factories and working class suburbs regardless of whether or not they were Basque. Supporters of the class-based approach were attacked on several grounds. First, because they advocated ties with Spanish political groups, they were labeled *españolista*, one of the worst epithets in the ETA lexicon. At the same time, being rather conventional marxists, they believed in the inevitability of social revolution once the economic and environmental conditions had reached the point where the workers would understand the true nature of their subjugation. At that point, the workers would rise more or less spontaneously. To seek to hurry that event by the armed action of small groups was adventurism and doomed to failure because the masses would not rise to support them. For this belief they were labeled too cautious and defeatist. One also frequently finds references to this group as "trotskyites," although what they borrowed from Trotsky is not at all clear.

The third important theme in the ideological struggle was very much influenced by events in the Third World during the 1960s, so its proponents came to be called "third-worldists" (*tercermundistas*). The leading spokesman for this approach was the son of a German industrialist living in Bilbao named Federico Krutwig Sagredo, although there were also a number of old Ekin members in this group. The principal ideas of this approach were derived from the various struggles in the Third World in the 1960s against Western European and American colonialism. The victories of the Algerian and Vietnamese revolutions against France and the Cuban triumph against the United States were held up as the correct models, and Frantz Fanon was the intellectual source for this approach. The tercermundistas believed Euzkadi was suffering from a colonial relationship just as surely as had Algeria or Vietnam under the French. In this case, the imperialist power, Spain, was closer to the colony and had penetrated its society and culture to a greater degree than was true in the other cases. But Euzkadi was a Spanish colony all the same. The only way to liberate the Basques was to wage a war of national liberation, a revolutionary war that would target as enemies all non-Basques and all members of the Basque bourgeoisie who would not cooperate in the struggle. So, whereas the culturalists chose ethnicity over class, and the marxists chose class over ethnicity, the third-worldists chose both and decided to carry on the struggle on both fronts simultaneously. More important, this approach was predicated on the assumption (borrowed from Che Guevara) that if the objective conditions for revolution were not correct, then the revolutionary elite (or vanguard) had the obligation to go on the offensive and begin the struggle in order to bring those objective conditions into being. The third-worldists stood for the most activist kind of struggle, one in which ETA would go on the attack, using urban guerrilla tactics to defeat a much stronger Spanish military and paramilitary establishment.

As the decade wore on and ETA's internal debates continued, the third-worldists gradually gained control over the organization. Many of the trotskyites were expelled in two major splits in 1966 and 1970. The remainder left more or less voluntarily in 1968. The culturalists split off on their own initiative in 1967. Each of these splits resulted in a proliferation of radical political parties, coalitions, and labor unions, as well as several groupings that defy easy classification. Each time one of these groups left ETA, those remaining tended more and more toward homogeneity of thought and purpose. As a consequence, ETA at the close of the decade had a more clearly defined ideology than it had had in the early 1960s. To be sure, there were still important schisms in the organization in the 1970s, but the fundamental ideological divisions had been completed by the time of the Burgos trial in December 1970. Significantly, as a result of these debates, splits, and consolidations, ETA emerged each time radicalized, more intransigent and more deeply committed to armed struggle.

The Early Years: 1959–64

For about the first year of its existence, ETA was not even known to the Spanish police. Then in 1960, following mass arrests of a group of EGI leaders, Spanish authorities became aware of ETA's creation and launched a search for its members. During these early days, ETA's actions were restricted entirely to meetings and discussions, circulation of papers and studies, and a few timid propaganda efforts such as painting their initials and slogans on the walls of buildings. Nevertheless, when the police finally uncovered the core of the organization in early 1961, most of the leadership was jailed. Following the short jail sentence, five key leaders—Txillardegi, Julen Madariaga, and José María Benito del Valle, from the old Ekin group, and Ignacio Irigaray and Javier Elósegui Aldasoro, more recent additions to the group—fled into exile just across the border into France.[3] To this day, many *etarras* from that period believe that the police uncovered the ETA leadership with the assistance of information provided by the PNV.

Despite the police crackdown on ETA, the organization managed to launch its first direct challenge to Spanish authority in 1961. The date chosen was July 18, the twenty-fifth anniversary of the military rebellion that began the Civil War. ETA attempted to derail a series of trains carrying Franco supporters to San Sebastián to celebrate his victory in the war. Characteristically for that time, the attempt was made with such precautions that it failed to derail even a single car, and there was not so much as one injury.[4] The response from the Spanish authorities was harsh and immediate. More than 100 ETA members (Ibarz cites 110 as the exact figure) were arrested, tortured, and sentenced to jail sentences ranging up to fifteen to twenty years. Another group of similar size was forced into exile in France. The

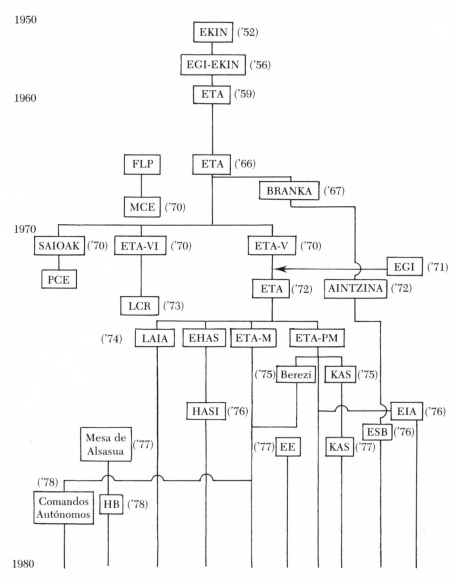

Figure 2.1.   Organizational Development of ETA, 1952–80.

effect on ETA's organization was devastating. The network of cells in Spain was thoroughly disrupted and took months to rebuild. More significant, perhaps, was the removal, either through exile or imprisonment, of a number of key figures from the Ekin days, leaving the organization in the hands of younger, more recent recruits.

If the wave of arrests and deportations set back for a year or more ETA's development within Spain, it also had the effect of giving the exiled leaders time to pause and begin to organize the movement on a little more solid basis. In France the exiles established themselves as an Executive Committee which, in early 1962, issued the organization's first declaration of purpose. "ETA," read the statement, "is a clandestine organization whose only objective is to obtain as rapidly as possible and using all the means possible—including violence— the independence of Euzkadi."[5] The Executive Committee divided itself into four subgroups called "fronts." Julen Madariaga was put in charge of the political front; Benito del Valle, the economic front; Ignacio Irigaray, the military front; and Alvarez Enparanza, the cultural front. Looking to the longer term, the committee established an eight-year plan of development. Divided into four two-year phases, the plan called for several years of training and propaganda, followed by two years of collecting weapons and money and of isolated terrorist actions. The final phase would culminate in a full-scale urban and rural guerrilla war in which ETA would seize power in the midst of general upheaval.

Of most lasting significance to the organization, however, was the Executive Committee's decision to convene the Primera Asamblea, or First Assembly, the first general meeting ETA had ever had. From this time on, the assemblies were to become the battleground for many major ideological debates within the organization, and opposing groups would take their identity and ideology from the resolutions and statements of principles approved at the meetings. At the time of the First Assembly, however, in May 1962, there was little of the acrimony that was to follow. The participants approved for publicaton (in an edition that eventually reached 30,000 copies) the first formal statement of principles.[6] In it, ETA asserted its identity as "a revolutionary Basque movement for national liberation, created in a patriotic resistance." The statement went on to advocate the creation of a federated Europe based on ethnonationalities, to declare its aconfessional position on religion, to reject definitively any kind of racism or belief that one race can be legally superior to another, and to oppose all kinds of dictatorial regimes, whether communist or fascist. Finally, the assembly confirmed and expanded the "front" organizational plan drawn up earlier by the Executive Committee and reorganized the fronts along five functional lines: internal publications and communications, cells and study groups, mass propaganda, legal actions (mass organizing), and military actions.[7] The old guard from Ekin remained in complete control of the organization.

In 1962 and 1963, however, the ideological debate was deepening.

ETA's first major ideological statement, written by Federico Krutwig Sagredo (under the pseudonymn F. Sarrailh de Ihartza) was a book called *Vasconia: Estudio dialéctico de una nacionalidad*, published in 1963 (with a prologue written in 1962) in Buenos Aires.[8] *Vasconia* made a great impact on ETA by introducing the notion of revolutionary war. Most of its criticism of the Basque nationalist bourgeoisie, including the Basque government in Paris, and of the French and Spanish Left political parties, had already been aired to a considerable degree in ETA's early writings. In his defense of revolutionary war as an instrument for gaining Basque independence, however, Krutwig was a seminal thinker and participant in the debate. Heavily influenced by the Algerian experience, Krutwig argued that ETA could mount a guerrilla war in both urban and rural areas, and spelled out how the organization should structure itself to accomplish this objective. Krutwig was not the only ETA theoretician during this period. A young economist named José Etxebarrieta, a former member of EGI, contributed some significant writings in which he showed how the ideas of Mao Tse-tung could be applied to the Basque struggle. Paco Iturrioz, a relatively new member of ETA but one destined to have an impact on the organization, put forward ideas that soon aligned him with the trotskyite branch of the movement. But this period belonged to Krutwig and to his notions of revolutionary war.

The debates within ETA took place against a background of economic difficulties, labor conflicts and strikes that began in November and December 1961 and lasted through October 1963. In May 1962, Franco decreed a state of exception (suspension of constitutional guarantees) for Asturias, Vizcaya, and Guipúzcoa provinces, and in June the decree was extended for two years and applied to the entire country. ETA became directly involved in these disputes by sponsoring a general strike in Vizcaya in October 1963 in support of some claims of dismissed workers. Although ETA played a relatively minor role in organizing the strike, it felt the full weight of the Franco regime's police power. Twenty-seven of its key members in Spain were arrested, including Paco Iturrioz.[9] The strikes and labor unrest of the 1960s forced ETA to examine its relationship to the working class in Basque cities. ETA leaders began to realize the need to link their earlier emphasis on ethnicity with an ideology that addressed the horrible conditions under which the workers labored and lived in the region. This change in ETA's ideology also forced the organization to rethink its approach to the thousands of non-Basque workers who had migrated to the Basque region since the early 1950s. These themes would all be debated extensively over the coming decade.

The Second Assembly was held in March 1963.[10] Again the meeting was dominated by the old Ekin group, but already ideological differences were becoming apparent. The eight-year plan drafted by the Executive Committee was turned down, and Krutwig's principles of revolutionary war were officially approved. The organization was given a geographical structure in addition to the five fronts designed the year before. Recognizing that the existing provincial structure was not appropriate for the waging of an armed insurgency, ETA divided itself into six geographic zones called *herrialdes.*

Six months after the Second Assembly, in a move connected with the strikes of October, ETA's leadership in Spain was decimated once again by arrests and deportations. In addition to Iturrioz, José Luis Zalbide, José María Ezkubi, Francisco Xabier Izco, and José Etxebarrieta were jailed, along with many others. Several key figures succeeded in crossing the border into exile in France, including Imaz Garay and Jon Etxabe. Faced with imminent disaster, the Executive Committee took steps to keep the organization alive until its next scheduled assembly. A small number of members were designated *liberados,* which meant that ETA would pay them a modest income that would relieve them of the need to earn a living and permit them to dedicate themselves to the movement. The principles of revolutionary war, approved in the Second Assembly, were published in a pamphlet entitled *Insurrección en Euzkadi,* which was distributed on an interim basis in early 1964 and approved later by the Third Assembly.[11] The herrialdes were restructured and a massive propaganda effort was approved by the committee.

ETA reached a major turning point in 1964. In April and May, the Third Assembly gathered to deal with the growing problems faced by the organization. Younger and more radical members challenged the authority of the old guard. The Ekin group continued to dominate, but their hold over the organization was slipping badly. In a series of resolutions, the Third Assembly broke definitively with the PNV, classifying that party as bourgeois and defining ETA as anticapitalist and antiimperialist. To strengthen the support they received from nonmembers who sympathized with their objectives, they established a parallel support organization to channel money, weapons, and other badly needed resources into ETA. Finally, the assembly drafted a statement of principles entitled "Letter to the Intellectuals," which suggested how much ETA had changed since its founding: ". . . for ETA the 'national' and 'social' problems are abstractions of the same reality, created in the development of capitalism in our homeland. And if the reality is a single unity it seems logical that the struggle undertaken to change it should be so as well."[12]

Late in 1964, several events combined to shake the movement loose

from the control of the Ekin group. In October, the French government expelled Madariaga, Txillardegi, Benito del Valle, and Irigaray
after French police discovered stolen weapons and documentation in
the offices of an export-import firm owned by Irigaray.[13] The four left
France to another exile in Belgium, but the distance between them
and Euzkadi contributed to the slackening of their grip. In addition,
the more radical Iturrioz and Zalbide had just left jail after having
served their sentences for participating in the 1963 strikes. Thus ETA
was left in the hands of leaders who wanted to turn the organization
into a revolutionary workers' party and make it part of a general socialist revolution throughout Spain. For the next six years the ideological
debate would center on the struggle to regain control of the movement
for ethnic Basques.

The Middle Years: 1965–67

ETA's Fourth Assembly, held during the summer of 1965, was the
first assembly to meet in Spain under clandestine conditions. With the
old Ekin group (Txillardegi, Madariaga, and others) far removed in
Belgium, new leaders began to come forward in the organization.
Some of them were from the trotskyite faction or what was called at
that time *la tendencia obrerista* (literally "the workerist tendency").
The head of this faction was Paco Iturrioz. The third-world faction was
also strong in the organization. The principal leader of this group was
José Luis Zalbide, who had also been jailed after October 1963. While
in jail, Zalbide had written the "Letter to the Intellectuals" that had
been approved by the Third Assembly in 1964. Later, under the pen
name K. de Zunbeltz, Zalbide would write another major work (also in
jail), *Iraultza (Hacia una estratégia revolucionaria vasca)*, finished in
1969 and published in 1975.

Important ideological and organizational steps were taken by the
Fourth Assembly. The assembly decided that the philosophy of its
previous guide, *La insurrección en Euskadi*, was too cautious and
conservative, and broadened it by adopting a revised version of "Letter to the Intellectuals" and by approving the "action-repression-
action spiral theory." This theory held that ETA could create the
objective conditions for spontaneous revolution by initiating armed
struggle and direct action against the Spanish police, military, and
Civil Guard. By means of specific attacks, ETA could provoke Spanish
authorities into an overreaction that would inflict heavy damage on
the civilian Basque population. In attempting to stop ETA, Madrid
would aggravate already strong but latent hostility against its policies

among the Basques, and the previously inert civilian population would then commit itself to support ETA's armed struggle. With each action, there would come a counteraction of such a repressive nature that ETA would benefit with an increased flow of members to its ranks and increased support (financial and otherwise) from the noncombatants. The end result would be a general inflammation of public sentiment in favor of ETA that would force Madrid to abandon the Basque country. What ETA did not calculate was whether the organization was strong enough to withstand Spanish counterinsurgent methods long enough to permit a mass uprising among the Basque people. When ETA leaders finally put into practice the action-repression-action spiral theory in 1968, they were rudely awakened to the reality of insurgent struggle.

Once again in 1965 ETA designed a new organizational structure. At the Fourth Assembly, the previously used "fronts" were replaced with "branches," or in Spanish, *ramas*. In addition to an Information Branch, an Activism Branch replaced the former Military Front and was responsible for conducting armed operations and for giving paramilitary training to the members. After 1966 this group, some thirty in number and led by Benito Zumalde (whose code name was *El Cabra*, "The Goat"), retreated to the mountains to carry on rural guerrilla warfare until 1968. The Fourth Assembly also created the Oficina Política, or Political Office, under the leadership of Paco Iturrioz. From its strategic location, the Political Office came to have a particularly important role to play in the crucial debates within ETA during these middle years of the 1960s.

Beyond its ideological and organizational decisions, the Fourth Assembly set in motion events that were to have decisive importance for ETA. The establishment of the Activism Branch and the decision to launch an armed insurgency implied the need for substantially increased financial resources with which to purchase weapons, explosives, and vehicles. As a consequence, ETA *comandos* were created to assault banks, factories, and other sites where large sums of money were known to be kept. The first of these robberies took place on September 24, 1965, when an ETA unit intercepted a courier of the Bank of San Sebastián. Two days later, one of the participants in the attack, José Zalbide, suffered an automobile accident and was recognized and arrested. Immediately after, a number of etarras implicated in the robbery fled into exile, including José María Ezkubi.

With Zalbide out of the way in prison and most of the other factions' leaders either in prison or in exile, the leaders of the tendencia obrerista now had unimpeded access to control of ETA. The mechanism for the takeover of the organization lay in Iturrioz's leadership of the

Political Office. The marxists began to establish their control over ETA by seizing the organization's newsletter, *Zutik*, which they began to fill with articles criticizing the linguistic-cultural and third-world approaches.

Opposition to the attempted takeover by the Political Office did not crystalize until the summer of 1966. Critics of the Political Office began to rally around two focal points. The first was Txillardegi, who represented and symbolized the culturalists within ETA. With him were the old Ekin leaders Imaz Garay and Benito del Valle. The organ for this group was the magazine *Branka*, published in Euskera from April 1966 until 1971. *Branka* had been founded as a medium of communication for Basque intellectuals. But in September 1966, Txillardegi and the others won control of the journal and began to use it to charge the Political Office with betraying ETA by attempting to link it with social revolutionary groups in other parts of Spain. Class-based common fronts of the sort advocated by Iturrioz and others of the Political Office, it was charged, were intrinsically damaging to Basque nationalism because they subordinated the national struggle to other dimensions of liberation struggles. In their place, Txillardegi and his allies advocated the creation of a Basque National Front composed of all groups for whom the Basque *national* struggle was the first and foremost objective. The Political Office group would be excluded from this front because of their association with the Spanish Popular Liberation Front through the Basque wing of that group, Eusko Sozialista Batasuna (Basque Socialist Union). For this sin, the Iturrioz group were labeled "españolistas" and "social chauvinists." They were also called *Felipes*, from the initials of the Frente de Liberación Popular.

Closely allied with Txillardegi and his group were the third-worldists, whose principal spokesman was Federico Krutwig, a new member of the organization. In addition to Krutwig, major figures in this faction were old Ekin leader Madariaga, the Etxebarrieta brothers José and Xabier (Txabi), José María Ezkubi, and a medical student named Emilio Lopez Adán, later to become well known for his writings under the pen name Beltza. Where Txillardegi used the magazine *Branka* as the outlet for the culturalists' attacks on the Political Office, Krutwig used his books *La cuestión vasca* (1965) and *El nacionalismo revolucionario* (1965) to publicize the position of the third-worldists. Krutwig and the third-worldists criticized the Political Office's "reformist" leanings. The Krutwig group was much more activist in orientation. They felt that the Iturrioz faction was too patient, preferring to wait until minor reforms had accumulated into the equivalent of a general social revolution. The third-worldists, in contrast, were impatient to launch the armed struggle immediately, and the working class would join the vanguard party as the momentum of the struggle developed.

The battle was thus joined between Iturrioz, the reformist marxists, and the Political Office, on one side, and the culturalists, Txillardegi, and *Branka*, in alliance with Krutwig and the third-worldists, on the other. The specific charge against the Political Office was that it had used *Zutik* no. 43 to call for all ETA militants to vote in the Spanish labor union elections scheduled for the autumn of 1966.[14] All other Basque political forces had agreed to boycott these elections, in large part because to take part in them would be to legitimize the state-controlled union system that was part of the Franco regime's apparatus of control. The use by the Iturrioz group of ETA's official organ to advocate participation in the elections was the mistake the other factions had been searching for to justify the expulsion of the marxists from the organization.

During the autumn of the year, several members of the anti-Iturrioz group, including Ezkubi and Madariaga, returned secretly to Spain to establish contact with their allies in the underground and to plan their strategy for removing the leaders of the Political Office. Fortunately for them, the Executive Committee of ETA was still under the control of the culturalists and the third-worldists, even though much of the apparatus of ETA in Spain had passed to the control of the trotskyites. To take advantage of this division of power, the alliance in the Executive Committee voted to expel Iturrioz and his comrades. Under the guidance of Ezkubi, the anti-Iturrioz factions worked to organize the upcoming assembly so that the group would ratify this decision. Ezkubi managed to mobilize most of the anti-Iturrioz forces to give himself a clear working majority in the next assembly.

The Fifth Assembly met in two phases, the first during December 1966 and the second during March 1967.[15] The struggle between Iturrioz and his opponents dominated the agenda of the first half of the assembly. Since Iturrioz and the other three etarras accused of espa-ñolismo and *liquidacionistas* had already been expelled by the Executive Committee a week before, they were not allowed to attend the assembly meeting. When a number of their supporters (Ortzi reports eleven in the group; Garmendia simply says they were one-quarter of the assembly) attempted to walk out to protest this measure, they were put under armed guard by the assembly's security committee.[16] Following this decision, the assembly heard a reading of the so-called Txatarra Report (labeled with the code name of the author), which spelled out the accusations against the trotskyites. The formal title of the Txatarra Report gives us the flavor of the accusations: "Analysis and Criticism of the Social-Chauvinist Españolism." Using the text of various issues of *Zutik* for evidence, the report found that the accused had been guilty of: "(a) españolist and legalist revisionism, in total opposition to the authentic revolutionary line of ETA; (b) sustaining an ideological system disconnected from reality, and therefore sustaining an idealistic system; (c) being a non-Basque tendency, introduced secretly into ETA, and having hidden from [the organization] their españolist socialist nature; (d) constituting a new breakout of social opportunism, and being, therefore, in total opposition to the revolutionary ideology of ETA."[17] Upon the conclusion of the report, the assembly heard additional material to support the accusations and then proceeded to vote on the measure. According to Garmendia (cited above) two participants abstained, one vote was annulled, and the remainder (probably about thirty) voted for expulsion. The first half of the Fifth Assembly closed with some discussion of the ideological positions to be adopted by the organization, and concluded with an admonition that persons desiring to be members of ETA had to accept the legitimacy of the principles therein adopted. The assembly also demanded that all members of ETA cut off all contact with the four expelled members and deny them all access to the organs of communication of the organization.

The expulsion of Iturrioz and the others in December 1966 was the first serious schism in ETA, but it was not to be the last. For a time, the expelled group took the name ETA-Berri (New ETA) and labeled those who remained in the organization ETA-Zarra (Old ETA). ETA-Berri continued to publish its own version of *Zutik*, which came to be called *Zutik-Berri (New Zutik)*. For two years, until the spring of 1969, ETA-Berri evolved into a maoist, class-oriented organization with fewer and fewer ties to Basque nationalism. In April and May of 1969, when police measures were resulting in the capture and imprisonment of many ETA leaders, ETA-Berri adopted a new name to avoid being identified as part of ETA. From that point on (August 1969) the group became known as *Komunistak* (Communists). The name was changed once again in 1970 to Spanish Communist Movement (*Movimiento Communista de España*, MCE). In this way, ETA served as the point of departure for a number of splinter groups that would occupy positions of radical intransigence throughout the Spanish and Basque political spectrum. From the point of view of ETA, of course, the schism removed one of the most serious challenges to the ideological purity of the organization.

While the first half of the Fifth Assembly removed one grave threat to ETA's internal unity, the second half, held in March 1967, dealt with the split between the two factions of the anti-Iturrioz group. Once the two allies had succeeded in driving the trotskyites out of ETA, they turned against one another in a struggle over ultimate control of the organization. The second half of the Fifth Assembly attracted all of the major figures who had been associated with ETA from its inception. Txillardegi and Benito del Valle came to represent the cultural approach. The Etxebarrieta brothers, Ezkubi, and Madariaga were there representing the third-worldist ideology (which was coming to be called "revolutionary nationalism"). Even Federico Krutwig attended.

The leftists, advocates of the third-world model, were clearly the dominant factor from the very beginning of the meeting. Txabi Extebarrieta was elected president of the assembly over a representative of the culturalist faction, Imaz Garay. Through the course of the meeting, as resolutions were presented and voted on, the culturalists lost virtually every vote. Some of their proposals were not even brought to a vote.

The revolutionary nationalists were intent on making the Fifth Assembly the point of departure for their own "great leap forward" into armed struggle. A new Political Office was elected to replace the expelled marxists. Its members came entirely from the third-world group, including Ezkubi and Txabi Etxebarrieta. Ideological changes were relatively minor, and echoed decisions already made by the Fourth Assembly. ETA was defined as a "Basque socialist movement of national liberation" committed to a "socialist affirmation," and the Basque working class was assigned the key role in the upcoming revolution. Basques who were members of the lesser and middle bourgeoisie would be allowed to participate in the struggle if they were willing to accept the principles of the revolution. The Fifth Assembly tried to combine social class and ethnicity in its ideology by coining the term Basque Working People (*Pueblo Trabajador Vasco*, or PTV), a classification that was used regularly even up to 1980. The PTV was identified as first and foremost an ethnic Basque unit. The Basque nation was defined as people of Basque ethnicity who had become conscious of their special language and cultural heritage and who felt the need to unite politically to preserve those features of their lives. Immigrants to the Basque region could join the struggle if "they assume[d] the sociocultural characteristics of the Basque people"; that is, if they learned to speak Euskera. If not, they would be contributing to Spanish colonial domination over the Basques and they would be rejected by the revolution despite their class affinity with the Basque workers. In general ideological terms, then, the Fifth

Assembly reaffirmed the basic outlines of the Krutwig philosophy of nationalist revolutionary war, to be waged against capitalism and Spain more or less simultaneously.

The Fifth Assembly made few changes in its tactics; the action-repression spiral was reaffirmed as the basic operating principle of the insurgency. There were a number of important structural changes, however. The former "front" organization was brought back to replace the now-discredited "branch" format. The four fronts were identified as cultural, political, economic, and military. In 1968, a Workers Front (Frente Obrero) was added to the list. But for now, the Military Front was the one that concerned ETA leaders the most. The general decision-making organs were to be the National Assembly, charged with meeting once a year to define ETA policy and operating principles, and the Executive Committee (sometimes called the Tactical Executive Committee or KET), responsible for the daily operations of the organizations. In addition, the Fifth Assembly created a kind of central committee, called (in Basque) Biltzar Txikia (BT) or Little Assembly, to monitor the activities of the Executive Committee to ensure ideological rigor and purity. The BT was to be made up of exiles who had no decision-making power per se, but who could convene a special assembly if they felt the Executive Committee had deviated from ETA's ideology. The Political Office was continued to provide the ideological support for the movement, and a special Strategic Command was set up to plan especially difficult operations. Below these offices there was a fairly complex network of cells that operated throughout the region and were responsible for guiding the work of the four fronts in their respective zones or neighborhoods.

Although the Fourth Assembly had produced the significant ideological statements linking Basque nationalism with revolutionary socialism, the Fifth Assembly was the strategic turning point of ETA. During the first half, as we have seen, the trotskyites of the tendencia obrerista were expelled. One month after the second half of the assembly, in April 1967, the chief figures of the culturalist movement—Txillardegi, José Manuel Aguirre, and Benito del Valle—submitted their resignations from ETA to the Executive Committee.[18] In their letters, the three explained that they could not accept the guerrilla tactics or the marxist-leninist philosophy adopted by the Fifth Assembly. From this point on, Txillardegi and the others continued their version of the struggle through (among other publications) the magazine *Branka*, for which they were called the Branka group. The ideological precepts of Branka could best be described as a mixture of Basque nationalism, social democracy, antimarxism, and rejection of armed struggle. With the withdrawal of Txillardegi and the others from ETA, a significant phase of the movement came to a close. Those who remained behind were in command of a newly reorganized clandestine political force with a coherent ideology and a commitment to armed struggle. Finally, many of the more moderate leaders of the third-worldists were forced into exile between March 1967 and February 1968. These included Madariaga from the Ekin old guard, Krutwig, and Beltza. The control of the BT over the Executive Committee was seriously weakened by the clandestine nature of the committee's work, and gradually through the first half of 1968 the BT lost effective control of the daily operations of the organization.

The net effect of these developments was to produce an Executive Committee composed entirely of members of ETA who were still at large on the Spanish side of the border. These men tended to be even younger and more radical than the leaders of the nationalist revolutionary war movement, such as Krutwig and Beltza. With no real opposition from within the organization and considerable momentum from the Fifth Assembly behind them, they launched a series of increasingly violent actions. Some were undertaken for propaganda reasons, while others, including ETA's first bank robberies, were carried out to obtain money and weapons. As the Spanish police and Guardia Civil reacted to violence with counterviolence, the predictable result was the first deaths associated with ETA.

In April 1967, a violent strike in Bilbao led to the declaration of a state of exception in Vizcaya province and a suspension of constitutional guarantees.[19] About a dozen members of ETA were arrested. The celebration of the Basque national holiday, Aberri Eguna, in Pamplona was broken up by police with beatings and arrests. Late in April, ETA members assaulted the Banco Guipuzcoano in Villabona (Guipúzcoa) and made off with more than one million pesetas. Demonstrations in Bilbao on May 1 were dispersed by police, with at least one youth wounded by gunfire. In the small town of Legazpia (Guipúzcoa) there was a gunfight between the Guardia Civil and the occupants of an escaping automobile. In June, there was a second bank robbery, this time in Arechabaleta (Guipúzcoa); and in August, there was another shooting between Guardia Civil troops and unknown persons fleeing in an automobile. In late summer, ETA leaders made one last attempt to launch a Basque National Front through what they called the Campaña del BAI.[20] The suggestion in the campaign literature and propaganda that the front would support armed violence turned away many moderate Basques; and the planned mass meeting on September 3 to launch the front was attended by only a few ETA members. In October, there was still another bank robbery in Villabona. In early November there was another gunfight between

Guardia Civil and suspected ETA members in an automobile in Deusto (Vizcaya), and later that month a sixteen-year-old boy, suspected (wrongly) of being a member of ETA, was killed by the Guardia Civil in a small town in Navarra. In December, an ETA comando attempted to blow up several buildings in Eibar and Elgóibar (Guipúzcoa), and in their attempt to get away through a Guardia Civil roadblock there was a wild shootout in which two of the four members were wounded. In the spring of 1968, a number of ETA members were arrested throughout the region. Many of them were beaten severely, suffering grievous wounds even before they reached the relative safety of the police station. In Vitoria, one of the etarras lost an eye during the beating; in Pamplona another lost his hearing. The celebration of Aberri Eguna in San Sebastián was again disrupted by police using helicopters and mounted patrols. More than three hundred were arrested. On May 1, of the nine cities where workers held mass demonstrations, six were in the Basque region. Throughout May, there were waves of bombings, automobile and bus burnings, and arrests and beatings in prison.

In retrospect, the turmoil from April 1967 to June 1968 could not have ended otherwise. There were so many violent clashes between armed men throughout the Basque country that eventually one of them had to lead to death. It was not without some prescience, then, that Txabi Etxebarrieta wrote in an internal document, "It is no secret to anyone that we will not end 1968 without a death." His was to be the first.

The Later Years: 1968–70

On June 7, 1968, near the little village of Aduna, about ten kilometers north of Tolosa (Guipúzcoa) and only about three kilometers from Villabona, the site of two recent ETA bank robberies, a car carrying ETA members Txabi Etxebarrieta and Iñaki Sarasqueta was stopped by a Guardia Civil roadblock. In the ensuing gunfight, a member of the Guardia Civil named José Pardines was killed, the first victim of ETA's violence.[21] The car sped southward toward Tolosa, where it was halted again by another Guardia Civil roadblock. Here, Txabi Etxebarrieta was hauled from the car and shot. Sarasqueta, although wounded, succeeded in escaping but was caught shortly after, tortured, tried in a military court, and sentenced to fifty-eight years in prison. (Soon after the first trial, Sarasqueta was tried a second time and sentenced to death. The second sentence was commuted.)

The reaction to all these happenings throughout the Basque country was massive. In every major city and most tiny towns and villages priests celebrated funerals and masses for Etxebarrieta for weeks following his death, despite a prohibition by the provincial governments. Mass demonstrations in Bilbao, San Sebastián, Eibar, and Pamplona, as well as in smaller cities like Ondárroa and Durango (Vizcaya) and Mondragón (Guipúzcoa), were blocked by police, who were met with stones and overturned cars. Etxebarrieta was converted into a national hero by the Basque population. In the months following his death, ETA's ranks swelled with new arrivals.

ETA now found itself in a serious dilemma. For three years, since the Fourth Assembly in 1965, the organization had espoused the action-repression-action spiral theory. Each repressive act by Madrid had to be answered by an even more provocative act, and so spiraling upward toward a massive conflagration. Here for the first time ETA was presented with an opportunity (or a challenge, depending on how one looked at it) to put its theory to the test. The organization did not retreat from the logical conclusions of its own theory. Its next step was crucial in the history of ETA, the Basques, and the Franco regime in general.

A police commissioner named Melitón Manzanas was returning to his home in Irún (Guipúzcoa) at about 3:15 on the afternoon of August 2, 1968, when he was shot several times at close range by a single gunman.[22] The attack occurred as Manzanas was about to enter his apartment. The only witnesses were his wife, who was opening the door to greet him, and his daughter, who was in an inner room of the apartment and failed to get a look at the killer. Only one other person saw the assailant flee from the scene, but the heavy rainfall prevented him from making a positive identification. Although the exact identity of the gunman was unknown, there was little doubt that ETA was involved. Manzanas had acquired a reputation as a brutal and sadistic prison official who (it was alleged) especially enjoyed beating and torturing Basque nationalists. He had in all probability been marked for assassination for some time. ETA was simply waiting for the right moment when public opinion would support the killing.

The reaction from Madrid was fierce. General Franco imposed a state of exception (a suspension of constitutional guarantees) on Guipúzcoa province on August 3 and renewed it for Guipúzcoa on October 31. On January 24, 1969, the state of exception was extended to cover Spain in its entirety.[23] It was not lifted until late March. The number of arrests and cases of police mistreatment of prisoners rose dramatically. In August alone, according to Ortzi, more than six hundred arrests were made in the Basque provinces. In 1969, nearly two thousand were arrested, and about half of these were retained in custody, tortured, and eventually tried and convicted of a variety of crimes against the state, none of which had anything to do with the Manzanas killing.[24]

There were, however, a series of arrests that were allegedly linked directly to the Manzanas murder, and their net effect was to almost destroy ETA. They began with the arrest of Gregorio Lopez Irásuegui and his wife, Arantxa Arruti, on the streets of Pamplona on November 7, 1968. Lacking evidence against him, the police released Lopez Irásuegui (he would be arrested again later) but kept his wife in jail. Despite her pregnancy, Arruti was subjected to torture and suffered a miscarriage. Eventually she was absolved of all involvement in the Manzanas killing.[25] Meanwhile Lopez Irásuegui, with the aid of Francisco Javier Izco de la Iglesia, attempted to get into the prison in Pamplona to rescue his wife on January 5, 1969. The attempt failed, and both men were captured. The weapon carried by Izco, a 7.65 mm Czech machine pistol, was confiscated and subjected to ballistics test, which showed it to be the weapon used to kill Manzanas. Izco was immediately charged with the murder.[26]

The arrests did not stop there but were broadened to include all of the members of the Central Committee, the Biltzar Txikia that allegedly agreed to kill Manzanas. In attacking this body, the Spanish court system was striking at the very heart of ETA. On December 11, 1968, José María Dorronsoro was caught in Mondragón. Xabier Larena was captured in Eibar on March 6, 1969. Jokin Gorostidi and his wife Iciar Aizpurua were arrested in the home of her parents in Deva (Guipúzcoa) on March 8. José Antonio Carrera was arrested on March 15. Victor Arana, Mario Onaindia, and Jesús Abrisqueta were captured in one of ETA's "safe houses" in Bilbao on April 9. One of the priests in the group, Jon Etxabe, was caught, along with three other members—Eduardo Uriarte, Jone Dorronsoro, and Enrique Guesalega—at a camp grounds in Santander province on April 11. The final arrest was that of the second priest, Julen Kalzada, on June 4, 1969, as he participated in a fast in the offices of the bishop of Bilbao. One other ETA leader, Mikel Etxebarria, was almost caught with the group in Bilbao on April 9, but he managed to escape even though wounded. In the ensuing gunfight a taxi driver named Fermin Monasterio was killed, allegedly because he refused to drive off with Etxebarria. His death was the third charged to ETA.[27]

If the arrests had stopped there, it is possible that ETA could have survived relatively unscathed. As it was, the Manzanas killing was simply the catalyst of the most massive crackdown by the Spanish police on ETA that had yet been seen. In December 1968 a military court asked for the death penalty for three ETA militants for burning the house of the mayor of a small town in Guipúzcoa. A number of other key figures, including two members of the rural guerrilla force of Zumalde ("Cabra"), were arrested. Andoni Arrizabalaga was sentenced to death after planting a bomb that failed to explode. Up until the wave of arrests in April, ETA had managed to remain more or less intact. After the arrests of Arana, Onaindia, Abrisqueta, Uriarte, Etxabe, Dorronsoro, and Guesalaga, all in less than forty-eight hours, the structure of the organization in Spain began to crack. Virtually every key leader on the Spanish side of the border was caught in these raids. Every one, that is, except the principal leader in Spain, José María Ezkubi, who managed to remain at large, although before long he too had to flee into exile, along with his wife, María Asunción Goenaga.

Many of the men and women arrested or deported in the period from August 1968 through April 1969 were themselves fairly new to the leadership of ETA. They had been placed in key positions only a year earlier, when another crackdown had sent such older leaders as Krutwig and Beltza into exile. Thus the new generation that now was forced to take command of the organization in Spain after the arrests of 1968 and 1969 was even younger and more untested and inexperienced than its predecessors.

The consequences of the Manzanas killing and the resulting mass arrests went far beyond a mere change in leadership. Some of the basic ideological principles that had guided ETA for several years now began to be sharply questioned. Many ETA militants asked whether the action-repression-action spiral theory might not be too costly a tactic, especially when the repression phase of the spiral left ETA so broken that it could not respond with an act of provocation. Furthermore, the spiral theory had been based on the assumption that ETA would have full control over events once the action-repression exchange began. Yet it was clear that many events beyond ETA's control, and even beyond the boundaries of the Basque region or of Spain itself, could intervene to complicate the prosecution of the spiral of action and repression. A specific case in point: the extension of the state of exception by Franco to cover all of Spain in January 1969 was at least partly due to student riots going on in other parts of the country, a fact that ETA could not have predicted or controlled but that worsened police pressure considerably.

A second aspect of ETA's ideology to be challenged during this period was its relationship with workers, both Basque and non-Basque. Etxebarrieta had been close to a number of labor leaders in the Basque region. After his death, ETA began to get closer to the clandestine unions, and an increasing number of non-Basques began to appear on the ETA arrest lists. When during the last half of 1968 ETA created the Workers' Front, charged with the responsibility of maintaining the organization's ties with the labor unions that were active in the Basque region, ETA, writes Ortzi, cast off the ambiguities and resentments it felt toward immigrants, and more non-Basques began to join the organization.[28]

The events of 1968 and 1969 were of momentous importance for ETA. The organization went through two entire generations of leaders in less than three years. A number of the key principles that had guided the movement since the middle 1960s were called into serious question. The consequence of all these changes was yet another internal debate over ideology, operating principles, and organizational structure. Incredible as it may seem after the internal struggle that the organization had gone through from 1965 through 1967, many of the questions that had been resolved in that era reappeared at the Sixth Assembly, linked to new factions and new faces.

The Sixth Assembly, held in August 1970, brought together a complex mixture of ideologies, personalities, and old and new animosities and alliances.[29] The mostly young and unknown militants of the Executive Committee were still (in ETA parlance) "virgins," because they had not been arrested and a police file did not exist on them (they were not "*fichados*"). Most of them had been somewhat to the left of ETA at the Fifth Assembly, but also rather more inclined to seek close ties with non-Basque workers and their unions and perhaps somewhat more cautious about military initiatives. Because of their relative youth and inexperience, however, the Executive Committee went to great lengths to please the various factions of older and more prestigious etarras, all of whom were in exile in France or Belgium. Thus, paradoxically, during the latter part of 1969 and the beginning of 1970, the Executive Committee explored openings toward both the Basque nationalist Right (with a call for a Basque National Front) and the Left (with a statement that the principal task of ETA was to create the Basque Communist Party). The new Executive Committee was reluctant to abandon the class struggle, but insisted that it be defined in the Basque case as a national liberation struggle, which in turn implied a national front with middle class Basques as well. The image projected by the younger leaders, then, was one of vacillation and confusion as they sought to placate first one group of ETA exiles and then another.

These exile factions were divided along lines that are already quite familiar to us. The faction closest to the existing Executive Committee, in both age and ideology, was composed of the few remaining survivors of the police suppression of 1968 and 1969. Under the leadership of José María Ezkubi after he reached exile, this faction was labeled the Red Cells (Células Rojas). Since they used the magazine *Saioak* to articulate their position, they also became known as the Saioak group. The fundamental belief that motivated the Red Cells was their conviction that ETA specifically, and Basque nationalism in general, was at heart influenced by middle class and lower middle class thinking and could not adequately meet the needs of the working class in the Basque region. They further held that liberation of the Basque region could not be undertaken while Spain remained under the control of a dictatorship and that the struggle would therefore have to be extended to the rest of Spain, the implication being that ETA must look for alliances with Spanish groups, something that was anathema to most of the older ETA members.

The factions that opposed this position were united by little except their disagreement with Ezkubi and the Red Cells. One group in the opposition consisted of older members of ETA's leadership, the generation that went into exile in 1967 after the Fifth Assembly, including (from Ekin days) Madariaga and Beltza. This faction, which continued to maintain cordial ties with the Branka group of Txillardegi, was probably the closest to what ETA had represented traditionally, emphasizing Basque ethnicity as key in the struggle. Another faction, much more militant, was composed of many of the survivors of the Military Front created by the Fifth Assembly. This group, led by Jon Etxabe, was referred to as the *milis*. Although the milis were staunchly anticommunist, they were also among the most radical and intransigent members of ETA in their insistence on armed struggle as the only way to gain independence. A third faction within the opposition was the revolutionary war group of Krutwig, which advocated armed struggle, although subordinating violence to the needs of a political-military structure and refusing to reject marxism out of hand.

The Sixth Assembly was held in the midst of this ideological turmoil. The principal participants in the assembly were the convenors, the Executive Committee and the Red Cells under the leadership of Ezkubi. Of the milis, only Madariaga agreed to attend. Beltza had already resigned from the organization, and the others could not run the risk of being discovered if they returned to Spain. The first action taken by the assembly, which was dominated by the Red Cells, was to expel Madariaga and the milis from the organization. Although Madariaga had to leave the meeting room, he was held under armed guard for a time so that he could not compromise the remainder of the meeting. With that action out of the way, the Executive Committee and the Red Cells began a bitter argument over the extent to which the latter could control the actions of the former from an exile base. Failing to find a suitable solution to the problem, the Red Cells and

Ezkubi formally submitted their resignations and left the meeting place and ETA. ETA had now been reduced in essence to the Executive Committee, since the committee had expelled several previous generations of leaders then in exile, and those who were not expelled had resigned in disgust.

While all these maneuvers were going on, the milis and the old guard in France and Belgium were making an effort to protect their position within ETA. Several days later, five members of the Biltzar Txikia elected by the Fifth Assembly—Eduardo Arregui, Etxabe, Beltza, Madariaga, and Krutwig—issued a letter announcing that all the participants in the Sixth Assembly were expelled from ETA for having tried to take over the organization. Their arguments were simple. First, the Executive Committee had no power to convene the assembly or to determine the list of participants, since that was a function of the BT. Second, recalling arguments heard from earlier days, the former (now expelled) Executive Committee and the Red Cells were guilty of españolismo and of trying to take ETA into the Spanish revolutionary marxist Left. In September, the Executive Committee fired back with a counterattack, accusing the milis of being racists and bourgeois. The rank-and-file members of ETA in the interior refused to line up behind any of the factions, and the general reaction among them seemed to be one of disgust and dismay. It was in this context that the Burgos 16 came to trial.

The Burgos trial, a military court-martial held under strict security and information controls, lasted from December 3 to December 9. It was surrounded by chaos.[30] There were repeated strikes during the trial, involving thousands of Basque workers. Street demonstrations erupted in Basque cities and resulted in bloody confrontations between the police and demonstrators. The Spanish government reacted with the declaration of a three-month state of exception in Guipúzcoa. In other Western European countries, mobs attacked Spanish embassies and called upon their own governments to break relations with Madrid. A number of European countries recalled their ambassadors for consultation. Inside the trial chamber, matters were hardly less chaotic. Motion after motion by the defense lawyers was rejected by the three senior army officers presiding. The defendants refused to address the court in Spanish and spoke only in Basque, which usually went untranslated for lack of qualified translators. All of the remaining fifteen accused (Arruti had been acquitted) admitted being members of ETA, and the room was filled with cries of "Long live ETA" and other rallying cries; but each one of the accused denied having anything to do with Manzanas's murder. Confessions presented to the court were denounced by the defendants as having been extracted by torture. Nevertheless, their convictions were a foregone conclusion.

The trial was greatly complicated by the kidnaping on December 2 of the honorary West German consul in San Sebastián, Eugen Beihl.[31] The kidnaping had been carried out by a comando under the orders of Jon Etxabe of the milis. It has been alleged that Etxabe and the milis decided to kidnap Beihl not only to put pressure on the Franco government to soften the punishment of the Burgos prisoners but also to win a propaganda battle with their opponents from the Sixth Assembly. At one stroke, the milis impressed Basques with their commitment to direct armed action against Spain. At the same time, the Beihl kidnaping gave the milis direct access to international media, which they exploited with the help of such spokesmen as Telesforo Monzón, an old fighter from the Spanish Civil War who had served in the Basque government and in the PNV until the 1950s, when the PNV approach became too timid for his taste. Monzón acted as intermediary between the milis and the press. The impact of the kidnaping was enormous, especially since it gave the milis an opportunity to show the world that they were reasonable but oppressed people who were reduced to desperate measures by Spanish oppression.

The ostensible purpose of the kidnaping was to pressure Franco into granting more lenient treatment to the Burgos prisoners. On December 22, after the trial was completed but before the court announced its verdict, Basque representatives issued a statement claiming that Spanish government officials had been in contact with them to secure Beihl's release. The Spanish government would only confirm that meetings had taken place between ETA members and "parties interested in securing the release of Beihl." The Basques claimed that a three-step arrangement had been worked out whereby Beihl would be released, the court would then announce its verdicts and sentences, and any death sentences would be commuted later by Franco. Spain would thus be spared the appearance of having given in to ETA's demands.

On Christmas Eve, Beihl was released unharmed and quickly transported to Germany. On December 28, the court met to hand down its verdicts. All of the accused except Arruti were found guilty. Six of the accused were given the death penalty: José Dorronsoro, Izco, Larena, Gorostidi, Onaindia, and Uriarte. The others were sentenced to a total of 341 years in prison. On December 30, Franco commuted all of the death sentences to 30 years in prison. The details of the Beihl agreement had been fulfilled. Franco had been able to satisfy his hard-line critics while at the same time offering a slight sign of generosity during the holiday season.

Although the Burgos prisoners had been sentenced to spend virtually all their remaining years in jail, by 1977 all of them were either back on the streets in Spain or in European exile. Several of them continued to play major roles in Basque politics through the 1970s, and became active in the Basque socialist movement following the restoration of democracy in Spain. As an organization, ETA emerged from this period confused, broken, and disorganized. Yet within three years, it had managed to pull itself together to carry out its most daring and spectacular attack.

CHAPTER THREE

ETA in the Last Years of the Franco Regime: 1971–75

During the 1960s, ETA had devoted much of its time and energy to internal quarrels over ideology and strategy. Several times during the decade these disputes led to splits within the organization. Remarkably, although each division left ETA weakened and drained, it seemed to possess an amazing ability to attract new members, to reorganize, and to return to the political struggle. Moreover, those remaining in control of ETA after each schism seemed hardened and more intransigent for their experience. As a consequence, ETA as an organization was increasingly radicalized and increasingly committed to armed struggle.

The struggles of the 1960s did not subside after the Burgos Trial or after the Sixth Assembly in 1970. Indeed, the passions and hostilities engendered by the debates of the 1960s spilled over into the 1970s, and the pattern of ETA's first decade (ideological dispute, confrontation, schism) was repeated several more times during the first half of the 1970s. Despite these internecine conflicts, ETA managed to keep itself intact during the last five years of Franco's regime. In fact it was during this period, when ETA was most seriously weakened by police suppression and internal quarreling, that the organization managed to carry out its most audacious and dramatic attack, the assassination of the prime minister of Spain. When the Franco years came to a close and Spain began its transition back to constitutional democracy, however, ETA was ill prepared to adjust to the changed political environment.

1971–72: ETA-V and ETA-VI

In early 1971 in the aftermath of the Burgos Trial, ETA had split into two significant factions. By far the stronger of the two was the group known as ETA-VI, the direct heirs of the organization that remained after the Sixth Assembly the preceding August. Not only did ETA-VI control the apparatus of the organization but it also had the greatest support from rank-and-file members operating in secret in Spain. Furthermore, ETA-VI was regarded as the principal benefici-ary of a key letter written by the most famous ETA members, the Burgos 16, from their jail cells. The letter was a blistering attack on conservative, right-wing, bourgeois Basque nationalists who, it charged, "while Txabi Etxebarrieta lay dying on a road in Euzkadi, went on handing out folklore calendars or writing novels." [1] These same bourgeois Basque nationalists, it said, faced with the challenge and the threat of a resurgent, socialist ETA, had decided to destroy the organization by infiltration and sabotage from within. The agents of this infiltration and sabotage effort were none other than the five for-mer ETA leaders (Madariaga, Etxabe, Arregui, Beltza, and Krutwig) who had signed the letter denouncing the Sixth Assembly, and who were now attempting to establish themselves as the chief rival of ETA-VI for control of the organization. As in the 1960s, the key debate turned on the issue of class versus ethnicity. The Burgos 16 letter leveled its attack primarily against the idea that the struggle for Basque freedom should be based on confrontation between Euzkadi on one side and France and Spain on the other. "To cause a confronta-tion between the national communities above the classes that com-prise them is," said the letter, "a bourgeois monstrosity. . . . The Basque people do not confront the Spanish people but rather the Spanish oligarchy; the Basque people are united with the Spanish people." According to the Burgos prisoners, ETA's Fifth Assembly had solved once and for all the conflict between national (read *ethnic*) liberation and social (read *class*) liberation by proclaiming itself a socialist organization in the marxist-leninist sense. By advocating the creation of a multiclass Basque "national front," the five "traitors," as they were called were trying to separate the Basque workers from their true allies, those in the working class organizations in all parts of Spain. As a response to this alternative, the Burgos prisoners advo-cated the creation of a workers' front that would fight for an indepen-dent Basque state, bilingualism, and the nationalization of the econo-mic holdings of the oligarchy.

Perhaps heavily influenced by the contents of this letter, the lead-ership of ETA-VI began to drift away from the ethnic, nationalist tendency in the Basque struggle and toward a closer association with the working class elements within the movement, and outside it as well. In all probability, these leaders miscalculated the social base from which such a struggle could be launched in Euzkadi. Either they overestimated the strength of the revolutionary sentiment within the working class generally, or they erred in their belief that Basque workers, forced to choose between class and ethnicity, would support a class-based struggle in preference to a national one. In either case, during 1971 and the first months of 1972 ETA-VI emerged as clearly committed to an insurgent struggle dominated by revolutionary socialism and only secondarily interested in Basque ethnicity and language. The serious miscalculations of its leadership, however, aggravated by a series of mistaken policy choices made by them, meant that by the end of 1972 ETA-VI had effectively destroyed itself as a major force in Basque politics.

The first error committed by ETA-VI involved the National Front meetings that were organized by a group of Basque leaders in early 1971. When the meetings were in their preliminary organizational stage, ETA-VI disdained the organizers and their efforts to form a common front, but by the time the meetings had begun in February, ETA-VI was demanding to be allowed to participate. They were finally permitted to on March 7, but at that meeting there was such tension over the official or unofficial nature of the meetings that the Basque Nationalist Party representatives walked out and never returned, thereby robbing the meetings of much of their significance. Nevertheless, ETA-VI distinguished itself primarily by advocating a five-point program that showed a strong socialist influence:

1. Violent destruction of the [Spanish] state and the imposition of popular armed councils of workers
2. The right of separation and reunification of the Basque nation, exercised through a Basque people's government composed of people's councils of workers
3. Socialization of the goods of the oligarchy, of the imperialists, and of the other counterrevolutionaries, without compensation
4. Effective equality of the Basque and Spanish languages and the encouragement of Basque popular culture
5. Political and labor union freedom[2]

As one can easily imagine, these proposals met with scant support from other participants in the front meetings, and ETA-VI was branded conclusively as marxist, and worst of all, españolista.

The second mistake made by the ETA-VI leaders involved their assessment of their social base and how that base was linked to the ideology and strategy of the organization. According to the analysis of José Mari Garmendia, ETA-VI leaders had become convinced that the social composition of ETA had changed over the years. While the organization had been dominated in its early years by students, intellectuals, professionals, and other middle class elements, ETA-VI believed that after Burgos the rank-and-file members tended to come from working class occupations and groups for whom Basque ethnicity and language were definitely subordinate to class interests. In this assessment, they were almost certainly wrong.[3] To be sure, the center of gravity of ETA did shift noticeably after 1970, away from Bilbao and other large cities toward the small towns of mountainous south and central Guipúzcoa, away from students and middle class professionals and toward the workers in the small plants and factories of that region. But ETA-VI misunderstood the peculiar mixture of class and ethnicity that characterized these members. They were not from the major industries of Bilbao and its suburbs, where Basque ethnicity had virtually disappeared, but instead from the interior zones of Guipúzcoa and Vizcaya where Euskera was still the dominant language and where issues of Basque ethnicity were still paramount. The new ETA members were coming from working class occupations and those of the lower middle class as well—there were office and administrative workers—but they were still overwhelmingly ethnic Basque, with strong ethnic and linguistic, as well as class, interests. In their move away from ethnicity and toward class as the central theme of the struggle, ETA-VI grew increasingly remote from its rank-and-file members and supporters.

The final error of the ETA-VI leadership was their relative inactivity during 1971 and 1972. The kidnaping of Eugen Beihl in 1970 by Etxabe and the comando from the milis faction had marked that group as the leading element in the armed struggle. By contrast, ETA-VI looked mild and timid, afraid to strike out against the Spanish state, unable to muster an organization that could carry out armed attacks. In March 1971, virtually the entire ETA-VI leadership in Vizcaya was arrested in several police raids, and the organization's leadership was badly shaken and disrupted. In December 1971, ETA-VI leaders called for a hunger strike of all Basque political prisoners to show their support for Basque workers who were about to enter into negotiations over new labor contracts. The prisoners, in an outstanding demonstration of resolve and discipline, began to strike, but the contract negotiations were delayed and the workers returned to their jobs, leaving ETA-VI looking extremely foolish and inept. Short of funds and experienced leaders, ETA-VI retired from the field of combat at precisely the time when other leaders were emerging as much more daring and committed to armed struggle.

As a consequence of all these factors, members of ETA-VI began to desert the organization in droves. The first major defection took place in early 1971; a second group broke away in the summer.[4] The defections included some of the most gifted and stoutly committed young members, such as José Miguel Beñarán Ordeñana "Argala" and Eduardo Moreno Bergareche "Pertur," both of whom would become major figures in ETA after Franco's death.

What was worse, there now appeared serious disagreements between ETA-VI leaders in exile in France and rank-and-file members and cell leaders operating clandestinely in Spain. The argument focused not so much on the merits of marxism as a philosophy as on the political and strategic ineptness of the ETA-VI leaders during the year and a half following Burgos. The cells operating in Spain wanted less rhetoric and more leadership, and their criticisms began to reach a level that was disquieting to the leaders in France.

To counter these internal criticisms and to try to stem the tide of desertions, ETA-VI held a series of meetings in 1972 that were regarded within the organization as the second half of the Sixth Assembly. In July, the group convoked a "preassembly" meeting of the Biltzar Txikia of ETA-VI, the purpose of which was to prepare for the second half of the Sixth Assembly. The meeting of the BT deteriorated into mutual recriminations, however, which led to still another split in ETA-VI, this time between the trotskyites, called *mayoritarios* because they were in the majority at the BT meeting, and their opponents, who found themselves in the minority and were therefore referred to as *minoritarios* or just *minos*. Members of the minos faction drifted away to other groups inside and outside of ETA, and some simply abandoned the struggle altogether. Ortzi asserts that despite this, the minos faction actually represented the majority of ETA-VI members, and their departure from the organization sealed its fate.[5] Near the end of the year, the remainder of the ETA-VI leadership held the so-called second half of the Sixth Assembly, but the only major decision to emerge from this meeting was a decision to join with the Revolutionary Communist League (Liga Communista Revolucionaria, or LCR) in the establishment of a new and expanded Basque wing of the Spanish parent revolutionary organization. In early 1973, ETA-VI and the LCR fused under the name of the latter, thereby ending the brief life of ETA-VI.[6]

No doubt one of the principal reasons for the short life of ETA-VI was the vigor and activism of its chief competition, ETA-V (so-called because it claimed to draw its inspiration from the ideological principles approved by the Fifth Assembly). Based solely on the slight personal and institutional following of the five authors of the August 1970 letter denouncing the Sixth Assembly, ETA-V in early 1971 had few members, scant resources, and no reputation to speak of, and was strongly opposed by the Burgos prisoners. By 1972, however, ETA-V had become the stronger of the two groups. After the decline of ETA-

VI in late 1972 and early 1973, ETA-V came to be referred to as simply ETA, indicating that it was synonymous with the organization in the minds of everyone.

There were a number of factors at work in the rise to power of ETA-V. Some involved the correct choice of ideological alternatives, while others had to do with the personalities of outstanding leaders. And there was an element of good fortune involved, too, especially in the international setting in the 1970s that formed the backdrop against which the drama was enacted.

The first factor in the success of ETA-V was probably the nature of its leadership at this particularly crucial moment. The key figure was Eustaquio Mendizábal Benito "Txikia," a leader so powerful that his code name became the symbol for this era in ETA's history, the "Era Txikia." Mendizábal was born in 1945 in the tiny town of Isasondo (1975 population, 983) in the Goierri region of Guipúzcoa.[7] In August 1968, while he was still studying for the priesthood in a Benedictine monastery, he took his first action as a member of ETA by helping set fire to the home of the mayor of Lazcano. He was attracted to Jon Etxabe and the mili faction, and took part in the kidnaping of Eugen Beihl in 1970. By August 1971, Mendizábal had risen to leadership in the organization, and he was to leave his mark on ETA-V for the next year and a half. He organized several large bank robberies in the fall of 1971 which netted about $100,000 for the group. He engineered the kidnaping of Lorenzo Zabala in January 1972, as well as that of Felipe Huarte in January 1973. Both kidnapings were carried out for political and labor-related reasons, but the Huarte action involved the payment of some $800,000 in ransom as well. Mendizábal was finally cornered and shot to death by police in the Vizcayan town of Algorta on Holy Thursday, April 19, 1973, as he attempted to make contact with another etarra in the local train station. After his death, he was eulogized throughout the Basque region; and his loss was mourned by many ETA members who saw in him the only leader capable of holding the organization together. Txikia had appeared at a crucial moment in the history of ETA, at a time when the organization desperately needed a strong and charismatic leader to bridge the generation gap between the ETA before the Burgos trial and the organization that was to carry on the struggle into the post-Franco period.

International events offered a favorable backdrop against which ETA-V could espouse its version of armed struggle, and with the resurgence of international armed insurgency, ETA-V seemed to be riding the crest of a wave of global significance. The rise of the Tupamaros in Uruguay through the late 1960s and into 1970 and 1971 gave ETA-V a valuable model that stressed links between a mass revolutionary movement and the leadership provided by a relatively small but activist armed group. The attack of the Palestinian group Black September at the 1972 Olympic Games in Munich offered another version of an audacious armed organization that seemed to promise positive results in an ethnic struggle. That neither of these two groups would be successful in their struggles during the remainder of the 1970s was of course not known to ETA-V at the time of their resurgence, and they seemed to provide a model for armed insurrection that fit the predispositions of many ETA members during the early 1970s. ETA in particular, and many Basques in general, had lost patience with the long-term strategies by the 1970s, and the daring of ETA-V caught the imagination of many young Basques.[8]

The second aspect of ETA-V that attracted the attention of Basque youth involved the now-familiar dispute over the relative importance of class and ethnicity. Whereas ETA-VI had alienated many of its earlier supporters by choosing class and socialism over ethnicity and nationalism, ETA-V prospered with exactly the opposite emphasis, on ethnicity over class as the organizing principle of the struggle. During the late winter and early spring of 1971, a number of Basque leaders convened a series of meetings, already mentioned above, whose aim was to create a multiclass Basque national front as the agency of a new liberation effort. Whereas ETA-VI fought (and fought with) the idea of the national front, ETA-V supported it. While ETA-VI tried to get the front to approve a revolutionary ideology that echoed a clear marxist-leninist influence, ETA-V argued for a program that was borrowed from more conservative Basque groups, including most expressly the Basque Nationalist Party's youth wing, EGI. Specifically, the platform suggested by ETA-V consisted of five points:

1. The unification of the Basque ethnonation by separating its two halves from both France and Spain, and the creation of a new political entity
2. The sovereign independence of this new state from both France and Spain
3. The restoration of the Basque language to the status of an official and functioning language (without necessarily eliminating Spanish from the Basque country)
4. Democratization of basic industries (which presumably meant turning them over to control by workers)
5. Nationalization of basic industries (without mention of compensation)[9]

The ideological themes sounded by ETA-V in 1971 and 1972 deserve some mention here, since they would characterize the approach of ETA through most of the rest of the decade and even beyond into the 1980s. Although the third-world arguments of the 1960s had been pretty well discarded by 1970, the notion of Euzkadi as a colony of Spain remained key in ETA ideology. According to this idea, the Basque ethnonation had been exploited economically, politically, and culturally by the Spanish oligarchy in league with foreign (read *British*) interests, the Basque oligarchy, who were willing to betray their ethnic comrades, and Spanish workers, who were lured to the Basque cities by the prospect of better jobs, housing, and so forth. While many in Basque society felt themselves oppressed by Spanish colonization—fishermen, farmers, artisans, and small businessmen, among others—only the industrial working class had the unity and level of mobilization necessary to lead the struggle. Nevertheless, the struggle could not be conducted solely by the Basque proletariat, because there were many other sectors of Basque society affected by the Spanish presence. Hence the idea of a Basque national front consisting of all Basque groups with an interest in eliminating the Spanish presence in Euzkadi. Since by their own admission the PNV and the Basque government were prepared to settle for the continued Spanish presence in Euzkadi as legitimized through a regional autonomy statute (similar to that of 1936), they were by definition excluded from the front. This point was moot, since the PNV had already excused itself from their meetings, and the government in Paris held to its long-standing position that the struggle had to be carried on through its offices.

The other major point in the approach of ETA-V involved the need for armed activism, and the relation between a militant armed faction and the mass of the workers, farmers, office workers, and others who were the popular base of the revolution. Here, ETA-V distinguished its own from earlier ETA ideology by advocating the kind of venture that in the past would have been called adventurous and liquidationist by advocates of a more cautious approach. The key document of ETA-V was the book by José Luis Zalbide entitled *Iraultza (Hacia una estrategia revolucionaria vasca).*[10] The central theme of *Iraultza* (the word for revolution in Euskera) was the need for armed struggle to maintain the momentum of the Basque fight for liberation. Without maintaining constant pressure on the sources of colonialist exploitation and imperialism in the Basque country (including, in addition to Spain and France, Britain and the United States), the Basque struggle was doomed to failure. So long as Spain controlled the apparatus of domination—the government and its bureaucracy, the educational system, the mass media, and the economy—nonviolent struggle would always lose, because the battle over individual personal loyalties played directly into the hands of the colonial powers. Only violence directed against the agents of colonialism and imperialism could raise popular consciousness about the aims of Basque liberation. As Zalbide put it, "The aim of the Basque revolutionary struggle in Euzkadi is the destruction of the apparatus of the Spanish state on Basque national territory."[11] Although armed activism would provoke the state to severe repression and inflict harm on the workers and other noncombatants, that was simply one of the costs of prosecuting the struggle. In a later version of *Iraultza*, Zalbide asserted that the main reason for the collapse of ETA in 1969 was the failure of the organization to remain on the offensive after the killing of Manzanas in August 1968. The lesson to be learned, he claimed, was the need for an armed vanguard which through its violent actions would keep constant pressure on Madrid. Efforts to organize the masses or to form a revolutionary party of the proletariat were too timid to carry the day. Only the daring of armed assaults could sustain the struggle over long spans of time.

The themes of internal colonialism and antiimperialism used by ETA-V leaders were not accepted in their totality by all ETA members. There were, as Gurutz Jáuregui has pointed out, several important defects in the theory. For one thing, it completely ignored the fact that the non-Basque workers in the Basque country were as exploited by industrial capitalism as were the Basque workers, but ETA's ideology made it practically impossible to reach out to this group to mobilize them as allies. Second, it failed to notice that much of the decline in the Basque language had resulted not from conscious Spanish policy but from the pressures of the mass media and other elements of industrialization and modernization that had become an integral part of contemporary Basque urban life.[12] But these flaws in the argument mattered little in the context of the struggle in the 1970s. In their effort to emulate the dramatic assaults of the Palestinians and the Tupamaros and to shake off the lethargy and inaction that had settled down over ETA after 1969, the leaders of ETA-V needed an ideology to support their decision to turn to armed struggle with renewed vigor. If *Iraultza* had not existed, they would have had to write it in 1971.

The activism of ETA-V seemed well suited to respond to the frustration and agitation felt by many Basque youth in the post-Burgos period. The stress on ethnicity over class interest also accorded well with the cultural and linguistic demands of these youth. Nowhere was the attraction to ETA-V felt more strongly than in the PNV's own youth organization, EGI. Throughout the 1960s EGI and ETA had felt a certain kinship, and their relationship had been warm but unofficial. Both the activism of ETA and their commitment to a unified Basque national front appealed to many EGI members, who saw their parent organization as both too conservative and too partisan. In 1970, at the time of the Sixth Assembly, EGI cells helped distribute copies of the "Manifesto" letter criticizing ETA-VI. EGI's position coincided fairly closely with that of ETA-V, particularly regarding their preference for independence, as opposed to simply regional autonomy, and for direct armed action, as opposed to the traditional Basque nationalist approach that counseled patience and nonviolence. After 1970 there emerged a faction within EGI known as EGI-Batasuna (for "unity"), which edged closer and closer to ETA-V. In 1971, EGI-Batasuna, which had a membership of about 500 on the Spanish side of the border, began to allow its operating cells to be used for certain nonviolent actions organized by ETA-V.[13] At about the same time, the idea of fusion surfaced on both sides. Former ETA leader Txillardegi advanced the notion of a new Basque national front based on his organization, Branka, as well as on ETA-V, but this idea failed to gain acceptance. In France, one of the key leaders of EGI-Batasuna made contact with Eustaquio Mendizábal in 1971 with the aim of fusing ETA and EGI. On Easter Sunday, 1972 (Easter always coincides with the Basque national holiday, Aberri Eguna), the two groups merged under the single set of initials ETA. From this point on, EGI-Batasuna and ETA-V ceased to exist, and a single unified ETA reappeared as a force in Basque politics. Of course much more had changed than simply the name of the organization. ETA was now infused with 500 youths as new rank-and-file members. In addition, the fusion brought them new respect from more conservative Basque nationalist forces. Most significant, the fusion added weight to the new ideology of activism that was sweeping the organization; the result was an increase in armed assaults during the period from 1972 through 1975.

After nearly a year of organizational confusion following the Sixth Assembly in August 1970, ETA-V finally began the long task of reconstruction with a so-called preassembly in the summer of 1971.[14] Without dwelling much on philosophical principles, since they had pretty much decided to follow those of the Fifth Assembly, the new ETA (which was still called ETA-V at the time) established a reconstituted Executive Committee and began to develop a new set of "front" organizations. At this meeting, apparently, the decision was made to renew armed actions and attacks under the direction of a renewed Military Front. Also created were fronts in cultural matters and workers affairs (the Frente Cultural and Frente Obrero).

The level of violence began to rise shortly after this preassembly meeting. In November and December, ETA teams attacked and burned or destroyed a number of shops and stores owned by known rightists in San Sebastián and other towns in Guipúzcoa. But the action that most clearly symbolized the emergence of the new ETA took place in January of the next year—the kidnaping of Lorenzo Zabala.

The Zabala kidnaping was a major event in the history of ETA, for not only was it the first kidnaping conducted as part of a labor dispute but it was also the first ETA armed action directed against a Basque. With this dramatic blow, ETA not only demonstrated that it had survived the Burgos trial and the police suppression of the period 1969–70 but also served notice that the final years of Franco were not going to be easy ones.

Lorenzo Zabala Suinaga was a middle-aged businessman, father of three children, a director of a factory in the Basque industrial city of Eibar, and—perhaps most important of all—a person of clear Basque ancestry who spoke Euskera.[15] On November 23, 1971, his company's workers had gone out on strike because the company had rejected the union's last wage offer. On December 1, the company had responded to the strike by firing all 154 of the striking workers. The 13 representatives of the workers had answered with a ten-day hunger strike in a local church. In this atmosphere, the leaders of ETA selected Zabala as their target. The new emphasis of ETA on attacking both industrial capitalism and Spanish colonialism seemed to call for an action of this sort. In their attempt to defend themselves against the charge of españolismo, the leaders of ETA-V had made Basque ethnicity the centerpiece of their ideology. Now, however, to reassure the workers that ETA could be counted on to defend their class interests, they had to direct their attack against an agent of capitalism but a Basque as well. The labor conflict of Zabala's company happened at just the right time, and gave ETA the chance it needed to intervene directly in a labor dispute against someone who spoke Euskera.

On January 17, while Zabala was parking his car in front of another of his company's shops in a nearby town, a team of four men surrounded him and forced him into another car and drove off. Despite the immediate establishment of road blocks throughout Guipúzcoa province, police were unsuccessful in discovering traces of Zabala or his abductors. The next day, ETA sent a note to the Bilbao newspaper *Hierro* setting forth the four conditions for Zabala's release: the rehiring of all workers without penalty for having been on strike; the payment of all wages lost during the strike period; the immediate increase of wage levels to those demanded by the strikers; and the recognition by the company of the bargaining rights of the committee elected by the workers before the strike began. On January 22, the directors of Zabala's company met and decided to accept the demands of the kidnapers, with some slight modifications. On that same day, the company signed a new contract with the strikers and the workers returned to their jobs. On January 24 at about 11:00 P.M., Zabala was found along a country road and returned safe and sound to his family.

Several days later, police accused eleven men of having been involved, directly or indirectly, in the kidnaping. What we know about these men tells us something about the kind of people who joined ETA in the early 1970s. The eleven ranged in age from twenty-two to thirty-six, with the mean being slightly over twenty-seven.[16] Five had been born in Vizcaya: two in Bilbao and one each in the small towns of Arrigorriaga, Ondárroa, and Miravalles. The remaining six were all from Guipúzcoa, and in fact all from the Goierri region in the southern and central part of the province: two from Mondragón and one each from Zaldivia, Eibar, Legorreta, and Isasondo. Apart from Bilbao, the average population of the birthplaces of the kidnap team was slightly less than 8,000 (1975 population). The average percentage of Euskera-speaking persons in the population of these birthplaces (again excluding Bilbao) was slightly less than 53 percent, nearly three times that of the Basque provinces as a whole. The eleven represented a wide range of professions: four were students (including two in engineering and one for the priesthood); two were factory workers; two were butchers; one was a truck driver, one a painter and paperhanger, and one a bank clerk. Three were married, and one had several children. A number went on from the Zabala kidnaping to leadership in ETA. In addition to Eustaquio Mendizábal, whom we have already met, the Zabala kidnaping team included Domingo Iturbe Abasolo "Txomin," who in 1981 was the leader of ETA (militar) in France; José Miguel Beñarán Ordeñana "Argala," who rose to be the head of ETA's Political Office and who died when his car was bombed in France in December 1978; José Miguel Lujua Gorostiola "Mikel," who in 1981 was in charge of the clandestine border crossings of ETA members back and forth between France and Spain; and Isidro María Garalde Bedialauneta "Mamarru," who in 1981 was in charge of logistics and training for ETA (militar), with special responsibility for explosives. The Zabala kidnaping was significant not only as a symbol of ETA's new ideology and strategy but also because it marked the emergence of a new generation of ETA leaders who would dominate the organization for the remainder of the 1970s and in fact into the 1980s.

The Zabala kidnaping unleashed a wave of violence unlike anything ever seen before in the Basque country, one that lasted some two years and culminated in the assassination of the Spanish prime minister in December 1973. The year 1972 saw a higher level of ETA activity than in any previous year. During the year, three bank robberies netted the organization about half a million dollars. An estimated forty attacks were carried out against the property of the Spanish state or against shops or homes of known rightists in the Basque region. During one period in mid-August, ETA attacks came at the rate of one per day.[17] The organization began to reach out beyond the frontiers of the Basque country to establish links with other insurgent organizations. In February, ETA leaders signed a joint communiqué with leaders of the Palestinian organization Fatah and with the Kurdish Democratic Party, and another in May with the Breton Liberation Front and the Irish Republican Army.[18]

All this activity was not without its human costs. Four members of ETA were killed by police or Guardia Civil during the year. In March, Jon Goikoetxea "Txapela" was shot to death in Elizondo; on September 2, two etarras, Benito Muxica "Xanxi" and Mikel Martínez de Murguia "Mikelon," were trapped in an apartment in Lequeitio and shot to death; and on September 20, Jonan Aranguren "Iharra" was killed trying to cross the border into France. On the other side, ETA took its fourth victim, a member of the Guardia Civil troop named Eloy Garcia, who was killed in a shoot-out with a group of etarras in an automobile in Galdácano in August.[19]

Following the kidnaping of Zabala and the integration of ETA-V and EGI-Batasuna, ETA (now known by the three letters only) began a period of expansion and increased activity unequaled in its prior history. The decline of ETA-VI, the new support given ETA by the Burgos prisoners, and the attractiveness of its new strategy of armed assaults won it new adherents by the dozens. But even as ETA was growing and becoming stronger during 1972, it was laying the base for the next round of internal disputes and eventual splits and divisions that would weaken it once again.[20]

The expansion of ETA affected not only its Military Front (FM, for Frente Militar), but its other operating units as well. In the summer of 1972 the Labor Front (FO, Frente Obrero) began to be organized in Vizcaya and in Guipúzcoa, and the Cultural Front (FC, Frente Cultural) also expanded significantly. This dual process of expansion and diversification caused increased tensions within the operating rank-and-file cells of the organization. Several factors aggravated this problem. For one thing, there was a severe lack of continuity between ETA of the Fifth Assembly and ETA in 1972. The new generation of etarras had come to the organization by various routes, including those through ETA-VI and EGI-Batasuna, and they lacked a common bond of experience and values. Second, the loose organizational structure encouraged competition among the various fronts, and below them, among the various cells of the organization. Since resources were scarce, there was sharp competition for a favored position with the Executive Committee, which in turn had grown rather out of touch with developments in Spain. On the Spanish side of the border, rank-and-file members were growing frustrated at the lack of leadership from the Executive Committee and the apparent lack of political coherence in the ideological approach of the leadership. To many of them, it looked as if the new ETA stood for nothing beyond opposition to the españolismo of ETA-VI. But the most serious problem lay in ETA's attempts to combine armed struggle and nonviolent activity in the same organization. Repeatedly through 1972 the armed attacks of the Frente Militar caused serious repercussions in the other operating arms of ETA. After the killing of the Guardia Civil member in Galdácano in August, police suppression of the organization was especially sharp. ETA members who were not in the Frente Militar suffered as much as if they had been a part of the armed attack units of ETA. In addition, the Frente Militar enjoyed considerable autonomy within the organization, partly because it was held in some awe by other members and perhaps partly also because it was feared by the others. In any case, members of the other fronts, especially the Frente Obrero, began to complain about the role of the Frente Militar within the organization. In the autumn of 1972, the organization convened another preassembly meeting to deal with some of these criticisms. The members of the Executive Committee refused to attend, whereupon the organization abolished the committee and replaced it with a new group of eighteen members. One objective of this restructuring was to reduce the bureaucracy of ETA and to decentralize, but a second important aim was to elevate the Frente Obrero to a position equal to that of the Frente Militar. The restructuring made the Frente Obrero the principal advocate of a political approach to struggle, in opposition to the Frente Militar, which continued to stress a military approach. Not surprisingly, the next schism of ETA was created by precisely this issue.

1973–74: ETA(m) and ETA (p-m)

In the fall of 1972, the Executive Committee of ETA received, quite by surprise, a piece of intelligence from one of its agents in Madrid that provoked considerable interest. According to this agent, one of Franco's most trusted advisors and the man generally regarded as the power behind the Franco government, Admiral Luis Carrero Blanco, had established a pattern of attending mass regularly at a specific church in one of Madrid's wealthy districts, and, more important, his protection was minimal, consisting of a sole bodyguard and a driver.

His kidnaping would be relatively easy and accompanied by little risk, but it would be a sensational blow against the Spanish state and could be used to extract major concessions from Franco. At that time, there were more than 150 etarras in prison, and it was believed that by kidnaping Carrero Blanco, ETA could obtain their release en masse. Wary of undertaking such an operation so far from the support network of ETA in the Basque region and unsure of the reliability of the information, the committee sent two members of one of its comandos to Madrid in December 1972 to confirm the report and return to discuss the operation with the committee. Thus began the planning for one of the most dramatic attacks ever launched by ETA, the assassination of the prime minister of Spain one year later.[21]

But at the turn of the year, in January 1973, the Carrero Blanco affair was still a distant operation. The attention of ETA's leadership was directed toward an action of much greater immediate import. Following the successful kidnaping of Lorenzo Zabala in 1972, the leadership had determined to carry out a second such operation, and awaited only the kind of labor dispute that would provide an appropriate context. By November 1972 such a conflict appeared, this time in the Torfinasa company in Pamplona, part of the enormous industrial and commercial holdings of one of Navarra's wealthiest families, the Huartes. (According to one source, the personal fortune of the Huarte family was estimated as equivalent to about $100 million.)[22]

In reality, labor troubles had been mounting for several years, not only in Navarra but throughout the Basque region. A series of strikes in the industrial areas around Bilbao in late 1971 had idled thousands of workers, and many hundreds of the strike leaders had been fired from their jobs. The strike in which Zabala's firm, Precicontrol, had been involved was one of fifteen such strikes that had taken place in Eibar in 1971. In November and December 1972, more than a dozen firms in Rentería and Eibar had been closed down by work stoppages. In January 1972, the Michelin plant in Vitoria had been closed by strikers, and this dispute led to mass demonstrations that had to be put down by police.

But in Navarra, the labor disputes became especially ugly, with considerable recrimination visited on both sides of each conflict. Because of his huge economic holdings, Felipe Huarte was a central figure in many of these disputes. In September, one of his many firms, Imenasa, was struck by angry workers demanding that the company negotiate a new contract with their elected representatives and not with so-called leaders chosen by the company's directors, who, it was charged, were nothing but puppets of the firm. By September 25, the strike had spread to other firms in Pamplona, and business leaders sent a letter to Madrid requesting special riot police to put down disturbances associated with the strike. On October 6, Imenasa simultaneously offered a slight increase in wages and fired all the strikers, but the next day the remaining workers rejected the offer overwhelmingly. A massive demonstration of solidarity with the Imenasa workers on October 9 had to be controlled by police, but it was sufficient to force Huarte to yield to workers' demands and reinstate the strikers.

Slightly more than one month later, on November 17, workers in another Huarte company, Torfinasa, went out on strike, and Huarte responded again by firing the strikers, and raising wages in his other companies to avoid solidarity work stoppages. At about this time, ETA decided that it had found the appropriate context for its next kidnaping.[23] This time, however, in addition to intervening in an active labor dispute, ETA decided to use the kidnaping to replenish its treasury, and a ransom payment of major proportions was added to the list of demands to be fulfilled to obtain Huarte's release. The leader and organizer of the kidnaping was Eustaquio Mendizábal. To assist him, ETA assigned two separate comandos, one to actually seize Huarte and the second to hide him during the phase of negotiations that would ensue.

Preparing the operation took a relatively long time, during which the labor dispute showed some signs of lessening. According to José María Portell, members of ETA met with leaders of the striking workers on at least two occasions, to deliver money to them to support the strikers and to urge the strikers to remain out for a period long enough to enable them to seize Huarte while the stoppage was still in effect. The strikers allegedly told the etarras that they (the workers) did not want anything dramatic to happen and were perfectly capable of bringing the strike to a successful conclusion without acts of violence. It is not clear whether or not the strikers knew that their benefactors were from ETA and that ETA was helping keep the dispute alive to provide a better reason for kidnaping Huarte.

In any case, on January 16, 1973, at about 7:30 in the evening, the four members of the first comando entered the Huarte home prepared to seize Felipe Huarte. Since he had not yet come home, they took the three Huarte children and the four servants to the wine cellar to prevent them from warning him when he did come. At 10:30, Huarte and his wife arrived, whereupon the kidnapers seized him and took him away in his own automobile, after leaving the other members of the household tied in the cellar. In the telephone book they left their ransom demands: 50 million pesetas (about $800,000) and the solution of the Torfinasa dispute according to the demands of the workers. By the time police were called, the kidnap comando had removed Huarte to a cave near Mendizábal's home town of Isasondo. Later, after transferring him to the custody of the second comando, ETA moved him again, this time to a "safe house" hiding place near San Sebastián. The labor dispute was resolved almost immediately, but the ransom payment was more difficult. After the transmission of a number of messages between the family and the organizers of the kidnaping, it was agreed to deliver the ransom in two payments through a network of intermediaries. The first payment of 25 million pesetas was made in Brussels on January 19; the second, in Paris on January 26. That same day at about 8:00 P.M., Huarte was released, tired and shaken, but basically unharmed.[24] Police charged some sixteen ETA members with conduct or support of the kidnaping, of whom eight were actually caught and brought to trial the following June.[25] The leader of the action, Eustaquio Mendizábal, was killed by police in April. Of the remaining seven, two were eventually absolved of complicity in the crime and five were never caught. None of the ransom money was ever recovered. It was said that Mendizábal and some of the other ETA leaders had had a falling out over the disposition of the ransom money, and that because of this, information was given to the police, which produced Mendizábal's detection and death some months later. While we do not have proof that this is true, it would not be startling to find out that it was.

The next six months or so were marked by an upsurge in ETA activity. On January 31, Mendizábal's comando assaulted a powder magazine near Hernani, in Guipúzcoa, and made off with 3,000 kilos of explosive. The explosive was hidden in the same secret hiding place where Huarte had been kept near San Sebastián. According to *Operation Ogro*, the standard account of the Carrero Blanco assassination, the explosives used to kill the prime minister were part of the 3,000 kilos stolen from the Hernani storehouse.[26] In March and April, there were a number of minor bombings in small towns in Guipúzcoa. The death of Mendizábal in April set the organization back slightly, but it returned to the attack in May and June with a series of bombings and a major bank robbery in Santurce.[27] During June and July, although ETA's direct attacks slackened somewhat, the trial of the accused Huarte kidnapers kept ETA's name in the daily press. In July and August, ETA returned to the offensive with several bombings of private homes and offices, the burning of a bookstore, a robbery, and a shootout with police in Guernica. Then, for reasons unknown to police, the organization retreated in mid-August and was not heard from for several months. There were two reasons for their withdrawal: preparations for the attack against Carrero Blanco, and the "legitimate" Sixth Assembly.

All during the winter and spring, an ETA comando had been living in Madrid to observe the routine of Carrero Blanco and to plan the kidnaping. The four men had passed themselves off to their landlord as professionals in a variety of occupations, including economics, and they said that they were in Madrid to conduct an industrial study for a corporation interested in investing in the area. They observed Carrero Blanco carefully as he came and went to and from mass at the Church of San Francisco de Borja, located in a wealthy neighborhood of Madrid near the American embassy. By mid-February, the plan had been set to kidnap Carrero Blanco as he attended mass. The plan would have required at least two more comandos in Madrid, some eight more men, as well as a number of automobiles and apartments in the city, all of which implied a major operation that required approval of the Executive Committee. At about this time, Mendizábal's death threw the organization into some confusion, and the plan was delayed. Then in June, Carrero Blanco was promoted from his position as vice premier to be the chief of government directly under Franco. This step brought with it not only a changed routine but many additional security forces to protect Carrero Blanco, which forced the comando to reconsider its plan. As August approached, the team decided to return to the Basque country to reconsider, as well as to attend the Sixth Assembly then being organized.

After two preassemblies, in the summer of 1971 and the fall of 1972, ETA was now ready at last to celebrate its version, the only legitimate one, it claimed, of the organization's Sixth Assembly. The leadership called this meeting the Sixth Assembly, so that everyone would understand that what had purported to be the Sixth Assembly in 1970 was nothing more than an illegal attempt by dissidents to seize control of the organization. Thus the 1973 Sixth Assembly, sometimes referred to as the "legitimate" Sixth Assembly, was the direct lineal descendent of the Fifth Assembly even though there was no one at the 1973 assembly who had attended the 1966–67 meetings.

The Sixth Assembly of 1973 took pains to avoid discussing issues of fundamental ideological importance. For one thing, most of those present believed that the principles adopted by the Fifth Assembly would serve as a basis for the organization for the time being, and there was no need to develop new ideological precepts. Furthermore, what the group suffered from most was lack of organization; after the disorderly 1972 preassembly and Mendizábal's death, it was not clear who, if anyone, was in charge. Finally, everyone feared a rupture between the Frente Militar and the Frente Obrero if questions of fundamental principle were raised at the meeting. It was decided, therefore, to hold a second half of the Sixth Assembly where these matters would be discussed.

What the organization did do was use the Sixth Assembly to refocus its efforts on armed struggle. According to Portell, the assembly made nine basic decisions:[28]

1. To maintain the organization's fundamentally military character
2. To intensify violent action
3. To gather together and train all of the exiled etarras in France
4. "To keep the action alive with collective attacks of personal reprisal" (the meaning of this statement is not clear)
5. To maintain morale despite arrests of key members
6. To choose a new Executive Committee, composed of Domingo Iturbe Abasolo "Txomin" (leader of ETA militar in 1981); José Manuel Pagoaga Gallastegui (killed in France in January, 1979); José Ignacio Múgica Arregui (arrested in September, 1975); and José Antonio Urriticoechea Bengoechea—an Executive Committee that was very promilitary and leaned decisively toward the Frente Militar
7. To designate new chiefs of operating comandos
8. To assign new nonmilitary functions to other members, including political and recruiting work and cultural affairs
9. To maintain close contact with Enbata, the Basque nationalist group in France

It is clear that none of these decisions has anything to do with general theories of insurrection, or the question of class versus ethnicity, or other similar basic principles. In 1973, ETA dedicated all of its energy to gearing its organization to undertake major armed assaults.

According to José María Portell, ETA in late 1973 consisted of about fifty to sixty members divided into operating cells or comandos of four to five men each. The organization was run by a directorate of about fifteen, at the center of which was the four-man Executive Committee. Perhaps in recognition of the inability of the organization to replace Mendizábal, no one was considered the leader of the group, however. The comandos were given maximum latitude to select their own targets, so long as the action contemplated was not of major importance. Membership of the comandos fluctuated, depending upon the skills and experience required by the particular operation. For a major action, the Executive Committee kept the comando on a very short rein to avoid mistakes of timing or execution.[29]

During the autumn of 1973, the message went out from ETA's Executive Committee to its operating cells to "make noise" (*armar ruido*). Something big was being planned and kept a tightly guarded secret. All the comandos knew was that they had to "make noise" to divert attention from the upcoming attack. Through the fall, then, the tempo of ETA attacks rose markedly.[30] There were several bombings and attempts at arson in November, as well as an unsuccessful attempt to kidnap the Spanish ambassador to the European Common Market, Alberto Ullastres. On November 28, two etarras, José Etxebarria Sagastume and José Luis Pagazaurtundua, were killed when a bomb they were assembling exploded accidentally. On December 6, police surprised an ETA member named Yosu Arteche in an ETA "safe house" in San Sebastián, and engaged in a running gun battle with him from 2:00 in the morning until 2:00 the following afternoon. Finally, because Arteche knew of what was being planned in Madrid and could not run the risk of being captured, he killed himself with his own pistol. From early November through mid-December, ETA had suffered one of its most serious blows since the arrests of 1969. Apart from the three etarras who had died, some thirty more had been caught and imprisoned. Nevertheless their "noise-making" had succeeded, for the plan to kill Carrero Blanco proceeded on schedule.

The assassination of the Spanish prime minister, one of the most dramatic armed assaults in the history of ETA, has been described repeatedly elsewhere. Here we need only summarize the basic details of the attack. Apparently, following the Sixth Assembly in August, the Executive Committee decided that since a kidnaping was impossible, ETA would attempt to assassinate Carrero Blanco, who was given the code name Ogro. The comando, now known by the code name Txikia after the slain Eustaquio Mendizábal, returned to Madrid, and in November managed to rent a basement apartment at 104 Claudio Coello street, along the route followed by Carrero Blanco as he left mass every day. On December 7, the comando began to tunnel under the street. The dirt extracted from the street was kept in plastic bags in the apartment. To explain the noise of the excavation, the etarras told their landlord that they were sculptors working on a statue. The tunnel extended under Claudio Coello street, and ended in the form of a T with a second tunnel running at right angles to the access tunnel from the apartment. By December 17, the tunnel was finished. Explosives had been brought by another ETA team from somewhere in the Basque region. It was subsequently discovered that the explosives were part of those stolen from the Hernani arsenal some eleven months earlier. The explosives, some 75 to 80 kilos of "Goma-2," were placed at the end of the tunnel along the horizontal part of the T and directly beneath the spot where Carrero Blanco's car would pass as he left church. To force his car over the correct spot and to cause his driver to reduce his speed, another car was double-parked next to the location of the tunnel and explosives.

The assassination had originally been set for December 13, but some technical difficulties forced a postponement until December 18. More problems caused a delay until December 19, but the visit of the American secretary of state Henry Kissinger to Madrid forced still another postponement, until December 20. On that fateful day at about 9:25 in the morning as Carrero Blanco's car passed over the explosives, the ETA *comando*, disguised as electricians working on cables along the street, detonated the charge. The force of the explosion threw the car over a five-story-high wall of the church and into the interior courtyard. The car's three occupants, Carrero Blanco, his driver, and his bodyguard, died instantly. The *etarras* ran off shouting that there had been an explosion of gas from the street, and in the general pandemonium that followed they made good their escape.

For several days, the authorship of the assassination remained unclear. Basque nationalists denied that ETA could have carried out such an attack. The Spanish Communist Party hinted darkly at other more mysterious assailants. On December 22, however, ETA issued a communiqué accepting responsibility. On Christmas Eve, two days later, ETA leaders held a press conference in France to which they had brought a group of blindfolded journalists and at which they demonstrated conclusively by their knowledge of the attack that ETA had indeed been responsible. The Spanish government officially charged six ETA members with the attack: José Miguel Beñarán Ordeñana "Argala," who would die himself almost exactly five years later in the bombing of his car in France; another member of the Executive Committee, José Antonio Urruticoechea Bengoechea; and four others— José Ignacio Abaitua, Javier María Larreategui, Pedro Ignacio Pérez Beotegui, and Juan Bautista Santisteban.

There seems little doubt that the assassination of Carrero Blanco had a major impact on the course of Spanish politics, probably making it possible for Juan Carlos to ascend the throne immediately after Franco's death. On the other hand, the killing had an even greater effect on ETA itself, and set in motion a series of events that would change fundamentally the character of the organization.

As I have already noted, the conflict between the Frente Militar and the Frente Obrero had been building for several years. The attack on Carrero Blanco was the catalyst that caused this conflict to erupt into a series of splits within the organization that negated much of the expansion of ETA during the preceding several years. These splits had the effect of separating even further the Frente Militar from ETA members who, by conviction or by character, were able and willing to try more conventional political tactics. As Spain left Francoism behind in 1976 and 1977, those members of ETA who could have led the organization into the new Spanish democracy had divided the organization a year earlier. As we shall see shortly, these members were predisposed toward a more political strategy to gain independence for Euzkadi, and became active members of the Basque system of political parties through the 1970s and into the 1980s. The etarras they left behind, the members of the Frente Militar, were ill prepared by temperament or philosophy to pursue democratic politics, and when the Franco era gave way to a new constitutional regime in Spain, they could not adjust to the changed circumstances. Had events turned out differently and had the more political members of ETA held the organization together to leaven its councils, the history of ETA and the history of Spain during the last half of the 1970s might well have taken an entirely different course.

The first splits came early in 1974, soon after the Carrero Blanco assassination. The Frente Cultural separated from ETA and joined with dissident members of the Basque labor union, Solidarity of Basque Workers (Solidaridad de Trabajadores Vascos, STV) to form the Basque Socialist Party (Euskal Alderdi Sozialista, EAS). At the same time, on the French side of the border, other members of the FC were forming the Popular Socialist Party (Herriko Alderdi Sozialista, HAS). In 1975, the two parties fused to form the Basque Popular Socialist Party (Euskal Herriko Alderdi Sozialista, EHAS). After Franco's death, EHAS would change its name to the Popular Revolutionary Socialist Party (Herriko Alderdi Sozialista Iraultzalea, HASI), which was to become one of the core parties in the coalition Herri Batasuna (HB).[31]

The more important split in 1974 was that initiated by events within the Frente Obrero. Calling the Carrero Blanco killing "the greatest error in the history of ETA" and accusing the Frente Militar of imposing its point of view on the rest of ETA, the leadership of the Frente Obrero declared itself to be free of the discipline of the organization.[32] The Executive Committee of ETA responded by expelling many of the FO leaders, who reacted in turn by resigning from ETA to form their own organization. This new party, which appeared by late 1974, was called the Patriotic Revolutionary Workers Party (Langille Abertzale Iraultzalean Alderdia, LAIA), and it, in turn, would form its own labor union, the Patriotic Workers Committee (Langille Albertzale Komiteak, LAK). LAIA would also form part of the Herri Batasuna coalition during the late 1970s.[33]

Despite the expulsion (or withdrawal, as one wishes) of many leaders of the Frente Obrero, the bulk of the Frente remained an integral part of ETA until later in the year. In June 1974, the Biltzar Txikia of ETA held a key meeting at which members of the Frente Obrero and of the Frente Militar disagreed sharply on future organizational structure, as well as on the role of armed struggle in ETA's strategy. (It should be noted in passing that a number of events inside and outside of Spain seemed to suggest the coming of a more democratic political system in the country: the "opening" of Prime Minister Arias Navarro in February; the fall of the dictatorship in Portugal in April, and of the military regime in Greece in July; and Franco's illness and the appearance in June of his imminent death.) The disagreement between members of the FO and FM carried over into the autumn and would be sharpened by still another dramatic act of violence: the bombing of the Cafe Rolando in Madrid.

In reality, armed actions of ETA had increased considerably since the spring of 1974, even before the Rolando bombing. In April, a member of the Guardia Civil was killed in Azpeitia (Guipúzcoa); in June, a second was shot to death in Ergoyen (Navarra). On September 13, at about 2:15 in the afternoon during the busy Madrid lunch period, a powerful explosive ripped through the Cafe Rolando on Correo Street, across from the headquarters of the Spanish government's Bureau of Security. Reports on casualties varied, but the *New York Times* listed them as nine killed and fifty-six wounded.[34] The responsibility of ETA for this tragedy has never been fixed precisely. According to the confessions of some of the accused, including Spanish leftists Eva Forrest and Antonio Duran, ETA supplied the explosives and the team that actually put them them in place, a young man and woman who, to my knowledge, have never been identified. In addition, participants in the plot used sanctuaries built into false walls and other hiding places constructed by several ETA members during the summer of 1974. On the other hand, ETA issued a comminqué on October 20, thirty-seven days after the explosion, denying any complicity in the attack. The delay in issuing the statement, said ETA, was due to their efforts to verify whether or not several of their members might have been involved on their own without ETA approval.

It was in this atmosphere that ETA held the next meeting of the Biltzar Txikia in October, a meeting that produced the final and most definitive split in the organization. At this meeting, according to Ortzi, the advocates of a unified political and military strategy found themselves in the majority.[35] Seizing the advantage of numbers, they proceeded to restructure the organization, deleting the four separate fronts and providing for a unified political-military organization down to the regional level, where the local directors would be responsible for both types of activity. In their opinion, the military struggle and

the effort to promote a mass organization would be mutually supportive. In addition, this group proposed the creation of a unified Basque
Left with a program that included the independence and reunification
of the Basque nation, the establishment of Euskera as the official
language, and the establishment of socialism and proletarian interna-
tionalism in the Basque country. According to Mario Onaindia in his
account of this development, the political-military faction of ETA was
closer to traditional interpretations of marxism-leninism because of its
commitment to a joint political and military strategy that combined an
armed party at the head of a mobilized proletariat.[36] In this approach,
they echoed the influence of similar organizations in Latin America,
in particular the Tupamaros of Uruguay. The first concrete step taken
by this faction after the BT meeting in October was to create Patriotic
Workers Councils (Langille Abertzalean Batzordeak, LAB), which
were directly involved, along with other underground unions, in
fostering the general strikes in the Basque country in December 1974
and June and September 1975.

Shortly after the October BT meeting, however, the group that had
found itself in the minority, the military faction, issued a manifesto
announcing its decision to maintain the strategy of a small clandestine
group dedicated to armed struggle.[37] This faction, directly linked to
the now-extinct Frente Militar, argued that it was premature to talk
about developing a mass-based organization. They argued that it was
essential to remain committed to the clandestine struggle of a tiny
armed group, in order not to be seduced by the false appearance of
democracy in Spain. The faction was apparently influenced by the
strategy of the Palestinian group Black September. In November
1974, it split off from ETA to form the group now known as ETA
(militar), or ETA(m).

Thus as 1974 came to an end, the basic outline of ETA as it was to
appear during the last year of Francoism and the first years of the new
Spanish constitutional regime had already been formed. The group
favoring a combined strategy of mass organization and armed struggle,
to be known henceforth as ETA (político-militar) or ETA (p-m), was
actually the more radical of the two, since it was deeply committed to
class struggle in the marxist-leninist sense in addition to the struggle
based on Basque ethnicity. The proponent of a strategy based solely
on a tiny armed group, ETA (militar), while less radical in an ideological sense, became the more dangerous and disruptive as the years
wore on, because of its greater commitment to armed action to prosecute the war against Spain and capitalism. Through the mid-1970s, the
more radical members of ETA(p-m) would grow restive and leave to

join the more dramatic and activist ETA(m), so that by the beginning of the 1980s, ETA(m) members would outnumber those of ETA(p-m) by about three to one.

1975: Franco's Last Year

The twelve months that preceded General Franco's death, from November 1974 to November 1975, were the most turbulent and violent in Spain since the end of the Civil War. Much of the violence stemmed from attacks launched by ETA, or from popular demonstrations in support of ETA members or objectives. Spain in general, however, and the Basque provinces in particular, were powder kegs on the point of exploding as the Franco regime drew to its inevitable close. Much of the disorder that attended the General's agonizingly slow death derived not so much from ETA's deliberate attacks as from massive unrest that spread through the Basque country and that manifested itself in three violent general strikes during the period. The two branches of ETA were swept along in these convulsive events that were, to some degree, not only beyond their control but beyond the control of the Spanish government or of any of the remaining fragile institutions of the Franco state. Both ETA(m) and ETA(p-m) were still uncertain about their strategies and ideologies for the post-Franco period, and the disorder of Franco's last year provided an unstable setting within which to develop them.

The spasms of violence began with the arrests of ETA leaders in November 1974, when the ETA(p-m) chief in San Sebastián, José María Apalategui, was detained, along with about 20 other major figures in the organization. On November 24, more than 150 Basque political prisoners began a hunger strike to demand amnesty, freedom for all political prisoners, and the return of all exiles from abroad. Several days later, ETA(p-m) joined the struggle with a call to all the workers of Euzkadi to conduct a general strike on December 2 and 3. According to *Le Monde*, more than 200,000 Basque workers walked off their jobs, and there were many other acts of defiance, including sit-in demonstrations in Basque churches and several bombings and bomb threats.[38] Practically the entire economy of Guipúzcoa was brought to a halt, especially in the Goierri region in towns like Beasain, Lazcano, and Villafranca. On December 5, the strike spread to bank employees, and virtually the entire financial system of the Basque provinces closed down. In Navarra and Vizcaya, the general strike coincided with other labor disputes that had been festering for some weeks, and together, they were severely damaging to the provinces' industry. On December 11, other left-wing organizations in the Basque region joined the strike, and added to the list of demands a number of measures having to do with inflation and unemployment.

Also in December, the level of attacks against the Guardia Civil and police increased measurably. On December 14, a Guardia Civil sergeant was wounded in Beasain. On December 17, two members of the Guardia Civil were killed in Mondragón. On December 18, an ETA comando was frustrated in its attempt to steal 25 million pesetas from a factory in Urdúliz, but two Guardia Civil members were wounded as the team made its escape. Also on December 18, police at a road block near Hernani machine-gunned a passing automobile, killing one of its occupants. On December 28, another ETA team assaulted the Banco de Bilbao in Vitoria and made off with 6 million pesetas, wounding a member of the Guardia Civil at a roadblock as they fled.

The period from December 1974 through January 1975 was one of great activity for ETA(p-m). In late 1974 the organization launched what it referred to as Herriko Batasuna, a movement for a Basque popular front.[39] The demands of this proposal included the following points:

1. The creation of a Basque government which would hold free elections
2. The dissolution of all the Spanish law-enforcement authorities in the Basque country and their replacement with a security force under the jurisdiction of the Basque government
3. Punishments to be meted out to the leading figures in the Francoist police state apparatus in the Basque region
4. Nationalization of basic industries, and measures to improve the conditions of life of the Basque workers
5. The adoption of a confederal system with other regional or national minorities within the Spanish state
6. Political and labor union freedom; amnesty and the return of exiles
7. The availability of funds to aid in the integration of non-Basques in Basque society if they wished to remain in the Basque region; to those who did not wish to be so integrated, guarantees that their ethnicity, language, and other rights would be fully protected under the new Basque autonomous regime

In January 1975, ETA(p-m) held the second half of the "legitimate" Sixth Assembly, the first half of which had been held in August, 1973. The outcome of this meeting was to make ETA(p-m) a more homogeneous organization that combined armed struggle with an intensified effort to organize workers' councils to serve as alternatives to local and municipal governments in the Basque provinces. In contrast to earlier assemblies, this one made an attempt to sketch out the framework for a Basque socialist state in the post-Franco Spanish political system, and it was clearly implied that such a state would be based on a loose federation of workers' committees from each town or neighborhood. At the same time, the old third-world argument in favor of a prolonged guerrilla war against the Guardia Civil was definitely rejected. As the Sixth Assembly put it, "Euzkadi is a revolutionary *foco* (focal point) isolated from the rest of the [Spanish] state, which makes easier the concentration of enemy forces in our territory. But the impossibility of military triumph does not exclude the possibility of political victory."[40] To force Madrid to negotiate the details of such a political outcome, however, it was necessary to keep up the pressure through even more dramatic acts of violence. As the assembly determined, it would pursue a "war of attrition (*desgaste*) based on the impossibility of defeating the enemy militarily, and with the objective of forcing a political negotiation whose terms would be determined by the balance of forces (*correlación de fuerzas*)." To accomplish this objective, the Sixth Assembly created a new organization, the *comandos especiales*, known also as the *comandos bereziak*. These special units were to be assigned assault missions likely to have a great impact on the "balance of forces." Ideally, these assaults would hurry along the day when the Spanish state would have to enter into the political negotiations ETA(p-m) expected. The third-world strategy of guerrilla struggle was abandoned, as well as the action-repression-action spiral theory from the 1960s. From now on, ETA(p-m) would force Madrid to the bargaining table by means of armed attacks that imposed such a heavy psychological cost on the Spanish state that it would have no choice but to negotiate.

For the next several weeks, during February and early March 1975, the Basque provinces returned to a wary silence. ETA(m) had withdrawn from active combat for the time being while its leadership worked through the ideological and strategic issues generated by its resignation from ETA.[41] Meanwhile, ETA(p-m) was gathering itself together for a renewed assault on the last remains of Francoism. The period of calm was not to last for long.

On March 30, ETA(p-m) shot and killed a police inspector named José Diaz Linares in San Sebastián, and on April 22 they killed a policeman named Morán in Algorta. On April 24, police arrested one ETA leader and killed a second in Ergobia. On April 25, General Franco decreed a state of exception for the provinces of Vizcaya and

Guipúzcoa, under which constitutional guarantees were suspended and a form of martial law was imposed. Some two to three thousand Basques were detained during the three months that this decree was in effect, and large numbers of them were tortured and held incommunicado for weeks.[42] Mobs of enraged rightists assaulted citizens in bars and restaurants and aboard buses and trains, and youths were beaten on city streets for no reason. The violence of a police state had given way to the violence of anarchy.

Perhaps sensing that they were close to producing chaos in Spain, ETA continued the attack. Shortly after the declaration of the state of exception, ETA(m) killed a Guardia Civil member in Guernica and a police inspector in Bilbao, and on May 14 they killed a Guardia Civil lieutenant in Guernica.

The reaction from Madrid was ferocious. In April and May, right-wing counterterrorist organizations launched a violent campaign against Basques in exile in France, a campaign that included bombings and arson attacks against Basque bookstores, bars, and commercial establishments. The French government claimed inability to deal with this threat, and the attacks proceeded unimpeded through the spring and summer.[43] On May 22, the Spanish government declared a state of absolute press censorship and secrecy about the events in the two provinces under the exception decree; and to publish any news of developments there was a crime against the state. In early June, the commanding general of Spain's Sixth Military Region (which included the Basque provinces), toured the Guardia Civil posts in Vizcaya and Guipúzcoa, and was quoted as telling the Guardia Civil that "although the mission of the Army is not to maintain public order, I want you to know that we are behind you."[44] The Basque Left countered with its second general strike, which began on June 11. In Guipúzcoa, more than 60,000 workers walked off the job; in Vizcaya, only about 15,000. In Navarra, more than 25 major firms were closed down by the strike.[45]

The state of exception decreed by Franco in April came to an end on July 25, but the violence and disorder continued unabated, leading to still another state of exception on August 26, this one to last until Franco's death nearly three months later. The specific cause of the disorders of August and September was the trial and impending execution of five convicted terrorists, two of whom were members of ETA. (The other three were from a radical Spanish leftist group known as FRAP, the Patriotic Revolutionary Anti-Fascist Front).

The arrest, trial, conviction, and execution of the two etarras outraged Basque public opinion as nothing had since the Burgos trial nearly five years earlier.[46] The first was a young man named Angel

Otaegi, who had been arrested in November 1974 in Azpeitia and charged with aiding the ETA team that had killed a member of the Guardia Civil troop in Azpeitia the preceding April. The government's case rested on the testimony of another etarra, presumably one of those who had taken part in the shooting, who had been arrested in October. In taking him prisoner, however, the police had shot him in the head, and the wound had rendered him speechless and paralyzed. It was under these circumstances that his testimony had allegedly linked Otaegi to the crime. According to the state's case, Otaegi had given room and meals to the assault team before the attack and had pointed out the victim to the attackers moments before they killed him. Otaegi admitted to being a sympathizer of ETA(m) but denied any knowledge of the specific crime. He was found guilty by a military court, and sentenced to death by firing squad in Burgos.

The second etarra was Jon Paredes Manot "Txiki," who had lived in hiding or in exile since 1974 and who had been associated with ETA(p-m) leaders Ignacio Pérez Beotegui "Wilson" and Miguel Angel Apalategui "Apala." Txiki was captured in Barcelona following an attempted bank robbery and was accused of taking part in attacks that had killed two policemen, one in March 1975 and the second in June. He likewise denied the accusations, and likewise was found guilty by a military tribunal in a trial filled with numerous defects of procedure that prevented his attorneys from mounting his defense. Txiki was sentenced to death by firing squad in Barcelona.

The response of Basque public opinion was still another general strike, the third in less than a year, that ran intermittently from August 28 through September 30. From August 28 to September 3, more than 150,000 workers stayed away from their jobs, and eventually more than 200,000 were idled by the strike.[47] The strike spread to the Basque region of France, where 1,500 demonstrated on August 28 in Bayonne and 1,000 in Hendaye the following day. A wave of protests rippled through the capitals of Western Europe. Pope Paul VI appealed to General Franco for clemency for all the prisoners. There were demonstrations in Lisbon, Paris, Brussels, Copenhagen, Athens, Rome, and Frankfort against the executions. The European Common Market issued a strong official condemnation, and the governments of West Germany and Holland recalled their ambassadors to Madrid.

In the face of all these pressures and mounting unrest, General Franco remained firm. While he did grant clemency to six other convicted insurgents, including two women and the etarra who had the brain injury, the executions of the five, including Txiki and Otaegi, were carried out on September 26. Almost immediately thereafter, the Spanish government revealed its intention to go ahead with the trial of fifteen other accused ETA members, including two accused of taking part in the killing of Carrero Blanco, José Múgica Arregui, and Ignacio Pérez Beotegui "Wilson." ETA responded to this announcement by attacking a government social security office in Barcelona and escaping with more than 3 million pesetas, wounding two policemen in the process.

On October 1, only a few hours before a mass demonstration in Madrid to support the Franco regime, unidentified gunmen attacked police in three separate areas of the capital, killing three of their victims and wounding a fourth. On October 5, three guardsmen of the Guardia Civil were killed and two more wounded in an explosion that destroyed their jeep on patrol in a mountainous area of Guipúzcoa southwest of San Sebastián. The next day, extreme rightists machine-gunned to death a Basque bar owner in reprisal for the ETA killings. In all, from January 1974 through October 1975, twenty-two police or Guardia Civil troops and fourteen civilians had been killed by ETA.

On November 22, General Franco died after a long and agonizing illness, thus bringing to a close one of the most turbulent and painful moments in Spanish and Basque political history. How ETA would respond to the challenges of the post-Franco environment was unclear, as were many aspects of Spanish politics. On the one hand, ETA(m) had apparently drawn back from its activist position of a year or two earlier. ETA(p-m) had been seriously weakened by the wave of arrests of some of its key members in June and again in September.[48] On the other hand, there were already signs of an increasing awareness within ETA that it would eventually have to adjust to the special demands put on it by a new, post-Franco Spanish democracy. Shortly before the Txiki and Otaegi executions, the organization had created a coordinating body known as the Patriotic Socialist Coordinating Council (Koordinadora Abertzale Sozialista, KAS), which was composed of the Popular Revolutionary Socialist Party (EHAS), the Patriotic Revolutionary Workers Party (LAIA), and ETA(p-m), as well as labor unions, and with the support (but not the active participation) of ETA(m).[49] In the years to come, as Spain made the transition to constitutional democracy and electoral politics, the KAS coalition would be a major actor in the Basque provinces and a central rallying point for the Basque Left.

CHAPTER FOUR

ETA in Post-Franco Spain: 1976—80

During the last half of the 1970s, Spain made what many people regarded as a decisive transition to constitutional democracy buttressed by a popular and charismatic monarch, King Juan Carlos. By 1977, most of the institutional trappings of Francoism had been eliminated. In 1977 and again in 1979, national parliaments were selected by democratic processes that met most of the criteria one would impose for judging free and open electoral systems. Also in 1979, for the first time since the Civil War, Spaniards enjoyed the opportunity of electing their municipal and provincial assemblies. In December 1978, the King promulgated the new constitution that would provide the institutional framework within which the transformation of the Spanish state would take place. All in all, it was in most ways an impressive show of Spain's commitment to undoing the Francoist state in short order.

For the Basques, the record of the first five years of post-Franco Spain was more mixed. On the surface there were substantial improvements in the institutions of self-governance, and the region obtained more autonomy than it had ever enjoyed before in modern times. The 1978 constitution contained explicit provisions for the creation of autonomous regional governments, and the document had barely been issued when Basque representatives submitted a proposed autonomy statute for consideration in Madrid. In October 1979, Basque voters affirmed their approval of the resulting draft statute, and in March 1980, the first autonomous Basque government was elected and began its labors.

The apparently peaceful transition to an autonomous government for the Basques masked some real and continuing difficulties for an autonomous Basque region within a democratic Spain. The issue of amnesty for Basque prisoners aggravated relationships between Euzkadi and Madrid throughout the late 1970s. Economic indicators like unemployment level worsened almost daily in the Basque country, and a state of panic began to creep into normally positive Basque perceptions of the future. Moreover, there were significant signs of a weakening commitment in Madrid to real autonomy for the Basques. The process of transferring powers to the regional government was agonizingly slow and each point required long and arduous negotiations.

It was against this backdrop that ETA played out its role in the transition to the post-Franco era. Relatively quiet during 1976 and 1977, ETA killed more people in 1978 than it had in all of the preceding years combined. In 1979 and 1980, Spain's Basque provinces acquired the unwanted distinction of being the site of more politically motivated violence than any other comparably sized territory in Europe. In 1980, of the 126 political killings recorded in Spain, 110 of them took place in the Basque provinces. Of these, 88 were committed by ETA. Why ETA chose to raise the level of its violence so dramatically, and how the organization managed to maintain its commitment to armed struggle under the changed conditions of Spanish and Basque politics, are the central questions to be answered about this phase of ETA's history.

1976–77: The Transition Period

During the two years following Franco's death, Basque politics was a maze of intersecting forces. As the region began to come to grips with the implications of the new regime in Spain, there was much experimentation with new political forms and strategies, crowned with varying degrees of success. As we look at the history of ETA during this turbulent period, we see a fascinating interplay of several key factors: a continuation of the armed struggle through increasingly dramatic acts of violence; new efforts to establish mass-based organizations, including political parties and labor unions; and a series of internal disputes and power struggles that were at once ideological and personal.

Seen in retrospect, the new post-Franco regime managed the transition to an operating constitutional democracy with remarkably little disorder, due primarily to the personal charisma and institutional power of the new monarch, King Juan Carlos.[1] Three days after he was crowned king, Juan Carlos proclaimed a general amnesty for nearly all of Spain's political prisoners and a reduction of prison terms for many of those who remained in jail. This initial amnesty was followed by a second in July 1976 and a third in March 1977. These amnesty measures were followed closely in Euzkadi, since most of the political prisoners were Basque. As a result of the decrees, nearly all these prisoners had been released by the second anniversary of Franco's death.[2]

Amnesty was not the only significant issue dealt with during these months. On a number of issues, including symbolic questions like the legalization of the Basques' right to fly their own flag, Madrid took a conciliatory position intended to soften Basque opposition to the Spanish government. Personnel changes were made at the senior levels of the Guardia Civil and the armed forces to give them a new and less Francoist image among Basques. Press censorship was relaxed, and by mid-1977 new Basque newspapers, like *Deia* in Bilbao and *Egin* in San Sebastián, appeared on the streets.

There were, of course, important institutional changes in Spain as well. In April 1976, the parliament approved new labor legislation that liberalized constraints on forming unions and engaging in strikes. In June, they approved the law that legalized political parties for the first time since the Civil War. In March 1977, the Basque Nationalist Party (PNV) returned to legal status. Its first public convention since the days of the Spanish Republic was an emotional event marked by the return from exile of a number of old PNV stalwarts from the 1930s and 1940s. In June 1977, free elections produced the first democratically chosen Spanish parliament since 1936.[3] This was the assembly charged with drafting a new constitution for the country, which would be promulgated officially by Juan Carlos about a year and a half later.

It is noteworthy, then, that despite these rather rapid transition measures from November 1975 to October 1977, popular sentiment in the Basque region remained decisively opposed to what was taking place in the rest of Spain and decidedly antagonistic to the new Spanish president, Adolfo Suárez.[4] For one thing, the level of street disorders rose markedly during 1976 and 1977. In March 1976, street demonstrations and strikes in Vitoria, the capital of Alava province, were brutally suppressed by riot police at a cost of five deaths. This violence was answered by a general strike throughout the Basque provinces, which saw about half a million workers walk off their jobs, and which eventually had to be quelled by police firing live ammunition over the heads of the strikers. In September, a young demonstrator named Zabala was allegedly shot in Fuenterrabia (Guipúzcoa) by a police officer who escaped with the aid of other police. This killing provoked another general strike throughout the province, which spread to the other Basque provinces and eventually involved some 700,000 workers before it ran its course by the end of the month. In March 1977, after the Guardia Civil had killed two members of ETA whom they had halted for a routine inspection of their car in San

Sebastián, the workers of Guipúzcoa went out on strike again, idling about 120,000. In March and again in May 1977, demonstrations in favor of amnesty for all prisoners had been forcefully put down by police, leaving more than half a dozen dead and scores injured.

The Basque region during these days was like a pressure cooker about to explode. Sentiments for change had been so sharply suppressed during the dictatorship of Franco that there had been little opportunity for the expression of dissent. With the dictator gone, Basques now sought to release the pressures built up over the preceding forty years. The new government in Madrid, on the other hand, counseled patience while it worked through the complicated and hazardous business of reform. After all, the new king and his new president had to be wary of pressures coming from the armed forces and new-Francoists that could wreck the democratic experiment if it gave too much freedom to the Basques too quickly. The consequence was that Basques saw their hopes for rapid change dashed time after time. Amnesty was granted, but not for all the prisoners. Even after a general amnesty was declared, it was still negotiated on a case-by-case basis. Party reforms were introduced, but some major Basque parties remained illegal through the 1977 elections. Freedom of dissent and association were protected, but the police still used extraordinary force to suppress mass demonstrations. And, of course, ETA remained a constant threat to public order in the region.

During 1976 and 1977, patterns of ETA activity were characterized by four central elements: the personal struggle for power within the organization; the changes in organizational structure and internal alliances; the level and nature of violent attacks; and the efforts to launch a mass-based organization that could compete in a democratic environment.

The first six months after Franco's death were marked by a number of armed assaults by ETA on a variety of targets. Continuing a series of attacks the organization had begun before November 20, ETA assassinated two Basque mayors who were alleged to be supporters of the Franco regime as well as police informers: Antonio Echeverría, the mayor of Oyarzún (Guipúzcoa) on November 24, 1975, and Victor Legoburu, the mayor of Galdácano (Vizcaya) in February 1976. Their victims during this period also included two members of the Guardia Civil, one killed by a bomb in Villafranca de Ordizia (Guipúzcoa) in January, and the second electrocuted by a booby-trapped Basque flag in Baracaldo (Vizcaya) in April. The organization also claimed responsibility for killing two Spanish policemen in France in April, as well as four civilians in separate attacks—a taxi driver, a bus inspector, a mechanic (later admitted to be a mistake), and a construction worker, all in February and March.

During 1976, however, ETA (político-militar) went through a major power struggle that was apparently touched off by the failure of two kidnapings carried out by the group to raise funds.[5] On January 15, 1976, four gunmen from ETA(p-m) entered the home of a Basque industrialist named Arrasate in the town of Berriz (Vizcaya) and kidnaped his twenty-six-year-old son, José Luis. For his safe return, the group demanded the payment of a ransom of $1.6 million, far beyond what the modest wealth of Arrasate would provide. The Arrasate kidnaping was roundly condemned by all Basque nationalist organizations, including even ETA(militar). On February 17, ETA(p-m) released the Arrasate youth unharmed but without having received any ransom payment, the first time they had given in to the pleas of a victim's family.

The second failure ended much more tragically. On April 7, an ETA(p-m) comando kidnaped and then killed a conservative Basque industrialist named Angel Berazadi. Responsibility for the killing has never been fixed precisely. Apparently, the man who actually did the killing was an etarra named Ignacio María Gabilondo who had joined ETA(p-m) in 1975 and who took part in a number of violent assaults both before and after the Berazadi killing.[6] The order to kill Berazadi came from another etarra, however, Miguel Angel Apalategui Ayerbe "Apala," the leader of ETA(p-m)'s Berezi Comandos. The Berezi Comandos had been created in January 1975 by ETA(p-m) for the purpose of carrying out high-risk armed assaults of great importance to the organization. As leader of the Berezi Comandos, Apala had assumed virtually complete control over the military arm of ETA(p-m).

Miguel Angel Apalategui came from the small village of Ataun in the heart of the Goierri region of south-central Guipúzcoa.[7] He was born in 1955 and grew up in a traditional Basque *caserío* or farm family, but he himself worked during his youth in a factory in a neighboring town. He had become involved with the Basque struggle from his early teens when he had taken part in some labor demonstrations in a nearby town, for which he was arrested and beaten in the police station. In May 1974, when he was about nineteen, ETA conducted a robbery of the factory where Apalategui was employed. In the police investigation of the attack, he was implicated, and an order was issued for his arrest. On June 1, while he was being stopped at a roadblock, Apalategui allegedly killed a member of the Guardia Civil and escaped into hiding. For the next year or so, Apala (as he now became known) took part in a number of ETA actions. When the split occurred between the mili and poli-mili factions, he sided with the p-m group, and rose within the organization to occupy the senior position in command of its military component, the Berezi Comandos.

Apala's rise to power collided squarely with the interests and personal ambition of the man who commanded ETA(p-m) after the 1974 split, Eduardo Moreno Bergareche "Pertur."[8] Pertur had headed the organization since the split with ETA(m), and it was primarily because of his influence that ETA(p-m) had developed its program of forming mass organizations that could link ETA to the working class. Before Franco's death, it was still unclear how this would be done. But as Spain moved toward a more open democratic system, it began to appear possible for certain elements within ETA to emerge as legal political parties or unions through which the organization could work with the people and mobilize popular support for its programs. Obviously, this step would be tied closely to some sort of negotiated cease-fire between ETA and the Spanish law enforcement authorities. Thus through 1976, ETA(p-m) factions fell to arguing over the merits of continuing armed struggle in the new Spanish democracy. Since he was the principal architect of ETA(p-m)'s "political" approach, one based on mass organizations rather than a small armed vanguard party, Pertur clashed with those who favored a continuation of the armed struggle. It is not surprising that the leader of that faction was Miguel Angel Apalategui "Apala."

While the Berazadi assassination was not the only source of disagreement between Apala and Pertur (a jailbreak of etarras engineered by Apala in April had failed miserably, and all the escapees had been either caught or killed),[9] it was apparently the issue over which the two broke decisively. According to one account, Apala had given the order to kill Berazadi against the express direction of Pertur. In any case, this kind of dramatic assault could only provoke Madrid to more repressive measures, which would work against Pertur's plan to gradually bring ETA(p-m) into the legal political system.

On July 23, 1976, Pertur and Apala met in the French town of St.-Jean-de-Luz to discuss their differences. Against the urging of his bodyguards, Pertur accompanied Apala on a drive out of town, and he was never seen again. Apala returned soon after to take over even greater power within ETA. Naturally, versions differ about the reasons for Pertur's disappearance (and presumed death). Pertur's family and closest associates blamed Apala and the Berezi Comandos for his death. The Berezi group affirmed that Pertur had been killed by Spanish police after they had been given information about his whereabouts from a spy who had infiltrated ETA. On the other hand, in January 1982, the Spanish right-wing counter-terrorist organization, the Apostolic Anticommunist Alliance (Alianza Apostólica Antico-munista, AAA), sent a communiqué to the Bilbao newspaper *Deia* claiming responsibility for the deaths of some twenty Basques includ-ing Eduardo Moreno Bergareche. Moreover, they claimed they had proof of their responsibility.[10]

In all probability we will never know for sure who killed Pertur. What we do know is that his death came at a decisive moment in Basque and Spanish political history. In the same month of Pertur's disappearance, July 1976, Adolfo Suárez took office as the new Span-ish president, and with King Juan Carlos's support, began to bring Spain into the modern era politically. Had Pertur lived, he might have been able to play a key role in adapting ETA to the new democratic politics. From mid-1976 onward, ETA(p-m) shifted increasingly to-ward the formation of a new political party. The Berezi Comandos and Apala, on the other hand, became restive within ETA(p-m) and would soon leave the organization. Once again, internal struggles over ideol-ogy and personality had intervened to split ETA into warring factions and to rob the organization of the talent it would need to participate in Spain's new democracy.

With Pertur gone, ETA now splintered into three divergent forces. The Berezi Comandos under Apala grew more and more intransigent and increasingly impatient with the political approach of the poli-milis. A second force involved the political faction of ETA(p-m), which, lacking a leader of the stature of Pertur, now began looking for ways to break out of the trap of violence that ETA had created for itself. The third element in the picture was a resurgent ETA(militar), which was beginning to renew its activities under the leadership of key cadres who had left p-m after rejecting its political strategy.

As far as armed struggle was concerned, the principal contenders within ETA were the Apala group, which we have already discussed, and ETA(m), whose chief leader was José Miguel Beñarán Ordeñana "Argala." Argala enjoyed considerable prestige within the organiza-tion for having participated in some of the most dramatic ETA actions, including the Huarte kidnaping and the Carrero Blanco assassination. After the split between ETA(m) and ETA(p-m) he had stayed with the poli-milis; but within months, he shifted to the more activist and violent mili faction. After Pertur's disappearance, the loyalties of etar-ras were divided about evenly between the Apala faction of ETA(p-m) and the Argala faction, one of the principal components of ETA(m). Both leaders prepared to launch some dramatic and shocking action with which to impress the rank-and-file members of ETA.

Argala struck first. On October 4, the president of the Provincial

Assembly of Guipúzcoa and a member of the Council of the Realm, Juan de Araluce, was machine-gunned to death on the streets of San Sebastián in the middle of crowded midday traffic. Four bodyguards were also killed and ten bystanders wounded. Araluce was not only the senior political leader in Guipúzcoa, but a member of the Spanish parliament and a trusted advisor of King Juan Carlos. Across the political spectrum, both Basque and Spanish leaders condemned the attack. The Spanish rightists proclaimed it to be still another example of "accelerating social deterioration" since Franco's death. Basque moderates criticized it as uncalled for in the reform atmosphere of post-Franco Spain. The Basque Left called the attack "adventurous," and said it risked provoking Madrid into harsh countermeasures. The day following the killing, bands of right-wing demonstrators went on a rampage in San Sebastián, firing shots into the air, smashing shop windows, beating bystanders, and destroying cafés and restaurants. Massive demonstrations were held in San Sebastián and Madrid calling for the army to take power and to seize control of the government. To their credit, Suárez and his interior minister Martín Villa remained calm and firm. They refused to declare martial law in Guipúzcoa and appealed to the citizens of that province to resist the temptation to panic. Under their leadership, the Spanish government weathered the crisis.

After the Araluce killing, an uneasy peace settled over the Basque country that lasted more or less unbroken until the following spring. During this interlude and with parliamentary elections apparently to be held sometime during 1977, the political faction of ETA(p-m) now began to develop some institutional expression of its strategy.

In October 1976, ETA(p-m) held the first half of the Seventh Assembly in Biarritz, France.[11] At this meeting, the majority of its members agreed to break once and for all with ETA(m) and to form a new political party based on four fundamental points. First, ETA(p-m) defined itself as a separatist party that recognized Euzkadi as an autonomous national base for the class struggle (that is, the Basque working class could never be liberated so long as capitalism remained in either Euzkadi or Spain). Second, it defined itself as a revolutionary organization at the service of the working class. It proposed a socialist society that would not be possible without the destruction of the oligarchy and the institutionalized violence employed by that class. Third, ETA(p-m) proposed a political structure, to be developed within the framework of a bourgeois democracy (rejecting thereby any notion of the dictatorship of the proletariat), which would be based on the power of the "autonomous organisms" of the Basque popular classes; ETA(p-m) would depend not just on a conventional political party structure but would attempt to involve workers, students, intellectuals, artists, and other groups that perceived a need to achieve independence for Euzkadi. Fourth, ETA(p-m) adopted the principles of democratic centralism, meaning that debate would be open and decisions made democratically, but policies once adopted would be rigorously enforced and further dissent would not be allowed. The new party that emerged from the Seventh Assembly was called the Basque Revolutionary Party (Euskal Iraultzale Alderdia, EIA).[12]

The growth of the Basque socialist movement during the 1970s was a complicated sequence of developments and part of the change in the Basque political party system in general. Almost immediately after the legalization of political parties in Spain in June 1976, a new party system began to appear in the Basque region and across all of Spain.[13] In all, at least 162 separate political organization had been organized in Spain by May 1977, although many of them faded from the scene after their first few trials at the ballot box. A number of these new organizations were based solely in the Basque region and appealed only to ethnic Basque voters. Several of them attempted to combine revolutionary socialism with Basque ethnicity.

The Basque political system of the later 1970s inherited three sets of parties from the 1930s: a Spanish Left, consisting of, principally, the Spanish Socialist Workers Party, PSOE, and the Spanish Communist Party (PCE); a coalition of Spanish Center-Right parties; and the Basque Center, occupied solely by the Basque Nationalist Party, PNV. In the elections of the 1930s, these three political forces divided the Basque regional vote approximately into thirds, but in the elections of 1936 the Spanish Right scored such gains in Alava and Navarra that they became the strongest of the three by some considerable margin (about 12 to 14 percentage points over each of the other two). The three groupings reemerged after 1976 in the Basque region, but they were joined by the new phenomenon of the Basque Left, and the votes of the region were now divided roughly into quarters.

During the electoral campaigns of the 1970s, at least four issues emerged that set the Basque socialist parties apart from the more moderate PNV. The first major issue had to do with the degree of cooperation Basque parties should offer Spanish parties like the socialist PSOE or the center-right Union of the Democratic Center, UCD. All ethnic Basque parties, including the PNV, took for themselves the title of *abertzale*, a Basque word meaning "patriotic." The farther to the left they moved, however, the more intransigent became the parties' interpretation of this label. The PNV cooperated with the Spanish Christian Democrats during the 1977 election campaign, and with the PSOE on repeated occasions on both the regional and national level, including in the Spanish parliament. The Basque Left parties explicitly rejected all such cooperation and accused the PNV of selling out because of its cooperation.

A second important question had to do with the territorial base for the Basque ethnonation, Euzkadi. The more radical Basque socialist parties demanded that Navarra be included in the Basque autonomous region, and that all Basque parties establish as a long-range goal the incorporation of the three French Basque provinces in the new union of all Basque peoples. The PNV, perhaps because of its traditional weakness in Navarra, was less intransigent on that score, and more ready to accept a regional autonomy statute that excluded Navarra, at least at the beginning. Further, the expansion of Euzkadi to include the French provinces was usually treated by the PNV as a long-range issue, included in party propaganda more for symbolic reasons than for any other purpose.

The third significant issue involved the exact nature of the ties between the Basque autonomous region and the rest of Spain. While the PNV seemed generally inclined to accept a form of federal status for Euzkadi, the Basque socialists argued strongly for a greater degree of separation, certainly to include the immediate expulsion of all Spanish civil and military officials (most especially, the Guardia Civil), and eventually of all Spaniards, once the Basque educational system had produced enough trained personnel fluent in the Basque language, Euskera, and skilled in the tasks needed to manage a complex industrial society.

The fourth issue had to do with the need for radical social and economic change. The PNV reaffirmed its faith in the free market and private property, although tempered by its recognition of the need to meet the social needs of a growing urban, working-class population. The Basque socialists, on the other hand, advocated substantial social change, including the nationalization of the Basques' major industries, using workers' committees to run the firms, and a tax and payment system to redistribute income.

The fact that the Basque socialist parties disagreed fundamentally with the PNV on these issues did not mean that they formed a common front in politics or that there was concensus among the Basque Left groups about either tactics or strategy. On the contrary, the Basque socialist parties were fragmented into numerous miniparties that seemed to spend almost as much time and energy attacking one another as they did their common adversaries, the PNV and the Spanish parties. Doubtless their strength would have been enhanced considerably if they could have avoided these internecine quarrels and developed a unified position on policy and electoral issues that would have made the most of their appeal for the voters.

From the time of the first half of the Seventh Assembly of ETA(p-m) through the winter and early spring of 1977, leaders of the emerging Basque Left worked to form a unified and coherent socialist political party that would represent unambiguously the interests of the Basque working class. One of the focal points of their efforts was the Patriotic Socialist Coordinating Council (KAS).[14] The platform of the KAS, known as the *alternativa KAS*, emphasized the need for the independence of Euzkadi from Spain, the establishment of socialism in the region, and the reunification of the French and Spanish zones of the Basque nation. In addition, the KAS proposed five specific points as preconditions for ending ETA violence: amnesty for all Basque political prisoners, legalization of all political parties, withdrawal from Euzkadi of all Spanish law enforcement authorities, including, especially, the Guardia Civil, incorporation of Navarra into the Basque regional community, without a referendum, and granting to Euzkadi the right to self-determination.[15]

Within the KAS, however, there were many who felt that the organization was too broad to represent fully the special interests of workers. In the eyes of many members of ETA(p-m), the KAS had arisen from and reflected the multiclass origins of ETA itself. It reflected what they referred to as a "populist character, although with the presence of working class positions."[16] There was a need, therefore, to build within the KAS framework a new party that could address specifically the issues that affected Basque workers. The establishment of EIA (Euskal Iraultzale Alderdia, the Basque Revolutionary Party) in late 1976 made that party possible.

In April 1977, EIA was launched with a mass rally in the working class suburb of Gallarta, across the Nervion River from Bilbao. In choosing this locale from which to begin its search for votes in the upcoming parliamentary elections, EIA was sending a clear message that it would count primarily on working class support, and only secondarily on the votes of ethnic Basques from the middle class, the professions, small towns, and farming communities.

The links between EIA and ETA(p-m) during this period were not at all clear. Although many leaders of EIA had been members of ETA(p-m) at one time, they rejected completely suggestions that EIA was nothing more than a front organization for ETA(p-m). On the other hand, the fact that ETA(p-m) and EIA were closely related, yet distinct, enabled their leaders to pursue different strategies simultaneously. When the KAS decided to boycott the June 1977 Spanish parliamentary elections, ETA(p-m), as a component of KAS, presumably had been consulted and had concurred in the decision. At the same time, a new coalition organization was created to contest the 1977 elections and to present the position of the Basque Left to the voters. This organization, known as Basque Left (Euzkadiko Ezkerra, EE), included in its coalition the new Basque Revolutionary Party, EIA. There were a number of other Basque Left parties and unions represented in EE, some of which could not participate officially in the 1977 elections because they were also members of KAS. However, since EIA was not a member of KAS (even though ETA(p-m) *was*), it could take part in the elections, and in fact became the principal factor in the success, limited though it was, of EE at the polls. Thus ETA(p-m) officially boycotted the elections while its political party, EIA, officially participated through the EE coalition. In the election, EE won about 5 percent of the total vote, while all parties of the Basque Left combined won slightly more than 11 percent.

The modest success of Basque socialism brought a number of important consequences. On the one hand, EE was entitled to one seat in the Spanish parliament elected in 1977, as well as to one seat in the Basque General Council (Consejo General Vasco, CGV), the body created by the Spanish Ministry of Interior in late 1977 to manage the transition of the region to autonomous status. Thus the Basque Left gained access to the formal organs of power and thereby to the various media by which it could communicate its demands to decision-making bodies. On the other hand, access to power created a number of difficult problems for EE. The party's tiny representation meant that it could accomplish nothing without entering into coalitions with similar parties, which immediately made it vulnerable to charges of selling out to the opposition. As a coalition member with much more moderate parties like PNV, EE had to modify its position on policy issues or run the risk of being left out of important discussions when key decisions were being made. A number of the smaller parties and unions, both inside and outside the EE coalition, began to criticize the EE leadership for moving toward the right to pacify the PNV and Madrid.[17] From late 1977 through the summer of 1978 a more intransigent alternative to EE began to attract considerable support from workers, students, and professionals, such as attorneys. (An important factor radicalizing the Basque Left was the slowness with which Madrid moved in 1977 and 1978 to accommodate Basque demands for regional autonomy. A considerable portion of the more radical Basque Left vote came from Basques who saw the elections as opportunities to send a message of protest to Madrid.)

The nucleus of this radicalized alternative to EE traced its origins back to the massive protests against the execution of Angel Otaegi and Jon Paredes Manot in September 1975, which led to the formation of the KAS. The KAS was composed of the Basque Popular Socialist Party (Eusko Herriko Alderdi Sozialista, EHAS), the Patriotic Revolutionary Workers Party (Langille Abertzale Iraultzalean Alderdia, LAIA), the Patriotic Workers Committee (Langille Abertzale Komiteak, LAK), and ETA(p-m), with the support of the Patriotic Workers Council (Langille Abertzalean Batzordea, LAB) and ETA(m). Following the 1977 elections, the KAS was made up of the Popular Revolutionary Socialist Party (Herriko Alderdi Sozialista Iraultzalea, HASI), which was the former EHAS, LAIA, a labor union coalition known as the Patriotic Socialist Coordinating Council (Abertzale Sozialista Koordinadora, ASK), again with the support of ETA(m). From this group, the Basque Left began to develop an ideology that combined radical Basque ethnicity with revolutionary socialism in a parliamentary electoral setting. This ideological approach was cited repeatedly not only by ETA(m) but also by the party that arose in its name, Herri Batasuna (HB).[18]

The dispute between KAS and EE/EIA involved differences of opinion over whether Basque socialist parties and coalitions should participate in Spanish electoral politics and the Spanish parliamentary process. This difference of opinion was also seen within ETA. In addition to the creation of EIA and its entry into conventional electoral politics, there were other signs in early 1977 that the leaders of ETA(p-m), who were the followers of Pertur, wanted very much to abandon armed struggle and return to normal political activity.[19] There were, however, members of ETA(p-m) who steadfastly opposed any such move. Most of these members were part of the Berezi Comandos groups under the leadership of Apala.

In the spring of 1977, the Berezi group launched a new offensive of armed attacks which, intentionally or not, had the effect of making it much more difficult for ETA(p-m) and EIA to work within the legal political structure being built around the 1977 elections. On March 12 an ETA(p-m) comando attacked a group of the Guardia Civil in Mondragón with machine guns, killing one and wounding two more.[20] On May 15, a representative of ETA(p-m) issued a communiqué announcing his group's decision to abandon its tentative experiment with electoral politics and its return to unrestrained insurgent violence.[21] Seen in the context of internal struggles within ETA(p-m), this communiqué was probably another attempt by the Berezi Comandos to force the Pertur group either to leave the organization or abandon their attempt to form a legal political party. In any case, the Berezi group followed the communiqué several days later, on May 18, by killing a policeman near the San Sebastián railroad station and by attacks on other policemen in San Sebastián and Pamplona.[22] On May 20, in its most dramatic assault yet, the Berezi Comandos kidnaped a well-known Bilbao industrialist named Javier de Ybarra.

The Berezi group of Apala was not the only obstacle to integrating ETA peacefully into the post-Franco political order. The Argala group within ETA(m) had also hardened its position against any kind of cessation of hostilities, as evidenced by the Araluce assassination of the previous October; and in the renewed offensive of spring 1977, the Argala group was also involved. On March 13, ETA(m) attacked several Guardia Civil troops in Oñate (Guipúzcoa), killing one and wounding two more.[23] In their communiqué following the attack, ETA(m) said, "Our action is an act of response" made necessary by the Spanish government, "which does nothing but make promises and halfway concessions, such as the pardon decrees of this most recent Council of Ministers [the Spanish Cabinet, RPC], but which refuses to suppress the fascist institutions and promulgate the measures necessary to reach a true democratization. . . . It is first of all a response, but also a warning. We have said that we do not wish violence, but we see ourselves forced to use it. If the total amnesty is conceded immediately, this response will be stopped, as we have already announced."[24] In June, ETA(m) launched its first attack against the Lemóniz nuclear power plant under construction in Vizcaya and against the company that was building the plant, Iberduero. As of mid-1981, ETA(m) had attacked Lemóniz or other Iberduero facilities or offices some 250 times and had caused four deaths and fourteen injuries (all Lemóniz construction workers).[25]

The Ybarra kidnaping and the events that surrounded it not only plunged Spain into a new crisis in the midst of the country's preparations for the parliamentary elections but also revealed once again the inner turmoil that was besetting ETA(p-m). On May 20, a group of men disguised as hospital orderlies entered the Ybarra home in Bilbao, tied and gagged the other members of his family, and made off with Ybarra in a stolen ambulance.[26] A prominent industrialist, banker, and politician, Ybarra was known to have been on ETA's "death list" since the beginning of the year. According to other members of the Ybarra family, the kidnapers demanded total amnesty for 'the twenty-three Basques still in Spanish prisons in return for his release. Although many observers thought the Suárez government would refuse to deal with these demands, late in the night of May 20 it was announced in Madrid that all twenty-three prisoners would be allowed to leave the country and go into exile. It would take time, however, to release them and arrange for other countries to receive them, and in the meantime Ybarra remained in ETA's control. By May 23, five prisoners were released and flown to Belgium. During the first ten days of June, thirteen more were released, including five to Norway, two to Austria, five to Denmark, and one allowed to remain in Bilbao. Thus even though by June 10 Madrid had made substantial progress toward releasing all of the Basques in prison, five were still held. Two of them were so-called historical prisoners, since they had been tried and convicted before December 15, 1976, and three were so-called new prisoners convicted after that date. Because there were still etarras in prison in June, several Basque Left parties announced that they would boycott the elections, but EIA declared its intention to proceed with its campaign and to present candidates, a move for which it was sharply criticized by many Basque leftists.

The whole matter was complicated greatly when on June 2, French police arrested Apala, the leader of the Berezi Comandos.[27] Since Spanish authorities believed Apala to be responsible for the Ybarra kidnaping, they requested that he be held for eventual extradition to Spain. On June 5, he was transferred to the French prison island of Porquerolle, where he was held along with an undisclosed number of other Basques, allegedly to prevent them from doing anything to disrupt the June 15 elections in Spain. Most of the others were released after June 15, but Apala remained in French custody. On June 21, the Spanish government officially requested that he be returned to Spain to stand trial for, among other things, the killing of Angel Berazadi; whereupon the French authorities changed Apala's status to "preventive detention" and transferred him to prison in Marseilles.

Meanwhile the fate of Ybarra was becoming more uncertain. Apparently in retaliation for EIA's participation in the June 15 elections, the Berezi Comandos formally separated from ETA(p-m) several days afterwards, which meant that the team that kidnaped Ybarra was for all intents and purposes beyond the control of even ETA(p-m).[28] More ominously, the Berezi Comandos responded to Apala's arrest and preventive detention with invective and increased demands. They charged that Apala had been turned into a counterhostage to bargain for Ybarra's freedom, and they now demanded a ransom of one billion pesetas (about $14 million) in addition to the release of the remaining Basques from prison. Despite the Ybarra family's great wealth, they could not reach that much cash in a short time, and so they sought to postpone the deadline of June 18 set by the kidnapers. The Berezi group never answered their appeals, and June 18 passed without news. On June 20, a message was sent to the family announcing Ybarra's "execution," with a map showing where the killers had left the body. When the Guardia Civil failed to find the body, a second note was received on June 22 correcting an error the searchers had made, and new efforts were made to locate the corpse. Ybarra's body was discovered about 25 meters from an old farmhouse in Navarra, wrapped in a plastic sheet. The victim had been shot once in the head, probably on June 18, the deadline set by his abductors. Virtually every significant political group in the Basque community spoke out against the barbarism of the act.

In France, meanwhile, the drama of Apala's extradition trial went on. On July 19, the French court in Aix-en-Provence rejected a Spanish petition for the return of Apala to be tried for the Berazadi murder, because the Spanish authorities had failed to provide the court with the correct kind of documentation. Nevertheless Apala was not freed. On July 23, Spain again requested that he be extradited, this time for the Ybarra killing. On August 2 and 9, the court met to hear this second request. During this entire time, there were street demonstrations throughout the Basque provinces to secure Apala's freedom, and on August 9, about five hundred Basques traveled to France to demonstrate outside the courtroom where his case was being heard. On August 9, the French court adjourned and announced that it would not decide the case until October 14. At this point, Apala began a hunger strike to prevent France from sending him back to Spain for trial. "If France delivers me up to Spain," he told attending physicians, "they will deliver a corpse." Again in early September, Apala's attorneys sought to have him released under bail, and they succeeded finally on September 6. Under the terms of his release, Apala was to report to the Marseilles police headquarters once a week. On Friday, October 7, Apala failed to appear for his weekly appointment. On October 11, the French court revoked his provisional freedom and issued an order for his arrest and return for hearing. From that date to this writing (September 1983), Apala has remained at large.

On October 8, the day after Apala broke the terms of his provisional release as well as the day after the Spanish parliament had agreed on a draft law providing for general amnesty, ETA gunmen shot and killed the president of the Provincial Assembly of Vizcaya, Augusto Unceta Barrenechea, and his two bodyguards. This brought to seventy-nine the number of political killings in Spain since General Franco's death, including forty-seven in the Basque provinces, and twenty-five, by ETA.[29] Ominously, the evidence showed that the Unceta killings had been carried out by an entirely new ETA group, one formed by a union of ETA(m) and the disaffected Berezi Comandos. Whether or not the Apala and Argala factions could suppress their ideological and personal difficulties sufficiently to enable them to work together was still an unanswered question. But for the time being, this new element (which still carried the title ETA (militar)) would introduce fresh waves of instability and disorder into Basque and Spanish politics. In November, ETA(m) killed a municipal police sergeant in Irun (Guipúzcoa) and, in Pamplona, the commander of the National Police in Navarra.

During the two-year period 1976–77, ETA was responsible for killing some twenty-six people, wounding seven, and kidnaping three, about the same level of violence observed during the last two years of the Franco regime, when they had killed twenty-seven, wounded sixty-three (fifty-six in one attack, the Rolando bombing), and kidnaped none.[30] The explosive mixture of a new and more radicalized element in ETA plus the growing frustration, unrest, and discontent among Basques generally, however, would shortly drive the level of violence to new heights.

1978–79: ETA Violence at a New Level

In a number of important ways, the nearly two-year span from December 1977 through the end of October 1979 marked a turning point in the history of ETA and of Basque-Spanish relations.[31] On the one hand, moderate Basque and Spanish political leaders succeeded in reaching a compromise agreement on a structure that would ensure the Basque region a certain degree of political and economic autonomy, although many intransigent Basque nationalists still believed that the arrangement contained many defects. On the other hand ETA, now divided into three aggressive factions, raised the level of violence to such heights that moderate Basque leaders finally turned against the organization and condemned its resort to armed struggle in a democracy. Moreover, in mid-1978 the Spanish government was forced to respond to heightened ETA violence with a counteroffensive marked by new antiterrorist laws and police measures that reminded many Basques of some of the worst features of Francoism.

In retrospect, the process of adopting a new Spanish constitution was surprisingly smooth and short. The parliament that had been elected in June 1977 began working on a draft document in August, and the new draft constitution was officially released to public scrutiny on January 5, 1978. After a long period of amendment and negotiation, the final version of the constitution was submitted to Spanish voters in a referendum on December 6, and promulgated by King Juan Carlos on December 28.

In this process, the Basques were active and aggressive, but frustrated. During the amendment process, Basque deputies to the parliament pressed for more than one hundred major changes to the draft, all of which would have either broadened the powers of any regional government or shortened the process by which such governments were created. As a tiny minority within the Cortes, the Basques, even in alliance with Catalan deputies, were powerless to secure these changes. Consequently, the new constitution offered a mixed set of advantages and disadvantages to the country's regional minorities. Because regional governments under the Spanish constitution depend solely on powers granted to them by Madrid, the Spanish experiment with regional autonomy more nearly resembles the British system of devolution than it does the American federal system. As a result of their failure to secure any improvements in the proposed constitution, Basque Nationalist Party leaders advocated that Basques abstain during the December 6 referendum to show their displeasure with the new law; and, indeed, abstention rates exceeded 50 percent in the four provinces as a whole and reached nearly 60 percent in Vizcaya and Guipúzcoa.

Nevertheless, if the Basques were to pursue their objective of regional autonomy, they would have to do it within the framework offered them by the Spanish constitution. The base for that effort was laid on December 31, 1977, with the promulgation in Madrid of the Pre-Autonomy Decree for the Basque and Catalan regions. The decree established for each region a "pre-autonomy" government whose job it was to prepare the administrative apparatus that would be needed to transmit power to an autonomous government once autonomy was achieved. In Euzkadi, this pre-autonomy government was called the Basque General Council. Because of the scant resources made available to the council, its efforts were disappointing.

The other major responsibility of the council, however, was to help draft a proposed autonomy statute once the constitution was approved. This task went quite smoothly, and the Basque deputies to the parliament finally agreed on a draft regional autonomy statute just one day after the constitution was promulgated. On December 29, 1978, the Basque deputies met in the historic city of Guernica to approve the draft statute and send it by air courier to Madrid, to start the long process of consideration by the parliament. Before that could begin, however, there intervened two more elections. In March 1979, a new Cortes was chosen, and in April, Spanish voters chose their municipal and provincial assemblies for the first time since the Civil War. After the new parliament was convened, the Basque statute was formally considered, and approved in July 1979 after long and difficult negotiation. During this bargaining, the statute was trimmed considerably from what the Basques had proposed, especially in the sensitive areas of the maintenance of public order and administration of justice. The leaders of the Basque Nationalist Party sensed, however, that the compromise statute was the best they could hope for and so they urged their followers to vote in favor of the statute, which the members did in large but not overwhelming numbers. On October 25, 1979, about 60 percent of the eligible Basque electorate turned out to vote yes to the proposed statute, which was then promulgated by the king and put into operation. This set the stage for the March 9, 1980, election of the first Basque government ever chosen by the people of the region as a whole.[32]

Given these advances in regional autonomy for the Basques, it might have been expected that ETA violence would decline. In fact, exactly the opposite occurred, and Spanish public opinion reacted with shock and amazement. In December 1977, the Spanish news-magazine *Cambio 16* reported the results of a public opinion survey that revealed that slightly more than one Spaniard in five (22.7 percent) was seriously worried about terrorism, compared with more than half the respondents who were concerned about unemployment (51.5 percent) and inflation (56.5 percent).[33] Eleven months later, in November 1978, a similar poll showed that the balance of public concerns had shifted dramatically. Terrorism now ranked as the second most pressing problem faced by the Spanish people. Slightly more than half (53.1 percent) now expressed grave worries about terrorism; a clear majority (63.1 percent) still worried considerably about unemployment; but somewhat fewer (43.0 percent) were concerned about inflation.

What had happened in the period between these two polls was that ETA insurgency had become one of the central issues facing the Spanish government. ETA(m), relatively quiet during the last half of 1977, launched a major offensive against the Guardia Civil and police units in the spring. A new ETA faction, the Comandos Autónomos, appeared in April. Not only did the absolute level of violence rise, but new targets were added to the list of ETA victims, including construction workers at the Lemóniz nuclear plant and senior officers in the armed forces in Madrid. Also during the spring, the Basque Left spawned still another radical political coalition, Herri Batasuna, that reflected the growing discontent and frustration among many working and middle class Basques. The Spanish authorities in Madrid, as well as moderate Basque nationalist leaders, reacted strongly against the rising tension and violence with a variety of countermeasures, none of which seemed to matter very much. By the end of 1978, the spiral of ETA violence and Spanish police counterviolence seemed headed clearly out of control.

Early in 1978, Argala, the leader of ETA(m), convened his lieutenants in France to consider the implications of events in Spanish politics over the preceding six months.[34] Apparently, the relatively low vote given to the Basque Left parties in the June 1977 elections, combined with the drive to draft and approve a new Spanish constitution, had convinced Argala that parliamentary tactics had failed and a new offensive of armed assaults was needed. Specifically, he had apparently decided that during 1978, while the constitution was being debated, the Spanish government would be especially vulnerable to a renewed ETA offensive and would be more willing to enter into negotiations to prevent the insurgency from spoiling this last phase of the consolidation of Spanish democracy. Because the Basque Left was such a small part of the Spanish political system, however, merely working through the parliamentary system would never make Madrid negotiate. The failure of EIA to force complete amnesty before the 1977 elections was one example of Basque weakness; the failure of the PNV to force changes in the draft constitution was another. Therefore, while Argala's ultimate aim was to negotiate an end to hostilities and an improved autonomy arrangement for Euzkadi, he reasoned that ETA(m) would have to increase its violence significantly to force Madrid into conciliations. His effort was given a sense of real urgency by his perception that once the constitution was approved, the Spanish government would have no incentive to negotiate and would be much less vulnerable to pressure from ETA. Therefore 1978 was a critical year in the timetable of ETA(m).

The upsurge in ETA violence was accompanied by a new hard line regarding the organization's objectives. In a communiqué published in the Basque press in mid-March, ETA answered the rhetorical question "Where is ETA going?" this way:

> Many people are wondering today, why is ETA still active after Franco's death and with the process of democratization of the Spanish state under way? ETA has not changed. What has changed is the awareness of a sector of the people toward our organization and what it represents and defends. These people thought that we were simply anti-Francoist patriots, and they never stopped to think about the definition that goes along with our initials: a Basque socialist revolutionary organization for national liberation. . . . Certain individuals, confusing reality with their desires, have seen ETA as they wanted it to be and not as it was. ETA will try to exist and to struggle in the most appropriate way for the creation of a Basque socialist state, independent, reunified, and Basque-speaking. We are supporters of the exercise of political su-

premacy of the proletariat, but we cannot affirm ex cathedra that said dominance has to be imposed by means of a violent explosion and a prolonged repression of the bourgeoisie. If the working class is permitted to organize and exercise its will freely, its seizure of power will occur peacefully and at the same time as it raises its awareness.[35]

The level of violence rose and fell several times during 1978. While January and February were relatively quiet, there were a number of attacks in March and April. The summer was made turbulent by the significance of its victims more than by the number of attacks, which remained rather low. In September, however, the tempo picked up, and the last three months of the year saw a spasm of violence unequaled in any previous period of ETA's history.[36]

In January and February, the ETA victim list included two police officers killed and two police and four Guardia Civil troopers wounded. In March, seven separate ETA attacks left six dead (two police, one Guardia Civil, two construction workers, and one ex-mayor) and thirty-five wounded (including fourteen in the Lemóniz nuclear plant explosion and fourteen in a bombing in San Sebastián). April's toll was only five wounded, but in May, ETA killed three Guardia Civil and wounded thirteen more, as well as wounding two other civilians, including one businessman. From the beginning of June through the end of August, ETA attacks killed eleven, including two senior army officers, three police, one Guardia Civil, and the well-known Bilbao journalist José María Portell. There were seven woundings during the period as well as one kidnaping (of the son of a Vizcayan industrialist).

The last quarter of 1978 was especially marked by ETA violence. In September, five were killed (all Guardia Civil or police) and two wounded. In October, the number killed rose to thirteen, of which six were from the Guardia Civil. In November, it rose again to fourteen killed (including five Guardia Civil troops and two police) and nineteen wounded. And in December, there were thirteen killed (including one Guardia Civil troop and five police). In all, during 1978, one faction or other of ETA accounted for sixty-seven killed, ninety-one wounded, and four kidnaped.[37]

Not only did ETA attacks increase during this period, but the organization attacked different kinds of targets than it had in the past. Of course, the Guardia Civil and the police continued to be the principal targets, but other kinds of victims began to appear on the list. In March, the Lemóniz nuclear installation bombing was the first time ETA had ever killed members of the working class. In May, ETA(p-m) kidnaped a Vizcayan industrialist named Iturregui and shot him in the leg, the first time that ETA's version of "kneecapping" was used to extort a "revolutionary tax" from a business executive. For the first time, there were several killings apparently to punish spies or police informers; and the assassination of Portell in June for allegedly trying to arrange a cease-fire between ETA and the government showed that it was dangerous for noncombatants to get too close to the organization. Other persons of senior rank were also targeted by ETA. An army general and lieutenant colonel were shot in Madrid in July (on the day after the parliament had approved the draft constitution). Victims included a Spanish navy captain in October, a judge in November, and two police chiefs in December. ETA now chose persons of rather more modest profession as well, including several taxi drivers, a grocery store owner, a bar owner, and several whose only "crime" appeared to be that they were friends of Guardia Civil members or police. In other words, as the level of killings went up, the range of potential victims expanded accordingly.

The upsurge in attacks by ETA(m) was only one of the reasons for increased violence in 1978. A second was the emergence of the Comandos Autónomos.[38] The origins of the Comandos Autónomos can be traced back to 1976, when a group of former members of the Frente Obrero who had refused to join the new workers' party LAIA merged with others from the Berezi Group of ETA(p-m) and from ETA(m) to form an entirely new faction unrelated to either of the other two groups. The Comandos Autónomos rejected ties to any already existing Basque Left group. For personal and philosophical reasons, members of the Comandos Autónomos rejected all forms of social control in which some give orders and others must obey. For this reason, they refused to be a part of any other branch of ETA, and they likewise rejected links to even the most radical parties on the Basque Left, including Herri Batasuna. According to press reports, the Comandos Autónomos were organized into cells at the local level, as were ETA(m) and ETA(p-m). While some attempt was made to coordinate these cells loosely, each was free to choose its targets and mode of attack as well as its explanations to the public. The first assault openly attributed to the Comandos Autónomos came on April 13, 1978, in an attack on a commercial establishment in San Sebastián. During 1978, they were allegedly responsible for killing a member of the Guardia Civil troop in Mondragón in August; two Guardia Civil in separate attacks in Marquina (Vizcaya) and Elgoibar in October; and the chief of police of Pasajes (Guipúzcoa) in December. The total membership of the Comandos Autónomos has probably never exceeded fifty, but because they are so loosely connected and so unpre-

speaking, the remainder of the year was fairly quiet, and December actually passed without a single death.

Despite news accounts portraying the October-November period as especially violent (allegedly because of ETA's attempts to sabotage the referendum on the autonomy statute), January and February were in fact the worst months of 1979. In January, ETA killed eleven and wounded five. Included among their victims were five members of the Guardia Civil, one policeman, the aide to the military governor of Guipúzcoa, and the military governor of Madrid. In addition, in an attack against a Guardia Civil member in Beasain (Guipúzcoa) on January 6, ETA killed his girl friend, the first time the organization had harmed a woman (and the only time, as far as I know, that they intentionally killed a woman through the end of 1980). In February, deaths from ETA violence declined slightly to eight, including four members of the Guardia Civil, the mayor of Olaberría (Guipúzcoa) the police chief of Munguía (Vizcaya) and a retired army lieutenant colonel. In addition, ETA(p-m) kidnaped three victims in February, including an executive of a construction firm, whom they shot in the leg,[44] the provincial delegate to Vizcaya from the Spanish Ministry of Agriculture, who was also wounded, and a director of the Michelin Tire Factory in Vitoria.

In March, three people lost their lives in an ETA attack, including the chief of police of Beasain. There were only two wounded, one of whom was the former mayor of Bilbao, Pilar Careaga de Lequerica. ETA also kidnaped the son of an industrialist in Algorta (Vizcaya), whom they released after the payment of a ransom of 2.8 million pesetas.

Also in March, Spanish and Basque public opinion turned its attention to the electoral process once again. Late the preceding December, after the promulgation of the new constitution, President Adolfo Suárez had dissolved the Cortes elected in 1977, and called new elections to produce a national legislative assembly with a new mandate under the terms of the constitution. These elections took place on March 1, with full participation by a wide range of Basque Left parties.[45] Although Herri Batasuna had not yet been legalized as a political coalition, the KAS officially supported participation in the elections by candidates as well as by rank-and-file voters.[46] It would be an understatement to say that the elections produced some surprises for moderate Basque nationalists. While the share of the vote given to the Basque Nationalist Party declined from its 1977 level (from 24.4 percent to 22.2 percent of the vote in all four provinces), the vote awarded to all Basque Left parties combined rose dramatically from 11.2 percent in 1977 to 21 percent in 1979. The Euzkadiko

Ezkerra coalition won 6.3 percent of the vote and retained its single seat in the Congress of Deputies, but Herri Batasuna won 13 percent of the vote and elected three members of the Cortes' lower chamber. One week later, HB announced that its delegates would refuse to occupy their seats in the chamber, beginning the coalition's use of the electoral process primarily as a mechanism for demonstrating a high level of voter discontent in the Basque provinces.[47] With the 1979 parliamentary elections, the Basque electoral system was in effect splintered into four segments of about equal strength: the Spanish Left (PSOE and PEC), the Spanish Center-Right (primarily the UCD of Adolfo Suárez), the Basque Center-Right (occupied solely by the PNV), and the Basque Left (principally EE and HB, the two coalitions linked with factions of ETA).

In April, the pace of ETA assaults rose once again. Ten persons lost their lives from ETA attacks during the month, including three members of the Guardia Civil and four policemen, three of whom were killed in a single assault in San Sebastián on April 8. The pressure of police actions was beginning to be felt, however. In April, the Guardia Civil succeeded in uncovering and arresting most of the members of one of ETA(m)'s most active comandos, the Comando Urola, which had primary responsibility for the Legazpia-Ezquioga area of Guipúzcoa.[48]

April was also the time for still another exercise in electoral politics. This time, the purpose was to select provincial assemblies and municipal councils, the first such elections held since the end of the Civil War forty years earlier. Again the Basque Left parties fielded a full list of candidates for most of the municipal and provincial seats, and again they showed surprising strength. Demonstrating the party's long-standing strength at the local level, the PNV won slightly less than 30 percent of the popular vote but elected nearly half (1,054 of 2,309) of the candidates chosen. The share of the vote given to the Basque Left rose once again, to 25.4 percent, with EE winning 5 percent (and 85 seats) and HB winning 15.1 percent (and 304 seats). Herri Batasuna thus became the second strongest party in the Basque provinces, running about one percent behind the Spanish socialist party, PSOE, in popular vote, but beating PSOE by nearly one hundred seats won. This was the first time in history that the vote given to all Basque nationalist parties combined rose above one-half of all votes cast (55.3 percent, to be precise). Again, the HB coalition officially called on its delegates to the various provincial assemblies not to assume their elected positions.[49] This time, however, delegates elected by the various HB coalition partners, especially those from the Basque Socialist

Party (ESB), chose to participate anyway, and several of the party's members took their seats on municipal councils.[50] The difference of opinion led to considerable tension within the coalition and was the cause of its splintering the following year.

While the total number of persons killed by ETA declined slightly in May, the level of public unrest and tension continued high. In the traditional May Day celebrations in Bilbao, members of ETA marched hooded with the demonstrators.[51] The following day, two Guardia Civil troops were machine-gunned to death in Villafranca de Ordizia (Guipúzcoa), one of ETA's strongholds. And on May 25, in one of ETA(m)'s most dramatic assaults of the period, one of their comandos killed a Spanish army general, two army colonels, and their driver in their car on a Madrid street.

The months of June and July were especially tragic, as some fifteen people were killed by ETA violence. Despite waves of new arrests by police, especially in Vizcaya, ETA(m) added four more victims to its list during the first half of June, including a factory owner in Vergara (Guipúzcoa) who was accused of being a spy, a retired Spanish army major, and a construction worker at the Lemóniz nuclear plant, killed by another bomb explosion.

While ETA(m) was carrying out its attacks on single individuals with firearms, ETA(p-m) launched a new campaign of exploding bombs in public places. The switch to this tactic was not completely without warning. Early in the year, police had estimated that ETA(p-m) had stored some 600 kilograms of explosive, and this quantity was augmented by the theft of some 1,000 kilograms of Goma-2 in Pamplona in early March.[52] In mid-June, some six bombs exploded almost simultaneously at widely separated spots in Guipúzcoa.[53] On June 27, ETA(p-m) announced that it was launching a bombing campaign to force the Spanish government to return to Basque prisons the hundred or so members of ETA who had been removed to Soria the preceding December.[54] The target, said ETA(p-m), would be Spain's tourist industry, then entering its most active period—specifically hotels, casinos, and the country's transportation network, particularly air and rail centers. The bombings began almost immediately thereafter, concentrated in Mediterranean coastal tourist resorts like Marbella and Benidorm. The actual explosions were preceded by telephoned warnings to police to indicate the approximate locations of the explosions, so that people nearby could be evacuated. By July 5, there had been more than a dozen bombings in some of Spain's most luxurious resorts.

During the first several weeks of July, ETA(p-m) suspended what it

later referred to as the first phase of the bombing campaign. Interpretations of the suspension vary. According to some reports, p-m
suspended the bombings because Madrid had withdrawn the special
military forces from around and within Soria Prison and had agreed to
begin discussions leading to the return of the imprisoned etarras to
Euzkadi.[55] Other reports suggested that ETA(p-m) did not want to
disrupt things unnecessarily while delicate negotiations were under
way in Madrid that concerned the proposed Basque Autonomy
Statute.[56]

Whatever the cause of the suspension, it eroded during July. On
July 29, according to ETA(p-m), negotiations over return of prisoners
to the Basque provinces broke down, and p-m decided to return to the
offensive with the "second phase" of the bombings. On that day,
between 1:00 and 1:15 P.M., three bombs exploded in Madrid. The
first, in a ticket office of the Atocha railroad station, killed three instantly and wounded more than thirty, one of whom would die four
days later. The second, in the ticket office of Chamartin railroad station, killed one and wounded dozens. The third, in the Madrid airport,
Barajas, killed one and wounded seven. Later that same day,
ETA(p-m) held a clandestine press conference at which they blamed
Madrid police for the fact that the explosions had taken such a high
toll. According to the spokesmen, the police had been warned more
than an hour and a half before the scheduled time for detonation.
Moreover, the bombs had been carefully placed in buildings with
large corridors and doors and good public address systems so that
evacuation would be easy. Nevertheless, if the police were going to
ignore such warnings, and in ETA(p-m)'s view place in jeopardy the
lives of innocent bystanders, then the organization would have no
choice but to suspend the bombing campaign. They also announced
that they had deactivated eleven bombs already placed, and they gave
out maps to show police the location of three bombs still to be exploded. Police subsequently destroyed the three bombs. A later communiqué, on August 2, confirmed p-m's decision not to resort to the
bombings, a decision which was greeted by Basque political leaders
with great relief and approval.[57] Several days later, Spanish authorities granted permission to return fourteen etarras from Soria to
Basque prisons, although nearly one hundred members of ETA remained. As always, the announcement was accompanied by claims
that the actions taken were planned in advance, and did not reflect any
negotiation with ETA(p-m) to get them to stop the bombings.[58]

From this point on to the end of the year, there was a steady if
irregular decline in ETA violence from the high level of the first half

of the year. In August, only three deaths were recorded, those of two members of the Guardia Civil and one policeman. In September, six lost their lives to ETA attacks: a bank director who had refused to pay an ETA-imposed "revolutionary tax," three senior army officers (including a major, a colonel and the military governor of Guipúzcoa), an ex-mayor, and the chief of police of Amorebieta (Vizcaya).

Despite the tension surrounding the upcoming referendum on the Basque Autonomy Statute, there were only four killings by ETA in October. ETA(m) killed three of these, including two police officials and a Guardia Civil trooper. ETA(m) was also responsible for the machine-gun attack on a San Sebastián cafe during lunch hour that wounded eight police and three construction workers but miraculously killed no one. The Comandos Autónomos took their fifth victim in October, a member of the PSOE and one of the few working class victims ever recorded by ETA. This attack resulted in an open split between ETA(m) and (p-m) and the Comandos Autónomos and in a mass demonstration by leftist unions against ETA violence.[59] During October, the Herri Batasuna coalition waged a strong campaign against approval of the proposed autonomy statute in the referendum, while ETA(p-m) was officially on record as supporting the statute and urging an affirmative vote. On October 25, voters in Alava, Guipúzcoa, and Vizcaya (Navarra was not included in the regional autonomy arrangement) went to the polls to register their opinion on the proposed statute. About 832,000 voted for the proposal and only 47,000 against, but about 620,000 abstained. As is the case in most abstention campaigns, the outcome was ambiguous and enabled both sides to interpret it as they wished.

Through the last two months of 1979, ETA(m) launched relatively few armed attacks. The only significant one was a machine-gun assault that killed three members of the Guardia Civil in Azpeitia (Guipúzcoa) in late November. Nevertheless, ETA(p-m) was once again in the headlines with its dramatic kidnaping of Javier Rupérez, an important leader of the ruling party UCD and chairman of the international relations committee of the party. Rupérez was kidnaped on November 13 by ETA(p-m), and held hostage for a series of demands that included amnesty for a number of etarras in prison, the return of the remainder from Soria to prisons in Euzkadi, and the withdrawal of all Spanish law-enforcement authorities from the Basque provinces. Despite repeated denials by both sides, there was apparently a round of negotiations that resulted in Rupérez's release on December 12, followed shortly by an announcement that twenty-six Basques would soon be released from prison and that the Spanish parliament would create a special commission to investigate charges of torture and mis-treatment of Basques in prison.[60] The rest of 1979 passed without incident.

The toll of ETA violence for the year was 72 killed, about 141 wounded, and 8 kidnaped.

1980: ETA at High Tide

ETA violence rose to an all-time high in 1980, although it continued to exhibit the same sort of cyclical rise and fall that we have seen in preceding years. ETA attacks rose in January and February, fell in the spring, but began to rise again in May and June, fell off to practically zero in August (the traditional festival month in the Basque region), and rose sharply through the autumn, only to turn down again sharply in December.

In January, eight people lost their lives in ETA attacks, including an army major who was also chief of the provincial police of Alava and two members of the Guardia Civil. However, the list also included two bar owners, a cemetery attendant, and a commercial agent, all of whom were shot either because of some alleged spying activity or for alleged rightist sympathies. Perhaps the most dramatic attack was a machine-gunning of a group of national police on a soccer field near their barracks in Basauri (Vizcaya) that left one dead and five wounded.

February was an especially bloody month in the Basque provinces. Some ten people were killed by ETA, including six members of the Guardia Civil who were shot to death in an ambush near Lequeitio (Vizcaya). In this attack, two members of ETA were also killed. The next day, rightist Spanish-Basque Battalion (BVE) killed two Basque civilians in retaliation, which meant that in all, ten persons had died as a consequence of the attack. Others killed during this month included an army major, a policeman, and a retired army lieutenant colonel. The only other notable event in February was ETA's first use of so-called high technology terrorism, the firing of a rocket against the Moncloa Palace in Madrid, an attack that produced no casualties.

On March 9, voters in Alava, Guipúzcoa, and Vizcaya went to the polls to elect the Basque parliament, the legislative assembly provided for in the Basque Autonomy Statute. Early in the year, the Herri Batasuna coalition had decided that it would present candidates for the Basque parliament, even though it continued to hold to its policy of not occupying the seats it would win.[61] This position prompted much debate within HB and caused the coalition to split apart, with the Patriotic Revolutionary Workers Party (LAIA) and the Basque Socialist Assembly (ESB) leaving the coalition.[62] Nevertheless, Herri Batasuna emerged as the second strongest party in the Basque provinces, winning 18.3 percent of the seats in the parliament (eleven out of sixty) and 17.6 percent of the popular vote.[63] Euzkadiko Ezkerra also showed strongly, winning 10.4 percent of the vote and six out of sixty seats. Thus the Basque Left won about 28 percent of the vote and slightly more than 28 percent of the seats in the new parliament. The PNV was the single strongest party, with 40.6 percent of the vote and twenty-five seats (41.7 percent). Because of Herri Batasuna's refusal to occupy its seats, however, the PNV constituted an absolute majority by the very slim margin of one vote (twenty-five out of the remaining forty-nine occupied seats), so they proceeded to organize the parliament as a dominant single party, electing as the first president Carlos Garaikoetxea, the PNV leader from Navarra. The Basque parliament met to begin its historic work on March 31.

Perhaps because of these developments in the electoral sphere, ETA violence declined in March and April. In March, only five were killed, including an industrialist who refused to pay the "revolutionary tax," two men accused of being informers, and a small child who accidentally kicked a bomb set by ETA to explode under a Guardia Civil Land Rover but which failed to detonate. In addition, the March casualty list included an army general and lieutenant colonel wounded in Madrid by a bomb which at the same time killed their driver. April was similarly quiet with only four killings, those of the chief of police of Vitoria and three members of the Guardia Civil, who fell in two separate attacks. Other events of significance during the period included the second firing of a rocket by ETA(p-m) against a government building, this time against the headquarters of the civil governor of Navarra in Pamplona (also without injury), and the kidnaping of Catalan industrialist Jesus Serra Santamans, who was released two months later after the payment of a ransom of 150 million pesetas (about $1.5 million). In early April, however, ETA(p-m) issued a communiqué stating its intention to continue the struggle, despite the launching of the Basque parliament and the Basque provinces' first autonomous regime since the Civil War.

The level of killing rose again sharply in May and June, with a total of seventeen dead in the two-month period. In May, ETA(m) killed nine, including four police (three in one attack in San Sebastián), two members of the Guardia Civil, and two business executives. Four police were also wounded in a bomb and machine-gun attack by ETA(m) in San Sebastián. ETA continued its attacks on executives of the Michelin Factory in Vitoria, too, by shooting and wounding its director of personnel, Jesús Casanova Salazar. In June, eight persons died from ETA violence. One of the dead was Luis Hergueta Guinea, a director of Michelin, the third victim from the anti-Michelin attacks and (excluding the Madrid bombings of July 1979) the first killing by ETA(p-m) since August 1978. In another incident, the Comandos Autónomos killed a retired Guardia Civil member and two of his friends in their car. Late in the month, ETA(p-m) announced a summer bombing campaign similar to its tragic actions of the preceding summer. As an ETA(p-m) leader recounted in an interview published in *Cambio 16*, the renewal of the bombing was decided upon as a consequence of the slowness with which Madrid was moving to grant real power to the Basque government.[64] Their specific demands included the immediate release of nineteen Basque prisoners, the removal of the director of the Soria prison, and the announcement of a referendum for the people of Navarra to determine whether or not they wished to join the Basque Autonomous Community.[65] In contrast to the events of the preceding summer, however, there were no immediate signs of negotiations between ETA(p-m) and the government, and the bombing campaign proceeded through late July and August but without injury to anyone.[66]

ETA activities declined slightly in July and to an even greater degree in August. During July, the principal target was the Guardia Civil. Two members of the Guardia were killed and three were wounded in an attack by ETA(m) in Orio (Guipúzcoa). Near the end of the month, ETA(m) exploded a bomb under the Guardia Civil convoy in Logroño, killing the convoy commander, a Guardia Civil lieutenant, and wounding thirty-four of the convoy. On July 26, an ETA comando made off with seven tons of Goma-2 explosive from a deposit in Santander province, the largest such theft in the history of ETA operations. August was, as usual, a period of relative quiet, broken only by the reprisal killing of a welder in Vizcaya and an attack on a newspaper editor in Pamplona. Although the editor, José Javier Uranga Santesteban, was only wounded by the attack, the assault provoked a mass demonstration against terrorist violence in Pamplona on September 1. Elsewhere, press reports suggested that Madrid police had located an important ETA comando operating in the Spanish capital and preparing some kind of spectacular strike, but by the end of 1980 nothing of the sort had occurred.[67]

The three-month period from the beginning of September through the end of November was one of the most violent in ETA's history: thirty-six people died at the hands of ETA, nearly half of all those killed during the year. In September eight were killed, including a national police captain, an army lieutenant colonel, a leader of the governing party UCD in Alava, and four members of the Guardia Civil killed in a single attack in Marquina. In October, the figure rose to fourteen killed: three policemen in a single attack in Durango; three Guardia Civil in a single attack in Salvatierra (Alava); an army lieutenant colonel; two telephone company employees in separate attacks in San Sebastián; and two key leaders of UCD in Guipúzcoa. In November, the number of killed remained at fourteen. The worst assault came in Zarauz (Guipúzcoa), where an ETA(m) team machine-gunned a bar, killing four Guardia Civil members and one bystander and wounding another member of the Guardia Civil and four bystanders. In other attacks in November, ETA(m) killed two Guardia Civil, two policemen, and the chief of police of San Sebastián.

As 1980 drew to a close, December seemed to bring a respite from ETA violence. There were only two killed during that month: a bar owner in Cestona (Guipúzcoa) and a police inspector in Eibar (Guipúzcoa). In all, in 1980, ETA had killed eighty-eight, wounded eighty-one, and kidnaped seven. In addition, there had been six etarras killed and nineteen others killed by anti-ETA rightists.

The violent spasms of the last quarter of 1980 provoked the moderate parties in the Basque provinces to mount still another mass demonstration against terrorism. On the last day of October, representatives of the PNV, the PSOE, and the UCD met to convoke a demonstration in San Sebastián to protest "against terrorism and for peace."[68] The call for the demonstration was joined by representatives from across the political spectrum, from communists to center-right Basque nationalists. The universities in the region agreed to close, and the faculty of Deusto University in Bilbao passed a resolution condemning terrorism. On November 2, a crowd estimated at 20,000 paraded in San Sebastián, harassed by pro-ETA counter-demonstrators who yelled ETA slogans and tried to interrupt the route of march of the parade. Most of the moderate Basque nationalists responsible for the demonstration claimed that it was proof that Basques wanted an end to violence from the police and Guardia Civil and from ETA.

On the day of the parade in San Sebastián, ETA members shot and killed four members of the Guardia Civil in a bar in Zarauz. They killed nine more victims before the year was over. Peace may have been what most Basques wanted at the end of 1980, but it was not what they seemed likely to get.

PART TWO

PATTERNS OF BASQUE INSURGENCY

CHAPTER FIVE

Patterns of ETA Violence: 1968–80

Like all insurgent organizations, ETA differs from more conventional political groups in two ways: in its need to operate clandestinely in a highly threatening environment, and in the fact that its principal objective is to inflict, or threaten to inflict, damage on people and property. In later chapters, I will discuss how ETA has dealt with the organizational and psychological imperatives arising from the stressful nature of clandestine insurgent operations. Here I wish to focus on the nature of ETA's use of violent attacks to further its own (and its constituents') objectives.

The key assumption here is, simply, that we gain important insight into the character of any complex organization by examining what it does as opposed to what it says that it intends to do. I believe that we can study patterns in ETA violence for important clues to the nature of the organization. I am convinced that in ETA's attacks we see not random, senseless killing and wounding but rather acts chosen with great attention to their possible impact on the political environment. Even since ETA's Fourth Assembly adopted in 1965 the action-repression-action spiral theory, the organization has demonstrated great concern for the instrumental role that violence plays in its strategy. Despite a fairly small number of unfortunate and tragic mistakes, there is considerable evidence that ETA plans its attacks with care to make them as much as possible symbolic and communicative and to minimize harm to bystanders and other noncombatants. We have some evidence that ETA attacks are discussed in substantial detail by high-level policy-making bodies of the organization before assignments are sent down to local cells or comandos for execution; and the historical record of selected comandos suggests that considerable time goes into the planning of attacks, at least three months and at times as much as a year. No doubt there have been a certain number of random killings and other attacks connected with ETA's struggle. It would be unrealistic and naïve to assume that a clandestine insurgent organization can control events perfectly to insure that all attacks go according to plan. Data to be discussed below suggest that in recent years there have been increasing numbers of revenge assaults, as ETA and ultrarightists have battled back and forth with killing and counter-killing. Despite these attacks and some fairly costly mistakes, I believe that ETA's record has been relatively free of unplanned or unsystematic violence, especially when compared with the records of other insurgent groups active in the 1970s. This chapter, then, is organized around the basic principle that ETA's attacks make sense and fit into some larger plan that helps define the character of the organization.

We run into a methodological problem of considerable proportions, however. What we have before us is a classic example of an attempt to capture for social science analysis data that resist being captured. In order for an ETA attack to show up in some data file, it must follow a complicated path of communications. First, an attack (and assassination, a wounding, a kidnaping) must occur in a way that warrants a report by the Basque or Spanish news media. It is obvious, for example, that the media will devote more coverage to some attacks than to others, depending upon such factors as the time and place of the attack and the status of the target. Second, the characteristics of the attack must justify news media or police speculation that ETA was involved. In the case of attacks involving machine guns and submachine guns, for example, much is usually made of the kind of ammunition casings left behind, since media observers in Spain believe that ETA has a tendency to use only a certain kind of ammunition (9 mm "Parabellum"). Casings of this type at the attack scene are usually regarded as one of ETA's trademarks and are so reported in press accounts. Third, for ETA to be credited with the attack, some person claiming to represent a branch of ETA must contact a news agency and claim that ETA was responsible. On occasion, these communications have gone to local Basque radio stations, but more often the contacts are made with one of the two major Basque newspapers, *Deia* of Bilbao and *Egin* of San Sebastián. Obviously, one has no way of knowing whether or not the claims are legitimate, but they are made frequently enough to create a certain pattern and an expectation that ETA attacks that are genuine will be followed by such a telephone call. Nevertheless, there are many obvious ETA attacks that are not claimed in this way, so we must infer their authorship by their characteristics. Fourth, the claim of responsibility must be duly reported by the news media, a step that seems to present little problem, since to have them reported is precisely why ETA went to the trouble of making the claim in the first place. Finally, the media reports must come to the attention of the social scientists who are gathering data on ETA attacks. Many social scientists will use Madrid newspapers such as *El país, Informaciones* or *Diario 16* for their data, but these newspapers will never cover events in the Basque country as intensively as *Deia* of Bilbao, for example. Thus the choice of source documents is of critical importance.

It is not surprising, then, to discover that even experts disagree on the number of attacks committed by ETA over the period 1968–80. (In table 5.1, for instance, we see the range of expert opinion on ETA killings.) For this reason, as well as to provide the data needed for other kinds of analysis, I have created my own data base, which will be used for all analysis here.

The data set from which my analyses are derived contains information on 287 killings, 385 woundings, and 24 kidnapings committed by

Table 5.1   *Variation in Estimates of ETA Killed, 1968–80*

YEAR	CAMBIO 16 3–30–81[a]	DIARIO 16 11–19–79[b]	PORTELL[c]	NEW STATESMAN[d]	HEWITT[e]	GUNTHER[f]
1968						
1969						
1970			8			
1971						
1972						
1973				134	4	
1974			36		17	
1975					21	
1976			19		20	
1977					10	
1978	67	64			55	53
1979	75				65	40
1980	98				42	

[a]Cited in Peter McDonough and Antonio Lopez Pina, "Continuity and Change in Spanish Politics," unpublished ms., p. 1.

[b]Cited in Juan Linz, "The Basques in Spain: Nationalism and Political Conflict in a New Democracy," in W. Phillips Davison and Leon Gordenker, eds., *Resolving Nationality Conflicts: The Role of Public Opinion Research* (New York: Praeger, 1980), p. 46.

[c]José María Portell, "E.T.A.: Objetivo, la insurrección de Euzkadi," *Blanco y negro*, June 29–July 5, 1977, p. 27.

[d]Julie Flint, "A Democracy under Threat," *New Statesman*, January 12, 1979, p. 46.

[e]From list provided author by Christopher Hewitt, Department of Sociology, University of Maryland–Baltimore County.

[f]From data provided author by Richard Gunther, Department of Political Science, The Ohio State University. These figures include only those killings clearly attributed to ETA by Gunther.

ETA (or which can reasonably be attributed to ETA) from June 7, 1968, through December 31, 1980. There is a small amount of duplication that comes from double-counting a kidnaping/wounding or a kidnaping/killing. An attack that wounds a victim who dies some days later from the wounds is treated as a killing only, however. My data have been drawn from nine primary sources, including two Basque newspapers and one Basque newsmagazine, and seven secondary sources.[1] Given the inherent ambiguities in data collections of this sort, the enumerations derived from the data set are reasonably close to those provided by both official and unofficial sources. For example, after the assassination of General Constantino Ortín Gil, military governor of Madrid, on January 3, 1979, the Spanish government released its official count, which showed ETA as responsible for killing 137 persons.[2] My count at the same time showed 130 deaths from ETA attacks. Soon after the end of the year, the *Washington Post* estimated the number of ETA killings for 1980 at 85.[3] My count for the year was 88. While no one really knows the exact number of victims of ETA attacks, I estimate that my data are no more than 3 to 5 percent away from the real figures.

Patterns of Violence: An Overview

From June 1968 through December 1980, ETA's violence affected directly slightly fewer than 700 people, of whom 287 were killed. Compared with brutal guerrilla wars in other countries, ETA's casualty levels are rather low. In Argentina, for example, more than 2,300 people were killed between July 1974 and August 1976. In Northern Ireland, more than 1,600 were killed in the seven-year period between 1969 and 1976. In many major American cities, there are more homicides in a year than ETA has committed in its entire history, although only rarely are the American killings part of an organized insurgency. In 1981 in the Washington, D.C., metropolitan area (with a population approximately that of the Basque provinces), there were 364 homicides, 226 of them with firearms. The significance of ETA's violence lies in the psychological effect of its attacks as opposed to the actual physical damage done by them.

In addition to the 287 killed, ETA's attacks have left 385 wounded (including one person wounded on two different occasions separated by a two-year period). The treatment of woundings from a statistical standpoint may be misleading. On the one hand, to include wounded casualties along with those killed, to count them as of essentially the same level, may inflate the figures unrealistically. One might argue that in many of these attacks, ETA really did not intend to cause any casualties at all, much less large numbers of killed or wounded. Particularly in the case of bombings that caused many casualties, the intent of the assailants (not to mention their identity or organizational affiliation) may be legitimately questioned. Such would appear to be the case in at least five such events:

the bombing of the Cafe Rolando in Madrid on September 13, 1974, which left 9 dead and 56 wounded (responsibility for the attack was subsequently denied by ETA)

the March 17, 1978, bombing of the Lemóniz (Vizcaya) nuclear plant while under construction, which resulted in 2 deaths and the wounding of 14 construction workers (ETA claimed they had telephoned a warning before the bomb exploded)

the bombing, on March 21, 1978, of the motor vehicle pool parking lot of the Spanish government ministries in San Sebastián, which wounded 14

the simultaneous bombings of the airport and two railroad stations in Madrid on July 29, 1979, which left 6 dead and about 100 wounded (ETA claimed it had telephoned a warning to the Madrid police some thirty minutes before the bombs exploded)

the bombing in Logroño on November 27, 1980, which killed 2 instantly and wounded 8, 1 of whom died the following January.

Were we to delete these five events from the list of ETA attacks, we would reduce the number killed by 20 and the number wounded by 191, which would have the overall effect of reducing the level of ETA-caused casualties by slightly less than one-third.

On the other hand, there are similar attacks in which it is obvious to the outside observer that ETA fully intended mass casualties. These include the following:

the machine-gunning of a group of national police playing soccer on a field adjacent to their barracks in Basauri (Vizcaya) on November 20, 1978, leaving 2 killed and 11 wounded

the machine-gunning of a café in San Sebastián during lunch hour on October 8, 1979, wounding 8 national police and 3 construction workers

the bombing of a Guardia Civil convoy in Logroño on July 22, 1980, killing 1 Guardia Civil lieutenant and wounding 34 troops

Whether or not an attack results in death, injury, or no harm at all is determined by a number of factors, not all of which are under the control of the assailants: the accuracy of their aim (if the attack is by firearms); the killing radius of the weapon (if it is by explosive); the density of the crowd within which the explosive is detonated; the speed with which the injured can be rushed to a well-equipped hospital; the health or physical condition of the victims; and so forth.

In view of these ambiguities, it seems appropriate to give readers as much information as possible and leave the interpretation to them. For that reason, in the analyses that follow, I provide the data in both aggregated and unaggregated form to facilitate informed interpretation and analysis.

Let us examine, first, the authorship of ETA-caused attacks (table 5.2). It will be noted that ETA(m) accounted for more than half of the killings recorded during the period, while about one-third were blamed simply on ETA (without distinguishing between subgroups), or were of unknown origin. ETA(p-m), in contrast, was held responsible for only a little more than 5 percent of the killings. On the other hand, ETA(p-m) was responsible for nearly one-third of the woundings charged to ETA (here the Madrid train-station and airport attacks bulk very large in the statistics), while ETA(m) caused only slightly more than four out of every ten injuries. The balance of responsibility was reversed for kidnapings, with ETA(p-m) accused of more than 60 percent, while ETA(m) caused only about 13 percent. Two additional points should be made from that table. First, the Comandos Autónomos committed relatively few assaults of any kind during the period; and second, a substantial number (about one-third of the killings and about one-fourth of the woundings) were committed by persons with unknown affiliation.

Let us next consider some important characteristics of ETA attacks, such as the kind of weapons employed, the site of the attack, and the size of the attacked group (tables 5.3–5.5). Our purpose here is to

Table 5.2   *ETA Attack Characteristics: Group Responsible*
(in percentages)

	N	ETA BEFORE 1974	UNKNOWN BRANCH OF ETA AFTER 1974	ETA (M)	ETA (P-M)	COMANDOS AUTÓNOMOS
Killed	287	2.8	32.1	55.0	5.6	4.5
Wounded	385	0.5	26.0	41.8	31.2	0.5
Kidnaped	24	8.3	12.5	12.5	62.5	4.2
All victims	696	1.7	28.0	46.3	21.7	2.3

Source: Data gathered from contemporary press reports. Calculations by author.

analyze the available data on these characteristics to determine the extent to which ETA sought to inflict casualties on innocent bystanders or to avoid such casualties. We will return to this theme later in the chapter when I present data on the characteristics of the victims chosen by ETA.

Table 5.3 statistics are drawn from my attack data set, but deal only with killings and woundings, since the weapons used in kidnapings are rarely reported, and in any case, seldom used. It would appear that the favorite weapon of ETA is the automatic firearm, the machine gun or submachine gun (also called the machine pistol). More than 25 percent of all killings were the product of such weapons, as opposed to about 15 percent caused by pistols and 14 percent caused by bombs or other explosives. On the other hand, bombs and explosives caused many more woundings than did the firearms, although automatic weapons caused about nine times as many woundings as did pistols. Overall, ETA casualties were divided about evenly between firearms and explosives, with each category causing about 45 percent, leaving 10 percent of unknown origin. The reader is reminded, however, that if we deleted the fewer than half-dozen high-casualty bombings referred to earlier, the balance between firearms and explosives would change dramatically.

Table 5.3   *ETA Attack Characteristics: Weapons Used*
(in percentages)

		FIREARMS				
	N	PISTOLS	AUTOMATIC WEAPONS	OTHER/ UNKNOWN	BOMBS/ EXPLOSIVES	OTHER/ UNKNOWN
Killed	287	15.7	27.2	22.6	14.3	20.2
Wounded	385	2.9	18.2	7.3	68.3	3.4
Killed and wounded	672	8.3	22.0	13.8	45.2	10.6

Source: Data gathered from contemporary press reports. Calculations by author.

The choice of weapons by an insurgent group is not a matter of random selection or even of availability, since we can assume that ETA has access to any sort of pistol, submachine gun, or explosive generally available. (The acquisition of weapons by ETA will be discussed in chapter 9.) Rather, different weapons possess different operating characteristics and differ in the injury they can inflict on intended (and unintended) victims. Pistols, for example, are more precise weapons than the others, and the risk of wounding bystanders with one is less. The problem with pistols is that they require some expertise in marksmanship, and generally, a closer approach to the victim. Machine guns and submachine guns have much greater range, and their higher rate of fire makes pinpoint accuracy less necessary. The major disadvantage of automatic weapons is that they tend to spray a wide area with lethal projectiles, and the chances of wounding bystanders are greater than, say, with pistols. Bombs are the worst weapon in this regard. Since there is usually some considerable lag of time between the placement of the explosive and its detonation, it is difficult if not impossible to predict how many people will be within its killing radius when it explodes. On the one hand, many bombs go off harmlessly, or at most damage property without harming people. On the other hand, in the worst cases such as the Madrid train-station bombings, the bombs explode in the midst of a large crowd. Whether or not ETA intended these explosions to inflict mass casualties is a subject of much polemical debate and can probably never be determined. We would conclude, however, that a tendency to use pistols during attacks signifies some effort by the group to control its violence and to protect bystanders. The use of bombs, on the other hand, would indicate that the assailants have relinquished a large degree of their control over the effects of their attack and that considerable casualties could result. Automatic weapons fall somewhere between these extremes.

Let us turn, next, to the site of ETA attacks (table 5.4). We notice immediately that a majority of those killed (52.2 percent) and more than three-fourths of those wounded (77.2 percent) were attacked in a public place in an urban area. About one out of every five persons killed and wounded by ETA was assaulted while in an automobile, jeep, Land Rover, bus, or other form of transportation while it moved along a city street. A second group, consisting of about one-fifth of those killed and more than one-third of those wounded, were attacked while walking on a city street or while in an airport or railroad station. About one-eighth of those killed and one-fifth of those wounded were attacked while in a bar, café, restaurant, or hotel. In contrast, relatively few ETA victims were attacked while on country roads or in their homes or places of work. (The exception to this observation lies, of course, in the category of kidnaping, where exactly half of all victims were taken from their homes.) Not surprisingly, there were almost no casualties inflicted by ETA during direct attacks on military or paramilitary installations, police stations, Guardia Civil barracks or road blocks, or the like. It is a rather widely accepted rule among urban insurgent groups like ETA that one avoids such direct assaults and confrontations with a target group like the Guardia Civil where it is on its home ground and can defend itself most effectively. On the other hand, a group that focuses its attacks heavily on public places like city streets, bars, and train stations is not really doing all it can to avoid harming bystanders.

The third attack characteristic I examine here involves the size of the groups in which the victims were attacked (table 5.5). We want to

Table 5.4   *ETA Attack Characteristics: Site of Attack*
(in percentages of victims attacked at each category of site)

SITE	KILLED	WOUNDED	KIDNAPED	ALL VICTIMS
City street, park, airport, train station	19.5	35.1	0.0	27.4
Automobile, bus	19.5	21.8	4.2	20.3
Bar, cafe, hotel	13.2	20.3	0.0	16.7
Rural road	2.8	1.6	0.0	2.0
Guardia Civil roadblock	1.7	0.5	0.0	1.0
Military or police installation	1.7	5.2	0.0	3.6
Private home	7.0	1.6	50.0	5.5
Workplace	5.6	6.5	12.5	6.3
Unknown	28.9	7.5	33.3	17.2
Total	99.9	100.1	100.0	100.0
(N)	(287)	(385)	(24)	(696)

Source: Data gathered from contemporary press reports. Calculations by author.

Table 5.5   *ETA Attack Characteristics: Size of Target Group*
(in percentages)

	N	SINGLE INDIVIDUAL	SMALL GROUP (2–5)	MEDIUM GROUP (6–10)	LARGE GROUP (11<)
Killed	287	49.8	38.3	4.9	7.0
Wounded	385	9.9	23.1	4.7	62.3
Kidnaped	24	100.0	0.0	0.0	0.0
All victims	696	29.4	28.6	4.6	37.4

Source: Data gathered from contemporary press reports. Calculations by author.

know whether ETA's victims were attacked while alone, or in small groups, or in large crowds. We see from these data that about half (49.8 percent) of all persons killed by ETA were attacked when they were by themselves, and another 38.3 percent were killed while in a small group of fewer than six. Very few killings involved medium-sized or large groups of people. In contrast, more than 60 percent of all woundings involved large groups—the Rolando bombing, for instance, and the Madrid airport and train-station bombings. About two-thirds of all casualties were suffered by persons either singly or in small groups, while the remaining one-third were inflicted on members of large crowds. (Again we can see the statistical importance of the half-dozen or so bombings in crowded public places.)

What is one to make of these data? It seems to me that we can generalize about ETA attacks in this way. Most of the time, ETA attacked either individuals or small groups of two to five people. These attacks were carried out with firearms, mostly automatic weapons such as submachine guns but often pistols. The majority of these attacks took place in public places in cities—in streets, bars, cafés, and restaurants. Despite the lack of control the assailants had over the killing radius of their weapons in crowded public settings, these attacks (which account for the bulk of ETA's victims) resulted in relatively few injured bystanders. On the other hand, ETA did make a few (between five and ten) tragic mistakes that involved the placing of bombs under uncontrolled conditions in crowded public places. The consequence of these errors were casualties in the range of two to ten killed and ten to one hundred wounded. I conclude from these observations, then, that most of the time ETA was careful to avoid harming civilian bystanders in its attacks but that its record is not flawless in this regard, and several very serious mistakes did result in the killing and wounding of numerous bystanders.

Patterns of Violence: Distribution of Attacks over Time

Let us turn to a consideration of the way in which ETA's attacks have been distributed over time (table 5.6). Do we see a patterns of attacks spread more or less evenly through the 1968–80 period, or are they concentrated in some way within that period?

We find that from 1968 through 1973, ETA was still relatively restrained (or weak, depending on how one looks at it) and was blamed for only 7 killings (although one was of the Spanish prime minister, Admiral Carrero Blanco, and therefore had a more-than-average impact). Through the turbulent years 1974 and 1975, ETA accounted for

27 killings, to bring their total to 34 by the end of 1975. Thus by the end of the Franco era, ETA had accounted for only about 12 percent of the killings for which it has been held responsible during the years 1968–80. Police or Guardia Civil killed at least 30 ETA members during this same period.

In table 5.7, we can examine in somewhat greater detail the rate of ETA killings from 1976 through 1980 and view them in relation to developments in Spanish and Basque politics that bore on Basque self-governance. We note that the level of assassination reached during the last two years of the Franco regime (13–14 a year) did not rise, and even declined a little, during the first two years of the post-Franco period, when the Spanish government initiated the transition to parliamentary democracy and a constitutional monarchy. It was only later that violence began to increase, to 67 killings in 1978 and to 72 in 1979. Most paradoxical of all, it was in 1980, when the Basques elected the first regional government they had ever had, that ETA killings reached a peak of 88. Thus it has been precisely during the

Table 5.6   *Distribution of ETA Victims over the Years 1968–80*

	KILLED		WOUNDED		KIDNAPED[a]		TOTAL	
YEAR	YEAR	CUM	YEAR	CUM	YEAR	CUM	YEAR	CUM
1968	2	2	0	0	0	0	2	2
1969	1	3	0	0	0	0	1	3
1970	0	3	0	0	1	1	1	4
1971	0	3	0	0	0	1	0	4
1972	1	4	1	1	0	1	2	6
1973	3	7	1	2	1	2	5	11
1974	11[b]	18	58[b]	60	0	2	69	80
1975	16	34	5	65	0	2	21	101
1976	17	51	0	65	2	4	19	120
1977	9	60	7	72	1	5	17	137
1978	67	127	91	163	4	9	162	299
1979	72[c]	199	141[c]	304	8	17	221	520
1980	88	287	81	385	7	24	176	696

Source: Data gathered from contemporary press reports. Calculations by author.

[a] Victims killed or wounded after kidnaping counted in both columns. Kidnaping does not include motorists whose seizure was incidental to the theft of their automobile.

[b] Includes 9 killed, 56 wounded in Rolando bombing.

[c] Includes 6 killed, estimated 100 wounded in Madrid airport, train-station bombings.

time when Basques were gaining a number of their objectives of regional autonomy that ETA has been most violent. This trend has confounded attempts at analysis of the ETA phenomenon, and has proven especially frustrating to Basque and Spanish political leaders in their search for a stable political order in the region. We will return to this theme again in chapter 10, as we attempt to assess the prospects for a restoration of civil order in the Basque country.

Patterns of Violence: Choice of Targets

Certainly, a key objective of this study must be to discover how ETA members define their political world, how they characterize the sources of their oppression, and how they separate the political universe into heroes and villains, friends and enemies, those to be attacked and those to be defended. I have examined the historical record for this kind of elusive detail by looking at the kinds of victims targeted for attack by ETA's assassination squads or kidnap teams. If, as I have argued, ETA's attacks are not random but in fact carefully chosen and planned, then the victims selected should reflect the organization's definition of its enemies. This kind of analysis is central to

Table 5.7   *Relation of the Number of ETA Killings to the Development of Basque Autonomy*

YEAR	NO. OF KILLINGS	AUTONOMY-RELATED EVENTS
1968–75	34	Franco regime in power; near-total suppression of Basque nationalist sentiment
1976	17	First Suárez government appointed; Cortes approves laws paving way for democracy; popular referendum approves transition
1977	9	First democratically elected Cortes chosen; Cortes begins drafting new constitution
1978	67	New constitution approved, giving legal status to autonomous regions; Basques submit proposed autonomy statute
1979	72	Second Cortes elected; municipal governments popularly elected; Basque referendum approves autonomy statute; Cortes subsequently approves
1980	88	First Basque parliament elected; Basque government chosen and formally begins work

Source: Data gathered from contemporary press reports. Calculations by author.

an understanding of how ETA translates its ideology into action through the attacks of the members. ETA is an organization whose ideology defines as the enemy both industrial capitalism (Basque or Spanish) and Spanish political domination, or internal colonialism. The data show, however, that ETA does not choose its victims in strict accord with this formula (table 5.8).

Overall, it appears that ETA has divided its targets about equally between military and law-enforcement personnel on the one hand and civilians on the other. The former category accounts for slightly more than 50 percent of all victims, the latter, about 46 percent, with the remainder unknown. Within the specific attack categories (killed, wounded, kidnaped) the balance changes dramatically. Among those killed, fully two-thirds were from the military or law-enforcement occupations or were directly related to the military or paramilitary struggle against ETA. As far as wounded victims are concerned, however, the large number of wounded bystanders injured by the several mass bombings discussed earlier causes the balance to shift

Table 5.8 *Distribution of ETA Victims by Profession/*
Occupation, Role, or Reason for Victimization
(percentages of victims in each class)

CATEGORY OF VICTIM	KILLED	WOUNDED	KIDNAPED	ALL VICTIMS
Military, law-enforcement	68.0	40.5	0.0	50.4
Guardia Civil	31.7	23.4	0.0	26.0
National police	14.6	13.5	0.0	13.5
Municipal police	9.1	1.8	0.0	4.7
Military	7.0	1.8	0.0	3.9
Spies/informer	5.6	0.0	0.0	2.3
Civilians	25.1	59.0	95.8	46.2
Pol figure/govt official	8.0	1.8	20.8	5.0
Industrial/business figure	2.4	2.9	70.8	5.0
Object of revenge/ retaliation/intimidation	4.2	0.3	4.2	2.0
Bystander	9.1	53.5	0.0	33.3
Accidental victim	1.4	0.5	0.0	0.9
Unknown/others	7.0	0.5	4.2	3.3
Total	100.1	100.0	100.0	99.9
(N)	(287)	(385)	(24)	(696)

Source: Data gathered from contemporary press reports. Calculations by author.

markedly, so that about six out of every ten wounded victims were civilians (more than half being bystanders). In contrast, virtually all of those victims who were kidnaped were civilians, the overwhelming majority being industrial or business figures.

Let us focus with more precision, then, on each specific subcategory. Apart from the many bystanders wounded by the half-dozen or so mass bombings, the single most heavily victimized category was the Guardia Civil. Nearly one-third (91) of those killed and nearly one-fourth (90) of those wounded were members of the Guardia Civil. The majority of these attacks were against single Guardia Civil members or small groups on patrol, either on foot or in an automobile or jeep. The favorite ETA tactic was to attack a Guardia Civil contingent in a vehicle while it was parked or stopped at a street intersection, or in an ambush on a country road. The great majority of Guardia Civil victims were in the enlisted ranks. The only officers of the Guardia who were killed were two lieutenants, one in Guernica in May 1975 and the other in Logroño in July 1980. This latter was killed in the bombing of the Guardia Civil convoy that left 34 wounded, the most massive assault on the Guardia in ETA's history. Given these data, it is easy to see why the Guardia Civil felt compelled to offer special bonuses in extra pay and vacation time to enlisted men who served in the Basque provinces.[4] It is also easy to understand why it would be the Guardia Civil that would be most restive and impatient with the seeming inability of the Spanish government to deal effectively with ETA.

After the Guardia Civil, the next most popular targets for ETA's assailants were the police, both national police (called, variously, Policía Armada, Policía Política-Social, and so forth) and municipal or local police. (The division in table 5.8 between national and municipal police is somewhat artificial, since in a number of cases the identification was not certain.) In all, ETA killed 68 police (23.7 percent of all killed) and wounded 59 (15.3 percent of all wounded). Slightly less than one-fifth of the victims were police officials or in the enlisted ranks. As with the Guardia Civil, most of these victims were attacked singly or in small groups while they patrolled on foot or in automobiles. In contrast to the Guardia Civil, however, a number of senior officials in the police force were killed, including the municipal police chiefs of Pasajes (Guipúzcoa) in December 1978, Mungía (Vizcaya) in February 1979, Beasain in March 1979, Amorebieta (Vizcaya) in September 1979, Vitoria in April 1980, and San Sebastián in November 1980, as well as the ex-chief of police of Santurce (Vizcaya) in December 1978.[5] In addition, ETA killed the commander of the national police in Navarra in November 1977 and the chief of the provincial police of Alava in January 1980. Both these officials were also active-duty Spanish army majors at the time of their killings.

Although the military victims do not bulk as large in the statistics as do other categories, no one would dispute the fact that their assassinations have probably caused more disruption of the Spanish political scene than those of any others. Because of the crucial importance of the Spanish armed forces to the democratic government, the assassination of senior military officers does more to jeopardize the Spanish democratic experiment than the assassination of an equal number of Guardia Civil enlisted men. It is probably for that reason that ETA has concentrated its assassination attempts almost entirely on senior officers. Enlisted men have been killed or wounded only when they were with a senior officer or officers at the time of an attack, as, for example, the drivers of military automobiles that were ambushed. Thus although ETA has killed only twenty members of the armed forces, among those members were the prime minister of Spain, Admiral Luis Carrero Blanco, killed in December, 1973; the military governors of Madrid (January 1979) and Guipúzcoa (September 1979); the aide to the military governor of Guipúzcoa (January 1979); two active-duty army generals (July 1978 and May 1979); three army colonels and one navy captain (two killed in May 1979, one in September 1979, and one in October 1978); two army lieutenant colonels (September and October 1980); and two army majors (September 1979 and February 1980). In addition to these active-duty officers, ETA has killed two retired army colonels, one retired army lieutenant colonel, and one retired army major. It has also wounded one army general, two air force colonels, and four army lieutenant colonels.[6]

The last category of attack targets under the military and law-enforcement heading consists not of uniformed members of the armed forces or the police but rather of persons whom ETA communiqués identified as spies or informers and as having been targets for that reason. By my count, some sixteen deaths fit into this category. The attacks were usually directed against people walking alone on city streets or driving alone in automobiles to home or work. The victims represent a wide variety of professions or occupations. At least three were former ETA members who were shot for having allegedly given information to the police. Another group of about half a dozen or so were bar owners or taxi drivers, and the remainder were from various occupations such as tailor, jewelry store owner, grave digger, automobile mechanic, and so forth. It must be emphasized that the only evidence we have that shows that these people were spies and informers is that contained in the ETA communiqués issued after each killing. In almost every case, the family of the deceased denied the accusations and challenged ETA to provide the evidence in the public media.

When we turn to civilians, we see that the largest single category of victims consisted of bystanders, 26 killed and 206 wounded. I have already discussed this category in some detail elsewhere in the chapter. The great majority of these people were the victims of bomb explosions, although a few were caught in a crossfire between etarras and police or Guardia Civil troops and lost their lives in the exchange of gunfire. Bystanders were fully one-third of all ETA victims of all kinds. We do not have any detailed information about these 232 people, but I have no reason to believe they are anything but a cross section of Spanish or Basque urban society.

The next most significant category of civilian victims were political figures and government officials, of whom ETA killed 23, wounded 7, and kidnaped 5. In addition to Prime Minister Carrero Blanco, the list includes a number of mayors and former mayors, prominent members of the Spanish political party Unión del Centro Democrático, and leaders of provincial governments in the Basque provinces. In particular, ETA killed the mayors of Oyarzún (Guipúzcoa) in November 1975, Galdácano (Vizcaya) in February 1976, and Olaberría (Guipúzcoa) in February 1979, and the ex-mayors of Echarri-Aranaz (Navarra) in January 1979, Bedia (Vizcaya) in September 1979, and Elgóibar in October 1980. They also wounded the ex-mayor of Bilbao in an attack in March 1979. Two of the most dramatic ETA attacks were those that resulted in the deaths of Juan María Araluce, president of the Guipúzcoa provincial government, who was machine-gunned, along with his bodyguards, in San Sebastián in October 1976; and of Augusto Unceta, president of the Vizcaya provincial government, who was killed in a similar manner in Guernica in October 1977. The list of political victims also includes five assassinated members of UCD, among them an executive committee member from Alava (killed in September 1980) and two from the executive committee of Guipúzcoa (both killed in October 1980). ETA's only attacks against members of the Spanish parliament have been the wounding of the information secretary of UCD in Madrid in July 1979 and the kidnaping of the UCD secretary for foreign relations in November 1979.

Industrialists and other business and commercial figures have not been prominent on ETA's attack lists except as kidnaping victims. Several kidnapings of industrialists were dramatic events in recent Spanish political history, including those of Felipe Huarte in Pamplona in January 1973 and Javier de Ybarra in Bilbao in May 1977. Most of the kidnapings ended happily in the sense that the victims were released unharmed, but at least half a dozen ended tragically with the death of the victims, including those of Ybarra and of Angel Berazadi in Elgóibar in April 1976. Beginning in 1978, ETA adopted its own modest version of the leg-shooting attack made famous in Northern Ireland in recent years. At least six or seven such attacks have been directed against industrialists and businessmen in the Basque region. In addition, several businessmen have been killed for allegedly refusing to pay the "revolutionary tax," but the evidence to support these claims is of course sketchy and subject to challenge. The business that has suffered the most from ETA attacks has been the Michelin Tire Company factory in Vitoria. In February 1979, a Michelin director was kidnaped and later released unharmed; in May 1980, the company's personnel director was wounded; and in June 1980, another director of the company was killed in Vitoria.

The most difficult category of victims to describe with accuracy is what I call the "revenge/retaliation/intimidation" category. On a few occasions, the ETA communiqué following an assassination made explicit reference to another killing for which theirs is a response in revenge. These are rather rare, however, and most of the time we must rely on press speculation about motivation. Because of the circumstances surrounding the attacks, I would definitely include in this category the sensational assassination of the Bilbao journalist José María Portell in June 1978, as well as the wounding of the Pamplona newspaper editor José Javier Uranga in August 1980. Most of the time, however, the killings involved more obscure individuals and motivations.

The final category we should look at is that of accidents, a classification I distinguish from that of bystanders because of the element of mistake or miscalculation involved. For example, in March 1980 a young child was killed in Azcoitia (Guipúzcoa) when he accidentally kicked a bomb lying in the street. ETA had planted the bomb beneath a Guardia Civil truck, but the truck had driven off before the charge exploded. On at least two occasions, ETA killed a person only to find that it had identified him incorrectly. On one of these occasions, ETA made financial restitution to the widow. Given the violence in Basque society in recent years and the weapons and explosives available to everyone, it is to me remarkable that I can find only six clear cases (four killings and two woundings) of accidental attack in the entire period from 1968 through 1980.

I would offer one final observation having to do with ETA targets: ETA has almost never deliberately attacked women. I have found only one killing (that of the girl friend of a Guardia Civil member, who was with him in his car in January 1979), and one wounding (of the ex-mayor of Bilbao) in which the intended target was clearly a woman.

I have not made an in-depth study of insurgent acts by groups other than ETA, but I have the distinct impression that compared to such groups, ETA stands out for the almost surgical precision with which it selects the times, places, and targets for its attacks. I believe that the data presented here support one of my basic propositions about ETA, that we are seeing here not random violence but violence carefully planned for the impact it is likely to have on Spanish and Basque politics. Our data show that ETA violence persists, and even increases, despite clear gains for the Basques in their struggle for self government. ETA's threat to the maintenance of public order in the Basque country has risen in almost perfect correlation with the increasing autonomy given the Basques. And finally we see that ETA's attacks have been directed primarily against the agents of the Spanish military, paramilitary, and law-enforcement presence in the Basque provinces and only secondarily against civilians, and to an even lesser extent against representatives of industrial capitalism.[7]

CHAPTER SIX

Characteristics of ETA Members: The Personal Factor

It seems to be fairly widely accepted among investigators of insurgent groups that their members generally suffer from distorted or distressed personalities, if they are not in fact insane. The prevailing view among students of political terrorism is that terrorists are, by definition, not psychologically stable, that they are not capable of supportive relationships with others, and that they lack a shared standard of rationality with their enemies. Not only are insurgents different, in this view, but they are different in a pathological way.[1]

Unlike these observers, I have not thoroughly investigated all contemporary political insurgencies or even a significant portion of them. My scope is reduced to this single case study. Therefore I have no wish to take issue with their more general observations about political terrorists (a term, the reader will note, that I refrain from using, especially in describing ETA). Nevertheless, my inquiry into the origins of ETA members and their life styles while members of the organization leads me to conclude that while insurgents in general may have distorted personalities, the overwhelming majority of etarras are well within the range of functioning and sane human beings; while terrorists in general may be seriously distressed, members of ETA suffer from no greater stress than are observed across Basque society generally, and certainly their level of stress is no greater than normal, functioning men and women can manage. I have concluded that while insurgents in general may have difficulty in establishing and maintaining warm and nurturant interpersonal relations, etarras have relationships with loved ones that are normal to the point of being mundane. Indeed, one of the sources of ETA's great durability over the past two decades has no doubt been the ability of etarras to seek refuge and solace, as well as material support, from among those whom they love and cherish. Etarras are not alienated people; they are, on the contrary, deeply embedded in the culture whose rights they fight to defend. This theme flows throughout this book, as the reader no doubt has noted. It is articulated most explicitly in the present chapter.

It is always something of a challenge to determine with any precision the important characteristics of the members of a clandestine insurgent organization. One reason for this is the secret nature of the organization and the consequent reluctance of its members to share information with outsiders. As a general rule, membership records or lists are either not kept or are fragmentary and unreliable. Police records are incomplete and may include many persons accused of criminal acts who are not members of the organization. In any case, police files are ordinarily not opened to outsiders; and when they are shared with journalists or social scientists, it is usually to influence the interpretation that will be given to the mass audience or the policy-making circles. These are general problems that affect any serious research about insurgent organizations. In the case of ETA there are additional problems that complicate our analysis.

Before we can begin to sketch out a profile of a "typical" ETA member, we must first grapple with certain ambiguities in defining what it means to be "a member of ETA." For one thing, as I shall discuss shortly, the process by which new members are recruited into the organization is usually a slow and gradual one, and it is difficult to say exactly when a young man crosses the threshhold of membership. A second ambiguity in defining ETA membership has to do with the various categories of membership that exist within the organization. As I describe in chapter 9, there are several classes of etarras, including *liberados, legales, enlaces, apoyos*, and *buzones*, each of whom has a specific role to play in the maintenance and support of the organization. Relatively few etarras carry weapons, and even fewer have carried out assassinations or bank robberies. A final definitional problem stems from the fact that in 1980 there were at least three wings of ETA whose members disagreed with one another, sometimes violently, and that had markedly different goals, strategies, and tactics. These wings are, of course, ETA (militar), ETA (político-militar), and the Comandos Autónomos. In addition, there are undoubtedly small groups of armed men who are not etarras in any strict sense of the word, since they do not take orders or receive support from the ETA chain of command. Nevertheless, they are capable of harming or killing people and then claiming credit for the attack as a subgroup of ETA.

My search for the social and psychological roots of ETA has led me to two quite different kinds of biographical information. The first consists of some forty-eight case studies of a wide range of ETA members spanning the history of the organization from the early 1950s to the present. The sources for most of this information were secondary books containing biographical data about a number of ETA members. In a few instances, newspaper accounts provided me with additional information. The set also contains several interviews which I conducted with ETA members in France in 1973. The studies are of some of the principal leaders of ETA throughout its history, such as José Miguel Beñarán Ordeñana "Argala" and José Luis Alvarez Enparanza "Txillardegi," as well as a number of simple rank-and-file members. They include members who founded the organization in 1959, as well as several who are still at large at this writing, and many in between. In short, they are as near to a cross section of ETA members as one could develop using the sources available.

These forty-eight case studies have been supplemented where necessary and appropriate by another data set derived from two sources. The first is a list of 245 Basque political prisoners in Spanish prisons as of October 1974.[2] After discarding unusable names, I have been left with a group of 171 etarras in prison during the last years of the Franco regime. While all I know from this list are the name and place of birth of each etarra in prison, it is surprising how much interpretation one can squeeze out of such scanty material. The second source is a list of 228 persons arrested during 1979 and 1980 for ETA crimes or for being members of ETA. For these persons I have somewhat more information, including the sort of offense they were charged with committing, their ages, occupations (in a few cases), and so forth. According to the Spanish government's own figures, from December 4, 1978, when Spain's antiterrorist law went into effect, until December 5, 1979, 652 persons were arrested for ETA-related offenses.[3] From that date until mid-1980, the number arrested was 329.[4] Thus my data set includes about 23 percent of all etarras arrested during the eighteen-month period from January 1979 through June 1980. I use these aggregate data, together with the case studies, to describe several important characteristics of ETA members: their social origins (family, language, class, etc.); the process by which they, as young Basques, are transformed into ETA members; and finally, what their lives are like within ETA and how they terminate their relationship to the organization.

The Roots of Insurgency: The Social Origins of ETA

Let us begin our description of ETA's members with some basic data on age and sex (table 6.1).

There is a prevailing view among many that ETA members are

generally very young, barely emerged from adolescence; and indeed, some insurgent groups may be forced to recruit youths in their teen-age years. Our data show, however, that on the contrary, ETA members tend to be in their middle to late twenties when they join the organization.[5] The cases drawn from our individual studies show a mean age of 24 years when joining the organization; the arrest records data show a slightly higher 25.2 years. These figures coincide fairly closely with those reported by Charles Russell and Bowman Miller, who found that the average age of ETA-V members arrested was 23.2.[6] For the entire sample of 130 etarras for whom I have age data, the range of entering ages spreads from youths of 16 to middle-aged men of 45.

Table 6.1   *Age and Sex of ETA Members at Joining or First Arrest*

SAMPLE	N	MEAN	RANGE	% MALE
Case studies	41; 48	24.0	16–35	93.8
Political prisoners, 1974	Unk; 171	—	—	95.3
Arrest records, 1978–80	89; 228	25.2	17–45	90.8
All samples	130; 447	24.8	16–45	93.1

Source: Data gathered from biographical case studies and contemporary press reports. Calculations by author.

The data on sex taken from table 6.1 reflect ETA's pronounced antipathy toward women in the organization. As one etarra told me in an interview in 1973, ETA opposed women in the organization be-cause "their place was in the home" and "they talked too much, especially to their parish priest." Fewer than one in ten etarras from the samples were female, and the few women who do manage to enter the organization are always found among the support or information cells. We have few if any actual cases of women taking part in an armed attack.

The third characteristic of ETA members that concerns us is social and economic background. On this subject there seems to be considerable disagreement. Using education as an indicator of social standing, Russell and Miller observe that "over 40 percent of the identified leaders and cadre members [of ETA-V] who have been arrested had some university training and many were graduates."[7] This would seem to suggest that etarras were drawn predominantly from the middle and upper classes, those best able to afford a university education for their sons. On the other hand, the Basque social historian Beltza has argued that some 40 percent of ETA's members during the 1960s and early 1970s were from the working class, and another 20 percent came from such lower middle class occupations as office worker and technician.[8] Still another observer, José María Portell, has suggested that ETA derived its early strength from the petite bourgeoisie, or lower middle class, including rural folk and small businessmen. In this connection, he cites (apparently in agreement) this observation by ETA leader José María Ezkubi: "The nationalist ideology that caused ETA to emerge in the 1960s is a typical product of the Basque intellectual strata as representatives of the petite bourgeoisie [*pequeña burguesía*]. Its characteristics include small-scale production based on a small industrial shop or family craft, or the small property based on small-scale trade, administered by a family. In both cases, with a few salaried workers."[9] One of the principal historians of ETA, José Mari Garmendia, asserts that ETA's leadership in the early days came from students whose origins were lower middle class, while after 1970 and the Burgos trial it tended to come increasingly from industrial workers in the smaller towns of western and central Guipúzcoa and eastern Vizcaya provinces, which were zones of relatively recent industrialization.[10]

The data in table 6.2 allow us to test these assertions, although the test is incomplete because of the scarcity of data. Of the 447 etarras in the sample, I can find occupational information about only 81, or close

Table 6.2 *Social Class and Occupation of ETA Members* *(in percentages)*

SAMPLE	N	WORKING CLASS	LOWER MIDDLE CLASS	MIDDLE CLASS	UPPER CLASS	STUDENT/ PRIEST	UNEM- PLOYED
Case studies[a]	46	28.3	30.4	8.7	4.3	23.9	4.3
Arrest records, 1978–80[a]	35	34.3	28.6	17.1	0.0	11.4	8.6
Both samples	81	30.9	29.6	12.3	2.5	18.5	6.2
Average, general population, Basque provinces[b]		47.2	23.6	12.4	6.0	NA	NA

[a] Data gathered from biographical case studies and contemporary press reports. Calculations by author.

[b] As of 1970. See Luis C.-Nuñez Astrain, *Clases sociales en Euskadi* (San Sebastián: Editorial Txertoa, 1977), p. 116, table 27. Data exclude the 10.8 percent in agriculture and armed forces.

to 18 percent. In particular, the sample drawn from Basque political prisoners in 1974 has no information at all about occupation or social class. Nevertheless, we can make some tentative generalizations based on these partial data.

As far as social class is concerned, the chances are about even that a typical etarra comes from a working class or a lower middle class background (about one-third of the sample of 81 members come from each class). The probabilities are somewhat lower that the member is a student or priest, and considerably lower that he comes from a middle class occupation (18.5 and 12.3 percent, respectively). Very few etarras in my sample came from upper class occupations. Relatively few were unemployed and living on unemployment compensation. If the etarra is an industrial worker, he is not likely to be employed in a very large factory, but rather in a small factory or shop (perhaps in a family-owned firm), or he may even be self-employed as a carpenter, a brick-layer, or in other manual labor. Those from the lower middle class are likely to be small shop owners or employees, office workers for commercial firms or government agencies or banks, or school teachers. Those from a middle class background will probably be lawyers, engineers, or economists, but few of them will still be practicing their professions, having left their careers to go over completely to ETA and its activities. My data are too scanty to permit any analysis of trends in class structure over the years, but it would appear that three classes—working, lower middle, and middle—have been represented within ETA to approximately the same degree that they are in Basque society generally, with the exception that the working class seems slightly underrepresented. In any case, one cannot say that ETA has been dominated by any single class or professional stratum over the years.

Several additional observations are of interest here. In my review of the 81 cases cited here, I found not a single instance of an ETA member who had come from a farming occupation or even a farming community. A number (including such well-known etarras as Miguel Angel Apalategui "Apala") grew up in the typical traditional Basque homes, the caseríos (in Spanish) or baserriak (in Basque), which are extended family units located close to small towns. The typical caserío is an agricultural enterprise something like the family farm in the American midwest. Crops are cultivated and some farm animals are kept close to the family dwelling (usually occupying the ground floor, while the family lives on the second floor). Nevertheless, in those few cases where we find an etarra still living in this environment, he almost invariably leaves the caserío during the day to work in a nearby shop, factory, or office, returning in the evening to his traditional home and family. (The implications of this life style will be explored in greater detail in chapter 8.)

The second point to be made is this: despite assertions to the contrary that one reads in the popular literature about ETA, very few etarras have come from the unemployed, according to my findings. In about 95 percent of the cases I investigated, ETA recruits were either employed or students. Moreover, the great majority of the *legales* (covert members) continued to work at their regular jobs even after joining ETA. This finding should put to rest the myth that ETA recruits from among some vast lumpen proletariat of unemployed youths who harbor serious grudges against society for denying them honest employment. I find little evidence that such is the case.[11]

From these observations, I want to turn next to a description of the family surroundings within which many etarras grew to adulthood and out of which they were recruited to ETA. Let us examine, first, their ethnic heritage (table 6.3). This examination is aided greatly by the

Table 6.3 *Ethnic Background of ETA Members*

sample	N	HAVING IDENTIFIABLE BASQUE SURNAMES			
		BOTH PARENTS (%)	FATHER ONLY[a] (%)	MOTHER ONLY (%)	NEITHER PARENT[a] (%)
Case studies[b]	48	54.2	27.1	14.6	4.2
Political prisoners, 1974[b]	171	40.9	34.5	8.8	15.8
Arrest reports, 1978–80[b]	228	43.0	23.2	14.0	19.7
All samples	447	43.4	28.0	12.1	16.6
Average, general population, Basque provinces[c]		51.0	——8.0——		41.0

[a] Includes cases in which mother's surname not known.

[b] Data gathered from biographical case studies and contemporary press reports. Calculations by author.

[c] As of 1975. See Luis C.-Nuñez Astrain, *Clases sociales en Euskadi* (San Sebastián: Editorial Txertoa, 1977), 168, table 43.

Note: A report issued by the deputy chief of staff of the Guardia Civil in early 1982 states that 72.6 percent of the "historical" members of ETA (those in the organization before December 15, 1976) were offspring of two Basque parents, while the percentage for members who had joined since 1976 had dropped to 58.5 percent. In contrast, while only 14.6 percent of the "historical" etarras were offspring of two non-Basque parents, the figure for the post-1976 group had risen to 23.1 percent. The report concludes that this means that ETA broadened its recruiting to include many non-Basques. See *Deia*, June 13, 1982.

fact that Basque family names are quite easily distinguished from Spanish family names.[12] Moreover, because most Basques follow the Iberian custom of using both paternal and maternal surnames, we can in most instances discern whether both parents were Basque or only one, and if the latter, which one. We can see from table 6.3 that between four and five of ten etarras were the offspring of two Basque parents (slightly below the average for the Basque population as a whole), while about one of six was the son of two non-Basque parents (less than half the average for the population of the Basque provinces generally). Also revealing is the fact that while only about 8 percent of the population of the Basque provinces is of mixed ancestry (one Basque and one non-Basque parent), fully 40 percent of ETA's members come from such ancestry. The consequence is that more than 80 percent of all etarras have at least one Basque parent, as compared with slightly less than 60 percent of the provinces' overall population.

The forty-eight case studies offer us only tantalizing glimpses of the role that ethnicity played in the family life and early years of these etarras. Apparently a number of them, such as Angel Otaegi and Miguel Angel Apalategui, grew up in families where Spanish was seldom spoken and where Basque ethnicity was taken for granted. Many others, like Andoni Bengoa, grew up in families where Spanish was spoken, but where Basque nationalism was ardently espoused and was often the topic of dinner table conversation. Still other cases were like that of José Luis Alvarez Enparanza "Txillardegi," who not only belonged to a family that was not particularly self-conscious about its ethnicity but who himself was not able to learn Basque until he was seventeen, and then without help and with little open encouragement or support. In a few cases, such as that of Jon Paredes Manot "Txiki," we see the son of two non-Basque parents completely reject his non-Basque ancestry and even change his name (from the Spanish, Juan, to the Basque equivalent, Jon) to fit into a pro-Basque peer group. We should note also that the fathers of ETA members did not as a rule suffer much for their nationalist sentiments; that is, they did not suffer to any marked degree more than others of their generation. Only Iñaki Orbeta (whose father spent four years in prison for his pronationalist sentiments) and an anonymous etarra I interviewed in France in 1973 (whose father died in combat in the Spanish Civil War) could be said to be seeking revenge for something done to their fathers. In the great majority of cases, the oppression felt by etarras was felt by Basques generally and was not something peculiar to their own families. Thus we have a mixed picture. In about half of the cases, the young etarra learned his ethnic intransigence in the home.

In many others, however, the radicalism of the youth far exceeded that of the father, not to mention that of the mother.

Let us linger a moment on this question of parental status in the home. Many authors have commented on the strength and dominant role of the mother/wife in Basque homes and families; and what little we know about the early lives of the etarras confirms that what was true of Basque society in general was especially true of etarra families.[13] It is striking to read again and again descriptions of a family in which the father is either deceased, missing, away from home for long periods, or not mentioned at all. The mothers of the etarras, on the other hand, are prominent in every story, standing solid as a boulder in the midst of turmoil that swirls about the family. Or, as we read in the account of the Apala case written by Miguel Castells (Apala's attorney), "At times when everything seems to be coming down around her, she [Apala's mother] remains strong and holds the rudder firmly."[14]

The formula of strong mother and subdued or absent father varies, of course, from case to case. For José Luis Alvarez Enparanza "Txillardegi," in his accounts of his youth, his father doesn't appear at all, and it is his mother who puts him on the road to political activism by helping him learn Basque at age seventeen. In a number of cases, including those of José Miguel Beñarán Ordeñana "Argala," José Martín Sagardía Zaldúa, and Angel Otaegi, the father died when the son was quite young, and the mother was left with the arduous task of rearing her offspring unaided. Others had the experience of Iñaki Orbeta, whose father spent several years in jail for his political views and then left home for work abroad (in his case, Venezuela), because the economic conditions in the Basque region offered little hope of maintaining a large family comfortably. Finally, we have cases like those of Miguel Angel Apalategui "Apala" and Jon Paredes Manot "Txiki," whose fathers stayed with their families but do not appear as significant in their sons' lives. Castells gives us an interesting account of how Apala's father was made so ill by the news of his son's extradition trial that he had to take several days off from his job to recover.[15] Virtually the identical reaction was exhibited by the father of Andoni Bengoa, who was so upset by the news that his son had joined ETA that he went to bed for several days to recover.[16]

Although we know something of the social class and occupation of the etarra as a young man, we know next to nothing about the social class of the family into which he was born. Of the nine or so cases about which information of this sort is available, it would appear that the families of ETA members vary in class origin as widely as do their sons grown to adulthood. While none of the etarras came from what we call an aristocratic or elite background, at least two had fathers who were employed in upper class professions: Iñaki Orbeta's father was a lawyer, and José María Ezkubi's a doctor. Txillardegi's father ran a printing firm with about forty employees. Argala's father was a construction laborer who started his own construction company with a prize he won in the state lottery. On the other hand, several etarras came from humble origins. José Martín Sagardía Zaldúa's father worked as a butcher and a truck driver and was working as a garbage collector when a heart attack killed him. Angel Otaegi's mother worked as a waitress in a hotel in San Sebastián and also managed the family tavern in their home town of Nuarbe. The family of Txiki was extremely poor and would probably best be classified as a peasant family in the process of becoming working class. Apala's father had started as a *carbonero* (maker of charcoal) working in the mountains of Guipúzcoa, and had managed to build up his modest caserío by virtue of many years of hard labor. The anonymous etarra whom I interviewed in 1973 was the son of a laborer who had died in the Civil War, leaving a widow and two sons in desperate financial straits. If there are clear patterns in all this, I have yet to see them.

Let us examine, next, the linguistic character of the towns from which etarras come (table 6.4). In all, we know the birthplace or town of origin of 320 ETA members, drawn from various samples. Slightly less than 45 percent of these etarras come from towns where more than 40 percent of the people speak the Basque language, Euskera; slightly less than 40 percent come from towns where less than 20 percent speak Euskera. These figures show that ETA tends to recruit from Basque-speaking regions, since only 19.3 percent of the people of the Basque region live in towns where more than 40 percent speak Basque, and about 66 percent live in towns where less than 20 percent speak Basque. I cannot assert that a person born in a town where, say, 60 percent of the people speak Basque will himself be Basque-speaking, but it does seem probable. The opposite proposition (that persons born in towns where no one speaks Basque will not speak the language) seems even more strongly supported by common sense. Thus, ETA's membership appears to be drawn most heavily from areas where Euskera is still predominant or is at least as widely spoken as Spanish. In this instance, ETA's origins appear to be rather different from those of the general society within which the organization operates.

Another significant difference in origin has to do with the size of the township of birth (table 6.5). About 40 percent of the people of the Basque provinces live in cities of more than 100,000, while about 25

Table 6.4 *Distribution of ETA Members, by
Use of Basque in Townships of Origin
(in percentages)*

| | | BORN IN TOWNS WHERE | | |
| | | LESS THAN 20% SPEAK BASQUE | 20–40% SPEAK BASQUE | MORE THAN 40% SPEAK BASQUE |
SAMPLE	N			
Case Studies	34	29.4	17.6	52.9
Political prisoners, 1974	151	39.1	16.6	44.4
Arrest records, 1978–80	135	40.7	16.3	43.0
All samples	320	38.8	16.6	44.7
Average for Basque provinces[a]		66.6	14.1	19.3

Note: All calculations used in the table have been made from data collected by Pedro de Yrizar and published in the early seventies, in "Los dialectos y variedades de la lengua vasca: Estudio linguístico-demográfico," *Separata del Boletín de la Real sociedad vascongada de los amigos del país* (1973), nos. 1–3. Data on birthplaces gathered by author from biographical case studies and contemporary press reports.

Table 6.5 *Distribution of ETA Members, by Size of
Townships of Origin*

| | | PERCENTAGE OF MEMBERS FROM TOWNS WITH POPULATION OF | | | | |
| | | LESS THAN 2,000 | 2,000– 10,000 | 10,000– 50,000 | 50,000– 100,000 | MORE THAN 100,000 |
SAMPLE	N					
Case studies	34	8.8	29.4	35.3	8.8	17.6
Political prisoners, 1974	152	8.6	10.5	43.4	7.2	30.3
Arrest records, 1978–80	135	8.9	14.1	36.3	20.0	20.7
All samples	321	8.7	14.0	39.6	12.8	24.9
Average for Basque Provinces[a]		8.0	15.5	24.5	10.5	41.5

Source: Data on birthplaces gathered by author from biographical case studies and contemporary press reports.

Note: Populations in table were those of 1975. See Talde Euskal Estudio Elkartea, *Euskadi: Ante las elecciones municipales* (San Sebastián: Ediciones Vascas, 1975), p. 11, table 1.1.

percent live in smaller towns of 10,000 to 50,000. Significantly, the distribution of etarras is exactly the reverse: about 40 percent of ETA members come from the small cities; about 25 percent, from the large metropolitan areas. The distribution of etarras among townships of other sizes corresponds almost exactly to that of the Basque population as a whole.

We conclude, then, that ETA draws its members predominantly from areas where Euskera is still spoken widely and from smaller cities of between 10,000 and 50,000 population. We will return to the question of the geography of ETA again in chapter 8, in the explanation of how etarras are distributed in clusters in specific regions of the Basque provinces.

Life in ETA: Insurgency and the Individual

It may be something of an exaggeration to say that the making of an etarra begins in the cradle, but almost certainly it begins quite soon thereafter. The process by which a Basque youth is transformed into a member of ETA is a long one full of detours and the exploration of competing alternatives. Even the actual recruiting is a gradual process which many potential etarras resist for months or even years. Once in the organization, most etarras live a fairly conventional life punctuated by brief flurries of hazardous activity. For the most part, they continue to live in the protective culture of their homes and neighborhoods, where they are buffered to some degree from the frustrations and anxieties of a clandestine insurgency. Most of them spend a relatively short time in the organization. Many are hunted down and captured or killed by police or the Guardia Civil; but a significant number simply leave the organization and return to a more-or-less-normal life, despite the threat of reprisals for having abandoned the struggle.

"[O]ne of the first requirements for a free man," writes psychologist Erik Erikson about the beliefs of the great Indian leader Mahatma Gandhi, "[is] the ability to express himself well in the language of his childhood. . . . For truth becomes a hazy matter indeed where most official business and much of everyday life of a people must be transacted either in a stilted and often broken [foreign language] or in a multitude of idioms offering no more than an approximation of intended meaning. And since this fact, in the long run, makes it both impossible and unnecessary to say what one 'really' means, it supports a form of habitual half-truth such as the English had come to consider 'inborn' in all Indians."[17]

So it was that many future etarras first encountered the notion of discrimination and deprivation when they emerged from the home and found themselves in a school where they could neither speak nor understand the language of instruction and were in fact punished for their inability to do so. Miguel Castells, for example, writes of his conversation with a cousin of Miguel Angel Apalategui, who tells us: "The first shock for a young person from Ataun is when he enters the Spanish national schools, and, whether you want to or not, you have to speak in Spanish. In Ataun we speak only Euskera. But the teacher, in a radical way with punishment and persecution, requires that in school one speaks only Spanish, and really the child when he enters doesn't know it. And later, as the child grows up, he continues to run up against different kinds of repression." [18] José María Portell, to cite a second case, tells a similar story of José María Ezkubi, one of the chief ETA leaders for the 1960s. Ezkubi was born to the well-to-do family of a doctor in the small village of Leiza, located in Navarra but only 20 kilometers from Tolosa and the Goierri region. At the age of seven, Ezkubi was taken to Pamplona, where he was enrolled in the Jesuit elementary school there. At the time, he spoke only Euskera, the language of his parents and his home. He recalls his encounter with Spanish education in this way: "When I got to the school, I realized that no one talked like me; I felt, then, a feeling of loneliness. I couldn't understand Spanish and the lectures of the teacher. They thought that I didn't want to study my lessons, and they punished me. This marked me deeply. And when I grew up I decided to do something for my Basque country." [19]

Even young Basques who did not speak Euskera as children felt the impact of Spanish government policies that suppressed not only this but other expressions of Basque ethnicity. Some, like Txillardegi, began to learn Euskera at a relatively advanced age (in his case, seventeen) and against formidable odds, including a proscription of text books in the language and an absence of teachers. But it was, after all, the language of his mother, and that fact eventually prevailed over the obstacles. Many others felt the presence of the Spanish government in their inability to enjoy simple expressions of folklore such as singing national songs, playing forbidden musical instruments, or wearing prohibited colors (red, green, and white, the colors of the Basque flag) in public. Eduardo Uriarte, for example, one of the Burgos 16, remembered vividly an event from his childhood when several youths were driven out of town by the mayor and the Guardia Civil for playing a Basque musical instrument, the *txistu*, in public without the prior approval of the governor of the province. [20] The cousin of Miguel Angel Apalategui, interviewed by Miguel Castells, tells us: "Ten years ago [in about 1967] in the festival in Aya, I was wearing a cap with four clusters of ribbons hanging from it. They [the police] grabbed me, they took off the ribbons and they took away my identity card, and they told me to come to Ataun the next day to get it. I went there, and they made me return home and come back with the cap that I had on in Aya. I went back with the cap. They slapped me around a little and yelled at me. And I had to remain quiet. The ribbons were the [Basque] colors. They gave me a fine of 500 pesetas [about $10] and they let me leave."[21]

These policies were used by the Franco regime to wipe out the last vestiges of Basque culture, and in truth, many of the worst practices were reversed soon after the Generalissimo's death. But while they were in effect, they had a significant impact on Basque youth and on ETA's ability to recruit new members. At one level, they served as a constant irritant, an enduring reminder of the oppressive nature of the Spanish state in the Basque country. Moreover, they forced the youth of the region to take their folkloric celebrations to distant mountain tops where they could not be observed by police or Guardia Civil troops. In earlier years, Basque mountain-climbing clubs (which exist in every town, no matter how small) had been used as a cover for clandestine meetings. During the Franco years, they served much the same purpose. And it was during the excursions of these clubs to their remote mountains that ETA chose to make many of the contacts that led to recruiting in earnest.

As Basque youth grew up and became increasingly aware of their deprivation, other factors came into play, factors that would move them along little by little toward their rendezvous with ETA. A significant number of them began as adolescents to wander restlessly and intensely in a search for solutions to the crises that afflicted them as individuals and their culture as a group. Few of these future etarras actually left the Basque country in their search; there were, it turned out, quite enough alternatives for them close to home. Their search focused on the possibilities for social change short of armed struggle. In all the cases for which I have data (very few, to be sure), the future ETA members tried other options first, and turned to ETA only when the others appeared to be futile. Nevertheless, this searching phase of their young lives played a crucial role in the development of rebels in several ways. For one thing, the wider the search ranged, the greater the likelihood that random events would touch the life of the rebel and push him little by little into a life of violence. In other words, the more a young Basque male looked for trouble, the greater the likelihood that he would find it. The Guardia Civil and the police were, after all, only too ready to play this role in the emergence of radicalized youths. On the other hand, the search made the groping youths painfully aware of those options that were not truly open but only appeared to be. For those who only dream of change, many roads appear open which testing reveals to be in reality closed. Without this test, the youth may never know which solutions to oppression are really possible and which are images created by the elite defenders of the status quo.

The searching phase in the lives of the etarras whom I studied assumed many different forms. A few, like Txiki, became enchanted with dangerous sports such as motorcycle racing and mountain climbing. "If they had not killed him," said one friend about Txiki, "he would have killed himself—against the pavement."[22] Others, like Argala, were subjected to a confusing and dissonant childhood, divided in their loyalties between a conservative home and church on the one hand and a need for militant rebellion and justice on the other. Their lives during this period oscillated from one extreme to the other until they could finally accept the identity of an etarra. But the great majority for whom I have data began their journey toward ETA in much less violent and less intransigent groups. Txillardegi helped form a number of illegal Basque youth and student groups during the late 1940s. The police break-up of one of these (Eusko Ikasle Alkartasuna) was a key factor in his radicalization in the early 1950s. Many young future etarras participated in strikes and demonstrations, which were flatly prohibited during the Franco era. Angel Otaegi worked with militant union organizers as well as with the PNV youth organization, Euzko Gaztedi (EGI), before joining ETA. Apala participated in strikes and demonstrations on a regular basis, even to the point of being arrested on several occasions. Mario Onaindia was active in various labor movements as a youth, while Jokin Gorostidi had been an active participant in a number of illegal Basque patriotic celebrations. In all cases, the police suppression of this early searching behavior played a key role in the psychological development of the etarras. They saw their earlier prejudices confirmed, and they became persuaded that only violence would suffice to gain their objectives. They discarded nonviolent options that were futile against a much stronger and intransigent enemy. This searching phase led almost inevitably to greater interest in ETA, and as we shall see, greater interest by ETA in the young men who were demonstrating their resolve and their commitment to Basque independence.

In all this change, the family appears to have played a surprisingly minor role. In only one case of the dozen or so for which I have information did the family actually support the youth's decision to join ETA. The widowed mother of an etarra I interviewed in 1973 actually encouraged her sons to join the Resistance to avenge their father's death. In all the other cases, however, the family was either neutral on the subject or actually opposed to ETA. The families of several etarras in my sample supported Basque nationalism but opposed ETA's violent tactics. In several cases, such as those of José Martín Sagardía and Jon Paredes Manot, the family had no overt political connections and little interest in politics. Apala's family was apolitical in the sense that it was not tied to any specific party. Apala hid from his mother the news that he had joined ETA, for she certainly would have opposed such a step, as would have the mother of Otaegi, who likewise would have tried to dissuade her son from joining. In at least one instance, that of Jon Etxabe, his mother did indeed try to persuade the young man to change his mind when she learned of his intentions to join the organization. It is significant that almost all of the families of etarras whom I investigated either played no role at all in the radicalization of their young sons or actually opposed it. In contrast, once the youth joined ETA and was caught, killed, or driven into exile for his actions, the family rallied around in a solid show of support for son and brother.

We come now to the critical event in the making of an etarra, his recruitment into the organization. The process is a slow and gradual one, and it is difficult if not impossible to say exactly when a young man crosses the threshhold of ETA and becomes a full-fledged member.[23] Typically, an older ETA member approaches a young prospective member while they are with a group on an outing or a mountain-climbing expedition. The ETA member who makes this first contact is the key to the whole process. Throughout recruitment, this person remains the contact between the organization and the prospective member. Once the youth decides to join, the contact etarra becomes his sponsor and guides him through his first tasks and assignments. Since the recruiter is a key member of the organization, ETA puts much emphasis on selecting etarras for recruiting duty, and recruiters are given a great deal of help in becoming proficient in their role. In particular, they must be very skilled in keeping up the enthusiasm and morale of the future etarra, for there will be many moments when the youth's commitment will wane and the organization will lose a new member if he is not bolstered in his decision.

After the initial contact is made, if the youth expresses interest in knowing more about the organization, the etarra will wait several months and then contact him again to invite him to participate in a simple operation, something like carrying packages of pamphlets to a drop point or delivering cans of spray paint to someone else for use in painting slogans on walls. To avoid security leaks, the organization is careful to give the potential member very limited information. Once the youth has proven his competence in the first exercise, the older member may ask him to participate in other operations of increasing danger and complexity, such as gathering information on the routine or schedule of bank employees in preparation for a robbery, for example, or driving a load of weapons to deliver to another ETA member. As the youth demonstrates his ability to carry out challenging assignments, he also invests considerable psychological energy in the operations of ETA, so that it becomes increasingly difficult for him to disengage from the organization. In addition, the organization now has certain leverage over him by threatening to divulge information about these early exploits to police authorities. At this point, which may come as much as a year after the first contact, the organization is ready to bring the young man into full membership. As far as I can tell, however, there is no formal oath taken by the new member. The older ETA member who made the contact will usually escort the younger to a meeting of a local cell of the organization and will in effect sponsor his young apprentice, after which the youth will be accepted as a full-fledged member.

If ETA takes a long time in recruiting each member, it can also be said that the potential member takes his time in considering. Young men approached to become etarras typically resist joining for a long time before they cast their lot with the organization. Virtually every case study reports that the young man resisted the first invitations to join, sometimes for as long as a year and a half or two, before finally deciding to become a member. The reasons for delay vary from case to case. Iñaki Orbeta thought that being a member of ETA would interfere with his university studies, which he wanted to complete before joining. Angel Otaegi waited until he had completed his military service. Others, like Jokin Gorostidi and Enrique Guesalaga, were involved in other organizations that were active in clandestine politics, and they waited to see what would be the fruits of those labors before finally deciding that ETA promised more results in a shorter time. In a few cases, young women joined the organization only after their husbands or boy friends had joined. In any case, the story has one constant: they all studied the organization, talked to many people about it, attended meetings of the local cells, and actively debated joining with friends and other ETA members. This process of deciding lasted a surprisingly long time and involved a great deal of soul-searching. We are seeing here not a dramatic conversion of a person from a simple uninvolved citizen to a flaming revolutionary over night. I find in all the case studies a surprising lack of any sort of "catalytic event," an incident so full of dramatic confrontation with authority that the issue of joining or not joining is made to stand out in stark relief, and the young man is thrust in an instant across the threshhold into ETA. Such events may have characterized the passage to revolution of famous rebels like Che Guevara or Lenin, but they are strikingly absent from the lives of the etarras of my sample.

It is difficult to generalize about what life is like for a typical etarra once he joins the organization, for there are many levels of membership, and many corresponding degrees of commitment in the lives of insurgents. The great majority of the members of ETA continue to live at home, either with their parents or, if they are married, with their spouses and children, and to work at their regular employment, either in an office or on a factory assembly line. Being a member of ETA is time-consuming, to be sure; and many members report having little time left over for the demands of their personal lives once they join. Yet at the same time it is not a commitment that demands all of a member's waking moments.

In general, there are three kinds of activities that occupy the time and energy of ETA members. The first involves what we might call consciousness raising. Young etarras are rather more highly politicized than many other Basques from their age group. Nevertheless, the organization believes that well-informed or well-indoctrinated members are in the long run more reliable and more competent at their jobs. So the organization has from its inception devoted much of its time to sponsoring study sessions or discussion groups whose purpose it is to increase the participants' understanding of contemporary political and economic matters as well as to raise complicated ideological issues for debate and resolution. Even senior members of the organization attend these meetings and participate in the debates, which are usually spirited. The meetings also afford young nonmembers the opportunity to see ETA in action and to hear some of its members discuss current concerns, and thus they often serve a recruiting purpose as well.[24]

The second general type of activity engaged in by ETA members is in support of the armed comandos of the organization. As I point out in chapter 9 in my discussion of the organizational structure of ETA, a high proportion of ETA members are involved in support functions such as gathering and transmitting intelligence about potential targets, carrying messages or supplies or weapons from one member to another, providing transportation for other members, offering food and shelter for members who are involved in some sort of armed action or fleeing from police pursuit, or simply producing or disseminating information about ETA or about political matters generally. Some of these functions are delegated to nonmembers who are serving their apprenticeship, while others are provided by older persons who are not etarras themselves but who desire to be of help to the organization. Most of these critical support functions, however, are performed by ETA comandos or cells whose assignments do not include armed assaults.

ETA support members are reported arrested almost daily in the local Basque press, so the following are cited merely as examples of the kinds of activities in which these members engage. In May 1980, for instance, police announced the arrest of members of an ETA intelligence cell (*comando de información*) which had conducted several operations in support of ETA. For four or five Sundays in a row, this comando monitored the schedule of the former mayor of Bilbao, Pilar Careaga, as she came and went to and from church, and passed the information to an ETA assassination team, which subsequently carried out an attack (nonfatal) on the former mayor. The comando also gathered information on the airports near Bilbao (Sondica) and Vitoria (Foronda), as well as on the Guardia Civil patrols that protected them. This information was given to an ETA comando, which attacked one of the patrols, killing one Guardia Civil trooper and wounding several others. The comando also gathered and provided ETA with photographs, blueprints, and other information about several electric power plants in Vizcaya, as well as lists of names of persons who occupied key roles in the plants. Finally, the comando gathered personal information about two national policemen who lived in Algorta, with the presumed objective of attacking them at some later date.[25]

The third kind of activity undertaken by ETA members is, of course, armed assaults on people and property, with the intention of either killing or injuring people, kidnapping them for ransom, or seizing money, weapons, automobiles, or other needed resources. My feeling is that fewer than half of the ETA members actually engage in violent action of this sort, but they are the ones who give the organization its special insurgent character and attract attention. Let us examine in some detail a few specific examples of ETA's assault cells or comandos. On November 20, 1980, police arrested all five members of an ETA(m) comando named "Kioto." Four of its five members lived in Amorebieta (Vizcaya), and the fifth lived in Larrabezúa, about ten kilometers away. This comando was accused of five killings:

On December 30, 1978, a taxi cab driver in the small village of Yurre, about 6 kilometers from Amorebieta

On May 17, 1979, a night watchman of a cement plant in Lemona, about 2 kilometers from Amorebieta

On September 30, 1979, the police chief of Amorebieta in Guernica, about 18 kilometers from Amorebieta

On March 24, 1980, a jeweler in Durango, 15 kilometers from Amorebieta

On October 23, 1980, a factory worker in Amorebieta itself[26]

On November 7, 1980, police arrested five members of the ETA(m) comando "Besaide." Three of the members lived in Mondragón (Guipúzcoa), one was from Oñate (11 kilometers from Mondragón), and the other was from Vergara (9 kilometers away). The group was accused of four killings:

On March 13, 1977, a Guardia Civil trooper in a bar in Oñate (wounding a second Guardia)

On January 30, 1979, a civilian, accused of being a police informer, in Anzuola, about 5 kilometers from Vergara

On February 8, 1980, a Guardia Civil trooper in Oñate

On July 18, 1980, an automobile mechanic in Vergara[27]

On April 17, 1979, police arrested two members of the six-person comando "Urola," based in the Goierri region of Guipúzcoa. Two of the commando's members were from Azcoitia, three were from Ezquioga (about 15 kilometers from Azcoitia), and the sixth was from Legazpia (about the same distance away). The commando was accused of the following actions:

On September 11, 1978, an attack against a Guardia Civil Land Rover in Ezquioga, which resulted in the death of two men of the Guardia Civil

On January 13, 1979, an attack on a Guardia Civil Land Rover in Azcoitia, which left one member of the Guardia Civil dead and another wounded. The comando left behind a booby trap bomb which exploded, killing two other Guardias.

On June 2, 1979, the assassination of the mayor of Olaberri (Guipúzcoa), about 20 kilometers from Azcoitia and ten from Ezquioga[28]

From these data we conclude that ETA comandos were given orders to conduct armed attacks about once every eight months, the average time separating the attacks listed above. The shortest period separating one attack from another was about four months; the longest, about twenty-two months. About half the attacks were conducted in the home town of members of the assault comando; the remainder were carried out in towns between 5 and 20 kilometers from the base village of the comando. As a general rule, comandos are composed of persons either from the same town or from nearby towns. These examples and the conclusions derived from them help us understand how ETA can recruit and maintain members who continue to live at home and work at their regular jobs. Their tasks as etarras, even those that involve armed assault, never take them far away from home. Their assignments are spread out over rather long periods of at least four or five months and sometimes more than a year. One gets the impression from reading these examples that service in an ETA *comando* is rather like working at a temporary parttime job, one that requires supremely dangerous and stressful tasks, but assigns them in such a way as to interfere as little as possible with the daily life of the perpetrators.

How does being a member of ETA affect the daily life of an *etarra*. How does he deal with family, loved ones, and friends?

There seems little doubt that joining ETA affects the relation of members with nonmembers. Friends of *etarras*, like those interviewed by Sanchez Erauskin in his book on Txiki and Otaegi, report that after joining the organization their former friend and comrade seemed totally absorbed by his new responsibilities and duties. Etarras have less time for the normal social life of a small Basque village. There is less time to make the rounds of the bars drinking wine or coffee and catching up on the gossip. In many cases, relationships with friends and family members deteriorate considerably. Light political banter that means little to most people begins to take on new and more serious meaning to a young man who has just joined an insurgent organization. The friends of newly recruited *etarras* often find them distant, difficult to reach, and easily aroused by political conversation. In most cases, however, the former friends and comrades know of their old friend's conversion, and they seldom hold it against him that he has somehow changed.[29]

If relationships with friends and family lose immediacy for new *etarras*, they paradoxically become even more important in a symbolic sense. Even though ETA members now have less time for friends and family, it has become more important for them to know that these people support them in their struggle. No matter how far away from their *caserío* they travel and how much time they devote to ETA, they remain steadfastly bound to the life of the traditional small Basque village. As we shall see in chapter 9, ETA has embedded itself organizationally in the everyday life of the Basque village. This it has done for strategic and tactical reasons, no doubt. Yet there is a personal and psychological dimension to this decision as well, for it is from small town traditional Basque culture that individual *etarras* derive their emotional strength, the unusual mixture of social, cultural, and psychological force that sustains them in a constantly failing guerrilla war.

I have described the relatively minor role played by the family in the transformation of a politically conscious youth into a member of an insurgent group. From the bits and fragments I have collected about the later lives of these young men, the family seems to play the same kind of role for active etarras. The family appears to have little to do with them, and plays only a small role in their maintenance and support. This changes dramatically whenever an etarra is captured or killed, for then the entire village, but especially the family, mobilizes in a major show of support for their friend and son or brother.

The principal support for active etarras, however, seems to come from the small circle of friends, job associates, and other ETA members who cluster together for mutual psychological support and assistance. This group may contain no more than half a dozen members, usually young men who have been close to one another since their early childhood. One of the most important social institutions in small Basque villages is the *cuadrilla*, a small group or gang of young boys (four to six members) who spend all of their time in various kinds of exploits with one another. In their youth, these groups may engage in relatively harmless acts of minor vandalism common to young boys in all cultures, such as breaking street lights or painting obscenities on walls. In Basque villages, however, the cuadrillas find other socially acceptable "targets of opportunity," and their harmless adventures may turn toward something a little riskier, like throwing stones at the passing car of some Guardia Civil troops. The reader can easily imagine how exploits like this can spiral into much more serious matters as the youngsters grow to adolescence. During the teenage years, however, many cuadrillas become more organized, and devote themselves to such group activities as mountain climbing, country outings, and informal discussion or study of important contemporary issues. The boys begin to make the rounds of local neighborhood bars, where they are gradually accepted into the adult Basque male culture. As they reach their twenties, Basque men may have stronger ties to the cuadrilla than to their own families. It is easy to see how the comando of ETA fits so readily into the youth culture of small Basque towns, for young Basques have already spent as much as a decade of their lives with a small group of intimate friends bound in tight cohesion against strangers from the outside. In this important respect, as in others, the culture of small Basque towns is ideal for nurturing a clandestine political organization.

If the relationships of etarras with other men are fairly simple, we can draw no such conclusions about their relationships with women. I have already remarked on the significant role played by Basque women in the family, and on the fact that mothers of most etarras seem to have been major figures in the lives of their sons. One can imagine, then, how a member of ETA would have an image of the ideal woman that, combined with his life style, would impose near-impossible demands on any wife, sweetheart, or lover. She would have to have the strength, resolve, patience, and durability necessary to carry the entire burden of the relationship. She would need to manage the family and rear the children, perform the day-to-day tasks of the family, see her husband or lover leave home at night never knowing where he was going or whether he would return, and endure all of this in silence and support, for years at a time. It is not surprising that I found few etarras who managed to maintain a normal family life under such circumstances.[30] Most about whom I have such personal data fell into one of two categories. Many had no real lasting relationships with women, even though they might have reached and gone beyond the conventional age for courtship and marriage in Basque society. Angel Otaegi, for example, was chided by his friends for being a *mutil zarra*, literally in English "old boy," but a phrase that connotes a man who has remained a bachelor too long.[31] In the case of others, like Apala and Txiki, we read no mention at all of any love or commitment they might have had to a sweetheart or lover. There were others, however, who solved the problem essentially by courting and marrying women who likewise had committed themselves to revolutionary struggle. Especially during the 1960s and early 1970s, when being a member of ETA did not seem such a hazardous matter, husband and wife "teams" were fairly common in the organization. Several of the Burgos trial prisoners were in fact married to one another, including Gregorio Lopez Irásuegui and Arantxa Arruti, and Juana Dorronsoro and Francisco Javier Izco de la Iglesia. Another early ETA leader, José María Ezkubi, was also married to an ETA member, María Goenaga. If the combined pressure of ETA membership on these couples was too great, we have no record of it. Most of these marriages survived as long as did the partners themselves, and as far as I know, they remained married well into their post-ETA period when they were no longer living a clandestine existence.

The picture of ETA life that I find from my investigation is one of a life that is significant and demanding, even difficult and hazardous, but not necessarily stressful enough to exceed the limits of normal and healthy personalities. Nevertheless, if we are to know why men (and on occasion, their women) join ETA, we must know how they can endure year after year of such a life, filled with a certain degree of danger and rewarded with success only sporadically if at all. Analysts of insurgency call these factors the "reinforcers," the elements of life that keep a person going in an organization when, rationally speaking, he should give up the struggle and return to a normal life.

In the summer of 1973, I had the opportunity to question several

members of ETA about their lives, their problems and successes, what
caused them despair and what brought them happiness. I concluded,
first of all, that these were not especially happy men. They had been at
their dangerous occupation for a number of years at that time, and the
thrill, if there ever had been one, had long since died away. They had
seen dear friends caught or killed, and they had witnessed the failure
of the Basque people to rise up in insurrection against the Spanish,
even after ETA had shown them the way. They were nostalgic over
the life they had to leave behind (this particular group was living in
France at the time), and they resented the fact that they were almost
constantly on duty, that the organization had the right to call them
away from whatever they were doing to carry out an operation on short
notice. Perhaps most of all, they were growing restive at the thought
that they were losing some of their most precious years in a struggle
that might in the end be regarded as futile and even a bit silly.

But they continued the struggle for a number of reasons that blend
both positive and negative reinforcements. On the positive side, they
received solid support from their close friends and from their spouses,
if they were married. They lived and moved about in a sort of hermeti-
cally closed compartment where one simply does not raise depressing
questions or challenge the ultimate victory of the organization. They
had learned to lower their expectations, to resign themselves to a long
struggle with little hope for immediate success. They had learned, in
other words, the psychological defense of insurgency, as expressed by
one of them this way: "A clandestine organization is living and dying
every day. There are people who quit. Tired people leave. New people join, and we train them, and then we do it all over again. You see
someone once, and then you never see him again. You don't ask questions, you just do your job."

There are also negative forces that discourage etarras from leaving
the organization, no matter how depressed they may become or how
much they may yearn for a normal existence. There is, simply put, a
fear of reprisal if one were to abandon the struggle and return to
civilian life. The source of the reprisals is disputed. Etarras claim that
Spanish secret police pursue ex-etarras after they leave the protective
cover of the organization, and settle old scores by gunning many of
them down, either in France, where many of them continue to live, or
in Spain. The official media and government version of all this is that
the killings are perpetrated by ETA gunmen who are punishing their
former colleagues for abandoning the struggle, and perhaps for delivering information to the enemy. No one can really know the complete story. In all probability, both forces are at work. But we do know

that former members of ETA are often the targets of armed attack after they leave the organization and attempt to return to normal life.

In reality, we need not make too much of the question of reinforcers, for the fact is that most men spend rather brief periods in ETA. I have no way to calculate such a statistic, but I would estimate that the average length of time that an etarra spends as an active member of the organization would be less than three years. What happens to them? Obviously, a number of them are killed in armed attacks, and others (probably fewer) are killed as a result of quarrels within ETA itself. Many, probably the majority, are caught and sentenced to long prison terms, and do not rejoin the organization once they are released. And of course, there are those countless etarras in insignificant support roles who simply blend into the environment after they "retire" from the organization. For some young Basques, ETA is a crucial end-point in their lives, the factor that gives meaning and purpose to an otherwise disorderly frustration. For many others, however, it is only a way station, a phase through which a youth must pass if he is to move on to other more complex and more conventional forms of struggle. In the long run, ETA's major contribution to Basque and Spanish politics may turn out to be its service as a crucial link bringing young Basques through their adolescence, radicalizing and training them, and then sending them back to attack the sources of their grievances through the institutions of conventional politics.

CHAPTER SEVEN

The Basque People and ETA: Sources and Dimensions of Popular Support

Sooner or later, debates about ETA usually touch on one of the most controversial aspects of Basque nationalist insurgency, the degree to which ETA is supported by the Basque citizenry. Arguments on this issue are not idle exercises. Supporters of ETA allege massive support among rank-and-file Basque citizens to use the threat of an expanded insurgency to lever increased concessions from the Spanish government. Opponents allege just the opposite, that the typical Basque citizen rejects ETA and its objectives, to argue for the opposite policy. Any comprehensive treatment of ETA, then, must include some analysis of popular support given the organization. My objective here is to portray the magnitude of popular support for ETA, to show how that support has risen or fallen, and to identify the location, social and ethnic, of the support.

The methodological obstacles to this kind of analysis are indeed formidable. There is, first, a problem of validity. Do the questions asked of respondents by survey researchers really tap pro-ETA or anti-ETA sentiment? There is considerable question on this matter. Survey researchers working in the Basque region do not usually ask bluntly, "Do you support ETA and its goals?" The questions are phraased obliquely, as for instance, "Do you agree or disagree that violent attacks must be condemned by everyone?" or to take another frequently asked question, "How would you classify people who engage in terrorism: patriots, idealists, manipulated people, madmen, or criminals?" Clearly, we cannot be certain that answers to questions like these are really measuring popular support for or opposition to ETA.

A second methodological problem stems from a lack of intersurvey reliability. A number of surveys have been conducted in the Basque provinces over the past six years or so, but only a few have been replicated using the same questions and the same techniques for drawing samples. If one is attempting to discern trends in pro-ETA or anti-ETA sentiments over time, he is forced to use questions and response data that are not comparable save in a very few instances.

Still another problem of interpretation involves the varying levels of support for ETA and its goals. When we look at available survey data from the Basque region, we find that the Basque people support to widely varying degrees certain aspects of ETA's struggle. Quite substantial numbers of Basques may advocate independence from Spain but still reject armed struggle to achieve that goal. On another dimension, we find that many Basques may reject ETA's tactics but still advocate a negotiated truce or ceasefire between ETA and Madrid in order to restore order and stability to the region. In other words, popular support for ETA rises or falls to some degree depending on how one defines such support.

A fourth recurring difficulty has to do with missing data. To a marked degree, respondents in the Basque provinces simply refuse to answer questions that seem to have something to do with ETA, terrorism, or just violence in general. These refusal rates are sometimes so high that they threaten to invalidate the entire survey. Moreover, they seem to show little pattern. For example, a survey conducted by Yale University sociologist Juan Linz and his associates in the summer of 1978 produced a refusal rate of only 10 percent; in late 1978, a survey conducted for the Spanish magazine *Cambio 16* was marred by a nonresponse rate of 45 to 48 percent; and in the summer of 1979, a second survey by Linz saw the "no answer" rate drop again to 15 percent. At least one analyst of Spanish public opinion surveys has suggested that 20 to 30 percent of the respondents always answer "don't know/no answer" in surveys dealing with political subjects.[1] If so, then Spain has one of the highest nonresponse rates in political attitude surveys taken in industrial democracies.[2] Another experienced analyst of Spanish public opinion, University of Michigan political scientist Peter McDonough, reports similar levels of nonresponse in surveys he conducted in 1978. It may be that Spaniards refuse to answer survey questions out of fear of reprisal; but McDonough argues that the high nonresponse rate is due more to a low level of political awareness or to a low salience of political affairs in the consciousness of the respondent population.[3]

We simply do not know why so many Basques often refuse to answer survey-takers' questions about politics or about ETA specifically. As some studies have shown, it is possible to persuade people to talk to interviewers even in politically tense and volatile situations.[4] But these examples are substantially different from the Basque case, where an entire generation has grown to maturity under strained and tense circumstances, first in the midst of the Franco regime, and then during the late 1970s surrounded by insurgent violence and police counterviolence. This kind of atmosphere does not encourage openness with strangers or responsiveness to the questioning of survey researchers.

A final issue has to do with the sources of survey data and the uses to which data are put once released to the public. In the highly charged political atmosphere of contemporary Spain, survey results that would otherwise go unnoticed are given wide coverage by the mass media, especially if they tend to support the policy position favored by the newspaper or magazine using them. In mid-1981, for example, the Spanish research organization FOESSA (Fundación para el Fomento de los Estudios Sociales y la Sociología Aplicada) released data showing that 50 percent of the respondents considered ETA members to be either "patriots" or "idealists," thereby causing considerable consternation among Spanish policy-making circles. Somewhat later it was revealed that FOESSA's survey had been conducted in late 1979 in the midst of a great deal of turmoil in the Basque region, and the results of the survey could not be taken to reflect conditions in 1981. As an answer to the FOESSA findings, the government's Center for Sociological Research (CIS) released the results of its own 1981 survey, which showed that only 13 percent of the Basque respondents viewed ETA members in a favorable light. This so-called "war of the surveys" was fought out in the various mass media in Spain in an attempt to influence the policy decisions that were under consideration.[5]

Popular Support for ETA: How Much?

When one asks how much popular support for ETA there is among Basque citizens, the answer depends largely on what is meant by support and on what aspects of ETA are being discussed. After reviewing the available survey data on the subject, I conclude that public support for ETA is divided into four more-or-less-distinct levels: support for armed struggle; advocacy of independence for the Basque people; viewing positively the members of ETA (as opposed to seeing them as criminals or lunatics); and favoring either acceptance or negotiation of ETA's demands in order to end hostilities, not necessarily because the respondent agrees with ETA objectives but because the violence is seen as an obstacle to restoration of public order and self-government in the region. Each of these layers of public support will be dealt with in turn.

Asking a respondent in a public opinion survey if he supports armed struggle to achieve regional independence is rather like asking the head of a family if he advocates bank robbery to provide his family with food and shelter. Naturally, viewed this way in the abstract, very few respondents in any sample would ever answer affirmatively to either question. The really crucial datum lies in how many persons would answer affirmatively *if all other measures fail*. If, for example, family heads could not provide for their loved ones in any other way than to resort to criminal action, how many would do so? If supporters of Basque independence could not achieve their goal in any other way, how many would advocate insurgent violence? Regrettably, public opinion surveys usually do not give us such discriminating information.

We do have, however, some general indication of the depth of positive sentiment for armed struggle from several surveys done in the Basque region over a six-year period (summer of 1975 to winter of 1981–82). The first survey,[6] conducted by Spanish sociologist Salustiano del Campo and his associates some months before the death of Franco, asked the respondents to indicate their preferred procedure for obtaining their desired form of government. Some 31 percent favored a referendum to decide the issue; 25 percent answered in favor of mass pressures but stopping short of violence; 12 percent chose some sort of decision process originating in Madrid (similar, one presumes, to the devolution procedure in the United Kingdom); and 5 percent chose "violent struggle." Significantly, 30 percent declined to answer this question. Those who favored violent struggle were distributed in a highly unequal manner, as one might expect. Among those who favored a federal solution to the Basque problem or advocated total independence of the Basques from Spain, 11 percent favored violent struggle as the best means to gain their objective. It would appear that in the closing, turbulent months of the Franco regime, popular support for armed struggle to gain Basque self-governance came from something between one-twentieth and one-tenth of the Basque population, depending of course on how one defines that population. We must remember, however, that the del Campo survey asked only for the *preferred* procedure for gaining the right of self-governance. The respondents were not asked how far they would be willing to go in the struggle if their preferred method (for example, popular referendum) did not result in the desired political outcome. We do not know, then, the depth of Basque frustration in mid-1975, except that there did not appear to be massive popular support for ETA during Franco's closing days. We must not forget, however, that at the time of the del Campo survey, any sort of pro-ETA response, or answer that suggested support for Basque independence could have violated Spanish law. Moreover, during the summer of 1975, two Basque provinces, Vizcaya and Guipúzcoa, had been placed under a state of exception by decree of General Franco, and constitutional rights had been suspended for a time to allow law-enforcement authorities to suppress popular expressions of unrest in the region. The time was not propitious to conduct a survey of Basque attitudes toward ETA. Nevertheless the del Campo study is still the starting point for our inquiry, not only because it may reflect Basque opinion during the Franco regime (and it is the only survey done during that period, to my knowledge), but also because it provides us with benchmark data against which we can measure subsequent surveys.

Since Franco's death, several surveys have attempted to uncover the extent of Basque support for armed struggle. One, conducted during the late summer and early autumn of 1978 by a Basque sociologist, José Ignacio Ruiz Olabuenaga, was released a year later in a report by the Bilbao Chamber of Commerce.[7] It found that 3.5 percent of the respondents advocated armed struggle to achieve Basque independence. A survey conducted for the Basque government in April and May 1979 showed that the percentage favoring armed struggle to gain independence had risen to 6 percent.[8] A third survey, also at the request of the Basque government, this time in the period December 1981–January 1982, showed that support for armed struggle had declined to about 3 percent once again. However, in May 1982, a survey was released by the Basque magazine *Euzkadi* which indicated that 8 percent of the respondents supported violent attacks by ETA against the Lemóniz nuclear power plant.

It would appear on the basis of these surveys that a hard core of about 3 to 6 percent of adult Basques support and actually advocate armed struggle or violence to achieve Basque independence. While this may seem to be an insignificantly small portion of the population, I estimate that it would still amount to between 56,900 and 97,000 adults in the Basque region.[9]

A second layer of ETA support involves preference for Basque independence. One of the central conflicts among Basque nationalists has been over the extent to which their nation could reasonably expect to be separated from Spain. Moderate Basques, including many leaders of the PNV, assert that complete independence is neither feasible nor desirable, since Madrid will never permit separation, and in any event

Euzkadi is too small to survive as an independent sovereign state. The ideological roots of ETA, on the other hand, reach back to a much more intransigent position that argues for complete separation and national independence. It holds that a policy of accepting regional autonomy within a centralized Spanish state simply plays into the hands of Spanish leaders who seek to buy off moderate Basques with this strategy of limited concessions. In any case, we expect most of the support for ETA to come from Basques who advocate complete independence for their nation. At the same time, a high percentage of those who favor independence probably support ETA, although many no doubt also support the PNV because of their dislike for ETA's violent strategy.

Table 7.1 presents the reader with data from fourteen separate surveys conducted from mid-1975 to winter 1981–82 which dealt in one way or another with the issue of Basque independence. (Indeed, we have more data on this question than on any other, because of its obvious policy relevance.) The del Campo study cited earlier, conducted in 1975, is again our base line.[10] It found that among Basque respondents, slightly less than one-third (32 percent) preferred autonomy for their regional form of government; 24 percent favored some sort of federal arrangement; 21 percent favored "the present form of government" (assumed to mean the Franco dictatorship); 6 percent preferred total independence; 6 percent professed to be indifferent to the form of government; and 13 percent declined to answer.

From this base of about 6 percent favoring independence, the accumulated surveys show steady increases in support through the next four and a half years. In the year following Franco's death, the percent favoring independence doubled to 12 percent.[11] During the course of the next three years, to mid-1979, the figure doubled once again, to the range of 25 to 26 percent.[12] During the turbulent year 1979, the figure increased once again by some 50 percent to about 36 percent or some three times its 1976 level.

The last three months of 1979 were an especially tense period in Basque and Spanish politics. With the referendum on the Basque Autonomy Statute held on October 25, the region was plunged into an intense round of political meetings and demonstrations. ETA violence increased significantly. From September 30 to November 30, ETA accounted for twelve dead and fifteen wounded, and it kidnaped a member of the Spanish parliament, UCD deputy Javier Rupérez (released unharmed on December 12). In the midst of this turmoil, the Spanish research organization FOESSA conducted a survey of the Basque region and found the results shown in table 7.2. Although the total in favor of independence does reach 63 percent, this includes those with "rather weak" and "very weak" desires for separation, so that it makes sense to me to reduce the figure to 36 percent, those with "strong" and "rather strong" desires for independence. This level of support is in line with the survey conducted by Juan Linz before the

Table 7.1 *Support for Armed Struggle and Independence among Basques, 1975–82 (in percentages)*

DATE		FOR ARMED STRUGGLE	FOR INDEPENDENCE
Summer	1975[a]	5.0	6.0
	1976[b]		12.0
	1977[c]		14.0
	1977[d]		15.0
	1978[c]		15.0
Fall	1978[e]	3.5	15.6
April–May	1979[f]	6.0	17.0
Spring	1979[g]		25.0
	1979[b]		26.0
	1979[c]		32.0
Fall	1979[h]		36.0
	1980[b]		18.0
Spring	1981[b]		12.0
Winter	1981–82[f]	3.0	23.0
Spring	1982[i]	8.0	

Sources:

[a] Salustiano del Campo, Manuel Navarro, and J. Felix Tezanos, *La cuestión regional española* (Madrid: Editorial Cuadernos para el Diálogo, 1977), p. 139, table 5.3; p. 175, table 6.7.

[b] Center for Sociological Research, as reported in *Cambio 16*, no. 502 (July 13, 1981), 20.

[c] Juan Linz, as reported in Richard Gunther, "A Comparative Study of Regionalisms in Spain," Society for Spanish and Portuguese Historical Studies, Toronto, Canada, 1981, p. 26.

[d] Instituto Consulta, as reported in *Cambio 16*, no. 502 (July 13, 1981), p. 20.

[e] *Clases sociales y aspiraciones vascas* (Bilbao: Cámara de Comercio, Industria y Navegación de Bilbao, 1979), chap. 9.

[f] Unpublished surveys conducted for the Basque government (see text note 8).

[g] Richard Gunther, Giacomo Sani, and Goldie Shabad, "Party Strategies and Mass Cleavages in the 1979 Spanish Election," American Political Science Association, Washington, D.C. 1980, p. 40.

[h] Foundation for the Development of Social Studies and Applied Sociology (FOESSA), as reported in *Cambio 16*, no. 502 (July 13, 1981), p. 20. See also *Deia* (Bilbao), July 7, 1981, p. 40.

[i] Survey conducted in spring 1982 for magazine *Euzkadi*, and published in *Deia*, May 7, 1982.

1979 referendum, which showed 32 percent favoring independence.

The data suggest that the percentage of Basques advocating separation has dropped steadily since the Autonomy Statute referendum in 1979. The two CIS studies, done in 1980 and again in 1981, show steady decline in percent of respondents favoring independence, from 36 percent in 1979 to 18 percent in 1980 and to 12 percent in 1981. In all likelihood, this 12 percent corresponds roughly to the 12 percent in the 1979 FOESSA survey who reported having "strong desires for" independence. In other words, while the level of support for independence did at one time reach some 36 percent of the Basque provinces' population (representing more than 585,000 adults), opinion on the issue fluctuated considerably, and declined after 1979 to what we might regard as a hard core of about 12 percent (equivalent to slightly more than 195,000 adults) who favor independence from Spain but who might not necessarily advocate armed struggle to achieve that goal.

The third layer of pro-ETA attitudes is based on a positive image of ETA despite some disagreement with them over goals or tactics. That is, many Basques may believe that ETA is a positive force in the political struggle of their region even if they believe that the goal of independence and the tactics of violence are unrealistic and unacceptable. A visitor to the Basque country frequently hears remarks such as "I don't agree with ETA's methods, but at least they force Madrid to bargain with the moderate Basque leaders." We can get

Table 7.2   *Changes in Basque Attitudes toward Independence, 1979–81 (in percentages)*

	FOESSA SURVEY 1979	CIS SURVEY 1981
Favor independence	63	12
"Strong desires for"	12	—
"Rather strong desires for"	24	—
"Rather weak desires for"	15	—
"Very weak desires for"	12	—
Opposed to independence	29	50
Favor centralized state	—	43
Favor autonomy	—	7
No answer/Don't know	7	38

Source: *Cambio 16*, no. 502 (July 13, 1981), p. 20.
Note: Categories showing no data were not used in their respective surveys.

some sense of the depth to which this layer extends by examining the data from surveys that show the proportion of the sample who have a positive image of ETA.

The first survey of this sort was the one conducted in the summer of 1978 by a team of researchers under the direction of Juan J. Linz.[13] Linz probed for popular support for ETA by asking respondents to tell the interviewer which of the following descriptions best fit "persons involved in terrorism": patriots, idealists, manipulated people, madmen, or criminals. About 10 percent perceived terrorists as patriots, while more than one-third saw them as idealists, another third perceived them as manipulated by outside forces, and only a small fraction classified them as madmen or criminals. Ten percent refused to answer the question.

More than any other, this layer of support for ETA appears to be highly volatile and oscillates wildly between extremes in very short periods of time. Only a few months after Linz conducted his first survey in 1978, the Ruiz Olabuenaga survey found that only about 18 percent of the respondents held a positive image of ETA. This finding is based on the percentage of the sample who disagreed with the statement "Violent attacks must be condemned by everyone."[14]

A third survey was that conducted in late 1978 by *Cambio 16* and printed in the magazine in January 1979, with full tabular data on attitudes toward ETA (see table 7.3). Apart from the problem of the high rate of refusals to answer, it seems clear that in the Basque provinces ETA was regarded favorably by something between 10 and 37 percent of the respondents, depending on how the question was phrased. For instance, about 32 percent thought ETA members were patriots and 37 percent disagreed that they were terrorists. On the other hand, only 10.6 percent disagreed that ETA represents a minority of the Basque people, and only 19 percent agreed that ETA is supported by a majority of the Basques. More than one-third believed that ETA's violence was unjustified in the context of Spanish democracy. And only one respondent in eight believed that ETA was the only organization that really represented Basque interests.

In the summer of 1979, Juan Linz followed up his earlier survey with the second study that has been mentioned, to determine shifts in Basque public opinion over the preceding year. He found that support for ETA had changed but slightly in the interim: 10 percent still saw ETA members as patriots (no change); about 25 percent perceived them as idealists (down from about 33); slightly less than 33 percent saw ETA as being manipulated from the outside (only a slight decline); about 25 percent believed them to be madmen or criminals (something of an increase); and about 15 percent declined to answer the questions.

Several months later, in the fall of 1979, the FOESSA study cited above found that 17 percent of the respondents considered ETA members patriots and 33 percent considered them idealists. In other words, half of the Basque sample had a favorable image of ETA. Another 42 percent thought them to be madmen, criminals, or manipulated by outside forces; and 14 percent declined to answer the questions. Finally, in a 1981 CIS study, only 13 percent of the sample reported positive feelings about ETA, with 2 percent seeing them as patriots and 11 percent as idealists. Forty-one percent perceived ETA members as madmen, criminals, or manipulated by outside forces. Significantly, nearly half the sample (46 percent) declined to answer the question.

Table 7.3   *Attitudes toward ETA in Spain and Basque Provinces, Late 1978 (in percentages)*

STATEMENT	AGREE		DON'T AGREE		NO ANSWER	
	ALL OF SPAIN	BASQUE PROVINCES	ALL OF SPAIN	BASQUE PROVINCES	ALL OF SPAIN	BASQUE PROVINCES
ETA members are patriots fighting for the liberation of the Basque people.	19.4	31.9	39.3	22.4	31.4	45.7
ETA represents only a minority of the Basque people.	52.6	43.6	15.3	10.6	32.0	45.7
ETA's violence has no justification today.	62.7	37.2	11.8	16.0	25.6	47.9
A majority of Basques support ETA.	28.8	19.2	38.9	35.1	32.5	47.9
ETA is the only organization that really represents the aspirations and interests of the Basque people.	13.4	12.8	50.9	43.6	35.8	44.7
ETA members are terrorists who should be pursued and eliminated.	47.8	17.0	22.3	37.3	29.9	45.7

Source: *Cambio 16*, no. 370 (January 7, 1979), p. 31.

Thus it appears that from 1978 to 1981 the proportion of the Basque population holding a positive or favorable image of ETA has fluctuated between 13 and 50 percent (equivalent, respectively, to 211,000 and 813,000 persons). It would appear that the image of ETA held by rank-and-file citizens is quite susceptible to public perception of current events and thus is quite volatile. Note, however, that the proportion holding positive views about ETA has never dropped below 12 percent, which seems a reasonable core figure for those favoring total separation from Spain. In all probability, that figure represents a kind of second-order hard core of ETA support of about 200,000 persons who are intransigent in their advocacy of independence for the Basque nation and who see ETA as a perfectly valid mechanism for attaining that goal.

The fourth and final layer of support for ETA contains those who, while not necessarily agreeing with ETA's goals or strategies, still feel that the Spanish government must come to some understanding with the insurgent organization before Basque political and economic life can be restored to smooth operation. There are many serious problems confronting Basque political leaders, including high unemployment, pollution, and urban congestion. These simply cannot be confronted productively so long as ETA remains a force in the region. Therefore, without making any kind of commentary on the validity of their goals or tactics, many Basques would urge Madrid to come to terms with ETA so that they (the Basques) can get on with the task of reconstructing their society. Apparently, this layer of pro-ETA sentiment accounts for about one-half of the adult Basque population.

In his 1978 survey, Juan Linz asked about the respondents' preferred methods for dealing with the ETA challenge. Five percent advocated accepting their demands, while 43 percent advocated negotiating a cease-fire with them. On the other hand, 38 percent favored the maintenance of authority, and 7 percent supported stronger counter-ETA measures, including the declaration of martial law. In his follow-up survey a year later, Linz found virtually no change in this dimension of popular opinion. Nearly half the respondents (48 percent) still believed that the best way to cope with ETA's challenge was to accept their demands or to negotiate with them. At about the same time (spring 1979), Richard Gunther found in his survey that 57 percent of the sample favored either accepting ETA's demands or negotiating with the organization as a means of putting an end to the insurgency.[15] Thus we can conclude that about half the adult Basque population (between three-quarters of a million and a million people) advocate either accepting ETA's demands or negotiating with them, if this would bring about an end to the violence in the Basque country.

(The data that deal with these latter two levels of support are summarized in table 7.4.)

Trends in popular support for ETA are complex and reflect the dynamics of public opinion at four different levels. The interplay among these levels is reflected in figure 7.1, which portrays changes in ETA-related attitudes among the Basque population from 1975 to 1981. Several conclusions can be drawn from examining this graphic and the related data. First, in answer to the question "How many Basques support ETA?" we can now respond "Somewhere between 5 percent (about 80,000) and 50 percent (800,000) of all adults, depending on what one means by support." Second, while there have been rather extreme shifts in levels of support, there does appear to be a discernible pattern of growth in support from the time of Franco's death to the period of late 1979–early 1980, at which point the lines begin to turn downward once again. The significant events of that period—the Autonomy Statute Referendum of October 1979 followed by the election of the first Basque government in March 1980—probably had much to do with this downturn in support for ETA. Nevertheless, there exists a hard core of ETA supporters that amounts to

Table 7.4   *Attitudes in Basque Provinces toward ETA and Negotiating with ETA (in percentages)*

DATE	HAVE POSITIVE IMAGE	FOR ACCEPTING DEMANDS/ NEGOTIATING
Summer 1978[a]	43.0 (est.)	48.0
Fall 1978[b]	18.1 (est.)	
December 1978[c]	32.0	
Spring 1979[d]		57.0
Summer 1979[a]	35.0 (est.)	48.0
Fall 1979[e]	50.0	
Spring 1981[e]	13.0	

Sources:

[a] Juan Linz, "The Basques in Spain: Nationalism and Political Conflict in a New Democracy," in W. Phillips Davison and Leon Gordenker, eds., *Resolving Nationality Conflicts: The Role of Public Opinion Research* (New York: Praeger, 1980).

[b] *Deia*, October 24 and 25, 1979.

[c] *Cambio 16*, no. 370 (January 7, 1979), p. 31.

[d] Richard Gunther, Giacomo Sani, and Goldie Shabad, "Party Strategies and Mass Cleavages in the 1979 Spanish Election," American Political Science Association, Washington, D.C. 1980, p. 45, table 10.

[e] *Cambio 16*, no. 502 (July 13, 1981), p. 20.

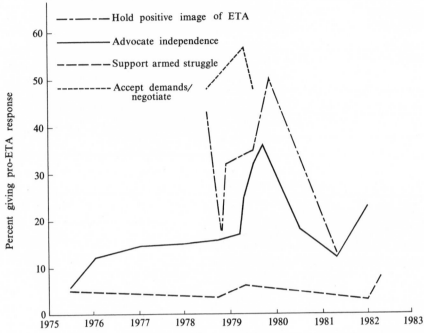

Figure 7.1.   Trends in Pro-ETA Attitudes among Basques.

perhaps as much as 10 percent of the Basque population, and certainly no less than 5 percent, that will continue to support the insurgency and to advocate violence to obtain Basque independence, no matter what happens with regard to Basque autonomy. At the same time, it is apparent that popular support among Basques for ETA is sensitive to changes in Spanish policy regarding regional autonomy. When policy decisions in Madrid constrain or block the development of an autonomous Basque regime, support for ETA climbs; when the Spanish government encourages autonomy, support for ETA declines.

Popular Support for ETA: Social and Ethnic Characteristics

Assuming that we have approached an answer to the question of how much popular support exists for ETA, we then come to ask where such support is located. Which social groups (defined in terms of class or ethnicity) support ETA most heavily?

To answer these questions, the surveys already cited are helpful but insufficient. To supplement them, I have chosen to work with vote data from the four elections held in the Basque region between 1977 and 1980.[16] Standing in for ETA will be the two radical Basque socialist political parties, Euzkadiko Ezkerra (EE) and Herri Batasuna (HB). I contend that the way in which the votes for EE and HB have been distributed over the past four elections in the Basque provinces (1977 and 1979 for the Spanish parliament; 1979 for provincial assemblies and municipal councils; 1980 for the Basque Parliament) will correspond approximately to the way in which popular support is distributed for ETA. Note that I do not contend that all those who vote for EE or HB are ETA sympathizers, although many undoubtedly are. I simply argue that the distribution patterns of support for ETA will correlate strongly with the distribution patterns of the votes for the two political parties that are most closely associated with ETA's ideological position in the Basque political spectrum.

I am presuming that there is a high degree of correlation between party identification and support for ETA. The greater the identification with the Basque socialist parties, EE or HB, the greater will be the probability of a person's supporting ETA. What is the evidence to support that presumption? For one thing, we know from surveys that supporters of these parties tend to have opinions on policy questions and issues similar to those espoused by ETA. The 1981 CIS study cited earlier found, for example, that 12 percent of the sample favored independence for the Basque region, while among self-identified supporters of Herri Batasuna the percentage rose to 52 percent, and for Euzkadiko Ezkerra, to 29 percent. The 1979 Gunther study found the same kind of distance between EE/HB followers and the general population. Whereas 25 percent of Gunther's sample supported independence for Euzkadi, the figure was 61 percent for HB supporters and 44 percent for EE.[17] On a related dimension, we also know that followers of Euzkadiko Ezkerra and Herri Batasuna tend to have much more positive views of ETA and to be much more supportive of ETA than do the rank-and-file population of the Basque region. Juan Linz found in his 1979 study, for example, that whereas only about 35 percent of the overall sample viewed ETA favorably, the proportion rose to 96 percent among HB followers (49 percent who classified them as patriots and 47 percent who saw them as idealists). Among those in the sample who identified themselves as supporters of Euzkadiko Ezkerra, 78 percent held a positive image of ETA.[18] Richard Gunther found somewhat the same tendency on the part of EE and HB supporters to view ETA favorably. For example, he asked respondents to place ETA on a "feeling thermometer" that would measure their attitude toward the organization. The higher the mean score, the more sympathetically ETA was viewed. In Spain as a whole, the mean ETA affect score was 0.65, indicating considerable hostility toward the organization. Among supporters of the PNV, the score was somewhat more positive, 3.01; while in the Basque population generally it rose even higher, to 3.46. But among supporters of EE, the pro-ETA score rose to 5.00, and among followers of Herri Batasuna, it was 6.4. On the subject of accepting demands or negotiating with ETA, Gunther also found much greater pro-ETA sentiment among HB/EE followers. Whereas only 14 percent of the Spanish population agreed that the government should accept ETA's demands or negotiate with the organization, in the Basque population generally (and among followers of the PNV), the figure rose to 57 percent. Among HB supporters, however, the figure was 83 percent, and among EE supporters, 87 percent.[19]

Not surprisingly, data drawn from the 1979 FOESSA study indicate that support for ETA and for independence comes primarily from those who consider themselves ethnic Basque or more Basque than Spanish (see table 7.5). Note that while only 12.8 percent of the total sample had "strong desires" for independence and 24.5 percent "rather strong desires," for those who considered themselves ethnic Basque the respective figures were 25.4 and 39.6 percent. Thus among *Basques* (as opposed to all residents of the Basque region), nearly two-thirds had what we might describe as a strong commitment to Basque independence. Data drawn from the same study show that a respondent's ethnic identity affects his or her image of ETA (table 7.6). Half of the total sample viewed ETA in a favorable light (17 percent as patriots, 33 percent as idealists), but among ethnic Basques, the figure rose to 71 percent (33 percent as patriots, 38 percent as idealists).

Other survey researchers have discovered similar tendencies. Juan Linz's 1978 study found that among persons born in the Basque region, 19 percent saw ETA members as patriots, and an additional 44 percent classified them as idealists. Among the group of respondents who were born in the Basque region and spoke the Basque language, 27 percent identified ETA members as patriots and 49 as idealists. Among immigrants to the Basque region, however, only 10 percent regarded them as patriots and only 30 percent as idealists. When asked to name the group or groups responsible for the violence then wracking the Basque region, persons of Basque ethnicity blamed first and foremost the forces from the extreme right (59 percent), and then, in order of importance, the Franco dictatorship (49 percent), the Spanish government and the extreme left (33 percent each), and the police (28 percent). Only 8 percent blamed ETA for the violence. In contrast,

Table 7.5   *Ethnonational Identity and Desire for Basque Independence, based on FOESSA Study, October 1979 (in percentages)*

DESIRE FOR INDEPENDENCE	SPANISH	ETHNONATIONAL IDENTITY				
		MORE SPANISH THAN BASQUE	AS MUCH BASQUE AS SPANISH	MORE BASQUE THAN SPANISH	BASQUE	TOTAL
Very strong	1.4	0.0	3.4	13.1	25.4	12.8
Rather strong	9.9	8.8	11.6	28.7	39.6	24.5
Rather weak	7.8	12.3	19.1	25.4	13.7	15.7
Very weak	13.5	17.5	19.5	5.7	6.5	11.6
None	57.4	57.9	39.7	21.3	9.8	29.2
No answer	9.9	3.5	6.7	5.7	4.9	6.2
N	141	57	267	122	386	973

Source: *Deia*, July 7, 1981.

Note: 1,011 people were interviewed. Thirty-eight (3.8%) either did not reveal their ethnonational identity or selected an identity not listed above.

Table 7.6   *Ethnonational Identity and Image of ETA, based on FOESSA Study, October 1979 (in percentages)*

IMAGE OF ETA	SPANISH	IDENTITY				
		MORE SPANISH THAN BASQUE	AS MUCH BASQUE AS SPANISH	MORE BASQUE THAN SPANISH	BASQUE	TOTAL
Patriots	0.0	2.0	7.0	16.0	33.0	17.0
Idealists	16.0	25.0	36.0	34.0	38.0	33.0
Manipulated	42.0	42.0	36.0	25.0	18.0	29.0
Crazy	16.0	9.0	6.0	9.0	5.0	8.0
Criminals	13.0	9.0	4.0	5.0	2.0	5.0
No answer	17.0	14.0	16.0	15.0	10.0	14.0
N	141	57	267	122	386	973

Source: *Deia*, July 7, 1981.

Of 1,011 people interviewed, 38 (3.8%) either did not reveal their ethnonational identity or selected an identity not listed above. Columns add to more than 100 percent because of multiple answers. Data rounded off in press report, which may have introduced very slight (less than 0.5 percent) errors.

immigrants to the Basque region were more prone to blame ETA (17 percent), although the extreme left (35 percent), the Spanish government, and the police also came in for their share of criticism.[20]

An ability to speak the Basque language, Euskera, is an important (but surprisingly not crucial) component of Basque ethnicity. That is, while nearly all Basque speakers consider themselves ethnic Basque, there are many people who do not speak Euskera but who still consider themselves ethnic Basque. By the same token, there will be many Basques who do not speak the language but who still support ETA, or advocate independence, or both. Richard Gunther, in his 1979 study, found that 23 percent of the sample advocated independence for the Basque country. Among immigrant non-Basque speakers, this figure was much lower, 9 percent. Among native ethnic non-Basque speakers, the figure rose to 24 percent. Among ethnic Basques who also spoke Euskera, the percentage rose to 39 percent.[21]

The other side of the coin is equally important: there are many who are ethnic Basques and who speak Euskera but who do not support the pro-ETA parties, Euzkadiko Ezkerra and Herri Batasuna. Here the Juan Linz 1978 and 1979 studies are extremely valuable.[22] Linz found that there were indeed more Basque-speaking people who preferred EE in 1978 or voted EE or HB in 1979 than was the case in Basque society as a whole. Linz found that 19 percent of his sample claimed to be able to speak Basque in 1978; 26 percent, in 1979. Yet among supporters of EE, the comparable figures were 48 and 30 percent, and among those who voted for HB in 1979, the figure was 42 percent. The significant thing about this is that the more moderate PNV registered almost exactly the same percentages: 40 percent among supporters in 1978, 47 percent among PNV voters in 1979. Indeed, the PNV clearly has more support among Euskera-speaking people than either of the two Basque socialist parties. Linz also discovered that in 1978, 16 percent of those who claimed to be able to speak Euskera were supporters of EE, while 26 percent of that group preferred the PNV. In fact, in the 1978 survey, the Spanish socialist party, PSOE, had as many Euskera-speaking supporters in the sample (16 percent) as did EE. Thus we can conclude that a feeling of Basque ethnicity is much more important as a predictor of support for ETA than is an ability to speak Basque. Moreover, Basque-speaking persons are probably more likely to support moderate PNV candidates and policy positions than they are members of the more radical Basque socialist parties.

These observations lead us to our final question: how is support for ETA distributed across the socioeconomic class system of the Basque population? Here the data are ambiguous but seem on balance to suggest that support for ETA spans several social classes. The 1975 del Campo study, for example, found that those advocating violent struggle for independence were relatively well educated (7 percent of those with a secondary or university education favored armed struggle, compared with 5 percent of the overall sample), relatively well-off financially (7 percent of those classified as having high income chose violence), and of the middle class in terms of social status (10 percent of salaried nonmanual workers supported violent solutions).[23] The 1978 Ruiz Olabuenaga study found something similar, in that more than half of the advocates of violent struggle came from the managerial and upper middle classes or sectors.[24] Richard Gunther's 1979 survey confirms these impressions. When matching occupational status against support for independence, Gunther found that 26 percent of both high- and medium-status occupational groups preferred independence, whereas only 18 percent of low-status occupation persons preferred separation from Spain. When he compared the respondents' subjective identification of their own class to their support for independence, Gunther also found that while 30.4 percent of upper and middle class persons favored independence, only 23.5 percent of lower middle class persons felt this way, and only 22.5 percent of working class respondents favored separation.[25] Moreover, Gunther also found that the Basque socialist parties drew the core of their support from the upper and upper middle classes. Fully 57.2 percent of those expressing a preference for regional left parties came from one of the upper or middle class categories. Nearly one-third (31.5 percent) came from mid-level public and private employees and technical professionals; 17.1 percent were owners, small businessmen, or independent artisans; and 8.6 percent were upper class professionals, land owners, or executives. In contrast, the lower middle class occupations such as low-level office workers, clerical employees, and small farmers accounted for only 9.5 percent of the parties' support. Slightly more than one-quarter (27.3 percent) came from the working classes, with skilled workers accounting for about two-thirds of these (17.6 percent as against 9.7 percent from unskilled labor).[26] Juan Linz found rather a different picture of class-based support for Euzkadiko Ezkerra in his 1978 survey. Linz found that only 8 percent of EE supporters were drawn from upper or upper middle classes, while 41 percent came from the lower middle class, and 49 percent came from the working class.[27] Hence the uncertainty over this aspect of ETA support.

What conclusions can we draw about the social characteristics of ETA's supporters? In ethnic terms, supporters appear to be predominantly, but not solely, ethnic Basque. They are rather more likely to speak Euskera than the average citizen of the Basque region, but not appreciably more likely than those who support the more moderate Basque nationalist party, PNV. In terms of social class, they are spread across all important social strata. If many come from the upper, upper middle, and middle strata of professionals and managers, ETA can also count on solid support in both the working and lower middle classes. Stated in a somewhat different way, ETA's supporters seem to be rather similar to ETA's members.

CHAPTER EIGHT

Geography and Insurgency: The Territorial Base of ETA

Students of insurgencies have generally argued that rural guerrilla movements require a substantial territorial base from which to conduct their operations.[1] In addition to a sanctuary to which they can retreat for rest and recuperation from the strains of battle, the insurgents need a zone where they constitute the sole legitimate government, where they can demonstrate to neutral civilians what can be expected if they come to power. All successful rural guerrilla insurgencies have had such a territorial base, from the Sierra Maestra region in Cuba to Mao tse-Tung's caves of Yenan.

My research suggests that ETA has also needed a geographical base from which to conduct operations, within which to recruit new members, and on which to ground its popular support among the citizenry. Far from being spread more or less randomly around the Basque region, the ETA phenomenon was, and is, concentrated in a rather well-defined region that amounts to no more than one-fifth of the area of Euzkadi. This region of maximum support for ETA has its own economic, social, cultural, and linguistic characteristics that set it apart from the rest of the Basque country. By knowing more about the geography of ETA, we will also know more about ETA itself.

The Geography of ETA Attacks

We have already seen, in chapter 5, several significant patterns in ETA's armed attacks, involving the weapons they use, the targets they select, and the way they distribute their attacks across time. Here I want to focus on the patterns we see in the territorial distribution of their attacks. I find that ETA does not spread its attacks evenly across

---

I wish to thank Mr. Carl Joseph Mehler II for the original cartographic work on which the maps in this chapter are based.

the Basque provinces; instead, the organization focuses them within a fairly clearly demarcated zone.

In the following table, 8.1, we can see how ETA has spread its attacks across the Basque provinces and beyond.[2] Nearly 85 percent of all ETA killings have taken place in the Basque region itself. The only significant level of assassination outside the Basque provinces has been in Madrid, where ETA has been held responsible for some 32 deaths: 9 in the Rolando bombing, 6 in the airport and train-station bombings, and the remainder from attacks on political leaders, government officials, and military and Guardia Civil personnel. The proportion changes somewhat in the category of woundings, where Madrid bulks much larger, again because of the high-casualty bombings that produced 156 wounded. Nevertheless, ETA has conducted the great majority of its violent attacks within the Basque region.

ETA's attacks have been fairly tightly clustered even within the Basque region, however (see tables 8.1 and 8.2). More than half the killings and woundings and more than one-fourth of the kidnapings have been concentrated in Guipúzcoa, with a population of about 700,000 (about one-fourth of the total Basque population) and an area of about 2,000 square kilometers (about 10 percent of the Basque region). Much more densely populated Vizcaya accounts for only

Table 8.1   *Distribution of ETA Victims by Location of Attack*
(in percentages)

LOCATION	KILLED	WOUNDED	KIDNAPED	TOTAL
Alava	5.9	3.9	8.3	4.9
Guipúzcoa	46.3	23.4	25.0	32.9
Navarra	4.5	2.1	12.5	3.4
Vizcaya	27.9	16.6	41.7	22.1
Total, Basque provinces	84.6	46.0	87.5	63.3
Madrid	11.2	41.6	0.0	27.6
Logroño	1.0	10.9	0.0	6.5
Other/Unknown	3.1	1.6	12.5	2.6
Total, other locations	15.3	54.1	12.5	36.7
Total, all locations	99.9	100.1	100.0	100.0
(N)	(287)	(385)	(24)	(696)

Source: Data gathered from contemporary press reports. Calculations by author.

Table 8.2   *Index of Attack-Victim Distribution*
(victims per thousand persons)

LOCATION	KILLED	WOUNDED	KID-NAPED	TOTAL OF VICTIMS	POPULA-TION IN 1975 (000's)	VICTIMS/1,000 POPULA-TION
Alava	17	15	2	34	238.0	0.14
Guipúzcoa	133	90	6	229	681.2	0.34
Navarra	13	8	3	24	484.0	0.05
Vizcaya	80	64	10	154	1,152.1	0.13
Total, Basque provinces	243	177	21	441	2,555.3	0.17
Madrid	32	160	0	192	4,513	0.04
Logroño	3	42	0	45	240	0.19
Total, above locations	278	379	21	678	7,310	0.09
Total, other locations	9	6	3	18		
Grand total	287	385	24	696		

Source: Data gathered from contemporary press reports. Calculations by author.

about one-third of all ETA victims during the period, while in Alava and Navarra the group has not operated to any significant degree.

It is possible to gauge the degree of concentration of ETA activity by calculating, for each province, the ratio between ETA attack victims and the population as a whole (table 8.2). We see that the overall ratio for the four Basque provinces, Madrid, and Logroño is 0.09 per thousand population. For the four Basque provinces alone, the ratio rises to 0.17 per thousand. Madrid and Navarra had the smallest proportion of attack victims, with ratios of 0.04 and 0.05 per thousand, respectively. Alava, Vizcaya, and Logroño provinces have ratios in the same range as that of the Basque provinces as a whole: 0.14, 0.13, and 0.19 per thousand, respectively. In Guipúzcoa, however, the ratio rises dramatically to 0.34 per thousand, twice the average for the four provinces as a whole. During the period, Guipúzcoa was the site of 133 killings and 90 woundings, of which 34 and 46 respectively took place in the capital, San Sebastián.

Let us focus next on the administration subdivisions within each province (see map 8.1). These subdivisions, referred to as *partidos judiciales* or judicial districts, are the units by which vote and census data are gathered and reported. Here, as elsewhere in this chapter, I will use these subdivisions to show links between ETA and other important social and economic factors.

Table 8.3 shows how ETA victims have been distributed across the administrative subdivisions within the Basque provinces. Within Guipúzcoa itself there are important variations in attack incidence, ranging from the high level of the Azpeitia region (0.53 per thousand) down to the lower but still above average level in the Vergara region (0.27 per thousand). Apart from the two districts in Vizcaya (Guernica

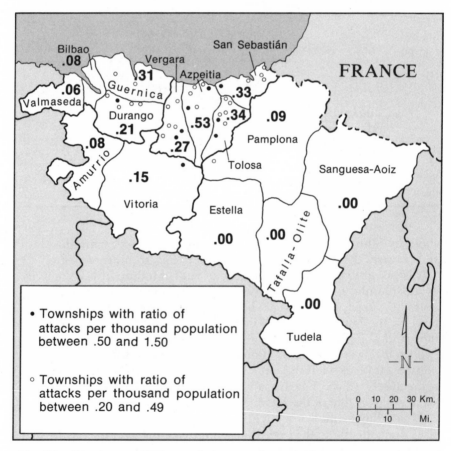

Map 8.1. Distribution of ETA Attacks by Township and Administrative Subdivision. Figures within each subdivision indicate number of ETA victims per 1,000 population in the subdivision.

Table 8.3 *Distribution of ETA Attack Victims by*
Administrative Subdivisions of Basque Provinces

SUBDIVISION	NUMBER OF VICTIMS	1975 POPULATION (000's)	VICTIMS/1,000 POPULATION
Amurrio (A)	3	36.3	0.08
Vitoria (A)	31	201.7	0.15
Azpeitia (G)	35	65.5	0.53
San Sebastián (G)	119	364.2	0.33
Tolosa (G)	32	93.4	0.34
Vergara (G)	43	158.1	0.27
Estella (N)	0	62.3	0.00
Pamplona (N)	24	256.2	0.09
Sanguesa-Aoiz (N)	0	47.6	0.00
Tafalla-Olite (N)	0	42.3	0.00
Tudela (N)	0	75.6	0.00
Bilbao (V)	35	431.1	0.08
Durango (V)	44	205.5	0.21
Guernica (V)	56	179.7	0.31
Valmaseda (V)	19	335.8	0.06

Source: Data gathered from contemporary press reports. Calculations by author.

at 0.31 per thousand and Durango at 0.21 per thousand), there are really no significant zones of ETA activity in the Basque region. (Map 8.1 portrays graphically this concentration of ETA attacks in a relatively small portion of the Basque region.)

Finally, let us examine ETA attack data at the level of the township or *municipio*. The units of analysis here are the 58 townships reported to have an electoral census of more than 5,000 people in 1979. While these towns account for only 11 percent of all Basque municipios, they account for more than 80 percent of the population. As depicted in map 8.1, ETA attacks have been confined to a relatively small number of the townships in the Basque region. The map shows those townships in which the number of ETA attacks per thousand population is greater than 0.20. The open circles represent municipios with between 0.20 and 0.49; the dark circles, townships with more than 0.50. Of the somewhat more than 500 townships in the four provinces, ETA attacks have been confined to fewer than 80, and in only 35 (those depicted on the map) does the number of attacks per thousand persons rise above 0.20. Of these 35 municipios, 25 are in Guipúzcoa,

8 in Vizcaya, and 1 each in Navarra and Alava (near the Guipúzcoa border). The townships are concentrated in a roughly crescent-shaped area of Vizcaya and Guipúzcoa, running from west-central Vizcaya south-eastward to south-central Guipúzcoa, thence north-eastward to a point where Guipúzcoa meets the French border. This concentration is not accidental, for it corresponds closely to other indicators of Basque ethnicity and political radicalism, a point to which I will return.

The Geography of ETA Recruitment

Let us turn, next, to the geographical base from which ETA members are recruited. This discussion follows on and is derived from the same data base as the analysis of the origins of ETA members that was developed in chapter 6.[3]

We focus first on the distribution of etarras by province, and find, probably not surprisingly, that ETA tends to recruit its members predominantly from the regions in which its attacks are concentrated: primarily Guipúzcoa province and secondarily, but still to a significant degree, the central and eastern parts of Vizcaya. (This finding supports the observation that I will offer in chapter 9, that ETA's operating cells launch most of their assaults close to the homes of cell members.)

Guipúzcoa, for example, has provided almost exactly half of the 341 etarras for whom province of birth is known, even though only about one-quarter of the Basque population lives in Guipúzcoa (see table 8.4). The proportion of etarras born in Vizcaya is almost the same as the proportion of inhabitants of the Basque region that Vizcaya holds: 41.6 percent for etarras, 44.6 percent for the general population. But the percentages in Alava and Navarra are significantly lower than those for the general population (2.6 and 8.6 percent in Alava, 4.1 and 19.9 percent in Navarra). If we calculate the index of ETA membership from each province, the ratio of etarras to province populations (table 8.5), we find that the ratio for the four provinces as a whole is 0.13 per thousand, which is almost exactly that of Vizcaya (0.12 per thousand). The ratios in Alava and Navarra (0.04 and 0.03) are about 75 percent lower than the overall ratio, but the ratio for Guipúzcoa (0.25 per thousand) is double the overall ratio.

We can focus our search for ETA's origins somewhat more narrowly by examining the distribution of etarra birthplaces across the administrative subdivisions within each province and by township (see table 8.6, map 8.2). Within Guipúzcoa, the Tolosa administrative subdivi-

Table 8.4   *ETA Members, Provinces of Birth*
(in percentages)

SAMPLE	N	ALAVA	GUIPÚZ-COA	NA-VARRA	VIZCAYA	NOT BASQUE
Case studies[a]	37	0.0	48.6	2.7	43.2	5.4
Political prisoners, 1974[a]	166	1.2	49.4	3.6	45.8	0.0
Arrest records, 1978–80[a]	138	5.1	51.4	5.1	36.2	2.2
All samples	341	2.6	50.1	4.1	41.6	1.5
Distribution of population in Basque provinces (%)[b]		8.6	26.8	19.9	44.6	

[a] Data gathered from biographical case studies and contemporary press reports. Calculations by author.

[b] As of 1970. See Luis C.-Nuñez Astrain, *Clases sociales en Euskadi* (San Sebastián: Editorial Txertoa, 1977), p. 162, table 40.

Table 8.5   *Ratio of ETA Membership to Total Population,*
by Province

PROVINCE	ETA MEMBERS	1975 POPULATION (000's)	ETA MEMBERS/1,000 POPULATION
Alava	9	238.0	0.04
Guipúzcoa	171	681.2	0.25
Navarra	14	484.0	0.03
Vizcaya	142	1,152.1	0.12
Total	336[a]	2,555.3	0.13

Source: Biographical case studies and contemporary press reports, various years 1960–80. Calculations by author.

[a] Reflects 5 eterras not from Basque provinces and 106 for whom place of origin not known.

sion leads all other jurisdictions, with a ratio of 0.45 etarras per thousand persons. (The practical effect of such a ratio would be, for example, to produce 5 members of ETA from a town of only 10,000 people.) The subdivision with the next highest proportion is Azpeitia, with 0.35 per thousand. The other two subdivisions are Vergara, with 0.22 per thousand, and San Sebastián, 0.16 per thousand. Outside of

Table 8.6   *Distribution of ETA Members by Administrative Subdivisions of Basque Provinces*

SUBDIVISION	NUMBER OF ETA MEMBERS	1975 POPULATION (000's)	ETA MEMBERS/1,000 POPULATION
Amurrio (A)	0	36.3	0.00
Vitoria (A)	9	201.7	0.04
Azpeitia (G)	23	65.5	0.35
San Sebastián (G)	59	364.2	0.16
Tolosa (G)	42	93.4	0.45
Vergara (G)	35	158.1	0.22
Estella (N)	1	62.3	0.02
Pamplona (N)	12	256.2	0.05
Sanguesa-Aoiz (N)	0	47.6	0.00
Tafalla-Olite (N)	0	42.3	0.00
Tudela (N)	0	75.6	0.00
Bilbao (V)	40	431.1	0.09
Durango (V)	37	205.5	0.18
Guernica (V)	46	179.7	0.26
Valmaseda (V)	16	335.8	0.05

Source: Biographical case studies and contemporary press reports. Calculations by author.

Guipúzcoa, only two administrative subdivisions have figures of any real significance, both of them in eastern and central Vizcaya: Guernica, 0.26 per thousand; and Durango, 0.18 per thousand. What this means is that for all practical purposes, ETA's members come solely from Guipúzcoa and the eastern two-thirds of Vizcaya. In other words, a geographical area that is only 19 percent of the territory of the Basque provinces and contains only 35 percent of its population has produced 75 percent of ETA's members.[4] Map 8.2 tells the same story in a more graphic way, and should be compared with map 8.1 to get the full effect of the concentration of ETA into a relatively small corner of the Basque provinces.

The Geography of ETA Supporters

In the preceding chapter, I used vote data for the Basque socialist parties, Herri Batasuna and Euzkadiko Ezkerra, as well as data on the ethnic and social characteristics of the members of those two parties,

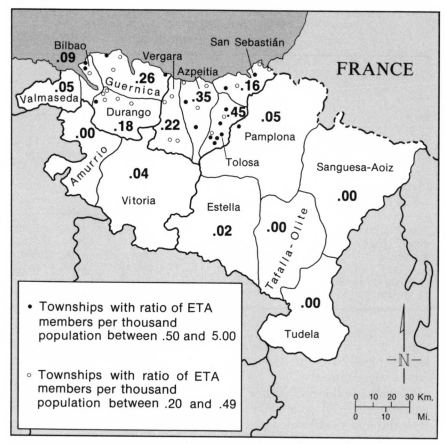

Map. 8.2. Distribution of ETA Members by Township and Administrative Subdivision. Figures within each subdivision indicate number of ETA members per 1,000 population in the subdivision.

as indicators of certain key dimensions of popular support for ETA. Here, I shall make use of the same data arranged geographically to examine how mass support for ETA is distributed across the Basque provinces.[5] In other words, we will use the distribution patterns of Basque socialist party voting data to suggest the areas in which popular support for ETA may be most heavily concentrated.

When we look at the data (table 8.7), we see that the Basque Left has scored major gains in each province as well in the region as a whole (2 to 23 percent in Alava; 9 to 31 percent in Guipúzcoa; 0 to 11 percent in Navarra; 5 to 24 percent in Vizcaya; and 4 to 26 percent in the overall region). The strengths of the Basque Left are in Guipúzcoa. EE/HB

Table 8.7   *Vote for Basque Socialist Parties in Four*
Post-Franco Elections, 1977–80, by Province
(percentages of total vote)

PROVINCE	1977 SPANISH PARLIA- MENTARY	1979 SPANISH PARLIA- MENTARY	1979 MUNICIPAL GOVERN- MENTAL	1980 BASQUE PARLIA- MENTARY	OVERALL AVERAGE
Alava	2.1	14.2	14.5	23.5	13.6
Guipúzcoa	9.4	31.3	27.7	31.1	24.9
Navarra	0.0	8.9	11.1	NA	6.7
Vizcaya	5.5	21.1	22.6	24.1	18.3
Overall average	4.3	18.9	19.0	26.2	15.9

Source: Robert P. Clark, "Recent Voting Trends in Spain's Basque Provinces," *Iberian Studies* 9, no. 2 (Autumn 1980); Robert P. Clark, "Basque Socialism at the Polls: An Analysis of Four Post-Franco Elections," Conference on European Studies, Washington, D.C., October 1980; Ramiro Cibrian, "El sistema electoral y de partidos en Euzkadi," *Papers: Revista de sociología* 14 (1980):71–79.

vote totals are about average in Vizcaya; the more conservative and less-ethnically Basque Alava and Navarra give rather fewer votes to ethnic socialism.

As we have done in earlier analyses, let us move our focus to the administrative subdivision or voting district. When the electoral data from the four post-Franco elections are arranged according to voting district (table 8.8, map 8.3), the pattern is quite unmistakable, even though the correlations are not quite as neat as we have seen in other instances. The four districts in Guipúzcoa and three districts in Vizcaya (Bilbao, Durango, and Guernica) are all above average in their support for Basque socialism. On the other hand, the remaining district in Vizcaya, Valmaseda, and the provinces of Alava and Navarra are all below average in their support.

Let us move to the same sort of township or municipio analysis developed earlier in this chapter. The objective of this analysis is to separate out the townships that have shown the strongest support for the Basque Left consistently over the four elections. To do this, I have calculated the difference between each township's votes for the Basque socialist parties and the share of the vote won by these parties in the region as a whole. This enabled me to classify the 58 municipios according to the number of times each had cast a percentage of its votes for EE/HB that was higher than the Basque socialist average. Those that voted above the four-province average (or three, in the case of 1980) on all four occasions have been designated as "strongly in favor" of the Basque Left; those that cast votes above the average three out of four times were classified as "moderately in favor." Those that voted above the average only twice were classified as "neutral"; and those that voted above average once, "moderately opposed." Those that never voted above the average in any election were listed as "strongly opposed." (Three municipios were unclassifiable because of insufficient data.)

The results of these calculations are contained in table 8.9 and map 8.3. The "strongly favor" category contains 16 townships; the "moderately favor" category, 13. The remaining municipios are distributed as follows: "neutral," 9; "moderately opposed," 8; "strongly

Table 8.8 *Vote for Basque Socialist Parties in Four*
Post-Franco Elections, 1977–80, by Administrative Subdivision
(percentages of total vote)

SUBDIVISION	1977 SPANISH PARLIA- MENTARY	1979 SPANISH PARLIA- MENTARY	1979 MUNICIPAL GOVERN- MENTAL	1980 BASQUE PARLIA- MENTARY	AVERAGE PERCENT- AGE
Amurrio (A)	2.0	16.7	23.5	21.8	16.0
Vitoria (A)	2.1	13.8	12.5	28.8	14.3
Azpeitia (G)	10.1	27.7	21.7	26.9	21.6
San Sebastián (G)	10.2	31.2	31.4	32.1	26.2
Tolosa (G)	12.1	34.9	23.8	36.2	26.8
Vergara (G)	6.1	31.2	24.9	27.2	22.4
Estella (N)	0.0	4.4	0.0	NA	1.5
Pamplona (N)	0.0	13.1	22.9	NA	12.0
Sanguesa-Aoiz (N)	0.0	6.2	0.0	NA	2.1
Tafalla-Olite (N)	0.0	4.8	0.0	NA	1.6
Tudela (N)	0.0	2.3	0.0	NA	0.8
Bilbao (V)	4.7	18.4	22.7	22.6	17.1
Durango (V)	4.5	24.4	20.1	23.9	18.2
Guernica (V)	5.1	28.4	21.5	27.6	20.6
Valmaseda (V)	2.1	13.8	12.5	28.8	14.3

Source: Robert P. Clark, "Basque Socialism at the Polls: An Analysis of Four Post-Franco Elections," Conference on European Studies, Washington, D.C., October 1980.

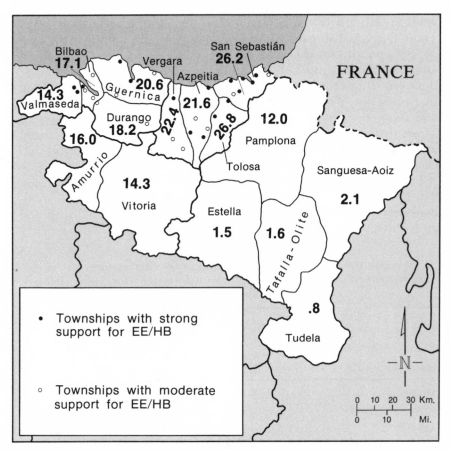

Map 8.3.   Distribution of Basque Socialist Vote by Township and Administrative Subdivision. Figures within each subdivision indicate mean share of vote given to the two Basque socialist coalitions in the four post-Franco elections. (In Navarra, the one exception, only three elections were held.)

opposed," 9. The province of each municipio is identified by the letter in parenthesis following each town or city name.

The 29 townships where Basque socialism is strongly or moderately supported fall into a pattern that by now should be familiar. They are all in either Guipúzcoa (17 townships) or Vizcaya (12), and the majority of them (all but 7) fall into one of the administrative subdivisions where ETA conducts most of its insurgent activity and recruits most of its members. It is hardly possible that this sort of pattern in the distribution of three related variables could be random. We are clearly seeing something significant in explaining the ETA phenomenon.

Table 8.9 *Support for Basque Socialist Parties in Four Post-Franco Elections, 1977–80, by Municipio*

CATEGORY OF SUPPORT	MUNICIPIOS			
Strongly favor	Andoain	(G)	Rentería	(G)
(above agerage in	Beasain	(G)	San Sebastián	(G)
4 elections)	Tolosa	(G)	Zarauz	(G)
	Elgóibar	(G)	Abanto	(V)
	Legazpia	(G)	Santurce-Antigua	(V)
	Hernani	(G)	San Salvador	(V)
	Oyarzún	(G)	Bermeo	(V)
	Pasajes	(G)	Guernica	(V)
Moderately favor	Villafranca	(G)	Lequeitio	(V)
(above average in	Mondragón	(G)	Lejona	(V)
3 elections)	Oñate	(G)	Amorebieta	(V)
	Zumárraga	(G)	Arrigorriaga	(V)
	Irún	(G)	Basauri	(V)
	Urnieta	(G)	Elorrio	(V)
	Santurce	(V)		
Neutral	Eibar	(G)	Portugalete	(V)
(above average in	Azcoitia	(G)	Guecho	(V)
2 elections)	Azpeitia	(G)	Ondárroa	(V)
	Zumaya	(G)	Galdácano	(V)
	Baracaldo	(V)		
Moderately opposed	Amurrio	(A)	Ansoain	(N)
(above average in	Llodio	(A)	Sestao	(V)
1 election)	Alsásua	(N)	Durango	(V)
	Pamplona	(N)	Bilbao	(V)
Strongly opposed	Vitoria	(A)	Tafalla	(N)
(above average in	Baztán	(N)	Tudela	(N)
no election)	Cizur	(N)	Valmaseda	(V)
	Burlada	(N)	Ermúa	(V)
	Estella	(N)		
Insufficient data	Vergara	(G)		
	Fuenterrabía	(G)		
	Munguía	(V)		

Source: Robert P. Clark, "Basque Socialism at the Polls: An Analysis of Four Post-Franco Elections," Conference on European Studies, Washington, D.C., October 1980.

Note: The four post-Franco elections were those of 1977 and 1979 for the Spanish parliament, the 1979 municipal elections, and the 1980 election for the Basque parliament. The degree of support was judged by the number of times the vote for EE/HB in each of 58 municipios was above the EE/HB average for the region as a whole.

The Geography of ETA: The Goierri

I am convinced that this concentration of etarras and their support-ers in Guipúzcoa province is not an accident either of history or of geography. The explanation for it lies in the very special social and economic character of this region. To understand better exactly what forces are working to produce such a fertile pro-ETA environment, let us look more closely at one specific area of Guipúzcoa, a region in the southern part of the province known as the Goierri.[6]

The Goierri has been mentioned by several authors as having spe-cial importance in the history of ETA. José María Portell reports that the Goierri region supplied more members to ETA than any other region in the Basque country.[7] And José Mari Garmendia, in his two-volume study of ETA, writes that after the Burgos trial and the split between ETA-V and ETA-VI, the principal source of members and of popular support for ETA was the Goierri.[8] This development, notes Garmendia, represented a major shift in support of the organization away from the intellectuals and middle class professionals of the larg-er cities like Bilbao and San Sebastián and toward the factory workers, small shop owners, and office workers of the part of Guipúzcoa where Basque language and ethnicity survive and flourish.

What are the principal characteristics of the Goierri that it should produce such an environment of support for Basque insurgency? Let us begin with the geography and terrain of the region. Map 8.4 nar-rows our focus so that we can examine it in greater detail. The Goierri is dominated by a series of mountain chains and ridges that divide it into three narrow valleys oriented roughly north-south. Each valley possesses its own river system, all flowing north and emptying into the Bay of Biscay. From west to east, these three rivers are, respective-ly, the Deva, whose valley contains the towns of Mondragón, Vergara, and Elgóibar; the Urola, where the towns of Legazpia, Zumárraga, Azpeitia, and Azcoitia are situated; and the Oria, on whose banks are located the towns of Beasain, Villafranca de Ordizia, and Tolosa. The lines of transportation and communication follow these rivers and valleys generally north and south, with the exceptions of the Tolosa-Elgóibar road, passing through Azpeitia and Azcoitia, and the road that connects Beasain with Vergara and Eibar.[9] To the south and east of this region the mountains rise to from 1,300 to 1,500 meters, the highest being Txindoki and Aitzgorri. Nearby to the southeast, in Navarra, lies the Sierra de Aralar range, a chain of mountains of be-tween 1,000 and 1,300 meters height which has for centuries held almost mystical significance for Basques as the geographical center of their nation. These natural borders have for hundreds of years sepa-

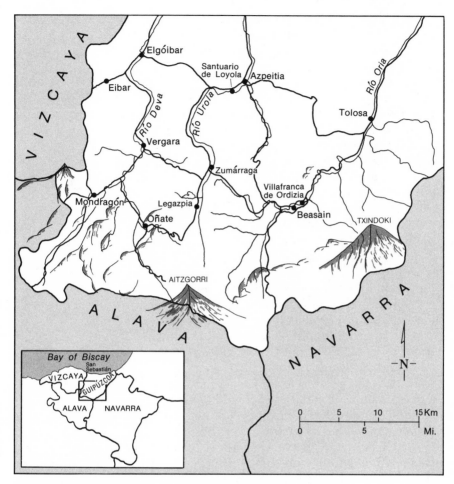

Map 8.4   The Goierri Region of Guipúzcoa Province.

rated this region of the Basque country from its neighbors, and shel-
tered its language and culture from the influence of immigrants, few of
whom ever settled there. Within the region, the mountains rise to only
600 to 1,000 meters, still sufficient to cut the area into numerous tiny
villages and mid-sized towns, the largest of which, Mondragón, has
only about 25,000 inhabitants. Since there are no fixed boundaries to
the region, and indeed, the region does not even exist as a specific
geographic place, it is somewhat arbitrary to establish its area and
population, but I would estimate that the Goierri covers about 1,000 of
Guipuzcoa's 2,000 square kilometers, and contains about 250,000 of
the province's 700,000 inhabitants. Since the industrial boom in the

area in the 1950s, the population has grown at the rate of about 3 percent annually, doubling about once each generation. The results of this demographic explosion have been disastrous for the quality of life of the region.

Industry came relatively late to the Goierri. It is true that there were some modest industrial beginnings during the last half of the nineteenth century, particularly in fields involving the transformation of metal products, such as the manufacture of weapons, sewing machines, and bicycles.[10] Nevertheless, the really heavy industrial development of the area came almost entirely in the 1950s, and particularly after the Spanish government began to stimulate economic growth through the investment and planning policies implemented in the late 1950s and early 1960s. Where there were half a dozen machine-tool factories in all of Guipúzcoa in 1940, by 1960 that number had risen to 111, most of them in the Goierri region.[11] Led by the Goierri-based manufacturing enterprises, Guipúzcoa has traditionally been the leading Spanish province in terms of metallurgical processing and light metal-goods manufacturing. Nearly one-fifth of the entire economic product of Guipúzcoa and more than one-third of the province's industrial product are derived from these industries.

Industrialization in the Goierri is distinguished by three important characteristics. First, the Goierri does not contain the iron and steel mills and shipyards of the Bilbao area. Its industry is concentrated instead in the manufacture of relatively small items that require the transformation of metal: weapons, home appliances such as sewing machines and refrigerators, bicycles, and machine tools. Second, to a degree not seen elsewhere in the Basque country, industry in the Goierri is situated in the very midst of traditional Basque culture, language, and life. Whereas in Bilbao, the city's heavy industry is staffed by mostly immigrant workers who live in massive working class suburbs with dense populations, in the Goierri, the factories or assembly shops are small enough to be located close to the small towns and villages that dot the area. There are few if any working class suburbs populated solely by non-Basque workers, since immigrants have generally not been attracted to industry in the Goierri. Thus an unusual combination of geography, industrial development, and culture has produced what may be a unique mixture of the economic aspects of industrial capitalism and the ethnic and cultural aspects of preindustrial society. Finally, industrialization in the Goierri has proceeded so fast and with so little planning that it has brought substantial dislocation and stress to what had been a fairly placid and tranquil region. The unleashed forces of industrial development seem to have condemned the residents of the Goierri to face most of the unrelieved ills of industrialization: air and water pollution, inadequate social services for an exploding population, deterioration of housing and social infrastructure, scant "green space" for parks and recreation, and others. José Miguel de Azaola was referring to the city of Eibar, but he could have been writing about any of a dozen similar towns in the Goierri when he wrote, "It is difficult to imagine a more atrocious promiscuity of factories and housing than that offered by the extremely narrow, humid, and dark corridor where this town has grown up against all logic and against the standards of hygiene, comfort, esthetics, urbanism, and simple common sense."[12]

I have already remarked on the central feature of society in the Goierri: the persistence of the Basque language and culture in contrast to their marked deterioration elsewhere in the Basque region. The family homestead, the caserío, is still an important socioeconomic unit in most of the Goierri, and Euskera is still the dominant language (see table 8.10 and map 8.5). In the administrative district of Tolosa, nearly two-thirds of all inhabitants still speak Euskera; in Vergara, the figure is more nearly half; but in Azpeitia, it exceeds four-fifths. In the

Table 8.10 *Relation of Indicators of ETA and Use of the Basque Language, by Administrative Subdivision*

SUBDIVISION	ETA VICTIMS PER 1,000	ETA MEMBERS PER 1,000	AVERAGE (%) EE/HB VOTE	% OF POPULATION SPEAKING BASQUE[a]
Azpeitia (G)	0.53	0.35	21.6	83.9
San Sebastián (G)	0.33	0.16	26.2	27.6
Tolosa (G)	0.34	0.45	26.8	64.5
Vergara (G)	0.27	0.22	22.4	49.5
Durango (V)	0.21	0.18	18.2	27.5
Guernica (V)	0.31	0.26	20.6	55.9
Amurrio (A)	0.08	0.00	16.0	1.0>
Vitoria (A)	0.15	0.04	14.3	1.0>
Estella (N)	0.00	0.02	1.5	1.0>
Pamplona (N)	0.09	0.05	12.0	14.0
Sanguesa-Aoiz (N)	0.00	0.00	2.1	3.9
Tafalla-Olite (N)	0.00	0.00	1.6	1.0>
Tudela (N)	0.00	0.00	0.8	1.0>
Bilbao (V)	0.08	0.09	17.1	1.0>
Valmaseda (V)	0.06	0.05	14.3	1.0>

[a] Robert P. Clark, "Language and Politics in Spain's Basque Provinces," *West European Politics* 4, no. 1 (January 1981), table 5.

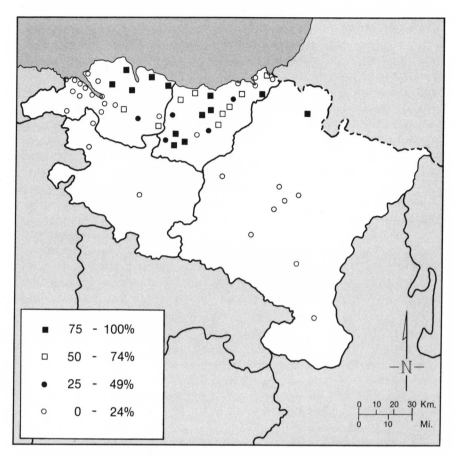

Map 8.5.   Distribution of Euskera-Speaking Population. (Townships larger than 5,000 persons.)

larger towns like Mondragón or Elgóibar, the proportion of Basque-speaking residents may drop to about half; but in small towns like Ataun (the birthplace of Miguel Angel Apalategui), the figure rises to nearly nine-tenths.

The confluence of all these forces has produced an unusual blend of traditional and modern in the lives of its residents. The dispersal of industries throughout the region and the closeness of factories and offices to the small farming communities and the caseríos means that young men and women can join a modern industrial work force or be employed in a managerial or administrative office and never leave their traditional surroundings. Throughout the Goierri, the predominant life style of young people of the last two decades has been to work in a small factory or in an administrative office while continuing to live in the traditional caserío where Euskera is still the prevailing language.[13] During the day, these young people live the life of the modern Spaniard, on the assembly line or in an office of a government agency or of a private concern in business or banking. At night, they return to their caserío to work with the crops and animals, to speak Euskera, to join the community of their friends at church or in a neighborhood tavern. Consider, for example, two of the best known etarras to come from the Goierri. Miguel Angel Apalategui, though born and reared in a caserío in tiny Ataun (2,119 population in 1975), worked in a factory in another town only 10 kilometers away, and continued to live at home and help with the work of the caserío until he was forced to flee into exile in 1974.[14] Angel Otaegi was born and grew up in the tiny village of Nuarbe, a cluster of twenty-two caseríos only 7 kilometers from Azpeitia, where Otaegi worked as a young man.[15] According to a member of Apalategui's family, in their neighborhood of San Gregorio, with a population of from 500 to 600, there have been at a single time as many as 11 etarras living in exile in France. It would seem reasonable, then, to estimate that Apalategui's neighborhood could have produced as many as 20 or 30 members of ETA over a two-decade period, a ratio of somewhere between 40 and 50 per thousand. If we were to multiply these cases by several dozen towns just like Ataun or Nuarbe, we would have some sense of the real impact of the Goierri culture on ETA's membership.

I am arguing, then, that to a significant degree, ETA is a product of a highly unusual socioeconomic environment, a blend of industrial production and premodern Basque ethnicity and language. The outcome is a life style, a set of pressing social and economic needs, and a configuration of political forces that create a fertile field within which ETA can recruit. The roots of ETA run deep into the Golierri and its caseríos, villages, and small cities. As we have already seen, ETA tends to concentrate its attacks in this region. It is also the zone in which ETA's members are most densely concentrated and where radical Basque socialist parties enjoy their heaviest voting strength. In my judgment, the coincidence of these three clusters of data (ETA attacks, member origins, and popular support) reflects a pattern that is not accidental. It is a product of the Goierri.[16]

CHAPTER NINE

ETA's Institutional Imperatives: Organization and Operations

All complex organizations, whether they are conventional and operate within the law or clandestine and aim at the overthrow of the political system, face certain common tasks to maintain themselves in good functioning order. These tasks are the institutional imperatives of the organization. This chapter describes how Ezukadi ta Askatasuna has performed those tasks, and how it has met its own special institutional imperatives.*

The functional requirements of an organization can be reduced to several broad categories. The organization must create institutional structures, or patterns of behavior, that ensure that crucial tasks will be performed. The foremost task facing a clandestine organization is the recruitment, training, and deployment of its members in such a way as to retain control over their actions without jeopardizing their security or the fate of their missions. The organization must also acquire badly needed resources, including weapons, money, vehicles, shelter, and intelligence information. Finally, the organization's leaders must channel or route information to ensure that operations are carried out in an effective and timely manner and in a way consistent with policy directives. This network of communications is usually referred to as a command and control system.

Organization

Until 1966 or 1967, to the extent that ETA leaders thought much at all about structure, it was mostly in terms of greater specialization and differentiation of the command and policy-making mechanisms that

---

*This description is based on information about ETA operations through the 1970s and 1980. While there will inevitably be changes in the organization through the 1980s, the description remains valid in broad outline.

governed the organization. Since there were relatively few members in those days and most of the key members had fled into exile in France, complicated hierarchical arrangements seemed unnecessary.

The first concrete step taken toward establishing more effective central control over the organization came in 1962 with the creation of the first Executive Committee. The committee was established in France to enable the organization to maintain contact with the remaining operating units, those that had escaped detection after the train derailment episode a year earlier. Of the pioneers on the Executive Committee, incidentally, none remained in power for more than several years, indicating how difficult it is for an insurgent movement to maintain continuity in leadership.[1] At the same time that the Executive Committee was established, ETA also created a fairly simple functional structure based on the idea of the four "fronts," operating units responsible for political, economic, military, and cultural affairs.

A few months later, in May 1962, ETA held its First Assembly, which was in itself an attempt to establish some more general legislative authority with which to hold the organization together. The assembly was given power to set general policy directions, with the understanding that the Executive Committee would actually run the organization on a daily basis. The First Assembly expanded and refined the functional command structure, replacing the four fronts with five "branches" responsible for internal publications and communications, cells and study groups, mass propaganda, legal actions (mass organizing), and military actions.

The basic structure of five branches was given an expanded infrastructure at the Second Assembly, held in March 1963. For the first time, ETA created a geographically based organization on the Spanish side of the border. The leadership at the Second Assembly rejected an organizational structure based on the existing provinces in the belief that it would not reflect the distribution of geopolitical forces in the Basque country, but they also wanted to avoid basing their new organization at the village level, which, they felt, would make it too parochial and insulated. The compromise was to create six *herrialdes*, or "popular zones," which would become the basis for a presumed future guerrilla activity. Three of these zones corresponded to the French Basque provinces as a unit and the provinces of Alava and Navarra. One herrialde covered the eastern part of Guipúzcoa, from about Tolosa east to the French-Spanish border. The fourth zone covered the eastern part of Vizcaya, from about Durango east, and the western and central parts of Guipúzcoa (the Deva River valley, and the towns of Vergara, Mondragón, Oñate, among others). The sixth zone encompassed the rest of Vizcaya province, primarily the city of

Bilbao and its suburbs. Each herrialde had an organization led by a regional chief who was given the title of *buruzagi*, or "head man." The buruzagis were given permission to carry firearms on a daily basis, but they were not yet completely committed to service to ETA. They were still only part-time members of the organization.

This situation was to change fundamentally between the autumn of 1963 and the spring of 1964. As a result of the wave of arrests and deportations that took place in September and October of 1963, ETA's organizational structure within Spain was practically demolished. In response, ETA created its first cadre of full-time local leaders who were known in the jargon as *liberados*, meaning that they had been freed from having to earn a living in conventional jobs and could dedicate themselves entirely to the tasks of insurgency. Each herrialde was to be put under the control of a liberado, although it was some time before there were actually enough full-time leaders in Spain to make it possible to afford this kind of structure.

The decision to create liberados and to put them in charge of the six herrialdes was an extraordinary step taken by the Executive Committee in exile in the midst of an emergency. The decision was ratified and refined at the Third Assembly, held in April and May 1964. To support the activities of the liberados, the assembly decided also to establish what were called Parallel Support Organizations (Organizaciones Paralelas de Apoyo, or OPA), whose assignment it was to provide ETA members with logistical support, shelter, money, or transportation whenever they needed assistance.

In October 1964, the French government detained several key ETA leaders, including members of the Executive Committee, and prohibited their residence in French provinces adjoining the Spanish border. Several were deported to Belgium. The effect was to cut off the exiled leaders from the herrialdes and the liberados on the Spanish side of the border. This separation from the exiled leaders strengthened the autonomy of the various zone organizations, who were forced to rely on their own initiative and ability to acquire such resources as money or weapons.

The next major change in ETA's structure resulted from the decisions of the Fourth Assembly, held in the summer of 1965. The existing branch structure was replaced by the Political Office, an Information Branch, an OPA Branch (charged with maintaining the support organizations), and an "Activism" Branch (a euphemism for military branch). This structure was in place for a year and a half, but its effectiveness was diminished seriously by the ideological and political struggles in ETA during that period. As we have seen, the Political Office was the focal point for these battles, and as a consequence the organization was hardly able or had the time to attend to external matters for most of 1965 and 1966.

After the failure of the Aberri Eguna celebration in spring 1966, ETA suffered the first major defection of a local operating *comando* when the leader of the military branch, Francisco Javier Zumalde ("El Cabra") resigned and led his force of about thirty into the mountains to conduct guerrilla operations. Although this group managed to escape detection and capture until 1968, they were not a significant factor in ETA's development. Nevertheless, they were a clear signal to ETA's leaders of what could happen if the organization let its subordinate units get out of control.

The Fifth Assembly of ETA, held in two phases—in December 1966 and in March 1967—was a turning point in the organization's history for both ideological and political reasons, as well as for the structural decisions that were made by the assembly.[2] At this meeting, the organizational structure of ETA became rather more complex and specialized, with several agencies and layers of authority added to increase the effectiveness of the organization. In itself, this series of steps revealed that the membership of ETA was growing, a development that required changes in organization.

After the Fifth Assembly, ETA's supreme policy-making group was called the National Assembly (in Euskera, *Biltzar Nagusia*). It was to meet at least once a year to give general policy direction to the organization, although it would not meet again after the Fifth Assembly for some three years. The criteria for eligibility to attend the assembly were always somewhat vague, although those in attendance always included the principal officers of the organization (those in the Executive Committee and the heads of the various branches), the chiefs of the regional or zone offices (the herrialde), and the heads of the subunits that made up the herrialdes. On the average, there were between forty and fifty top leaders of ETA at the assembly meetings.

Below the National Assembly, power was split between two working executive committees and two relatively independent chains of command, one in Spain and the other in exile. On the Spanish side of the border, daily operations of the organization were placed in the hands a new body called the Tactical Executive Committee (KET), a body charged with overseeing the activities of all the liberados and all the heads of the zone organizations, now referred to as herrialdeburus. The head of each herrialde was responsible for organizing within his zone the operations of ETA in each of the four fronts, political, economic, cultural, and military. Each herrialde was divided into subunits called *mesa de zona*, and each *zona* was further subdivided into units that encompassed only a single village or cluster of villages,

called *mesas de pueblo*. At the base of the organization were established three-man cells called *irurkos*, a word derived from the Basque
word for three, *iru*. The irurko was the forerunner of the cell or comando that came to be the operating core of the organization after its
revival in 1971.

ETA's leadership in exile, primarily in France, attempted to set up a
parallel chain of command north of the border, but it quickly fell into
disuse. The counterpart to the Tactical Executive Committee was the
so-called Small Assembly (in Euskera, the Biltzar Txikia), which was
intended to oversee and monitor the operations of the committee, and
if necessary, convene the National Assembly to set new guidelines for
operations. There were also set up two other exile organizations, one
in charge of ideological and political matters (similar to the ill-fated
Political Office), and the other the High Strategic Command (Alto
Mando Estratégico), a group apparently intended to oversee armed
operations but which never really functioned. The events of the summer of 1968 and the resulting police repression and Burgos Trial
intervened at this point to virtually wreck the organization. When it
emerged into prominence again, after 1971, it was with an entirely
new set of operating structures and mostly new leadership. We therefore do not really know whether an organizational structure like the
old one, divided into an operating wing in Spain with real power and
an exile wing in France with mainly symbolic power, could provide
effective leadership to the organization. What we do know is that
through early 1968, when it became clear that the KET could not
function effectively if it had to answer to the Biltzar Txikia for its
actions, the committee began to substitute its members for the exiles
on the BT. By the summer of 1968, that process had been completed
and the membership of the two bodies was identical, whereupon the
KET ceased to exist and the BT operated on Spanish soil exclusively.

Between 1968 and 1975, ETA went through a period of great turmoil and upheaval and its organizational structure underwent
wrenching changes. The violence and police suppression of 1968 and
1969, the Burgos Trial, and the split between ETA-V and ETA-VI
virtually destroyed the organization. The new generation of leaders,
headed by Eustaquio Mendizábal, provided a bridge to the 1970s, but
Mendizábal's death in 1973 once again threw the organization into
disorder. The splits following the Carrero Blanco assassination in
1973 and the Café Rolando bombing in 1974 also contributed to its
weakening. Finally, ETA had great difficulty adjusting to the new
climate of Spanish democracy after 1975. On the one side, the Berezi
Comandos, the Comandos Autónomos, and ETA(m) advocated increased armed action, and on the other, the followers of Pertur within

ETA(p-m) looked for ways to build a legal Basque socialist party to contest elections and build mass support.

As ETA(m) developed during the late 1970s and into the 1980s, its organizational structure was a blend of the small secret cell operating at the local level and a single operating directorate in France.[3] The middle ranks of the hierarchy, the herrialdes and the mesas del pueblo, no longer performed major roles in the organization, but the local cell, the comando, and the directorate in exile remained central features of ETA.

The small cell has been important as an operating unit of ETA from the time of the organization's founding in 1959. In fact, the roots of ETA as an organization can be traced to similar cellular organizations that existed in the Basque country as long ago as the 1920s. In those early days, mountain climbing clubs, called *mendigoitzales*, helped keep alive a spark of resistance during the dictatorship of Primo de Rivera. After the Spanish Civil War and especially after World War II, the Basque underground depended greatly on the strength and integrity of the cell structure spread throughout the four Spanish provinces and into France. After 1952, in the Ekin period of the organization's history, the five-person cell was practically the only organizational structure to develop.

At the base of ETA(m), the most significant organizational structure is the cell or comando, composed of three to five men (and occasionally, a woman). Each comando is assigned a small area of operations covering a single town or at most several towns near one another. The members of the comando all come from neighboring towns or villages. They usually live and work in their home towns, where they are well known by large numbers of townspeople. Generally, they continue to live at home with their parents and brothers and sisters, although if they are married, they may have started a home of their own with wife and children. Each comando is known by a code name, usually in Basque, and generally taken either from the names of other ETA members who have been killed or captured or from place names like those of rivers or mountains. As is customary in clandestine organizations, the members of the comando work in complete secrecy and are completely cut off from the rest of the organization. At most, they will know the names of one or two other etarras from whom they receive messages transmitted by the leaders of the organization. It is doubtful that anyone knows how many operating cells there are at any given moment in the Basque provinces, but arrest records give us some clue. From September 1 to December 25, 1978, police claimed to have arrested the members of 46 ETA cells, of which 30 belonged to ETA(m), 6 to ETA(p-m), 7 to the Comandos Autónomos, and 3 to other (or unknown) organizations. Even after this, however, police estimated that there were still about 140 cells operating in the region. As of March 1981, it was estimated by the Spanish news magazine *Cambio 16* that police had broken up more than 400 comandos of ETA in the preceding three years without impairing the organization's effectiveness. This fact suggests that at any given time there are between 100 and 200 cells of 3 to 5 members each operating on the Spanish side of the border, which would mean an active membership of between 300 and 1,000 etarras at that time. This general range corresponds fairly well to the estimates on membership that I discuss below.

Contemporary press reports in the Basque country carry articles almost every day on the arrest or trial of members of an ETA comando. For a sense of how one such comando was organized, equipped, and managed, let us consider a specific example, understanding that, within limits, there are one to two hundred similar cells operating throughout the Basque country all the time. On November 7, 1980, police arrested five young men in Mondragón (Guipúzcoa) and charged them with belonging to an ETA comando named Besaide (apparently for a mountain near Mondragón on the Giupúzcoa-Vizcaya border).[4] The five included a 29-year-old carpenter from Mondragón, a 27-year-old construction worker from Oñate, a 23-year-old skilled laborer (exact field not recorded) from Mondragón, a 28-year-old industrial machinist from Mondragón, and a 28-year-old office worker from Mondragón. All but one were living in the towns of their birth, and the fifth was living in Vergara, only 9 kilometers from his birthplace of Mondragón. Two of the five were married. The group was accused of (and apparently confessed to) committing four separate armed attacks which left two Guardia Civil dead and one wounded and two civilians dead. Three of the four attacks were made in the towns of residence of the comando members (two in Oñate and one in Vergara), and the fourth was carried out in Anzuola, only about 4 kilometers from Vergara. The attacks were spread out over more than three years, with the first coming in March 1977, the second in January 1979, the third in February 1980, and the fourth in July 1980. The news account does not record what the comando did between attacks, but presumably it was not active. In addition to capturing the five members of the comando, police found a weapons cache (called in ETA parlance a *zulo*) containing one British-made Sten Mark II submachine gun (for some reason, always referred to in the Spanish press as "Stein" guns), four 9 mm pistols of the Colt 1911A1 or Browning HP 35 variety (three of which were in all probability manufactured in factories no more than 20 to 30 kilometers from the place where they were used), two revolvers (a .38 special and a .357 Magnum), large quantities of ammunition for all these firearms, four hand grenades, 12 kilograms of Goma-2 explosive, electric detonators, wigs, dark glasses, and materials for making bombs, including cables and batteries.

As we have seen there are several membership roles within ETA at the comando level. In late 1963, ETA's leaders created the class of member known as the liberado, and known increasingly during the 1970s and 1980 as *ilegales*. Liberados are well known to the police and have a police record (they are referred to in ETA jargon as *fichados*, meaning they have a *ficha* or card on file in local police headquarters that identifies them as etarras). Since they cannot move freely because of their known ETA connections, the organization makes the most of their condition by paying them a modest salary and thereby freeing them from the need to earn a living. The liberados are usually the ones who participate in armed actions, including bank robberies, bombings, kidnapings, and shootings.

A second category of ETA member is called the *legal*, which means that the member is not known to the police and can continue to work at his or her job. The legales are further divided into several subcategories, depending on what kind of service they perform. Legales provide much of the intelligence and communication for the organization. One subcategory of legal is called *enlace*, or link. The enlace is usually employed as a courier for information too bulky, too urgent, or too sensitive to convey through conventional means such as telephone or the mails. Another specialized subcategory is called *buzón* (literally, "the mailbox"), whose task it is to serve as the drop point for messages, weapons, and other items that pass through ETA's command and control network. A third kind of task is performed by the *informativo*, a member who gathers information about future targets of ETA operations such as banks, factories, or persons who have been marked for assassination.

A third category of membership is called the *apoyo* (literally "support"). The apoyos are members who supply food, shelter, clothing, transportation, false documentation, and other logistical support to the liberados when they are on an operation or fleeing from the police. Many apoyos may in fact not be members of the organization at all but simply providing shelter for friends of their sons or daughters. Others may be the owners and residents of apartments or houses where ETA has constructed elaborate hiding places behind false walls or in staircases where their members can evade pursuers. (This is apparently an old tradition going at least as far back as the Spanish Civil War and perhaps even farther.)

When we look at arrest records for an indication of how these various functions in ETA are distributed among its members (table 9.1), we find, first, that a majority of those arrested were liberados engaged in direct action or armed attacks for ETA(m). A relatively small percentage of those arrested were part of the information and support network of the organization, but these data almost certainly understate the true importance of the legales. At least one press report has indicated that there were as many support comandos or cells as there were liberados, and that the former played a crucial role in supporting the armed attacks of the latter.[5] In all probability, fewer legales are arrested because they are unknown to the police and their work exposes them to less danger.

Table 9.1   *Division of ETA Membership by Function*
(based on arrest records; N=214)

FUNCTION	PERCENTAGE
Liberado; armed operations	56.5
Buzón; enlace	5.1
Informativo	18.7
Unknown	19.6

Source: Press reports of arrests of ETA members from January 1, 1979, through June 30, 1980. Calculations by author.

If the comando is the operating arm of ETA, the head or directorate of the organization is a body of about thirty-five to forty men who live in various places (their exact whereabouts are a carefully guarded secret) on the French side of the border.[6] At the head of the organization is an Executive Committee composed of seven men (see figure 9.1).[7] In 1980, the leader of ETA(m) and of the Executive Committee was Domingo Iturbe Abasolo "Txomin." Born in Mondragón in 1944, Iturbe left his job as a factory worker in 1968 to join ETA as a liberado in France, and continued to be a major figure in the organization. He was believed by police to have been involved in the assassination of Prime Minister Carrero Blanco and in the Cafe Rolando bombing as well as in the kidnaping of Eugen Beihl. He was accused of taking direct part in six kidnapings, fourteen bank robberies, and twenty killings. He exercised complete control over the organization by holding a monopoly of its weapons and money. Iturbe was one of Europe's most wanted fugitives, and was hunted not only by Spanish and French police but also by the secret right-wing assassination squads that operate in southern France. He was protected by four well-armed bodyguards, and changed his residence and automobile about once a

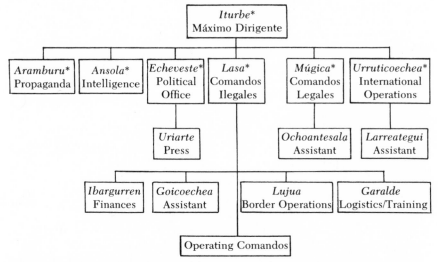

Figure 9.1. Organization Table of ETA (militar) Directorate as of February 1981.
Sources: "Todos contra ETA," *Cambio 16*, no. 487 (March 30, 1981); "Así es la organización interna de ETA(m) y sus dirigentes," *Deia*, May 5, 1981.
*Members of Executive Committee.

week. He was shot (for the third time) in May 1979 by a rightist assassination team in Biarritiz, France, and again in February 1980 by three French policemen dressed in civilian clothes.[8]

Iturbe's second in command was Juan Lorenzo Santiago Lasa Michelena "Txiquierdi," born in Rentería (Guipúzcoa) in 1955. Lasa was regarded as one of the *duros* of ETA. He joined ETA(m) after he had split off from ETA(p-m) when the Comandos Berezi left it in 1977. Police alleged that he had been through terrorist training in Algeria, Libya, and South Yemen. He was accused of having killed seven police or Guardia Civil, the mayor of Oyarzún, a Spanish army general and lieutenant colonel, and a Spanish supreme court judge. Within ETA, he was in command of the so-called *comandos ilegales*, sometimes called the *comandos especiales*. These were the operating comandos staffed with etarras known to the police and responsible for carrying out the more difficult armed assaults ordered by the organization.

In addition to being in direct command of the operating comandos of ETA, Lasa had several assistants responsible for specific aspects of the organization's operations. Carlos Ibargurren Aguirre "Nervios" was born in 1940 in Guipúzcoa, and up to the end of 1978 had been accused of killing several members of the Guardia Civil and of participating in several bank robberies. At that time, he was elevated to an executive position within ETA, first in the area of international operations, and then as the organization's finance officer, a position he held in 1981. Miguel Antonio Goicoechea Elorriaga "Txapela" was Lasa's chief assistant in managing the comandos especiales. He was born in Baracaldo in 1957. In 1976 he received training in Algeria, and later killed a police sergeant and wounded three others, killed two Guardia Civil troopers in San Sebastián, and shot to death two policemen in a San Sebastián bar. Miguel Lujua Gorostiola "Mikel" was Lasa's chief assistant in charge of moving etarras and their weapons across the Spanish-French border. He was born in Bilbao in 1947 and joined ETA in 1966. He took part in several bank robberies and bombings as well as the Zabala kidnaping. He was one of the key persons in the organization in the acquisition and movement of weapons and explosives. Finally, Isidro María Garalde Bedialauneta "Mamarru" was responsible for logistical support (especially weapons) and training for the operating comandos. He was born in Ondárroa (Vizcaya) in 1951. He was accused of participating in a number of kidnapings and robberies. His responsibilities included supplying members of the comandos with weapons and explosives and training them in their use.

The third member of the Executive Committee was Eugenio Echeveste Aranguren "Antxon," the etarra responsible for the operations of the Political Office. Born in Pasajes de San Juan (Guipúzcoa) in 1951, Echeveste joined ETA(p-m) in 1976, and went over to ETA(m) with Lasa Michelena in 1977. After the death of Argala in December 1978, Echeveste was placed in charge of the organization's political operations. In this role he was responsible for the ideological training of new members and for ensuring that the armed operations of ETA followed a correct ideological line. In this position, then, he was the person chiefly responsible for deciding who would be assassinated and when. Echeveste had an assistant named Eloy Uriarte who handled the press relations of the organization.

The information-gathering and intelligence functions of ETA(m) were performed by José Luís Ansola Larrañaga "Pello el viejo," another native of Guipúzcoa, born in 1936. He had a long history of participation in armed attacks and was responsible for some dozen victims, including the mayor of Galdácano. His responsibilities included the creation and supervision of comandos de información on the Spanish side of the border and the analysis of such information before the planning of specific attacks. He also functioned as a sort of general administrator of the directorate and was responsible for its support and infrastructure.

The fifth member of the Executive Committee was ETA's chief of propaganda, Juan Ramón Aramburu Garmendia "Juanra." Aramburu was born in Villafranca de Ordizia in 1953, and joined ETA in 1972. For some years, he was part of a *comando legal* operating in Beasain and allegedly carried out numerous robberies and armed assaults. It was his responsibility to explain ETA's armed attacks to the general population of the Basque country, and to disseminate propaganda throughout the area. He also conducted classes in ideology for etarras in the operating comandos.

Francisco Múgica Garmendia "Artapalo" was the sixth member of the Executive Committee, and was responsible for supervision of the comandos legales. He also was a native of Guipúzcoa, born in Villafranca de Ordizia in 1954. He allegedly participated in planning meetings that led to the death of Carrero Blanco, and himself killed an officer and an enlisted man of the Guardia Civil. He also participated in several kidnapings. He shared responsibilities with Juan Angel Ochoantesala Radioloa "Kirru," who was born in Ondárroa in 1954 and who belonged to ETA after 1973. Ochoantesala was trained in Algeria as well as France, and was accused of several killings, including that of the mayor of Galdácano.

The seventh and last member of the Executive Committee was Juan Angel Urruticoechea, who was responsible for the international links of ETA. Little is known about him, except that he supervised the operations of the ETA office in Brussels, through which the organization channeled its relations with helpful governments and with forces in the international terrorist network.

The leadership of ETA, and its supporting structure of houses, automobiles, communications, training camps, weapons supplies, and so forth, were located primarily in southern France near the Basque towns of St.-Jean-de-Luz, Hendaye, Bayonne, and Biarritz. There is considerable debate over the real role of the French government in the whole affair. Spanish authorities have complained that Paris is too lenient with ETA; and the Basques have criticized the French for harassment of innocent Basques, as well as for allowing secret right-wing assassination teams to operate with impunity against Basques in France.

Before the death of Spanish Prime Minister Luis Carrero Blanco in 1973, the French government had generally ignored the existence of ETA on the French side of the border, so long as ETA did nothing to whip up nationalist sentiment among French Basques. The organization conducted its meetings and established its training facilities on French soil with little interference from Paris. After the Carrero Blanco assassination and the subsequent dramatic secret press conference conducted in France by four hooded etarras who claimed to be the authors of the attack, Paris could hardly afford to continue to ignore

ETA's operations on its territory. In early 1974, the French government officially prohibited all separatist organizations, including ETA, but also organizations from Corsica, Breton, and other regions of France. Despite this prohibition, little was done by Paris to control or suppress ETA. In truth, the French government had little reason to want to cooperate with Franco. Not only did France disagree with the totalitarian rule of General Franco, but they were also angered by the support Spain gave to agents and former members of the French Secret Army (OAS) after that group had fled Algeria following the end of the war there. Thus through 1975 France did little if anything to discourage ETA from using French territory for sanctuary.

Beginning in 1976, however, there was a significant change in French policy toward ETA.[9] While nothing was done to break up ETA headquarters or to dislodge any of its training facilities, French authorities did toughen their attitude toward political refugees in a number of key areas. Permits to work and to live permanently in the country became difficult to obtain. Refugees suddenly found serious obstacles to their obtaining official refugee status, which had formerly been granted fairly easily. Police surveillance of refugees was increased, and ETA leaders were harrassed by French authorities almost constantly. Their homes were broken into and searched, and items removed, without warrant and without charges of criminal conduct. Their political rights were severely circumscribed, and they were allowed virtually no freedom to take part in any form of organized political expression. On almost any pretext, police accosted Basques in their homes or places of employment to interrogate and intimidate them.

The most worrisome aspect of French policy during this period was the preventive detention of refugees on one of the prison islands just off the French coast.[10] As of January 1977, ten Basques associated in one way or the other with ETA were confined on the prison island of Yeu. These eight men and two women had been detained, removed from their homes or taken off the streets, and sent into confinement without being charged with the violation of any French law. They were held for months in detention on Yeu without trial or legal counsel. This French policy of unwarranted preventive detention continued throughout the decade of the 1970s and into the 1980s. As of December 1981, there were some fifteen Basques under such detention or confinement on French soil, five on the island of Yeu and the remainder in small French villages near the Alps, as far as possible from the Spanish border.[11]

The next major change in French policy toward ETA began to emerge in the summer of 1978, when Madrid was beginning to toughen its measures of internal security.[12] On June 30 (two days after the assassination of José María Portell), in a press conference in Madrid, French President Valery Giscard d'Estaing said that the emergence of Spain as a democracy would cause his government to reexamine its policy toward Spanish exiles, since they would no longer have any reason to be considered political refugees. As a consequence, he went on, France would no longer issue to Spanish citizens, including Basques, the highly prized cards that would identify them as political refugees, and they would receive thenceforth no special privileges from their status. On January 12, 1977, the Spanish foreign minister, Marcelino Oreja, called on his French counterpart to request that Paris formally put that decision into effect. In response, Paris announced that no further political refugee cards would be handed out and that all persons with cards still in effect would shortly be receiving a letter advising them of the early expiration of that status. Thus from January 30 onward, Basques were unable to obtain French approval of their status as political refugees, which interfered considerably with their ability to find housing and employment.

Concurrently with this decision, French police began to round up Basques in general and etarras in particular, for deportation or detention or simply to relocate them in other parts of France. On January 30, twenty-four Basques were detained, principally in Bayonne, Biarritz, St.-Jean-de-Luz, and Hendaye. Four were released within twenty-four hours, but thirteen were sent to live in a remote part of France and seven were handed over to Spanish police at a border post in the Pyrenees. The next day, January 31, nine more Basque refugees were detained, of whom two were sent to live in distant villages. By mid-February, seventeen Basques had been removed from their homes and escorted under police guard to new residences in other parts of France. On the following March 5, these seventeen were removed forcibly once again and sent to still another residence where allegedly they could be monitored more easily by French police. To a greater or lesser degree, this kind of treatment has continued to characterize French policy toward the Basques in general and ETA in particular.

One thing that the French government has never done, however, much to the consternation of Madrid, is grant the Spanish government's requests to extradite known ETA members who have been detained in France.[13] The first such request from Spain was the famous case of Miguel Angel Apalategui "Apala," which caused a tremendous mobilization of Basque public opinion and demonstrations against the extradition.[14] The request was denied by the French courts, as were the following twenty-nine such requests for extradition covering the period of four years from the summer of 1977 to the summer of 1981. In the spring of 1979, for example, Spain asked for the return of two members of ETA, Mikel Goikoetxea and Martín Apaolaza, who countered with a hunger strike and mass protests until the French court decided in their favor and denied the petition from Madrid.[15] In February 1980, three well-known ETA leaders, Txomin Iturbe, Jokin Gorostidi, and Eugenio Echeveste, were detained by French police following a shooting incident in Biarritz in which Iturbe was wounded by French policemen in plain clothes.[16] The three were accused of illegal possession of weapons and incorrect documentation. Gorostidi was released, but Iturbe and Echeveste were sentenced to three months in jail. The Spanish government immediately petitioned for their extradition on the grounds that they were key ETA leaders (as, indeed, they were). The request was denied. Another recent case involved another etarra, Tomás Linaza, who was arrested in Paris following his return from a trip to Mexico. In this case, the Spanish request was approved by the French courts but was denied by the French prime minister on instructions from the French president Mitterand. As of June 1981 there were pending eleven more requests from Madrid for extradition of known ETA members under French control. It seemed unlikely that any of them would be more successful than the preceding thirty had been.

The victory of French socialists in the 1981 presidential and parliamentary elections had little effect on French policy toward ETA, contrary to what one might suppose. Ideologically, President Mitterand and his advisor on such matter, Regis Debray, were probably in sympathy with the struggle of ETA in behalf of revolutionary socialism. Despite the fact that French socialists favored increased autonomy for the country's regions, however, they excluded the Basque region, where separatist sentiment was too strong, and ETA was well advised not to do anything that might stimulate stronger separatist feeling in France's Basque region. They knew that if they did, Mitterand would not hesitate, to suppress the organization. Thus in 1981 and 1982, relations between ETA and the French government were characterized as an uneasy truce wherein each side agreed to avoid steps that would provoke the other. The result was that ETA's command structure managed to survive in southern France, much to the dismay of the Spanish government.[17]

Operations

The student of insurgencies can learn much from examining the organizational structure of ETA, but it is only when we look in detail at its operations that we begin to get the feel of the organization and the way it conducts its affairs. In general, the various operations of an insurgent organization can be reduced to the categories of recruitment and training of members, acquisition of other resources, including money, weapons, and information, creation and maintenance of an internal communications network, and conduct of its armed assaults. In addition to these, this section will discuss briefly ETA's alleged ties to the international terrorist network and thereby to the Soviet Union and other countries.

Recruitment of new members has always been a top priority for ETA since its founding. According to José María Portell, ETA began to recruit actively as early as 1961, when, again according to Portell, they succeeded in winning sixty-five new adherents to their cause.[18] They concentrated their efforts in three institutions: Deusto University in Bilbao, Catholic Church youth groups, and mountain-climbing clubs. In the early years, the organization recruited entirely among ethnic Basques, and while it was not required that one speak Basque to become a member, new members had to at least demonstrate their intention to learn the language. By 1968, ETA had altered its recruiting to focus on the offspring of non-Basque immigrants to the region, and the lists of arrested Basque militants included more and more non-Basque family names.[19] ETA has always dedicated considerable energy and resources to the recruitment of new members, as we have already seen in chapter 7. The success of the recruitment effort is demonstrated by the organization's ability to maintain a reasonably large core of members even during times of sharp repression by the Spanish authorities.

Given the ambiguities surrounding the definition of ETA membership and the difficulties in gathering data on this subject, it is hard to estimate the size of the organization and how it has changed during its existence. Nevertheless, I have made such an attempt, the results of which are reflected in table 9.2 and figure 9.2. As nearly as I can tell, ETA's membership rose slowly from the early 1950s to the early 1960s, when it increased sharply to about 250 to 300. Thereafter, it rose sharply once again until 1968, when it peaked at about 600. In the aftermath of the Manzanas killing and the Burgos trial, waves of arrests and deportations reduced the size of the organization to rather fewer than 100. The figure rose again after the killing of Carrero Blanco, to somewhere in the neighborhood of 100 to 200. After Franco's death in 1975 the organization grew steadily, especially in the 1978–79 period, when membership peaked once again at about 500. Sources differ considerably on the size during this period, however, and it could have gone as high as 2,000 (although I am inclined to

Table 9.2   *Estimated Size of ETA, 1952–81*

YEAR	ESTIMATED SIZE	SOURCES AND REMARKS
1952–59	Ekin-EGI "Generation"	
1952	6	Half-a-dozen founding members of Ekin.
1953	18–20	Two cells added to original group.
1954–56	50	Estimated only.
1957–59	?	Ekin formally merged with EGI. No way to know correct size.
1959–67	Old Guard "Generation"	
1959	50–70	ETA founded July 31, 1959.
1960	300	Interview with José Luis Alvarez Enparanza "Txillardegi" in *Garaia* 1, no. 1 (September 2–9, 1976):25.
1961	200–250	After train derailment affair, police suppression resulted in the jailing of 110, exile of like number. Organization practically wiped out. Mercé Ibarz, *Breu historia D'ETA 1959–1979* (Barcelona: La Magrana, 1980), p. 64. During first year of serious recruitment, ETA attracted 65 new members. José María Portell, *Los hombres de ETA* (Barcelona: DOPESA, 1974), p. 96.
1962	?	
1963	250–300	After Bilbao strike, 27 principal ETA leaders jailed and several more went into exile. Estimate assumes leader:follower ratio of 1:10. Gurutz Jáuregui Bereciartu, *Ideología y estrategia política de ETA: Análisis de su evolución entre 1959 y 1968* (Madrid: Siglo XXI, 1981), p. 225.
1964–65	?	
1966	300–450	ETA convoked an Aberri Eguna celebration in Irun; 250 people attended. Ortzi, *Los Vascos: Síntesis de su historia* (San Sebastián: Hordago, 1978), p. 188. The Activism Branch ("El Cabra") formed, with 30 members. Ortzi, p. 189. Attendance at first half of Fifth Assembly about 45. Ortzi, p. 192; José Mari Garmendia, *Historia de ETA*, 2 vols. (San Sebastián: L. Haranburu, 1979), 1:221.

Table 9.2, *continued*

YEAR	ESTIMATED SIZE	SOURCES AND REMARKS
1967–74	The Burgos and "Txikia" "Generations"	
1967	?	
1968–69	600	200 members in Bilbao area. 600 arrested following Manzanas killing. Ibarz, pp. 82, 85. 862 Basques arrested for political crimes in 1969. Luis C.-Nuñez Astrain, *La sociedad vasca actual* (San Sebastián: Editorial Txertoa, 1977), p. 121, table 48.
1970	100–200	396 arrested in 1970. C-Nuñez Astrain, p. 121. 108 Basques in prison as of February, 1972. Iñaki de Zabala, "Informe sobre Euzkadi" (Basque Nationalist Party in exile, 1972, Mimeo).
1973	100–200	316 arrested in 1973. C.-Nuñez Astrain, p. 121. Does not include members of EGI-Batasuna.
1974	100–200	315 arrested in 1974. C-Nuñez Astrain, p. 121.
1974–81	ETA(m)–ETA(p-m) "Generation"	
1975	300	632 arrested in 1975. C.-Nuñez Astrain, p. 121.
1976	300	290 arrested in 1976. Claire Sterling, *The Terror Network* (New York: Holt, Rinehart and Winston, 1981), p. 176.
1977	400	Sterling, p. 196.
1978	300–400	About 200–250 arrested during second half of 1978. *Deia*, December 21, 1978; *Cambio 16*, January 7, 1979.
1979	300–400	1979 membership estimated at well over 200. Risks International, *Regional Risk Assessment: Europe* (Alexandria, Va.: Risks International, 1979), p. 37. Julie Flint, "A Democracy under Threat," *New Statesman*, January 12, 1979.
1980	At least 400–500; estimates as high as 2,000.	Spanish Interior Minister Juan José Rosón quoted as saying 20 percent of ETA members in jail or on trial, only 700 of 2,000 etarras known to police. *Deia*, December 6, 1980. 329 etarras arrested between January 1, 1980, and July 15, 1980. *Deia*, July 19, 1980. 265

Table 9.2, *continued*

YEAR	ESTIMATED SIZE	SOURCES AND REMARKS
		etarras in prison as of December 1, 1980. *Deia*, December 3, 1980.
1981	500	394 members of ETA(m) arrested and 118 released on bail, January 1–October 30, 1981. *Cambio 16*, November 11, 1981. 499 members of ETA (all branches) arrested December 1980–May 1981. *Deia*, May 22, 1981. A report by the deputy chief of staff of the Guardia Civil estimated ETA membership in early 1982 at 500. *Deia*, June 13, 1982.

doubt such a high figure). I would estimate that in 1981, the membership of all branches of ETA was about 500, plus or minus 100.

It is a matter of some importance to know how these ETA members were distributed among its three competing branches: ETA(m), ETA(p-m), and Comandos Autónomos (see table 9.3). From these

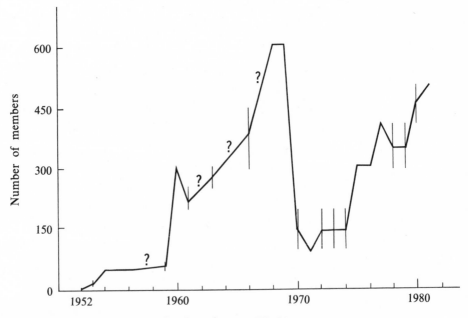

Figure 9.2.   Estimated Membership of ETA, 1952–81.

data, it appears that about two-thirds of all ETA members were in ETA(m), about one-quarter in ETA(p-m), and about one-tenth in Comandos Autónomos. If these percentages are approximately correct, then out of an estimated active and at-large membership of about 500, ETA(m) could count on perhaps 300, ETA(p-m) on about 150, and Comandos Autónomos about 50.

Once members have been recruited, it is necessary to give them some basic training in the skills they will need to survive in such a hazardous enterprise. From the time of the resurgence of the organization in the early 1970s, ETA has maintained secure training facilities in southern France where its members can receive instruction in weapons, combat techniques, explosives, communications devices and channels, information gathering, and so forth. A few members have been sent abroad for training in foreign installations, which I shall discuss shortly. The basic training course for new members that is conducted in France lasts about two weeks.[20] While there is some ideological instruction, new members are told virtually nothing about the organization, so that if they are captured soon after their return to Spain, they cannot reveal any details that might assist police in uncovering other comandos or finding other members. Once the training

Table 9.3 *Distribution of ETA Members by Organization (based upon arrest records; percentages)*

	ARRESTED 1/79– 7/80[a]	ARRESTED 1/80– 7/80[b]	ARRESTED 12/80– 4/81[c]	IN PRISON 12/80[d]	IN PRISON 1/81[e]	IN PRISON 10/81[f]
ETA(m)	65.0	68.1	70.6	61.1	57.7	56.7
ETA(p-m)	21.5	27.1	18.5	20.0	23.5	33.0
Comandos Autónomos	7.5	4.7	10.8	16.2	16.1	10.3
Other, unk.	6.0	0.0	0.0	2.6	2.7	0.0
N	214	339	286	265	298	97

Sources:
[a]Collected by author from contemporary press reports, January 1979–July 1980.
[b]*Deia*, July 19, 1980.
[c]*Deia*, April 2, 1981.
[d]*Deia*, December 3, 1980.
[e]*Deia*, January 14, 1981.
[f]*Deia*, October 29, 1981. Applies only to ETA members in Carabanchel prison.

course is completed, the new members are sent back to their villages or neighborhoods to resume life as it was before they joined ETA. They continue to live at home and to work at their jobs, to frequent their old hangouts and to meet with their old friends. Unless they are on an assignment, they are forbidden to carry weapons that might attract the suspicion of the police. And there they wait for further orders.

Apart from gathering new recruits and training them, the most pressing need for any clandestine organization is the acquisition of other key resources, including weapons and explosives, money, transportation, shelter, and information.

Finding weapons and explosives has never seemed to be much of a problem for ETA. The international market in illegal arms is so widespread and accessible that practically any kind of weapon can be obtained in almost any quantity desired. The trade routes followed by these illegal weapons reach out of Spain to France and then to other neighboring countries, including Belgium, Switzerland, Germany, and the Netherlands. By most accounts, Paris and Brussels are the focal points for the trade. The weapons, once purchased, are usually transported by truck in false containers and packing crates. Most of them are delivered to ETA leaders in France, from where they are subsequently distributed to comandos at the time they are needed.[21] In recent years, French and Belgian police have made several arrests in an attempt to uncover the organizations that are conducting this illegal weapons trade. At least one such arrest involved a high official in the French customs service. Nevertheless, it seems highly unlikely that there will ever be a satisfactory solution to this problem, given the virtually uncontrolled manufacture and distribution of light weapons around the world since World War II.[22]

What ETA cannot buy in the international arms markets of Western Europe it can always steal from arsenals in Spain and neighboring countries. In January 1982, following the daring rescue of the father of famous Spanish singer Julio Iglesias from his ETA(p-m) kidnapers, Spanish police obtained leads that took them to a caserío near the Vizcayan town of Erandio. There they uncovered a huge cache of weapons which, said police, amounted to 95 percent of the arms held at that time by ETA(p-m). Discovered in the cache were some 336 shot guns, 1 rocket launcher (of the type used in the Moncloa Palace attack in 1980), 7 rifles, 4 machine guns, 4 pistols, 4 revolvers, 50 kilos of explosive, and other articles associated with armed assaults (bulletproof vests, for example). According to police, the shotguns had all been stolen from a weapons factory in Elgóibar in December 1977. Since they were all still in their original wrappings, they apparently had not been used in the intervening four years. In a somewhat similar case, also in January 1982, French and Belgian police revealed the theft of 541 revolvers (.357 Magnum) by suspected ETA members. The weapons had been manufactured in Guernica and assembled in Bayonne, France. They were being shipped in a large single container to Liege, Belgium, when they disappeared.[23]

The individual operating cells of ETA never seem to be at a loss for weaponry. From press accounts of the capture of members of a comando, which also frequently detail the weapons and other materiel taken at the same time, it appears that ETA comandos are about as well equipped with weapons as conventional infantry detachments in the Spanish army. For example, from September 1 through December 25, 1978, police arrested the members of 46 ETA comandos, of which 33 were comandos de acción and 13 were comandos de información. If we assume that each assault cell had 4 members in it, this would mean that police had arrested 132 etarras whose assignment involved armed attacks. At the time of these arrests, police also confiscated the following weapons: 30 submachine guns, 21 shotguns, 63 pistols, 45 extra magazines, and 1,900 cartridges. This works out to about 3.5 weapons per comando, or just slightly less than one per person. The ammunition found with these weapons was enough for only about one-half to one magazine per weapon, which suggests that ETA rations its ammunition fairly strictly, and probably provides its comandos with only enough for one assignment at a time.

Whether by preference or of necessity, ETA's arsenal has been stocked almost entirely with weapons from Spain, other Western European countries, and the United States. The preferred submachine guns include the 9 mm Vigneron, made in Belgium; the 9 mm Uzi, made in Belgium and Israel; and the 9 mm Sten Mark II, made in Great Britain. Some special comandos, including especially the bodyguard units that protect members of the Executive Committee, are equipped with the Ingram submachine gun, manufactured in the United States. This remarkable weapon weighs only 7 pounds and is only about 11.5 inches long, yet it fires a 9 mm bullet at the rate of 900 rounds per minute. Precisely because it has such a high rate of fire, however, ETA has usually not entrusted its use to ordinary comandos, since inexperienced gunners will exhaust ammunition too quickly and leave themselves vulnerable to counterattack.[24] ETA has also frequently used automatic and semiautomatic rifles, including the American-made M-16 and the Belgian FAL. Their preference for pistols includes the Browning 9 mm HP 35 made in Belgium and several varieties of pistol made in Spain, including the "Star," the "Astra," and the "Firebird." All of these latter models, ironically, are manufactured in substantial quantities in factories in the Basque cities of Eibar and Elgóibar, in the very heart of ETA territory.[25] Although one occasionally sees photographs of alleged etarras practicing or training with heavier weapons such as rocket launchers, the fact is that they have almost never used weapons of this size. I know of only four instances through December 1980, in which ETA units fired a rocket launcher against a real target.[26] The first use of this kind of weapon was against the Moncloa Palace, the headquarters of the Spanish prime minister in Madrid in February 1980. The other three attacks, all in 1980, were against the headquarters buildings of the civil governors of Guipúzcoa, Navarra, and Vizcaya. The attacks caused some building damage but no casualties. While weapons of this sort are easy to acquire, they are usually quite old and unreliable and therefore not frequently used. According to markings on the launching tube left behind at the Moncloa Palace, the weapon had been sent to an American army unit for use in Korea in 1951! One can only speculate on the path that weapon must have followed to end up in the Spanish capital nearly thirty years later.

Aside from firearms, the principal weapon of ETA has been an explosive referred to as Goma-2. This explosive, manufactured in both Spain and Portugal, is widely used throughout Spain as a blasting agent in construction, quarrying, and so forth. According to one press report, there were in the early 1970s about 270 major deposits of explosives and blasting agents in Spain, and ETA has successfully assaulted several of these in the Basque region.[27] The explosive used to destroy the automobile of Prime Minister Carrero Blanco, some 80 kilograms of Goma-2, was part of a load of 3,000 kilograms stolen by an ETA comando from a powder magazine in Hernani (Guipúzcoa) January 31, 1973, nearly one year before the assassination. The explosive had been stored in a hollow wall in a garage warehouse in an apartment house complex in a town near San Sebastian, and had escaped detection for a year before it was used.[28] As far as is known, the largest theft of explosives carried out by ETA took place on July 24, 1980, in Soto la Marina, in Santander province. In this action, an ETA comando consisting of six men and one woman, all disguised as Guardia Civil troops, made off with 8,000 kilograms in a stolen truck. Some nine or ten hours passed before the theft could be reported by the guards of the powder deposit, who had been captured and chained to a tree in a country area. By that time, the explosive had been removed to a warehouse in Amorebieta (Vizcaya) from where it was taken in smaller lots across the border into France. By the time police discovered the hiding place, all but 300 kilograms had been removed. In this one theft alone, ETA obtained enough explosive for nearly one hundred bombings of the magnitude that killed Prime Minister Carrero Blanco.[29]

Next to personnel and weapons, the most important resource for ETA is money. Since the mid 1960s, ETA has never had any problems securing funds to support their activities. In general, their funds come from three sources: bank robberies, kidnap ransom payments, and the so-called revolutionary taxes.[30]

The first theft of money committed by ETA took place in September 1965, when an ETA team held up a bank messenger and robbed him of the bank funds he was carrying. The organization's first bank robbery occurred on April 21, 1967, when it struck the offices of the Banco Guipuzcuano, in the town of Villabona, making off with more than one million pesetas. From that operation up until mid-1977, ETA had obtained more than 60 million pesetas (about $1 million at then-effective exchange rates) from its bank robberies.[31] During 1978 alone, ETA committed about fifty bank robberies which netted the organization more than 250 million pesetas (about $4 million). The most spectacular robbery was that carried out by ETA(m) of the Sestao factory of Altos Hornos de Vizcaya resulting in the theft of more than 76 million pesetas.[32]

The second major source of ETA's funds has been the ransom payments made to rescue kidnap victims. In the beginning, ETA kidnapped people to extract political concessions, as with the German consul Eugene Beihl, or to force concessions in a labor dispute, as was the case with Lorenzo Zabala in 1972. In January 1973, with the kidnaping of Felipe Huarte, the organization discovered that it could combine a political statement with a demand for ransom and turn what had been a simple political strategy into a moneymaker. The Huarte family responded to the kidnap demands with a ransom payment of 50 million pesetas (a little less than $1 million), delivered in Brussels and Paris in two installments. Apparently there was a disagreement within ETA over the disposition of the funds, but nevertheless the lesson was not lost on future generations of ETA leaders. Most of the subsequent kidnapings involved demands for ransom in addition to requirements of a more political nature. In 1978 alone, known ransoms paid by Basque industrialists to ETA exceeded one-quarter of a million dollars.[33] The largest ransom paid was $1.5 million for the release of Catalan businessman Jesus Serra Santamans, who was kidnaped in April 1980 and released unharmed two months later. In all, ETA has probably received more than $10 million in ransom payments from their various kidnapings.

The "revolutionary tax," a technique learned from the Irish Republican Army (IRA), is the third major source of ETA funds. Beginning in

1976, ETA sent letters to several hundred individuals demanding payments of between $12,500 and $25,000 a year. Each letter threatened the recipient with death if he did not deliver the required payment to an intermediary by a certain date. These letters were sent out periodically. In May 1978, for example, *El país* reported that ETA had sent out such letters to "dozens" of Basque industrialists, demanding payment of 10 million pesetas to finance the "people's struggle." The money was to be delivered to one Otxia in St.-Jean-de-Luz or Biarritz and was to come in used bank notes with mixed serial numbers.[34] By the end of 1978, according to a British press report, ETA had levied its revolutionary tax on about eight hundred wealthy Basques.[35] From other press accounts, we can infer that the great majority of those on whom the tax is levied usually end up paying it, even if they might resist in the beginning. When the tax was first levied, the reaction of most industrialists was to ignore the letters. Then in May 1977, ETA kidnaped and assassinated the well-known Bilbao industrialist Javier de Ybarra. It was known that Ybarra had refused to pay the tax and had been threatened with death for doing so. Subsequently, ETA (one or the other of its branches) carried out a number of killings and woundings of businessmen, including the following:

In May 1978, a businessman named Pedro Luis Iturregui was kidnaped and shot in the leg near Munguía.

In October 1978, an industrialist named Jacinto Zulaica Iribar was kidnaped and wounded near Orense.

In February 1979, an executive of a construction firm named Jesús Molera Guerra was kidnaped and wounded near Baracaldo.

In September 1979, a bank director named Modesto Carriegas was killed in Baracaldo, allegedly because he refused to pay the tax.

In March 1980, an industrialist named Enrique Aresti y Urien was killed in Bilbao, allegedly for refusing to pay the tax.

In May 1980, an industrialist named José Araquistain Leceta was kidnaped and wounded in Durango, for unknown reasons.

Also in May 1980, a businessman named Ramón Baglieto was killed in Azcoitia for unknown reasons.

In June 1980, the president of the Vizcaya Pharmacists Association, José María Lecea, was shot in the leg, for unknown reasons.

In September 1980, a Cuban businessman named Pedro Abreu Almagro was kidnaped and held prisoner for two months. The motive was unknown, but press speculation centered on his refusal to pay the tax.

After this rash of killings and woundings of people who had refused to pay the tax, most preferred to pay it rather than run such a risk. During the first four months of 1980, press reports speculated that ETA had already collected more than 800 million pesetas that year from the tax. In late April 1980, however, a respected industrial leader named Juan Alcorta published an open letter in the Bilbao newspaper *Deia* in which he refused to pay ETA the 20 million pesetas it had demanded of him. The public reaction from both business leaders and Alcorta's workers was strongly positive. Many people praised the industrialist for taking a strong stand on such a dangerous issue. By the end of 1980, Alcorta had not yet been harmed for his defiance of ETA.[36]

From the standpoint of logistical support, the key requirements for ETA involve transportation and shelter. For certain members who have needed an automobile on a more-or-less-permanent basis, the organization has bought one through legitimate channels, to avoid attracting attention and suspicion. The assassination team that killed Prime Minister Carrero Blanco bought several automobiles during the year they were living in Madrid. Key leaders of the organizaton have a number of automobiles and vans at their disposal, which they change rather frequently to confuse would-be attackers. Often, however, the organization needs a car for only a short time to carry out an assault or a bank robbery. In these cases, the comando meets its needs simply by stealing a private automobile or a taxi cab. After tieing or handcuffing the driver to a tree in some secluded area, the comando uses the car to carry out its assignment, then abandons it and switches to another car to make an escape. According to one press report, from September 1976 to February 1978 there were thirty-two of these so-called "momentary kidnapings" (*secuestros momentáneos*) involving the theft of an automobile for assault or robbery.[37]

The problem of finding shelter is likewise relatively easy to solve, given the extensive network of supporters and "safe houses" that are spread through the Basque country. Virtually every village in the region, at least in Vizcaya and Guipúzcoa, contains not just an operating comando of ETA but at least one house where the owners are sympathetic to the cause and can be counted on to provide food and shelter with no questions asked. The etarra executed in September 1975, Angel Otaegi, was convicted of providing this kind of aid to two youths, unknown to him, who appeared from nowhere asking for lodging for a night or two. Otaegi provided them with help, but claimed no knowledge of their mission, which turned out to involve a killing. Otaegi was subsequently convicted of being an accomplice to the assassination. A number of "safe houses" have been altered by ETA to include false walls or floors that conceal elaborate hiding places where etarras on the run from police can escape detection and capture. According to the Risks International report, ETA sent one of its members, José María Arrumberri Esnaola "El Tanque" to Argentina to study with Argentine guerrillas the construction of such hiding places. Upon returning to Spain in April 1974, Arrumberri built at least eight in Madrid alone, one used in connection with the Cafe Rolando bombing in September of that year. On a number of occasions, these hiding places have also been used as "people's prisons" to keep kidnap victims safe from detection.

The final element in a successful insurgent operation involves the transmission of information safely, securely, and clearly. From ETA's very earliest days, its use of conventional communications channels such as telephones and the postal service has been impeded by government surveillance. Under the Franco regime, mail was opened with regularity, and personal telephones were monitored with few restrictions. In a counter effort, ETA tried to infiltrate the local telephone company offices to discover where the telephone bugs were being planted, but of course they could never use these media with any security. Since 1975, the Spanish government has continued its close surveillance of communications channels, although with the advent of democracy there are more controls on such surveillance and greater demands for public reporting. For example, in April 1981, the Spanish minister of interior, Juan José Rosón, reported to the Congress of Deputies that from December 1, 1980, through March 24, 1981, his ministry had conducted 373 telephone monitoring projects (all under the authorization of the antiterrorist law and duly authorized by the appropriate court), and had carried out 10 surveillances of individual use of the postal service (which, one presumes, means that they had systemically opened the mail of ten different persons).[38] For the period from June 1981 through October, 1981, according to Rosón, the number of telephone surveillances rose to 502, of which 266 had been concluded and 236 were still in effect at the end of October.[39] While the minister did not say as much, one infers that the great majority of these were conducted in the Basque country and were directed against ETA. Since 1979, ETA has assassinated some employees of the telephone company, and one might presume that they were marked for killing because of a supposed link between them and the telephone bugging operation. For most purposes, then, ETA has had to consider normal modes of communication closed to it.

For this reason, ETA over the years has built up an elaborate network of couriers and drops that have been difficult for Spanish authorities to intercept or penetrate. There are two basic elements of this network. The first is a chain of more-or-less-secure locations, such as bars or movie theaters, where messages can be delivered and picked up. This chain of drops extends throughout the Basque country and well into France. The second is the courier system, the key to ETA's command and control network. The couriers, the buzones, are frequently women or older men who can no longer afford to run the risks of armed combat with the police. Many comandos have their own special buzón, but there are many buzones who operate on what we might call a free-lance basis, offering their services to anyone who needs them. The assignment of the buzón is to carry messages or packages from one ETA comando to another, particularly if the information or material to be transmitted is sensitive or incriminating.

In June 1979, the arrest of a number of ETA couriers in Bilbao disclosed many interesting details of the life and work of the buzones.[40] One courier, a forty-three-year-old factory worker, was accused of receiving in a bar in Guernica letters sent to him from ETA leaders in France, and of subsequently sending them on to various comandos in Vizcaya. He was also accused of receiving a package containing explosives and weapons and holding it until it was picked up by another etarra. A second courier, a forty-four-year-old factory worker, had received letters delivered to him at his home and had carried them across the border to deliver to another buzón in the French city of Hendaye. He was also accused of receiving two packages, each containing five million pesetas, part of a payment of a revolutionary tax, which he was to send on to ETA headquarters in France. He was further accused of having prepared a typed version of a letter from an ETA leader denying responsibility for a recent bombing, and delivering the typed copy to the office of the newspaper *Egin* in Bilbao. A third buzón, a forty-two-year-old electrician, was accused of hiding in his home a bag containing cameras and hand grenades and subsequently delivering them to an ETA comando in the Guecho (Vizcaya) area.

All of these various resources—weapons, money, information, shelter, and so forth—come together in the conduct of ETA's armed operations. We know very little about how these operations are actually carried out, but we can piece together some of the basic elements from press accounts and secondary sources. The process begins, typically, with a decision, made at the highest levels, to carry out a specific kind of attack against an identified individual. We have evidence that these decisions are not made lightly or in the heat of debate, but are carefully thought out and their possible impact discussed. On occasion, they are sparked by an unexpected piece of intelligence. For example, ETA decided to kidnap Prime Minister Carrero Blanco after it had received an unsolicited tip from an informant in Madrid about Carrero

Blanco's habits of church attendance.[41] On most occasions, however, the decision to attack a specific person results from ETA's analysis of the situation facing it and a discussion of how the attack in question would help or hurt the organization. The decision to kidnap Lorenzo Zabala in 1972 was made precisely because he was both Basque and an industrialist, and ETA's leaders wanted the working class to understand that their struggle was not just one of nationalists against Spain but also of workers against capitalism.[42]

Once a decision has been made to attack a given individual or facility, a specific comando is assigned the task. If the target is a relatively unknown and unprotected person, such as a bar owner or a Guardia Civil trooper, the assignment will probably go to a comando legal stationed in one of the small towns near the site of the planned attack. If, however, the target is a person of considerable importance and attacking him will mean combat with bodyguards or other difficulties, the organization will give the job to one of seven comandos ilegales, the special units of the most hardened and experienced ETA members whose names and faces are well known to police. As of March 1981 there were two such comandos in San Sebastián, two in Bilbao, and one each in Vitoria, Pamplona, and Madrid. These comandos especiales are the closest thing ETA has to professional killers. Their members never see one another until the moment they come together to carry out their assignment. They do not even know of one another's whereabouts, and all business among them is carried out by couriers. They are paid a salary of less than $200 a month and provided with lodging and transportation.

When the assignment has been made, it is transmitted, together with any needed special equipment or information, to the comando charged with carrying out the task. The assigned comando has available to it a vast network of intelligence sources and couriers to support its operations. If it thinks it necessary, the comando may go back to ETA headquarters with requests for clarification, more information, or special weapons or equipment, which are usually delivered without unusual delay. As far as we can discern, the operating comando is left pretty much alone to choose the exact way in which the attack will be carried out, particularly as to time and location. Once the attack has been made, the elaborate ETA support network comes into play once again. "Safe houses" are made available to shelter the comando members or to hide the kidnap victim. The courier system transmits followup information about the attack to ETA headquarters and to the mass media. The transportation network is brought into action to move the comando members away from their hiding place and to safety in France. And then the entire operating system slips back into inaction, awaiting the moment when a call from France will set it in motion once again.[43]

One of the most controversial aspects of ETA involves its alleged contact with the so-called international terrorist network, and through that network, with the Soviet Union and other countries that support revolution, such as Libya. The core of the thesis that ETA is a part of such a network has been expounded by Claire Sterling in her book *The Terror Network*. According to Sterling, the Basques are a gallant and oppressed people, and ETA might have begun as an honest attempt at countering that oppression; but over the years, and especially since 1976, ETA has naïvely allowed itself to be used by Soviet agents and the representatives of other international terrorist groups, particularly the Irish Republican Army and the Italian Red Brigades, who have no real interest in Basque nationalism but who are using ETA to destabilize Spain. No matter what the Spanish government does in the way of concessions, ETA's international links will continue to keep the insurgency alive. The implication is that without interference from outside by the Soviets and others, ETA would have subsided and perhaps have even ceased to operate.[44]

While I do not agree with this assessment of the international links of ETA, it is impossible to deny that they do exist. Let us consider what little we know of the record here. There is no question that ETA has sent a number of its members abroad for training in the use of weapons, explosives, and tactics. As early as 1964, ETA sent an unknown but probably small number of members to Cuba to be trained in kidnaping and sabotage.[45] During the early 1970s, ETA established informal links with leaders of the IRA, but the exact role of ETA in the European terrorist network seems vague. Sterling and others are convinced that ETA was and is a full member of this network, along with the IRA, the Red Brigades, the Baader-Meinhof Gang, and others. In 1980, however, an Italian magazine, *Panorama*, published a report that indicated that efforts to bring ETA into the network had failed, and that ETA remained the only significant insurgent group in Europe that had not joined the international union.[46]

It is known that during the late 1970s ETA sent a number of its members to be trained abroad, primarily in four countries: Algeria, Libya, Lebanon, and South Yemen.[47] Although the Spanish police release this kind of information to the news media rather readily, Spain's Foreign Ministry cannot protest directly to the governments involved, because the evidence of such training is largely circumstantial. The most important training site seems to be Algeria, although the number of etarras trained there varies according to the source. Sterling says that 143 members of ETA(m) were sent to train in Algeria, but I frankly find that number rather high, since at the time this was supposed to have happened (late 1975 or 1976) there were barely twice that many in the entire organization.[48] The most recent Spanish police report on the subject indicated that some 20 etarras went to Algeria to train at an undisclosed time near the end of 1976, but this information was provided by an etarra named José Arregui Izaguirre, who died under police interrogation (or torture, as one prefers) in early 1981, so I would not consider it especially reliable.[49] One confirmed incident, however, does indicate the existence of a network of training facilities for etarras in the Middle East. On May 23, 1980, Dutch authorities arrested four members of ETA(m) at the Amsterdam airport. The four were returning from South Yemen, where they had admittedly taken part in paramilitary training for a period of four months, along with eight other etarras and several Palestinians.[50] This incident produced the first, and to my knowledge only, case in which the Spanish government formally protested a foreign government's allowing ETA members to be trained on its territory. There is no record of South Yemen's reply to the protest, but one doubts that it was very responsive.[51] In early 1981, there were reports that about 20 members of ETA had gone to Nicaragua and El Salvador for training, but the evidence was scanty and both governments denied the accusation. It is occasionally alleged that in the 1960s several etarras went to Uruguay and Argentina for training, but if such a thing did happen, it was almost certainly an isolated case or two and not a part of formal policy on the part of either ETA or the Latin American guerrilla groups.

In January 1981, a Spanish magazine *Policía española* (*Spanish Police*) published the most comprehensive list yet compiled of ETA's alleged foreign contacts over the years.[52] According to its article, etarras have gone for training to South Yemen, Lebanon, Czechoslovakia, Ireland, Uruguay, Cuba, and Algeria; ETA has received weapons and economic assistance from Czechoslovakia, Ireland, the Soviet Union, China, and Libya; and etarras have sought refuge and sanctuary in France and Belgium, as well as Venezuela (where, incidentally, ETA has maintained an office practically from the beginning).[53]

Without denying the existence of these ties between ETA and other countries and insurgent groups, I find the argument unconvincing that these connections provide ETA with a critical margin of support and that without this outside support ETA would cease to exist (with the obvious exception, of course, of their sanctuary in France). Some etarras may have received paramilitary training abroad, but many more received the training they needed in ETA's own camps in southern France. The weapons traditionally employed by ETA's comandos are relatively easy to master, and it is doubtful that etarras really had to go all the way to Algeria to learn how to fire a Sten submachine gun. If etarras have made extensive use of heavier weapons such as rocket launchers that would require considerable training and practice, that fact has escaped my notice. I also find it difficult to believe that ETA depends on the Soviet Union or China for weapons and money. I have already observed that ETA's weapons come from Western Europe and the United States, and the group's preferred explosive, Goma-2, comes from Spain and Portugal. Whatever the group needs can be bought with readily available funds or stolen from powder magazines or arsenals in Spain itself. As far as money is concerned, ETA has demonstrated convincingly, I think, the ability to extract by force from the Spanish and Basque economy the funds it needs to prosecute its strategy effectively. The combination of bank robberies, kidnapings, and revolutionary taxes has produced literally millions of dollars in the last several years, and I doubt that ETA needs more than that to survive. All other resources needed by the organization, such as shelter and transportation, are provided, either willingly or not, by the host population. When one adds to this the tendency of Basques to mistrust foreigners, we have what I think is a convincing case that foreign assistance, no matter how great, has never been, nor could it become, the critical factor in keeping the ETA insurgency alive.

Postscript: 1982

During 1982, several of the better known ETA(m) leaders mentioned in this chapter were arrested and held for varying periods in French prisons. In June, Domingo Iturbe "Txomin," Mikel Lujua Gorostiola "Mikel," Carlos Ibargurren "Nervios," and some thirty other etarras were caught up in a police sweep in Biarritz. Most of the arrested members were held without charges, but Iturbe was officially charged with illegal possession of a firearm. In November, two ETA leaders, José Luís Ansola "Pello el viejo," and Carlos Ibargurren (for the second time), were arrested in St.-Jean-de-Luz and charged with plotting to assassinate Pope John Paul II during his trip to Spain. To my knowledge, none of these arrests led to trial or extradition.[54]

CHAPTER TEN

ETA and the Spanish State: Challenge and Response

Clandestine insurgent organizations like ETA do not, of course, operate in a vacuum; they function in the midst of complex pressures both in support and in opposition to them. Spanish government policy toward ETA has undergone several major changes over the years. While the Franco regime ruled Spain, policies toward all dissident groups were harshly suppressive. For about two and a half years after Franco's death, until the summer of 1978, the new democratic government relaxed a number of the more oppressive laws and police state practices. But, from mid-1978 through 1980, many of the policies and practices reminiscent of the Franco approach to security were reinstated. How these changes in policy have affected levels of ETA violence is a complex question. In answering it, we shall bring this study to a close with some thoughts on self-sustaining insurgent violence.

Domestic Security Policy under Franco

On July 18, 1936, when the military uprising led by Generals Mola, Sanjurjo, and Franco touched off the Spanish Civil War, the rebel generals proclaimed "Spain is a unity. All conspiracy against this unity is repulsive. All separatism is a crime that we will not pardon."[1] This proclamation was followed ten days later by one of the first decrees issued by the rebels' governing body, the Committee of National Defense, which extended the declaration of war to the entire Spanish territory and which made it a military offense to bear arms, possess flammable or explosive substances, or oppose in any other way the military uprising. On June 23, 1937 (after the fall of Bilbao to the rebels and the flight of the Basque government into Santander province), the same committee formally declared the provinces of Vizcaya and Guipúzcoa to be traitorous and disloyal, thereby depriving them of their special economic privileges (still enjoyed at that time by Alava and Navarra).

Although the Civil War ended in April 1939, insurgent pressures did not; so, on March 2, 1943, the earlier proclamations concerning armed opposition were codified and made a part of Spain's post–Civil War judicial system. This step was followed four years later, on April 18, 1947, by the Decree-Law for the Repression of Banditry and Terrorism, the so-called "law against the maquis."[2] These two decrees, plus the Code of Military Justice promulgated in July 1945, provided the legal framework for the Spanish government's approach to insurgency until 1960.

In the late 1950s, the upsurge of violence and political disorder throughout Spain, but especially in the Basque provinces, made it clear to the Franco government that new measures were needed to meet the challenge. The result was the Decree-Law on Military Rebellion, Banditry, and Terrorism promulgated by General Franco on September 21, 1960. This new law established four broad categories of punishable offenses. "Crimes of military rebellion" included the dissemination of false or tendentious information to cause disturbance in public order, international conflict, or a decline in the prestige of the state, its institutions, the government, the army, or the authorities. It also prohibited joining, conspiring, or taking part in meetings, conferences, or demonstrations intended to accomplish any of the above-stated goals. The category included strikes, sabotage, or any analogous act which had a political objective or which caused serious disturbance of public order.

The other categories of offense were defined in a similarly broad fashion. Terrorism, for example, was defined as attacks against public security, terrorizing the inhabitants of a particular location, revenge or reprisals of a political or social character, or disturbing tranquility, order, or public services; causing explosions, fires, the sinking of naval vessels, the derailment of trains, interruption of communications, landslides, floods, or the employment of any other means or artefacts that could cause great danger; the possession of arms and munitions, explosive apparatuses or substances, flammable items, or other lethal devices; the manufacture, transport, or supply of any such items; and the mere placing of any such substances or artefacts, even if they failed to explode or otherwise malfunctioned.

Armed attack and kidnaping were defined to include armed robbery, with or without intent to use weapons to threaten or harm the victims; assault on any industrial or commercial establishment or on any person charged with the custody or transportation of any valuable items; and the taking or holding captive of any person. Banditry was defined as living in or otherwise forming armed groups whose intent was to engage in banditry or social subversion; any act of assistance given to such groups, even though such assistance might not in itself constitute complicity with a criminal act; and any act designed to take advantage of the fear or disorder caused by any of the above acts, by threatening harm or by exacting retribution in the form of money, jewels, or any other kind of goods, or by compelling any person to engage in any activity or to desist from any activity.

The penalties called for in the 1960 Decree-Law were severe. The death penalty was required for any of the punishable offenses if the offense resulted in the death of any person, whether or not that person was the intended victim. In cases where the death penalty was required by the law, the courts were prohibited from considering extenuating circumstances when they assigned punishment. Life imprisonment was required for armed attack, kidnaping, and terrorism. Lesser jail sentences, from twelve to twenty years, were prescribed for other crimes under the categories of military rebellion and banditry.

Perhaps the most significant feature of the 1960 decree-law was its assigning of jurisdiction for hearing the cases. Persons accused of having violated the law were judged not by a civilian court but by a military tribunal. In a subsequent modifying decree of December 2, 1963, this provision of the 1960 law was suspended, and punishable offenses were transferred to a new set of courts called Tribunals of Public Order. With the upsurge of violence after 1967, however, the original provision was reinstated by the Decree-Law of August 18, 1968, and the offenses of banditry, military rebellion, and terrorism were returned to the jurisdiction of military courts, where they remained until the entire law was revoked following Franco's death. These provisions were strengthened, and preventive detention of suspected terrorists was authorized by a new Decree-Law on the Prevention of Terrorism, promulgated on August 28, 1975, in the midst of the violence and turmoil of Franco's last days in power.

Thus the Franco regime's approach to internal security was essentially a military one. Spain was divided into military regions, whose boundaries were used to determine the jurisdiction of each military court. The four Basque provinces lie in the Sixth Military Region, whose headquarters are in the city of Burgos. For this reason, military trials of persons accused of ETA activity in the Basque region were held in Burgos. The most famous of these was the December 1970 trial of the fifteen men and women accused of aiding or perpetrating the assassination of Melitón Manzanas. The trial of Angel Otaegi was also held there, as were many others.

Placing the trials for terrorism and related offenses under military jurisdiction altered substantially the protection of the human and civil rights of the accused.[3] Defense was hampered significantly by the military surroundings. Trials were customarily conducted in secret. The press and family of the accused were usually denied access to the courtroom, although in the case of the more controversial trials, public opinion usually forced them to be opened to a small group of outsiders, including family members. Until 1963, defense attorneys had to be active-duty military officers, but that provision was deleted from the 1968 decree. Defense lawyers were often given only a brief time to prepare the defense of their clients. Appeals were processed literally in a matter of hours. Defense attorneys were not allowed to cross-examine adverse witnesses or to question the validity of evidence presented by the state. The accused were led into the courtroom in handcuffs or chains, and the courtroom was under heavy guard. Often, the members of the court were armed. Testimony of the accused was restricted to matters directly related to the crimes alleged. No evidence could be introduced concerning the use of torture or coercion in the extraction of confessions. Basques were not allowed to address the court or to testify in the Basque language, and no interpretation between Euskera and Spanish was permitted. No extenuating circumstances could be adduced to explain the behavior of the accused. On the other hand, the trial attorney representing the state was given a free hand to develop evidence to convict the accused. There could be no appeal from the jurisdiction of the military tribunal. The military court itself was the final arbiter of any dispute over its jurisdiction, and there was no higher court to which this issue could be carried.

One of the most disturbing aspects of the army's jurisdiction over matters relating to dissent and political opposition was that the military courts were used to try persons accused of acts that were not in themselves insurgent or life-threatening. In 1969, for example, of the some 1,100 cases heard in military courts throughout Spain, 867 (or nearly 80 percent) involved acts that would not be considered crimes in a democratic political system: attending political meetings or demonstrations, distributing literature, belonging to political organizations that opposed the state, and so forth.[4] Few of us would deny a state the use of legitimate self-defense procedures to protect itself against violence and insurrection. The problem with the use of military courts in Franco Spain was that they were used to suppress all dissent and political opposition no matter what form they took.

The use of military courts and military justice in cases of political dissent was only one half of the Franco regime's approach to dealing with its opponents. The other half lay in the juridical device known as the "state of exception." One of the most important challenges to a political regime is to protect fundamental human rights under conditions of stress, disorder, and crisis. Through use of the state of exception, the Franco government repeatedly set aside constitutional protections available to all Spanish citizens in order to free the police and Guardia Civil to impose the official violence of a police state.

The state of exception was one step short of martial law. It was a temporary abrogation by the government of six rights theoretically preserved and guaranteed by the Fuero de los Españoles: freedom of expression, privacy of the mails, freedom of assembly and association, right of habeas corpus, freedom of movement and residence, and freedom from arbitrary house arrest.

In the Spanish case, during the transformation of a regime of law into one of arbitrary coercion, the most significant abrogation was that affecting the right of habeas corpus. When the right was in effect, persons detained by the police had to be brought before a court for arraignment within seventy-two hours of arrest. There were ample provisions for securing legal counsel and for informing family or friends of the whereabouts of the detainee. When a state of exception was in effect, however, the right of habeas corpus was suspended. Persons could be arrested and held at any location for any length of time without anyone being informed of their whereabouts or even of the fact that they had been arrested. The courts, lawyers, and family were completely helpless to come to the aid of the detainee. Under these conditions, police brutality was encouraged and even protected. Confessions extracted by torture were particularly common during states of exception. People were imprisoned and tortured more or less continuously for weeks without any charge having been brought against them and without their ever having seen an attorney or appeared before a judge.

The state of exception also led to extralegal violence by rightist vigilante groups. Freed from government restraint, these groups assaulted political leaders and ordinary citizens in the street and in other public places and created their own reign of terror quite apart from the state-sanctioned violence of the police and Guardia Civil. The most active right-wing group in the Basque country during the Franco years was the organization known as the Guerrilleros de Cristo-Rey (Warriors for Christ the King). The Guerrilleros combined fervent Catholicism with a self-appointed mission to advance the Franco crusade. They attacked prominent opposition leaders throughout Spain, but they were especially virulent in their attacks on separatism in the Basque provinces and in Cataluña. Because they operated with impunity during states of exception, there is no way of knowing how

Table 10.1   *States of Exception in Spain, 1956–75*

DATE OF DECLARATION	MONTHS DURATION	AREA AFFECTED
February 10, 1956	3	All Spanish territory
March 14, 1958	4	Asturias
May 4, 1962	3	Asturias, Vizcaya, Guipúzcoa
June 8, 1962	24	All Spanish territory
April 21, 1967	3	Vizcaya
August 3, 1968	3	Guipúzcoa
October 31, 1968	3	Guipúzcoa
January 24, 1969	2	All Spanish territory
December 4, 1970	3	Guipúzcoa
December 14, 970	6	All Spanish territory
April 25, 1975	3	Vizcaya, Guipúzcoa
August 22, 1975	3	All Spanish territory

Source: Luis C.-Nuñez Astrain, *La sociedad vasca actual* (San Sebastián: Editorial Txertoa, 1977), p. 126, table 49.

much damage they did or how many people fled into exile to avoid their assaults. One account asserts that right-wing groups operating in the Basque provinces committed eighty-five "actions" (including two that resulted in deaths of the victims) during the eighteen-month period following the state of exception declared in the spring of 1975.[5]

A state of exception was declared in part or all of Spain twelve times from 1956 until Franco's death in 1975 (see table 10.1). Only one of these, that covering Asturias in 1958, did not affect the Basque provinces. Of the remaining eleven, five covered all Spanish territory; one covered Asturias, Vizcaya, and Guipúzcoa as a group; one covered Vizcaya alone; three covered Guipúzcoa alone; and one covered Vizcaya and Guipúzcoa as a group. In the span of 178 months from February 1956 to Franco's death in November 1975, at last one Basque province was under a state of exception for 56 months or about 31 percent of that time. According to José María Portell, an estimated 8,500 Basques were directly affected during these states of exception either through arrest, imprisonment, and torture or by fleeing into exile to avoid the police or vigilante groups.[6]

Data on the nature of police repression in the Basque country during Franco's regime are, as one might expect, difficult to obtain and in any case highly polemical. Table 10.2, however, presents some information on these matters for the period 1968 through 1975. Arrests of etarras tended to come in waves, particularly when stimulated by some especially dramatic threat to public order or assault. The prin-

Table 10.2   *Police Repression in Basque Provinces, 1968–75*

YEAR	ARRESTED	EXILED	IMPRIS-ONED	YEARS SENTENCED	FINES ($ US)	WOUNDED BY POLICE
1968	434	38	—	—	—	—
1969	1,953	342	862	786	110,833	—
1970	831	128	396	1,104	432,167	416
1972	616	—	328	226	71,667	216
1973	572	—	316	635	16,667	178
1974	1,116	320	315	786	636,043	105
1975	4,625	518	632	—	—	—

Source: Luis C.-Nuñez Astrain, *La sociedad vasca actual* (San Sebastián: Editorial Txertoa, 1977), p. 121, table 48.

Note: Data were not available for 1971. Figures are for all arrests in Basque provinces, including both ETA and non-ETA.

cipal waves of arrests came in 1961 following the train derailment, in 1963 and 1964 following the Bilbao strike, in 1967 and early 1968, in 1968 and early 1969 following the assassination of Manzanas, in 1972 and 1973 culminating in the killing of Eustaquio Mendizábal, and in 1975 in an effort to deal with the disturbances surrounding the executions of Txiki and Otaegi. For example, according to Mercé Ibarz, some 110 members of ETA were arrested and a like number exiled in 1961 after the attempted train derailment.[7] In 1963 after the Bilbao strike, 27 principal ETA leaders were jailed and several more went into exile.[8] After the Manzanas killing, according to Ortzi, more than 600 were arrested.[9] In 1969, certainly one of the worst years of the entire Franco period, there were an estimated 1,953 persons arrested, of whom 890 were subjected to mistreatment, 350 to moderate torture, and 160 to severe torture. Some 150 went into exile during the same period.[10] Estimates range rather widely as to the number of Basque political prisoners in jail at any given moment. One list of such prisoners, prepared by the Basque Nationalist Party in February 1972, records 108 names.[11] On the other hand, the list supplied in the book *Operation Ogro*, current to October 1974, contains 245 names, many of which appear to be the same as on the February 1972 list.[12] José María Portell reports that there were more than 240 etarras in prison in early 1974.[13] Mercé Ibarz asserts that when Franco died in November 1975, there were 749 Basque political prisoners and more than 2,000 Basque men and women in exile (although she does not say that all of them were associated with ETA).[14]

The last two states of exception declared by General Franco before his death were especially brutal. The first, which lasted from April 25 to July 25, affected only the four Basque provinces. The second, which lasted from August 22 until Franco's death on November 20, covered Spain in its entirety.

The first state of exception followed a wave of bank robberies, street shootings, and assassinations in the Basque provinces during early spring. After the suspension of constitutional guarantees was declared, police and Guardia Civil troops sought to suppress not only the violence, but all popular support for Basque separatism. During the first thirty days of the exception decree, 198 people were arrested in Vizcaya alone, not counting an unknown but significant number taken to police headquarters or Guardia Civil barracks for interrogation and eventual release without charges.[15] Police roamed at will through the major cities of the Basque provinces, stopping citizens in public places to request their documentation. Young people gathered in bars or restaurants were singled out for special attention, and police raided these establishments regularly to seek out ETA members or other political activists. More than 150 youths fled into France to avoid the searches.[16]

The most complete report of the effects of the state of exception was provided by a team sent in July 1975 by the human rights organization Amnesty International to investigate charges of police brutality.[17] The following were among the findings of the Amnesty International investigation:

1. Although the exact number of detainees was unknown, AI found conclusive evidence that mass arrests took place in Vizcaya and Guipúzcoa provinces at levels far higher than official statistics claimed. As of May 27, 1975, the Spanish government claimed that 189 people had been detained, of whom 90 had subsequently been released. AI found evidence that more than 1,000 persons had been detained in each of the two provinces, and that more than 500 of these were held by authorities for more than seventy-two hours without notification of family, consultation with an attorney, or formal charges being brought.

2. While the state of exception was in effect, the civil governors of the two provinces ordered the rearrest of a number of detainees after they had been released by a judge. In addition, the governors ordered the removal of detainees from police stations or Guardia Civil barracks and their transportation directly to prison, thereby circumventing the judicial process.

3. The AI mission received "personal and direct evidence" of the torture of 45 detainees during the state of exceptions. Further, the investigation revealed "credible and convincing evidence that torture

was systematically used against a *minimum* of 250 Basque detain-ees"[18] in the two most seriously affected provinces. Torture was used against many more people, in all four Basque provinces, AI affirmed, but the evidence was somewhat more circumstantial. Every victim interviewed by the mission had been tortured at least once a day during his or her period of imprisonment. Some had been tortured as many as five times a day. Sessions lasted from thirty minutes to six hours. One victim reported thirty sessions of torture in twenty-one continuous days. Five of the torture victims interviewed had been illegally transferred from one province to another to circumvent the rule prohibiting detention for more than seventy-two hours without charges or notification of legal counsel.

The nature of the torture indicates that it was used as a systematic technique to punish and suppress Basque nationalists and was not a series of isolated and irregular violations of law by a few police. All three major law-enforcement authorities in the Basque prov-inces—the two police forces and the Guardia Civil—participated in the beatings and torture. The methods of torture included, to quote the AI report, "severe and systematic beatings with a variety of contu-sive weapons, *falanga* (beatings on the sole of the feet), burning with cigarettes, near drownings by being submerged in water while sus-pended upside-down, enforced sleeplessness, and forms of psycho-logical stress, including mock executions, sexual threats, threats to relatives, and the technique known as *el cerrojo* (the frequent fasten-ing and unfastening of bolts on the cell doors in order to keep prison-ers in perpetual fear that the torturers have returned)."[19]

4. AI found that torture was used for two reasons: to obtain informa-tion or confessions that would enable the security forces to combat the ETA challenge, but also to intimidate the Basque population into submission and frighten it into abandoning support for the Basque nationalist cause. Even when detainees had no knowledge to reveal, torture was employed to intimidate them and the general Basque population as well as to seek revenge for the assassination of two policemen during May.

Domestic Security Police in Spain, January 1976–July 1978

Within months after his death, the system of repression that General Franco had built began to crumble as Spain groped its way back toward democracy. By the time a year had passed, virtually the entire legal structure of Franco's domestic security policy had passed from the scene. Nevertheless, as the tempo of ETA's insurgency picked up in late 1977 and 1978, elements of the old Franco system began to reappear through new antiterrorist legislation. By the end of the decade, Spain and the Basque country were once again living under laws and institutions which, as far as internal security was concerned, closely resembled the old Franco system.

The period from January 1976 to July 1978 saw a series of policy steps taken in Madrid to appear conciliatory toward Basque public opinion and toward ETA itself. Despite an upsurge in right-wing counterviolence in the Basque provinces, the Spanish government took steps to change the legal framework of its domestic security policy, and sought to put into effect a number of amnesty decrees that would free most Basque political prisoners. There was also an abortive attempt to negotiate a cease-fire with ETA. Its failure, however, brought conciliation to an end and launched the repressive measures so reminiscent of the Franco years.

On February 6, 1976, less than three months after Franco's death, King Juan Carlos and Premier Carlos Arias Navarro formally abrogated fourteen articles of the August 1975 Law on the Prevention of Terrorism. Jurisdiction over alleged political crimes was returned to the civilian Tribunal of Public Order and mandatory death sentences were eliminated.[20] This action dealt only partially with the 1960 and 1975 antiterrorist laws, however. Within Spanish legal circles, pressure continued to build to do away with the laws completely. As the liberalization of the Spanish political system continued through the summer of 1976, many observers felt that a system of separate institutions for "political" and "ordinary" crimes was incompatible with democracy. Accordingly, in late December 1976, King Juan Carlos signed the decree that formally abolished the Tribunals of Public Order, and returned to civilian jurisdiction all politically related crimes, including those that were of a so-called terrorist nature.[21] Only attacks against military personnel and installations remained subject to military courts and military codes of justice. Thus one year after Franco's death, King Juan Carlos had done away with virtually all of the dictator's internal security structure, and hoped thereby to win over key elements within the moderate Basque nationalist leadership.[22] The new regime of laws to deal with extraordinary threats to public order or internal security lasted less than one month.

On December 11, 1976, a small group of gunmen from a leftist Spanish revolutionary organization known as GRAPO entered the office of Antonio María Oriol y Urquijo in Madrid and forced him into a waiting car. As the price for his release, the group demanded the freeing of some two hundred political prisoners, including eight

Basques who were being held for assorted killings and other attacks. Because of the prestige of the victim, a top political advisor to King Juan Carlos, the kidnaping was a sensational and dramatic assault on Spanish public order. A little more than a month later, on January 24, 1977, the same group kidnaped a senior military official, Lt. Gen. Emilio Villaescuesa, president of the Supreme Military Tribunal. At about the same time, in a series of unrelated attacks, seven persons lost their lives in politically related violence in the span of less than a week. Spain's fragile democracy was coming perilously close to self-destruction.

Faced with this challenge, the Spanish government responded by returning to a number of counterinsurgent legal and police devices that it had worked so hard to dismantle.[23] All political demonstrations were banned, and police were given wide search and arrest powers. In Spanish legal terminology these measures stopped just short of a declaration of martial law. Police were given the power to detain suspects for up to ten days for questioning without formally charging them. They were also permitted to enter private residences to search and to gather evidence without securing search warrants. People could be arrested without warrants. Police also had authority to intercept telephone messages and to open mail without court authority.[24] These emergency provisions were withdrawn relatively quickly after the threat subsided, but the incident showed how easy it was to push the new Spanish regime back into the Francoist police-state methods when the threat to public order grew to menacing proportions.

One year later, in the spring of 1978, Spain began the long road back to Francoism without Franco. The return to police-state tactics was preceded by a series of provocative ETA attacks that included the following:

May 1977: ETA killed a policeman in San Sebastián and kidnaped the well-known Bilbao industrialist Javier de Ybarra.

June 1977: ETA killed Ybarra when its demands allegedly were not met.

October 1977: ETA killed the president of the Vizcaya Provincial Government, Augusto Unceta Barrenechea, and his two body-guards.

November 1977: ETA killed a municipal police sergeant in Irún and the commander of the National Police in Navarra.

January 1978: ETA killed a police inspector in Pamplona and wounded two policemen in Eibar and two Guardia Civil troopers in Bilbao.

February 1978: ETA wounded two Guardia Civil troopers in Villarreal de Urrechua, Guipúzcoa, and killed a municipal policeman in Santurce.

March 1978: ETA wounded three policemen in Bilbao, killed two policemen and wounded three more in a single attack in Vitoria, killed a retired member of the Guardia Civil in Aduna, Guipúzcoa, killed two construction workers and wounded fourteen more in a bomb explosion in the nuclear plant at Lemóniz, Vizcaya, killed the former mayor of Castillo y Elejabeitia, Vizcaya, wounded a bar owner in Durango, and wounded fourteen civilians in a bombing in San Sebastián.

April 1978: ETA wounded a Guardia Civil troop in Lejona, Vizcaya, wounded a court employee in Azcoitia, wounded two policemen in San Sebastián, and wounded a Guardia Civil troop in Hernani.

Faced with this level of insurgent violence, the Spanish government began to draft an antiterrorist law that would reinstate a number of the old Franco devices for dealing with terrorists.[25] The draft legislation appeared in early May. On May 20, fourteen Basque nationalist political parties, mostly on the left of the political spectrum, condemned the move, accusing the government of creating a climate of terror "that might justify the putting into effect of some antidemocratic and repressive laws against the public will." At that point in Spanish history when the leading democratic parties and political forces were engaged in debating the new draft Spanish constitution, the appearance of such a new law would, according to the Basque critics, muzzle dissent and stifle debate. The proposed law would, in addition, give a blank check to what the critics called "reactionary forces."

On June 8, the draft antiterrorist law was introduced in the Spanish parliament for debate. Debate and discussion on the proposed law had just begun when the assassination of the Bilbao journalist José María Portell on June 28 produced a dramatic new climate in support of vigorous government measures to curb terrorism. The Congress of Deputies of the Spanish parliament unanimously passed a resolution condemning all terrorist actions and calling on the government to take prompt and effective steps to stop them. From the communist leader Santiago Carrillo to the rightist Manuel Fraga, all parties condemned the attack and called on the government to crush ETA.[26] The Spanish minister of interior, Rodolfo Martín Villa, called for the prompt introduction of measures against terrorism. That very same day, June 29, the Council of Ministers met, and at the request of Minister Martín Villa, approved the pending draft antiterrorist bill as a decree-law. The practical effect of this step was to put the bill into effect in its entirety without waiting for the Cortes to act on it. Among other provisions, the new decree-law authorized the police to hold persons arrested for more than seventy-two hours if they first notified the appropriate judicial authority, who had the power to deny the request; but the burden of action rested with the court to stop the detention, not on the police to defend and justify it. Police were also given the right to intercept telephone and mail traffic with persons suspected of affiliation with insurgent groups. The law also specified that amnesty or pardon would not be permitted in the case of any crime dealt with in the law. Likewise, courts were not permitted to release prisoners on bond before trial.

The reaction from Basque politicians of all ideological positions was strongly negative. The spokesman of the Basque Nationalist Party in the parliament, José Angel Cuerda, denounced the decision by the Cabinet to resort to the decree-law technique to put the draft bill into effect. "Don't talk to us," said Cuerda, "about the urgency of the draft antiterrorist bill, since the Congress has had time since last June 8, at which time said draft bill was presented, to have studied it in depth. The truth is that the government doesn't want the parliament to enact this legislaton because it fears it will be trimmed by amendments."[27] Three prominent leaders of the Basque Left, Miguel Castells, Juan María Bandrés, and Daniel Barandiarán, characterized the decree-law as the thirteenth time since 1956 that the Basque country had been under a state of exception.[28] The leader of the Basque Revolutionary Party, Mario Onaindia, declared, "The anti-terrorist plan is a new state of exception for Euzkadi. It is a serious attack against the freedoms of all citizens, but especially against those of the [Basque] nationalists, for which we have fought so hard." Nevertheless, once approved by the parliament's special Commission on Legislative Urgency, the decree-law went into effect on July 1, 1978. In all, Spain had lived under a regime of law and protection of civil rights almost exactly one year and a half.

Closely related to the debate over the legal framework of Spanish counterinsurgency policy during the early post-Franco years was the equally acrimonious conflict over general amnesty for political prisoners. From General Franco's death until October 1977, the amnesty issue was one of the sharpest points of disagreement between Basque nationalists and the Spanish government.[29] During the period from 1969 through 1974, there were between 100 and 250 members of ETA in Spanish prisons for politically related crimes (table 10.3). During Franco's final days, however, the number increased dramatically to nearly 750. Until these Basques were back on the streets as free men and women, there was little hope of bringing peace to the Basque country.

Table 10.3 *Basques in Spanish Prisons for Politically
Related Crimes against the State, 1969–77*

DATE	NUMBER	SOURCES AND COMMENTS
August 1969	114	Of 209 political prisoners. José Mari Garmendia, *Historia de ETA*, 2 vols. (San Sebastián: L. Haranburu, 1980), 2:239.
February 1972	108	Iñaki de Zabala, "Informe sobre Euzkadi" (Basque Nationalist Party in exile, 1972, Mimeo).
October 1974	245	Julen Agirre, *Operation Ogro*, trans. Barbara Probst Solomon (New York: Ballantine, 1975), pp. 150–58.
November 1975	749	Mercé Ibarz, *Breu historia d'ETA 1959–79* (Barcelona: Magrana, 1981), p. 119.
November 1976	150	Robert P. Clark, *The Basques: The Franco Years and Beyond* (Reno: University of Nevada Press, 1980), p. 277.
March 1977	103	*Diario de Navarra* (Pamplona), March 29, 1977.
May 1977	23	Clark, p. 296.
June 1977	5	Clark, p. 297.
October 1977	29	At time of passage of amnesty legislation by Spanish parliament. *Washington Post*, October 15, 1977.

On November 25, 1975, just three days after Franco died, King Juan Carlos freed nearly all of Spain's political prisoners and reduced the prison terms of many of the remainder. About 1,000 political prisoners were to be given their immediate freedom, and about 700 would have their sentences reduced. By November 28 about 250 had already been released. However, this amnesty affected only those convicted for lesser crimes such as distribution of illegal propaganda or belonging to illegal organizations. The amnesty decree left unaffected some 250 to 350 (nearly all members of ETA) who had been convicted of or were suspected of terrorist crimes, called *delitos de sangre*, or "blood crimes." On July 30, 1976, the king decreed a second amnesty that would free all political prisoners except those sentenced for terrorist acts. The regime estimated that this decree would free about 400 to 500 of the remaining 650 political prisoners. The fate of the remaining 150 Basque prisoners became the focal point for deteriorating Basque-Spanish political relations for the next year.

Throughout the fall and winter of 1976–77 there was much turmoil and disorder in the Basque country, most of it stemming from the amnesty issue. In September, there were massive demonstrations and general strikes which brought hundreds of thousands of Basques into the streets to protest the failure of the Spanish government to grant a total amnesty for all prisoners. Following the assassination by ETA of Juan de Araluce in San Sebastián in early October, right-wing mobs also took to the streets, smashing shop windows, invading bars and coffee shops and beating the patrons, and committing other acts of intimidation. In November, a number of Basque nationalists formed provincial pro-amnesty associations to bring pressure to bear on the Spanish government to free the remaining prisoners. Their slogan was "*Extera Gabonetarako,*" "Home for Christmas." The associations organized rallies to emphasize the Basque public's strong support for a prompt and total amnesty as well as to raise money for the families of those still in prison. They provided medical aid to the recently freed prisoners to help correct some of the physical ailments from which they suffered after so many years of harsh prison life. The associations also toured Western European capitals, including Paris and Brussels, to conduct public hearings and press conferences to publicize their grievances.

There was to be no general amnesty, however, and the prisoners were not home by Christmas. Instead, the Spanish government, under Premier Adolfo Suárez, hardened its position on amnesty for the remaining 150 or so etarras. The Araluce assassinations in October, followed by the kidnaping of Antonio María Oriol in December and of Lt. Gen. Emilio Villaescusa in January, plus rising pressure from rightist political forces and the Spanish military, combined to transform the government's amnesty policy from one of leniency to one of extreme rigidity. From the Oriol kidnaping in December until the following March 1977 there was no general extension of the July 1976 amnesty decree. Prisoners were released on a case-by-case basis, which caused the amnesty program to move slowly if at all. By the spring of 1977 there were still slightly more than 100 etarras in Spanish jails.

As the first democratic parliamentary elections drew near, however, Premier Suárez entered into negotiations with a number of opposition political forces, including the Basque Nationalist Party, over the conditions under which they would agree to participate in the elections. In mid-March, Suárez issued the government's third amnesty decree, which provided for a complicated procedure for rehearing all of the cases that had been decided by the now-defunct Tribunal of Public Order, in anticipation that the new court system would prove more lenient and would result in the release of most (95 percent was the government's estimate) of the remaining prisoners. There were still in prison, however, some dozen or so members of ETA whose cases would be so inflammatory to Spanish rightists that the government simply could not tolerate allowing them back on the streets. The solution for this tiny group was to grant them freedom on the condition that they would go into exile, strictly prohibited from ever returning to Spanish territory.

The Suárez proposal was decidedly unacceptable to the pro-amnesty associations, who now launched new mass demonstrations to put renewed pressure on Madrid. In March, and again in May, the associations organized pro-amnesty weeks in San Sebastián, which led to mass demonstrations, police suppression, and at least five deaths and more than fifty injuries. The agony of the amnesty issue was aggravated severely by the May 20 kidnaping of Javier de Ybarra and his death on June 18.

Apparently in response to the Ybarra kidnaping (something the Spanish government never would admit), Madrid approved, on May 20, the freeing of the remaining twenty-three etarras on the condition that they would go into exile, never to return to Spain. Nevertheless, by the time of the 1977 elections, five etarras still remained in prison.

On October 14, 1977, the Spanish parliament approved legislation that would grant total amnesty to all political prisoners. The bill was passed in the Congress of Deputies by a vote of 296 in favor, 2 against and 18 abstentions. The Senate passed the same day by a vote of 196 in favor, none against, and 6 abstentions. For the first time since July 18, 1936, Spaniards were not at war with one another.

In theory there should not have been any members of ETA in prison by this time. Nevertheless, notwithstanding the intentions of the Spanish government, there was never a time during the summer and fall of 1977 when Spanish prisons were entirely cleared of ETA prisoners. In October 1977, when the general amnesty law was passed, the number of etarras in prison had once again risen to twenty-nine, and it continued to rise steadily for the next three years. The last etarra to be amnestied was Francisco Aldanondo Badiola "Ondarru," who was released on December 9, 1977. (Aldanondo was pursued and killed by the Guardia Civil some two years later, in October 1979.)[30] On numerous occasions in the ensuing years, the Spanish government stated that there would be no more amnesty program. All persons with ETA after the October 1977 amnesty law were to be considered to be attacking a democratic state without justification, and their acts would be looked upon as common crimes to be judged and punished accordingly.[31]

This account has so far focused solely on the legal and institutional framework of Spanish internal security policy, especially as that policy affected ETA. Of equal importance during this same period, however, were the unofficial efforts made by intermediaries to arrange a cease-fire between ETA and the Spanish government. It was the failure of the most promising of these efforts in mid-1978, in fact, that caused Madrid to reverse its policy of conciliation and to launch a new program of repressive measures against ETA.

Obviously it is difficult to know for certain, but I would estimate that between 1977 and 1980 there were at least half a dozen attempts to negotiate a cease-fire between ETA and the Spanish government. There is considerable evidence that these efforts reached their peak, and nearly succeeded, during the spring and summer of 1978. The assassination of José María Portell, followed by the return of the Spanish government to the suppressive tactics of a police state, may have destroyed any chance to arrange an end to the insurgency.

If we are to make sense of the continuation of ETA violence in post-Franco Spain, we must first understand why attempts at negotiation seem always to fail. There are on either side of the struggle persons who genuinely want the conflict to end. But there are also many who have a vested interest in seeing it continue, and they are usually well situated to see to it that attempts at negotiation are frustrated. Lest this all seem excessively conspiratorial, let me add that, even with the best of intentions on both sides, the obstacles to a negotiated settlement are formidable, perhaps insuperable. Without genuine commitments on both sides and a substantial degree of mutual trust, however, there will be no movement toward a cease-fire regardless of how rational such a step might appear from the perspective of an outsider.

From all indications, certain elements within ETA wanted to enter into negotiations leading toward a cease-fire as early as the spring of 1977. In an interview published in the Spanish magazine *La actualidad española*, two representatives of the Pertur faction of ETA(p-m) declared their group's willingness "to abandon violence totally if [the government] lets us move about in the light of day."[32] This interview should be placed in context. In April 1977, following the disappearance and presumed death of their leader Eduardo Moreno Bergareche "Pertur" and following the Seventh Assembly, ETA(p-m) had formed its own political party. It seems likely that there were some within ETA(p-m) who wanted to seize the opportunity to declare a truce. On the other side, however, the Spanish government was still very fragile and uncertain of how far it could press in the transition to democracy (the first parliamentary elections were still several months away, and the new constitution more than a year and a half into the future), so there was no response from Madrid to this overture.

The year 1978 was the decisive period for negotiations. On February 1, newspapers in Bilbao published a communiqué from ETA(m) announcing its wish to discuss a cease-fire and naming five basic points as the minimum needed to get discussions underway.[33] The five points, known as the "KAS alternative," were the following:

1. Total amnesty for all political prisoners (at the time there were an estimated fifty Basques in prison)
2. Legalization of all political parties, including those whose program included the creation of a separate Basque state (at that time prohibited by Spanish law)
3. Expulsion from Euzkadi of the Guardia Civil and all Spanish police forces
4. The adoption of measures to improve the working and living conditions of the masses and especially of the working classes, and the satisfaction of their social and economic aspirations as expressed by their representative organizations
5. An autonomy statute that encompassed as a minimum these points:
   a. Recognition of the national sovereignty of Euzkadi
   b. Euskera as the principal official language of Euzkadi
   c. Law-enforcement authorities to be under the control of the Basque government
   d. All military units garrisoned in the Basque country to be under the control of the Basque government
   e. The Basque people to possess sufficient power to adopt whatever political, economic, and social structures they deemed appropriate for their own progress and welfare

Clearly there were elements within the five-point ETA(m) statement that would be unacceptable to any Spanish government and perhaps even to many Basques. There were, on the other hand, certain points that were not only feasible but had been accomplished by 1980. Therefore the issue was one of desire to negotiate. The spokesman of the Spanish government, Interior Minister Rodolfo Martín Villa, focused on the extreme points and classified the entire package as unacceptable, declaring, "The government has never had contacts with ETA and never will have."[34] Those disposed to negotiate could have opened discussions by attempting to deal with the easier of the points, to test exactly how hard ETA's line would prove to be. In the last analysis, however, there was no one at this time willing to take such a step, and the initiative died. One month later, ETA(m) issued a second communiqué accusing the Spanish government of turning a deaf ear toward Basque needs, and threatening to raise the level of violent action.[35]

The issue emerged once again in the spring. Upon his arrival in late March to assume his position as Bilbao's new police chief, José Sainz Gonzalez issued a statement to the press: "I am ready to take the first step to enter into a dialogue with ETA."[36] In mid-May, the transitional Basque government, the Basque General Council, urged the Spanish government to undertake discussion with ETA in the hope of some kind of breakthrough. By June, something important was definitely underway. Interior Minister Martín Villa was reported to be meeting with an unnamed Basque representative to discuss negotiations. Martín Villa's counterpart in the Basque government, José María Benegas, held an important meeting with leaders of the Basque socialist parties that comprised the KAS. Bilbao journalist José María Portell was rumored to be preparing for a meeting with the head of ETA's Political Office, José Miguel Beñarán Ordeñana "Argala," who was known to be one of the chief proponents of a cease-fire within ETA.[37]

On June 28, the Madrid newspaper *El país* carried a story with the headline "The Government and ETA Prepare Bases to Negotiate." At almost the exact moment that the edition was appearing, José María Portell was assassinated in front of his home as he was preparing to leave for work.[38] I have already described how this event turned the Spanish government away from any interest in conciliation and back toward the repressive measures of the Franco era. Almost exactly six months later, on December 21, Portell's contact within ETA, Argala, was blown up in his car outside his home in the French Basque town of Anglet.[39] His death probably eliminated whatever interest in a cease-fire remained within ETA(m).

All the surviving parties to the discussions immediately denied that there was any attempt at negotiation. Martín Villa stated categorically that while he had indeed chatted with Portell in February 1978, the conversation was only a general one about terrorism and ETA, and that Portell had never acted, either directly or indirectly, as an intermediary between the Spanish government and ETA.[40] Following Argala's death, ETA(m) issued a communiqué flatly denying that he had ever been a contact person with anyone regarding a cease-fire, and that rumors to the contrary were planted by Madrid to discredit Argala in Basque circles.[41] On the other hand, an old friend of Portell's, Juan Felix Eriz, claimed that Martín Villa had lied, and that Portell had indeed arranged to meet with Argala about the time that he was killed.[42] In February of the following year, José María Benegas affirmed that "the government tried to negotiate with ETA on three occasions last summer."[43] In March 1979, the German newspaper *Frankfurter Allegmeine* published an interview with a leader of the Spanish socialist party, PSOE, Alfonso Guerra, in which Guerra claimed that Martín Villa himself had met in Switzerland with ETA leaders and that he had continued to have secret contacts with them during the summer of 1978.[44] Furthermore, as long as the discussions were under way, ETA avoided any provocative action, but every time Martín Villa denied having these discussions in the press, ETA carried out some daring assault as if to remind him of their intransigence. The interview went on to assert that in public, Martín Villa always denied any contact with ETA, out of fear of provoking the rightists in Spain's military and in its ultra-right-wing parties.

Who was responsible for the deaths of Portell and Argala? Elements within ETA(m) claimed responsibility for Portell's killing, but those specifically responsible have never been brought to justice. Persons within the KAS told me in December 1978 that Argala had been killed by Spanish secret police working on the French side of the border; but the version reported most frequently in the Spanish media was that he was killed by members of ETA(m) who opposed negotiation with Madrid. In particular, it was alleged that Argala had been killed by his chief opponent within ETA(m), Miguel Angel Apalategui "Apala," who had also been accused of involvement in the disappearance and presumed death of Pertur some two and a half years earlier. Obviously, responsibility for these matters cannot be ascribed with precision. For our purposes here, it is sufficient to cite this case as the last and best hope for a peaceful settlement of the conflict between ETA and Madrid. That it failed was due, it seems clear to me, to the opposition of powerful elements within ETA and in the neo-Francoist Spanish ultra-Right, who have vested institutional and personal interests in seeing the conflict perpetuated.

Despite the conciliatory posture of the Spanish government in 1977 and early 1978, ETA had to contend with the counterterrorist activity of various groups that emerged from the neo-Francoist Spanish right. These groups began to form during the spring of 1975, when they were little more than armed bands that roamed the streets of the larger Basque cities, intimidating citizens and occasionally breaking into bars or cafés to beat the customers, particularly young men. As the end of the Franco era neared in the fall of 1975, this rightist violence increased in intensity and tempo. In the months following Franco's death, the groups began to solidify and to form organizations from which they could carry out anti-ETA action. As we have seen, one such organization, Guerrilleros de Cristo-Rey, had existed since 1975. It was joined by the Basque-Spanish Battalion (BVE, for *Batallón*

Vasco-Español), ETA Antiterrorism (ATE, for Antiterrorismo ETA), Armed Spanish Groups (GAE, for Grupos Armados Españoles), the Apostolic Anticommunist Alliance (AAA, for Alianza Apostólica Anti-comunista), and several other, minor, organizations. Not much is known publicly about these groups, and it could very well be that the same group used different names to evade detection or to make itself appear more powerful than it really was.[45]

The first attack officially attributed to forces of the extreme right was a bombing of a bookstore in April 1975 in the French Basque town of Hendaye, where many Basque refugees lived.[46] The first killing attributed to rightist groups occurred six months later, in October, when a Basque named Ignacio Echave was killed in a hotel in Elorrio, Vizcaya. During 1975, attacks from right-wing groups resulted in two deaths and five wounded. In 1976, the toll of rightist killings rose to three, with thirteen woundings and two kidnapings. In July, Eduardo Moreno Bergareche "Pertur" was kidnaped and never seen again. Only in January 1982 did the AAA formally claim responsibility for his death (along with those of some twenty other persons).[47] In 1977, there were no deaths associated with rightist attacks, but there were sixteen wounded and numerous bombings and other assaults. In 1978, there were four deaths, twenty-three woundings, and three kidnapings. One of the killed was the wife of Jon Etxabe. On December 21, as already noted, the ETA leader Argala was killed when his car was blown up in the French town of Anglet. The responsibility for that attack has never been assigned.

Domestic Security Policy in Spain: July 1978–December 1980

During the second half of the period under review, Spanish internal security policy turned 180 degrees from its position of the preceding thirty months. Vigorous antiterrorist legislation provided the juridical framework for strengthened police and paramilitary operations aimed at total suppression of ETA. There were new waves of political arrests, and the number of Basques in prison reached levels not seen since Franco's death. Reports of torture in prison once again became public, and rightist counterterror squads increased their activity. There were isolated and sporadic attempts at negotiation, but they were uniformly unsuccessful.

The special 1978 Decree-Law on Antiterrorism remained in effect in one form or another for nearly two years and a half. It was approved as emergency legislation by the Spanish parliament as Law 56/1978 on December 4 with the title "Special Measures toward Crimes of Terrorism Committed by Armed Groups." The law was expanded by a special Decree-Law 3/1979, promulgated by the king of January 6, 1979, with the title "On the Protection of Citizen Security."[48] The basic law was renewed by government decree in December 1979. Finally, in mid-October 1980, after twenty-seven months, the government submitted to the parliament new draft legislation to combat terrorism. The draft law was very much like the antiterrorist decrees and laws that had been inherited from the Franco years. The term *terrorism* was defined broadly and loosely to cover a long list of acts, as well as any degree of collaboration with those perpetrating the acts, both before and after the commission of the act itself. The law provided for the suspension of a number of important constitutional guarantees, including the guarantees against preventive detention and search without warrant and the protection of privacy in the use of the mails and telecommunications. Detention for up to ten days incommunicado and without charges was permitted.[49]

Not surprisingly, the strongest opposition to the proposed draft came from Basque political leaders in the Congress of Deputies. On repeated occasions throughout the parliamentary debate, the Basque Nationalist Party attempted to amend the draft to soften its effects, but to no avail. Press reports suggested that some Spanish leftists also opposed the law, but when the final vote was taken on October 29, out of the 350-member Congress of Deputies, 298 members voted for the bill, 2 voted against, 8 formally abstained (including the seven PNV deputies), and the remainder were not present. Thus Spain enacted, through democratic methods, a special legal regime for dealing with insurgent threats to public order that was virtually identical to the one used by General Franco throughout the 1960s and early 1970s.[50] (The special legislation was still in effect in the fall of 1982, and probably will continue to be for as long as ETA remains a genuine threat to Spanish internal security.)

Discussion of the legal framework of Spanish and Basque internal security policy would be incomplete without a brief mention of the role of the government of the Basque Autonomous Community in the maintenance of public order.

From the outset, the most sensitive and controversial aspect of the Basque Autonomy Statute had to do with the maintenance of public order. The statute permits the Basque government, with headquarters in Vitoria, to establish its own police force, which it had managed to do by mid-1982. However, the statute also established a special mixed Basque-Spanish Security Board (Junta de Seguridad) whose job it is to coordinate the security forces of the two governments in the Basque region. The board contains in equal number members named by the Basque and Spanish governments and is chaired by a person named by Madrid. According to the Autonomy Statute, Spanish police and security forces (including the Guardia Civil and the army) can intervene in the Basque region under three conditions: when requested to do so by the Basque government; when the decline of order threatens the security of the Spanish state and when the intervention is approved by a majority vote of the Security Board; or when the Spanish government determines that such intervention is necessary for it to carry out the obligations entrusted to it by the Spanish constitution. In this latter case, due notification must be given to the Spanish parliament, which may cancel said intervention. Finally, the statute carries this reminder of the ultimate authority of Madrid: in cases of a declaration of a state of alarm, exception, or siege (all of which imply a suspension of constitutional guarantees), the Basque police forces will come under the jurisdiction of the regime, civil or military, that is established in the region by the Spanish government. Since its creation (which was delayed more than a year for various political and bureaucratic reasons), the Security Board has played an insignificant role in the internal security policy of the region. The Basque government did indeed recruit and begin in 1982 to train its own police force of some 680 men, with a budget of about $22 million.[51] Since this force was to be only lightly armed and was to concentrate primarily on traffic control and related aspects of public order, it seemed highly unlikely that native Basque security forces would become involved in counterinsurgent activity for some years to come.

After early 1978 and particularly after the promulgation of the Anti-Terrorist Decree-Law in July 1978, the number of ETA members in prison rose steadily to the point where, by October 1980, there were as many etarras in prison as there had been during the Franco years. By late 1978 or early 1979, there were more than 100 etarras in prison. By October 1980, this number had risen to 231; by December 1980, to 265; and by January 1981, to 298 (see table 10.4).

During the period from October 1978 through May 1981, a period of thirty-two months, some 350 members of ETA (including 30 women) were tried by the Audiencia Nacional, Spain's supreme tribunal for this kind of judicial case (see table 10.5).[52] According to one source, trials of ETA members account for about 40 percent of all terrorist cases in Spain, with the left-wing Spanish group GRAPO accounting for about 35 percent and various other rightist and leftist Spanish groups making up the remaining 25 percent. The 350 members of ETA were convicted of some 428 criminal acts (and found innocent of some 142 others, one should add), and sentenced to a total of 1,185

Table 10.4   *Basques in Spanish Prisons for Politically Related Crimes against the State, 1978–81*

DATE	NUMBER	SOURCES AND COMMENTS
December 1978	97	This is a minimum number, those transferred to Soria prison in late 1978. *Diario vasco* (San Sebastián), December 28, 1978.
January 1979	111	*Diario vasco* (San Sebastián), January 4, 1979.
February 1979	130	*Deia*, February 7, 1979.
October 1980	231	*Deia*, October 22, 1980.
December 1980	265	*Deia*, December 3, 1980.
January 1981	298	*Deia*, January 14, 1981.

Table 10.5   *ETA in the Spanish National Court System, 1978–81*

PERIOD	CASES	PERSONS TRIED	GUILTY VERDICTS[a]	YEARS SENTENCED	YEARS SENTENCED PER PERSON
October 1978–December 1979	26	67	72	173	2.6
January–December 1980	61	162	222	637	3.9
January–May 1981	39	121	134	375	3.1
Totals and average	126	350	428	1,185	3.4

Source: *Deia*, December 18, 1981.

[a] Number of guilty verdicts exceeds number of persons tried, because many were convicted of multiple crimes.

years in prison, for an average of 3.4 years per person.[53] In all, the cases involved 542 separate criminal acts, including 28 killings, 114 illegal possessions of arms or explosives, 53 automobile thefts, 50 armed robberies, and 130 acts of collaboration with ETA. The heaviest sentence during the period was 34 years and 6 months, given to a member of ETA(p-m), Victor Garay, for 4 acts of armed robbery. A member of ETA(m), José Miguel Azurmendi, received a sentence of 34 years for a terrorist killing; and Lorenzo Alcain received sentences totaling 29 years and 6 months for two unsuccessful attempted homicides.

One of the most worrisome aspects of the treatment given to ETA members in prison had to do with the way in which they were moved about from one prison to another, without notification of family or lawyers. Often the prisoners were removed to detention sites distant from their homes, making it inconvenient for family and attorneys to contact and assist them. The most inflammatory of these cases was tried in December 1978. Following the assassination of José María Portell in June, the Spanish minister of interior, Rodolfo Martín Villa, went to West Germany to discuss antiterrorist measures being developed there. Upon his return, he announced that security measures around prisons containing terrorists would have to be strengthened, especially in those cases in which the terrorists were held near their homes and could obtain support and assistance in case of an escape attempt. By the close of the year, it had been decided that it would be more feasible to move the prisoners in question from their current prisons to several in other parts of Spain where security provisions were tighter and where the facilities were newer and in a better state of repair. In addition, in mid-December, the Interior Ministry alleged that it had discovered a plot to launch a major jail escape of the etarras who were at that time in prisons in the Basque provinces. Accordingly, under orders of the interior minister, 97 members of ETA were removed from their jails and sent to a maximum security prison in Soria, about 110 miles south of Bilbao. Once in Soria prison the etarras, together with some 36 members of GRAPO, were under the control of two companies of special antiterrorist army troops instead of the normal prison guard force. Because the move took place in secret, without notification of family members or lawyers, it violated the basic rights of the prisoners. The transitional Basque government, the CGV, protested the move, as did all of the Basque nationalist political parties. There were massive protests and demonstrations all over the Basque country through the end of December and into January. Three years later, however, in January 1982, there were still 110[54] members of ETA in Soria, 70 from ETA(m) and 40 from ETA(p-m).[55]

Another violation of prisoner rights had to do with the mistreatment and torture of ETA members under police jurisdiction, either at the police station before they had been formally charged or in the prison itself while they were awaiting trial or serving their sentences. Amnesty International, the London-based human rights organization, was most concerned about the opportunity for abuse of prisoners under preventive detention by police or the Guardia Civil. According to AI's special report on Spain, as well as its annual report for the period May 1, 1980, to April 30, 1981, the various changes in Spain's legal system after the summer of 1978 removed many of the institutional protections of the rights of detainees and prisoners who had been arrested for suspected terrorist activity.[56] In its reports, Amnesty International focused especially closely on four aspects of the treatment of suspects and prisoners. First, the laws governing terrorist acts made it possible for the police or Guardia Civil to hold persons in preventive detention for periods of up to ten days without charging them or bringing them before a court for arraignment. In theory, police needed court permission to hold suspects more than seventy-two hours, but in practice the courts seldom if ever exercised control over this form of prisoner abuse. Second, as the AI report put it, "the danger inherent in prolongation of custody in the sole hands of the police is exacerbated by the fact that it is almost always accompanied by an order of 'incommunicado detention.'" That is, persons being held during this period of preventive detention could be, and usually were, denied right to see legal counsel. Third, the organizational structure of the Spanish judiciary, centralized in Madrid, made it highly unlikely in practice that any Spanish judge would travel to the remote Basque or Catalan provinces to investigate personally police requests to hold suspects for up to ten days without charges or counsel. Finally, the procedures whereby detainees could make complaints about their treatment were clearly inadequate to ensure that abusive police or Guardia Civil would be punished for the mistreatment of prisoners. Interrogation was carried out in most cases by police officers out of uniform, so that subsequent identification was difficult. Since prisoners were denied access to legal counsel, and their friends and family usually did not know where they were or even that they had been arrested, they had difficulty producing corroborating evidence or testimony against abusive police. There was no requirement that prisoners be given regular medical examinations, and prisoners had no right to medical care if they were injured during interrogation. When police doctors did examine them during interrogation, the doctors were not compelled by law to record their findings in a place accessible to parties to any future action for maltreatment.

Not surprisingly, the Amnesty International mission in October 1979 found "on the basis of all the evidence obtained by the mission, and in particular the medical reports [of 14 claimed torture victims], . . . that maltreatment amounting to torture has occurred in police stations in Madrid, Barcelona and Bilbao between September 1978 and June 1979."[57] Examples of torture include the following: death or threats of mutilation made to the detainees themselves or to their families; mock executions; *la bañera* (having one's head forced into a bathtub filled with a mixture of water, blood, vomit, excrement, and food remnants and kept there until near-suffocation); mental and physical exhaustion through deprivation of sleep and being forced to remain in strenuous positions for long hours; beatings about the head, body, genitals, soles of the feet, and fingers; suspension by hand-cuffed wrists from a bar for long hours; electric shocks; *la moto* (literally, "the motorcycle," a form of punishment involving extreme pressure on the knees and lower legs, causing severe pain); and sexual threats and humiliation.

As the reader might imagine, the subject of torture in prisons is one of considerable polemic and heated debate in Basque and Spanish political circles. Neither side seems disposed to grant the validity of the perspective or evidence of its adversary. On October 14, 1979, for example, a Basque youth named Mikel Amilibia was arrested by the Guardia Civil, held in their headquarters in San Sebastián for three or four hours, and then transferred to police headquarters, where he was held incommunicado and without charges until October 20. When he was released, he claimed to have been tortured, and exhibited marks on the inside of his thighs where he claimed electrodes had been placed. An examining physician confirmed the cause of the injury. Leading Basque politicians denounced the police and Guardia Civil for mistreating Amilibia, but the official Spanish government position was that the youth had burned himself with red hot coins in an attempt to discredit the Guardia Civil. With no evidence and no explicit accusations against a specific individual, the government did not press charges.[58]

In these matters, the elected members of Spain's parliament found themselves virtually helpless to restrain the police and Guardia Civil in their alleged mistreatment of prisoners. In December 1979, in the midst of charges of torture in prisons, the parliament created a special commission to investigate the validity of the charges and to ascertain whether or not Basques were being mistreated. After much delay, the commission finally arranged to visit detention sites in the Basque region to verify for themselves the extent of the abuse. Upon their arrival in July 1980, they were denied access to a number of Guardia Civil and police installations on the grounds that the installations were the property of the Ministry of Interior and that visits to them could be arranged only with the express permission of the minister, who denied his approval. Thus the elected representatives of the Spanish people returned to Madrid without having been allowed to visit the sites where the torture and abuse allegedly took place. Without such key information, the commission quietly recessed for the customary Spanish August vacation and as far as I can determine was never heard from again.[59]

The point of the lance, as far as the Spanish government's policy toward ETA was concerned, consisted of police and paramilitary operations (to which, in 1981, were added operations of Spain's regular army and navy units). Through the late 1970s and into 1980, there were stationed in the Basque provinces some 12,000 Guardia Civil troops (out of a total of 64,000 in all of Spain) and some 6,000 Policía Armada (out of a total 40,000), in addition to the normal police and constabulary forces one would expect for a population of about two and a half million. Thus while the Basque provinces accounted for about 3.5 percent of Spain's territory and about 7 percent of its population, about 17 percent of the nation's paramilitary strength was committed to the maintenance of public order in the region.[60] In addition to sending a large percentage of their paramilitary manpower to the Basque provinces, Spain's law-enforcement authorities also spent more on those forces. Police and Guardia Civil troops sent to the Basque provinces were especially selected for the assignment and given additional technical and psychological training before reporting for duty. As an added incentive to accept duty in Euzkadi, they were given double vacations and a bonus of 30,000 pesetas (about $300) a month. While in service in the Basque country they were given extra support personnel in office and administrative jobs and the best available equipment. After three years service in the region, they were given their choice of assignment elsewhere in Spain; and those who completed five years' service were given a special medal for valor.[61]

Table 10.6 suggests the extent of police and paramilitary action from the summer of 1978. I do not have data on arrests before July 1978, but from scanning secondary sources, one infers that arrests of ETA members were not nearly as frequent as those recorded subsequently. While there was some fluctuation over the period 1978 to 1981, there were on average 40 to 50 etarras arrested per month. If this is accurate, then somewhere between 1,440 and 1,800 members of ETA were detained during this period. The reader may recall from chapter 9 that I estimated the size of ETA at between 300 and 400 in 1978 and 1979, between 400 and 500 in 1980, and at 500 in 1981. Unless these data are substantially in error, a number equal to the entire membership of ETA was detained by Spanish authorities at one time or another during the period 1978 to 1981. That the organization continued to function despite these arrests is due, in all probability, to a combination of two factors: ETA's ability to recruit new members to replace arrested ones, and the tendency of Spanish courts to release members on bail at the rate of about one release for every four arrests.[62]

After the spring of 1978, even before the passage of new antiterrorist legislation, one of the principal instruments of Spanish anti-ETA policy was the force of special police or paramilitary trained and equipped to deal with insurgent threats. In March 1978, following the bombing of the Lemóniz nuclear plant under construction, a bombing that killed two and wounded fourteen workers, the director of security of the Ministry of Interior promptly dispatched his assistant, José Sainz Gonzalez, to replace the police chief of Bilbao. The appointment of

Table 10.6   *Rate of ETA Arrests, 1978–81*

PERIOD	NUMBER	ARRESTS PER MONTH	SOURCES AND COMMENTS
September 1– December 25, 1978	184 (est.)	46.0	Estimate of 4 persons in each of 46 comandos arrested. Mass arrests date from September 1, 1978, and arrival of Roberto Conesa in Bilbao. *Cambio 16*, no. 370 (January 7, 1979).
January 1– December 4, 1979	468 (est.)	42.5	According to *Deia* (Bilbao), December 6, 1979, 652 etarras arrested June 30, 1978–December 4, 1979. The cited figure represents 652 minus the 184 (est.) arrested in last third of 1978.
January 1– July 15, 1980	329	50.6	*Deia*, July 19, 1980. 132 were arrested during first 3 months of 1980 (44 per month). *Deia*, April 2, 1980.
December 1, 1980– March 24, 1981	296	74	Report of Minister of Interior Juan José Rosón to Congress of Deputies. *Deia*, April 2, 1981.
March 24– May 21, 1981	203	101.5	Report of Minister of Interior Juan José Rosón to Congress of Deputies. *Deia*, May 22, 1981.
June 1– October 30, 1981	71	14.2	Report of Minister of Interior Juan José Rosón to Congress of Deputies. *El país*, October 30, 1981.
January 1– October 30, 1981	410	41.0	Report of Minister of Interior Juan José Rosón to Congress of Deputies. *Deia*, December 30, 1981. Note: *Cambio 16*, no. 519 (November 11, 1981), reports 394 arrested during same period.

Sainz, reputed to be one of the leading experts on ETA, was accompanied by the creation of a special antiterrorist police unit to investigate suspected terrorist attacks and assist local police units in tracking down the perpetrators.[63] In July, following the assassination of José María Portell, Spanish Interior Minister Rodolfo Martín Villa consulted with West German experts about that country's highly regarded antiterrorist program, including training and equipping of antiterrorist forces.[64] After Martin Villa's return to Spain, the decision was made to create special antiterrorist units to deal with attacks while they were in progress, something on the order of S.W.A.T. teams as they are used in municipal police forces in the United States.

The anti-ETA effort began in earnest in September with the arrival in Bilbao of a special counterterrorist unit of about fifty men under the command of police commissioner Roberto Conesa.[65] The group began by scanning police records for clues to contact between ETA members and persons involved in quasi-public (but still illegal) political parties and labor unions. Police surveillance of these latter individuals was increased to obtain leads to the whereabouts of ETA leaders. A number of the members of the openly operating Basque socialist parties, such as HASI, LAIA, and KAS, were detained and questioned intensively. Even a few members of the legalized Basque National Party were arrested and questioned.

It seems virtually certain that at about this same time, Conesa also managed to place at least one and perhaps several spies in key positions within ETA. Before this, ETA had been invulnerable to such infiltration, especially at the higher levels of the organization. There had been attempts to infiltrate the organization; but the spies and informers were almost always intercepted and killed or intimidated and driven out before they could cause much damage. The strange case of Tomás Sulibarria suggests something of what was taking place in 1978, however. Sulibarria, whose code name was Tomi, was first arrested in Bilbao on August 14, 1978, while distributing pamphlets demanding amnesty for political prisoners. Since the preceding May, police had pursued him, suspecting him of being the head of an ETA cell in Bilbao. A short time after his arrest, he was released by the police. On August 30, he was kidnaped from a restaurant in the French Basque town of St.-Jean-de-Luz, taken to a remote country area near Mundaca in Vizcaya, and shot in the neck. Badly wounded, he was picked up by two youths and rushed to a hospital. ETA(m) issued a communiqué the next day claiming responsibility for the attack and accusing Sulibarria of being a police spy. Sulibarria survived, and was sent to prison for a year and a half. All the time, he denied ETA's accusation. Upon his release from prison, he returned to Bilbao, where he worked as a bank clerk. Two months later, on June 3, 1980, while he was walking on a street in downtown Bilbao in mid-morning, Sulibarria was shot and killed by a man and woman, both about twenty-five years old, who managed to escape undetected. ETA(m) claimed responsibility for this second attack also, again accusing Sulibarria of being a police informer. In mid-December 1978, several months after Sulibarria was shot the first time, a member of the Basque Revolutionary Party (EIA) in the small town of Ermua was approached by four men who attempted to bribe him to reveal the names of ETA leaders, for which they would pay five to ten million pesetas (roughly $50,000 to $100,000) per name. He was also invited to pass information to persons who had allegedly infiltrated ETA, and he was warned that if the information were not correct, his contacts within ETA would "do to him what they had done to 'Tomi.'" The possibility exists, then, that Sulbarria was killed not by etarras but by Spanish agents who had infiltrated the organization and were punishing him for passing on false information.[66] Press accounts suggest that on at least one other occasion, in November 1980, the capture of a number of ETA cell leaders was made possible by information gathered from informants within the organization.[67] Thus it would be reasonable to assume that in late 1978, Conesa had managed to penetrate ETA's organization with several spies.

Whatever his source of information, it apparently was sufficient to enable Conesa and his men to carry out one of the biggest waves of arrests of etarras since ETA had been founded. From September 1 through December 25, 1978, Conesa's group uncovered 46 ETA cells and made an estimated 184 arrests, captured more than 100 firearms, 76 kilos of explosive, 6 automobiles, 48 million pesetas (nearly half a million dollars), and innumerable objects associated with false identities, such as disguises, false papers, and so forth.[68]

The Conesa group's effort during the last four months of 1978 was only the first of several extending through the next three years. In January and February 1979, the special antiterrorist group launched a major hunt for the 36 "most wanted" members of ETA. While they did not capture any of the 36, the search did lead to the arrest of more than 50 etarras during the first ten days of February.[69]

One year later, on February 1, 1980, an ETA ambush near the small Vizcayan town of Ispaster left six Guardia Civil men dead and provoked still another major build-up of antiterrorist forces in the Basque region.[70] The principal elements involved in the February 1980 buildup came from the National Police and the Guardia Civil. From the National Police came a 120-man force called the Special Operations Group (GEO, the Grupo Especiales de Operaciones), especially selected, armed, and trained for dealing with urban insurgencies, and modeled after the West German antiterrorist police unit that rescued the Lufthansa airliner hijacked to Mogadishu by members of the Baader-Meinhof group in October 1977. The GEO was equipped not only with German Mauser assault rifles but also with such heavy equipment as helicopters and armored cars. The Guardia Civil detachment, some 450 strong, was called Rural Antiterrorist Units (or Groups), or by its initials UAR (or GAR). As the name suggests, these units were primarily used to patrol rural areas, particularly along routes where ambushes were likely. Within the UAR there was still another special unit called the Special Intervention Group (GEI, Grupo Especial de Intervención), a force of some 23 men committed solely to crisis intervention in cases such as aerial piracy, hostage-taking, and so forth. These groups were likewise equipped with the latest weapons, communications gear, and transport, including helicopters and armored vehicles. The combined force, together with the regular Guardia Civil and police forces and the Conesa group, were placed under the control of a Spanish army general, José Saenz de Santamaría, who had achieved a distinguished record as a military commander and had also served as chief of staff of the Guardia Civil. In addition to having special authority as the sole head of the combined forces for public order in the Basque provinces, General Saenz de Santamaría was named as an envoy of the Spanish government by action of the Spanish Council of Ministers, which gave him special powers in the provinces that in certain ways rivaled those of the provincial governors.

At the time, it was believed that build-up of anti-ETA forces would ensure that the campaign against terrorism in the Basque region could be pursued without resort to the use of Spanish regular army troops. In September, the minister of defense, Agustin Rodriguez Sahagun, told a press conference, "I do not believe in the efficacy or in the need for the intervention of the armed forces in the struggle against terrorism."[71] Six months later, by the spring of 1981, Spanish regular army troops were committed to the war against ETA.

During 1979 and 1980, negotiations and rightist counterviolence continued to be important in the struggle between ETA and the Spanish government.

There were, during the period, renewed attempts to negotiate between ETA and Madrid, but they were frustrating and futile. During the summer of 1979, contacts were made between ETA(p-m) and the government in an attempt to halt p-m's bombing campaign.[72] The kidnaping of UCD deputy Javier Rupérez in November 1979 occasioned a flurry of negotiations which led eventually to the freeing of

26 Basque prisoners, although the government denied any connection between their liberation and the release of Ruperez.[73] After the attack by ETA(p-m) with a rocket launcher against the Moncloa Palace in February 1980, the organization attempted to use the threat posed by this new weapon to initiate talks, but the government refused to listen to their demands.[74] In March 1980, French police raided the apartment of ETA leaders in Bayonne and discovered documents alleging that they had had contact with PNV officials, but the PNV discounted the documents as having been planted to discredit them before the upcoming elections for the new Basque parliament.[75] Also in March, the president of the Catalan government, Josep Taradellas, claimed that he had gone to France to meet with ETA leaders at the express request of King Juan Carlos and Premier Suárez; but the latter promptly denied it, and many Basques were angered at this attempt to interfere in their affairs.[76] In May 1980, at the time of the attempted censure motion against Suárez in the Spanish parliament, the PSOE leader Felipe Gonzalez claimed that there had been attempts at contact between Suárez and ETA; but Suárez denied it, although again Benegas made it clear that there had indeed been such attempts, and more than once.[77] In the summer of 1980, ETA(p-m) once again tried to enter into negotiations with Suárez to avoid another summer bombing campaign like that of 1979 that had been so costly to all concerned, but the government refused to consider the overture.[78] In September 1980, ETA(p-m) issued a statement announcing its desire to arrange a truce.[79] Through the end of 1980, however, none of these efforts had produced anything lasting. As the head of the Basque Nationalist Party, Xabier Arzalluz, put it in September 1980 in a classic understatement, "I have tried to negotiate with ETA, but it is not easy."[80]

In 1979, the tempo of right-wing assaults rose measurably. There were 11 deaths, 37 woundings, and 4 kidnapings attributed to rightist groups during the year. On January 13, an etarra named José Manuel Pagoaga Gallastegui "Peixoto" was machine-gunned to death in St.-Jean-de-Luz. On May 4, ETA leader Domingo Iturbe "Txomin" was machine-gunned by three individuals in Biarritz. It was the third time since 1975 that Iturbe had been wounded by rightists. On June 25, a Basque exile named Enrique Gomez "Korta" was shot to death in front of a bar in Bayonne. On August 3, a Basque refugee named Juan Lopategui was shot to death and his two companions wounded in an attack in Anglet. On September 13, a Basque exile named Justo Elizarán Sarasola was machine-gunned in Biarritz, and died twenty-three days later. On September 28, a member of the San Sebastián city council representing the Basque socialist party Herri Batasuna was killed. The GAE claimed responsibility.

The year 1980 was even worse: 21 killed, 55 wounded, 2 kidnaped. On January 17, the GAE claimed credit for killing Carlos Saldise, a member of the Pro-Amnesty Committee of Lezo, Guipúzcoa. An attack on a bar in Alonsótegui, claimed by GAE, resulted in 4 deaths and the wounding of 11. On February 3, BVE assassinated 2 youths, a man in Ondárroa named Jesús María Zubikarai and a woman in Madrid named Yolanda Gonzalez Martin, allegedly in retaliation for the ambush by ETA of 6 members of the Guardia Civil several days earlier. On April 19, a supporter of Herri Batasuna was killed at the front door of his home in Hernani. On February 8, Txomin Iturbe was attacked for the fourth time, again in Biarritz, although this time the attack was carried out by French police dressed in plain clothes.[81] On June 11, the BVE kidnaped a member of ETA named José Miguel Etxebarria "Naparra." On the following July 3, a telephone call from BVE announced that Naparra had been killed. His body had not been discovered by the end of 1980. In two attacks, on August 30 and September 7, BVE and AAA shot and killed 3 HB supporters. On November 25, the BVE attacked a Basque bar in Hendaye, killing 2 and wounding 10. After the attack, the assailants were able to cross the border into Spain, causing protests from Basque political leaders as well as the French government for what apparently was complicity between the attackers and Spanish customs officials and the Guardia Civil. On December 30, José Martín Sagardía Zaldúa "Usúrbil" was killed by an explosive charge placed in his car in Biarritz.

In all, as best we can calculate, from April 1975 through December 1980 right-wing groups were responsible for 509 separate attacks on Basques in either France or Spain. These attacks killed 41, wounded 149, and kidnaped 11. Approximately one-fourth of the killings took place in the French Basque region, particularly around the cities of Biarritz, Bayonne, and St.-Jean-de-Luz. About the same number were concentrated in the Andoain-Urnieta-Hernani region of Guipúzcoa, on the main road that connects San Sebastián with the Goierri area. The remainder were scattered through Guipúzcoa and Vizcaya. Few if any took place outside these two provinces, in other regions of Spain.[82] The AAA has claimed responsibility for 20 of the killings, or almost half, while most of the rest have been attributed to the BVE.

Very little is known about these militant rightist groups. Apparently, the BVE was commanded by a retired Spanish army lieutenant colonel who spent time in Argentina training (or training with) rightist vigilante squads there. This official allegedly ran the organization from Madrid, from where orders, supplies, and weapons were sent to the operating cells of the organization in France and in the Spanish Basque region.[83] The only cell of the BVE to be uncovered by police was broken up in early March, 1981, following the assassination of Francisco Javier Ansa Zirkunegi in Andoain. The cell was found to contain only two permanent members, although a third person was arrested for having been associated with the group in a support role. The leader of the cell was a thirty-two-year-old unemployed man from nearby Andoain who had a long history of participating in rightist causes, and had been accused before of taking part in attacks on leftists in Guipúzcoa. Police also found six shot guns, two pistols, and a revolver, with considerable ammunition for the weapons. In addition to the killing of Ansa Zirkunegi, the cell was charged with seven other assaults, which had resulted in six deaths and two woundings. In other words, this one cell of only two people had accounted for about one-third of all the killings charged to or attributed to the BVE. This suggests that the total strength of the BVE was probably no more than thirty to forty.[84]

According to press accounts (which admittedly are little more than informed speculation), these rightist assault groups recruited their members from one of two sources. On the Spanish side of the border, the groups employed primarily neo-Francoist political extremists with close ties to the country's internal security apparatus, including the National Police and the Guardia Civil. The two men convicted of killing Yolanda Gonzalez in Madrid in February 1980 had both served in the national security forces, one in the Guardia Civil and the other in the intelligence service that reported directly to the office of the prime minister.[85] It would appear that, although considerable sums of money did change hands to finance these killings, most of the BVE cells in Spain were staffed by men who did so out of political conviction and who were not hired killers.

Matters on the French side of the border were quite different. Here the assassinations of at least eight and perhaps as many as ten Basque exiles and ETA members were carried out by hired teams of mercenaries who operated out of bases in Marseilles and other parts of the French Mediterranean coast. These teams were composed primarily of Frenchmen formerly with the French Secret Army in Algeria, although other nationalities were represented in the groups. The machine-gun attack on the bar in Hendaye which left two dead and ten wounded was allegedly carried out by two Frenchmen and an Algerian. There were probably no more than twenty such assassins. Versions differ on the cost of a murder, from $100,000 per victim to $10,000 per member of the assault team. The money to finance the killings allegedly came from various sources, including wealthy Basque industrialists who did not wish to pay the revolutionary tax, wealthy Spaniards who wanted to reestablish Francoism in Spain, and even Mafia leaders around the Mediterranean coast who found ETA(p-m)'s summer bombing campaigns in 1979 and 1980 "bad for business."[86]

Spanish Counterinsurgency Policy and ETA Violence

Government policies to counter insurgent violence are no different from other public policies; in the long run, they must be judged by how effectively they solve the problem of civil disorder in the country and how much they cost in terms of material resources, human lives, and individual liberties. By way of conclusion to this discussion of Spanish counterinsurgent policy from 1976 through 1980, I offer the reader some data and analysis that relate changes in that policy with fluctuations in ETA insurgent violence through the period.

In performing this analysis, we are fortunate to have an almost perfect test case with which to work. If we consider the five-year period from January 1, 1976, through December 31, 1980, as our span of time for analysis, we see that it is divided exactly in the middle as far as Spanish internal security policy is concerned. As we have seen, halfway through the period, on July 1, 1978, Spanish policy reversed itself completely. For the preceding thirty months, Madrid's domestic security policy had emphasized dismantling the structure of the Francoist state. For the two and a half years following July 1, 1978, however, Spanish internal security policy came more and more to resemble that of the Franco regime.

The question, then, is this: what was the effect of the sharp turnabout in Spanish policy on July 1, 1978, on the level of ETA violence? Let us refer to the information in figure 10.1. The chart depicts changes in levels of ETA violence on a monthly basis from January 1976 through December 1980. The line portrays the number of ETA victims recorded in the Basque press each month. Along the right margin of the figure are listed some key events in Basque and Spanish political affairs, including elections, amnesty decrees, and antiterrorist legislation.

It is obvious from simple inspection of the figure that ETA violence was much higher after July 1, 1978, than it had been before. During the thirty-month period before July 1, 1978, the average number of ETA victims per month was only 3.87. The organization attacked 5 or more victims in only four of the thirty months in the span. After July 1, 1978, when Spain's vigorous and repressive antiterrorist policy was in

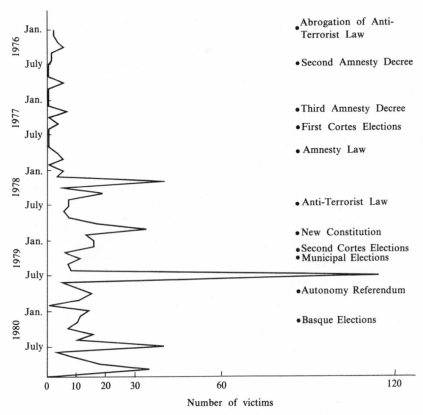

Figure 10.1.   Changes in Levels of ETA Violence, by Month, 1976–80.

effect, ETA averaged 15.97 victims per month, and the number of ETA victims exceeded 5 during twenty-five of the thirty months in the period.

It would be simplistic to suggest any direct cause-and-effect relation between these two sets of data. The rise and fall of ETA violence is a complex phenomenon linked to general and specific conditions in the Basque provinces, internal policies and disputes within ETA itself, and even international developments. I am not suggesting that Spain's new antiterrorist policy after July 1, 1978, *caused* ETA's violence to rise, although there is strong evidence that the change in policy in Madrid destroyed chances for a cease-fire that was being negotiated through the spring of that year. On the other hand, while the increase in ETA violence in the spring of 1978 (especially the Lemóniz bombing in March) probably did play a major role in provoking Madrid into its policy changes, the threat from ETA was certainly not the only reason for these changes. Other developments in Spain, including the drafting of the new constitution, undoubtedly also played an important role.

What we can say definitively, however, is that the new Spanish counterinsurgency policy did little if anything to restrain or limit ETA violence. Despite the implementation of vigorous measures that imposed a heavy cost on the Basque civil population, Madrid was unable to halt ETA's insurgency during this two-and-a-half year period, and in fact ETA attacks increased during the period. (The counter argument, that *without* the policy ETA's violence would have been even worse, is of course impossible to prove one way or the other. I find it difficult to imagine how ETA's violence could have been much worse during this period, regardless of what Madrid might have done.) If there was a solution to the recurring problem of ETA insurgency, at least as far as the 1976–80 period was concerned, it did not lie in an attempt to reimpose the Francoist regime in the Basque region.

In Conclusion: Some Thoughts on Self-Sustaining Violence

Violence done to others for one's instrumental purposes always seems to have a certain pathological character. While we may understand intuitively and even empathize with the violence done to one another by estranged lovers or drunken quarrelers or lunatics, when one man shoots another for "political" reasons, "in cold blood" as it were, we rebel against trying to find rational explanations for the act. Such is the case especially if the shooting is done by persons not in the employ of a bona fide national army and in uniform but rather by members of a relatively undisciplined and uncoordinated insurgent group whose political claims are unrecognized by the outside world. Moreover, if it appears to us that the insurgents have access, however defined, to other channels of protest and dissent, we are even more likely to condemn what they do as especially blameworthy. In any event, only rarely do we subject such behavior to rudimentary tests of evidence and analysis. Only rarely do we stop to ask why people should seek out and remain in a life of violence, frustration, and hazard when there are so many other attractive alternatives available to them.

That ETA is a puzzle to most outside observers, as well as to most Spaniards and to a goodly number of Basques, seems obvious. That so many young men seek such a dangerous life, and stay in it long after most of us would have abandoned it, strikes many as irrational. How are we to account for such puzzling behavior? The questions are simple, but they demand complex answers. By way of conclusion to this extended essay, I should like to advance a number of propositions that might explain ETA's approach to insurgency. I have divided these explanations into two categories, according to whether they emphasize the external social, political, and economic setting within which ETA operates or the internal dynamics of the insurgency itself. By itself, no single explanation will suffice. The final answer to our puzzle probably lies in a mix of all or most of these propositions.

One approach to explaining the ETA phenomenon is to focus on the political, social and economic environments that supposedly influence ETA's behavior.

One set of environmental explanations deals with the changing character of the Spanish political system. One such proposition, for example, holds that increased ETA violence is due to the increasingly permissive and liberal policies of the Spanish government. According to this proposition, insurgent groups are always more active in liberal democracies, where they can hide behind the protection afforded them by their constitution, than they are in dictatorships where the state is free to suppress them. In post-Franco Spain, according to this explanation, where the press is relatively free to expose police-state abuses and where courts protect the rights of the accused, ETA will exploit the openness of the society with greater and more audacious violence. Ironically, the exact opposite proposition can also be advanced, namely, that ETA's activities are a response to a harsh state of repression. The Spanish police and the Guardia Civil have police powers very nearly as broad today as they were in Franco's era, and in 1980 there were just as many Basques in prison for political crimes as there were in 1975. Treatment of prisoners, although somewhat improved over conditions in the 1960s and early 1970s, is still bad enough to have drawn criticism from international human rights groups like Amnesty International.

A variation on this theme has to do with the slowness of or the incompleteness of gains made by moderate Basque nationalists. Many, perhaps a majority, of the Basques believe that Madrid has doled out their autonomy at an agonizingly slow pace, and that the 1979 Autonomy Statute leaves major gaps that prevent the Basque provinces from exercising full control over their own destinies. There have undoubtedly been unnecessary delays in the pace of devolution of regional powers to the Basques, particularly in areas like education and taxation. There are no doubt gaps in the structure of power grants by Madrid, especially in critical areas like law enforcement and the administration of justice. Nevertheless, we must still ask why ETA insists on defining their struggle in the most uncompromising and intransigent terms possible, including demands for full sovereignty for their country and the forced inclusion of Navarra in the regional grouping without consulting the Navarrese people through a referendum. Why does ETA choose to struggle for goals that many people think are clearly impossible? Why does ETA choose to raise the stakes, if not to perpetuate a struggle that many Basques regard as well on the way to completion or even conclusively finished? For the answer to these questions we must turn to another dimension of the struggle, to be addressed shortly.

Still another kind of explanation would focus on the economic cramp, inflation, high unemployment, and the decaying social structure that afflict the Basque provinces. In the opening chapter, I summarized the dismal economic record of the Basque provinces since the mid-1970s. The reader will recall that the hardest hit were Vizcaya and Guipúzcoa, precisely those in which ETA is strongest. The possibility exists that ETA is the product (not the cause, as many have argued) of the region's economic decline. Unemployment rates of 18 percent translate into perhaps as much as a third of the young male population out of work. Are these unemployed youth the raw material from which ETA recruits its comandos? Data presented in chapter 6 suggest that the answer is negative, since the vast majority of ETA members are employed in some normal job.

Each of the preceding explanations involves some aspect of the political or economic environment in the Basque provinces. We could also, however, consider explanations that examine the changing goals of ETA as a group struggling for the liberation of its homeland. For instance, some might hold that capitalism is the real enemy of the Basques and that the struggle for national liberation is not complete until that aspect of the struggle has been concluded. The central idea of this proposition is that the real target of ETA is not Spanish colonialism but industrial capitalism and social conservatism. These forces are represented in the Basque political spectrum by the Basque Nationalist Party, the dominant political party of the region, and the governing party in the Basque parliament since the March 1980 elections. The mere fact that the Basques have their own regional government is of no significance to ETA so long as that government remains under the domination of the same exploitative capitalist forces that govern all of Spain. If ETA, or any faction thereof, were solely a revolutionary socialist organization that defines its struggle on the basis of class, not ethnicity, then we would expect it to continue the war not only against Madrid, but also against its fellow Basques who represent industrial capitalism and middle class conservatism. But ETA is not such an organization. ETA defines itself by its acts (if not by its rhetoric) as a revolutionary organization based first on Basque ethnicity and only secondarily on social class. The organization is strongest in regions where the Basque language is spoken and where Basque ethnicity is best preserved. Its targets are predominantly not the symbols of industrial capital but rather the agents of the Spanish military and paramilitary presence: the Guardia Civil, the police, the armed forces, and the spy networks that they employ.

Another proposition is a variation on the action-repression-action spiral theory. It suggests that ETA's objective is to mount a general social revolution in the Basque region, and the organization realizes that the only way to accomplish that goal is to provoke the Spanish Right and the armed forces into some sort of clumsy intervention, either in Madrid or in the Basque region, which will cause the downfall of the Spanish government. The next step would be a second Spanish Civil War, with general social upheaval following in the wake of the inevitable turmoil. Out of the ensuing chaos, the Basque Left would seize the opportunity to mount a general social revolution. This kind of apocalyptic theory has always struck me as improbable; and the withdrawal of ETA from provocative violence immediately after the coup attempt of February 23, 1981, suggests that such a proposition is too extreme, even for ETA.

In chapter 9, we considered the proposition that the international terror network supports and encourages insurgency. The reader will recall that the proposition assumes that external assistance from socialist countries that support revolution, principally the Soviet Union, routed through Libya, Yemen, or Palestinian groups, makes it possible for ETA to survive and continue the struggle. I find such an explanation also improbable. ETA obtains what it needs from local sources, and in any event would find cooperating with foreign forces to be alien to its cultural biases. I do not, obviously, include here the aid ETA receives by being allowed to stay in southern France. Without that sanctuary, it would indeed be seriously hampered but on the other hand, it is not at all clear what Paris can or wants to do about ETA's presence on French soil.

Whatever their validity, all of the foregoing propositions are derived from what is basically a rational choice model of complex organizations. Most of us regard a complex organization as a rational response to a set of environmental circumstances or problems that call for a specific kind of institutional solution. When the circumstances change or the problems are solved, the organization must change as well or it will cease to exist.

Regardless of the strengths of this approach to the study of conventional organizations, it has clear limitations when we try to apply it to organizations that operate beyond the law, in the high-risk world of political insurgency, and whose repertoire of strategic choices includes armed violence and political murder. Groups like ETA often engage in behavior that appears to outsiders as irrational, counterproductive, or wholly unwarranted by circumstances. When these groups behave in this way, we become frustrated at our inability to deal with them "rationally," with concessions that seem to us to be reasonable or through counterforce that we presume will raise the costs of continuing the insurgency to an unacceptable level. We label as crazy or irrational groups that do not seem to comprehend when their historical role has come to an end, or to sense when they can most effectively pursue their own self-proclaimed goals or objectives through nonviolent means.

To examine insurgent behavior at this level, I believe we need to apply different kinds of models, new analytical approaches that work with the inner dynamics and tensions of insurgent movements rather than with the external circumstances that condition their actions. Of these new kinds of models there are two broad sets: those that deal with the psychocultural dimensions of the struggle and those that deal with the peculiar dynamics of self-sustaining revolutionary violence.

Some observers, for example, have suggested that ETA members are imitating role models from their culture. Ever since the Spanish Civil War, young Basque men have been challenged to live up to the heroic exploits of their older brothers, fathers, or uncles. This influence has been especially strong within the Basque Nationalist Party, but as I pointed out in chapter 6, it does not seem to have played much of a role in the development of ETA. Clearly, evidence of this kind of influence is difficult to tease out of secondary data. In the scanty information we have about the life histories of ETA members, however, fathers are relatively minor characters, older siblings seem to play no role at all, and the immediate family generally discourages the youth from joining the organization.

Another way of approaching the issue from a psychocultural perspective would be to explore whether or not ETA members are "high risk" personalities. There are, it seems, people endowed with the psychological capacity to define as acceptable a risk that most of us would characterize as intolerably high. There is even a good possibility that certain cultures contain more of this kind of person than do others. After considerable investigation, I have come to the belief that Basque culture may be one of these and that ETA may indeed contain an unusually high number of high-risk personalities. If this were discovered to be the case, then we would know much more than we do about ETA behavior, and we could understand better why the organization raises the stakes of the struggle just when such an act seems most inappropriate. The challenge in this kind of research is, of course, the discovery of confirming data.

Still a third way to look at this dimension of the phenomenon is to test the proposition that Basque political culture encourages violence. There has never been a study of Basque political culture as far as I know, but I have suggested elsewhere (*The Basques: The Franco Years and Beyond*) that violence plays virtually no role in that culture. ETA is an anomaly as far as the rest of Basque culture is concerned. Basques do not support or practice violence on either an interpersonal or an intergroup level, and traditional Basque culture does not support ETA behavior. Nevertheless, there does exist in Basque culture a certain respect or admiration for clandestine political groups and underground political activity, and that feature of Basque political culture would surely influence the degree to which non-ETA members would give support to ETA and would protect its members from discovery and arrest.

As the reader can appreciate, the difficulty in applying these propositions lies in the remoteness and inaccessibility of the evidence. I would like to suggest still a third approach, one that seems to me to offer the most promising new framework within which to analyze ETA's puzzling behavior. I suggest that ETA is caught in the grip of forces that are created by insurgent violence itself and that tend to make the violence self-sustaining, almost apart from the wishes of the participants or the objective conditions that led to the insurgency.

One such proposition suggests that ETA is now being used for revenge or grudge killings. Wars, and especially civil wars, seem to spawn feuding that persists perhaps for a generation after the main struggle has terminated. The presence of revenge or grudge killings in the ETA record over the past two years suggests that something like this is beginning to occur in the Basque case. If so, then violence linked to ETA may persist for a generation, although at declining rates, as old scores are settled, previous attacks are avenged, and the Basque social order gradually purges itself of this contaminant.

Another possibility is that ETA attracts sociopaths who use the organization to act out their personal disorders. Insurgent groups may attract disturbed persons who seek to act out their distress under the cover of the legitimacy of a political struggle. There is no reason to believe that ETA has been able to protect itself from being used in this way. As important as this dimension must be, I see little probability that the outside investigator will be able to find the necessary evidence, although one clue would be the extent to which non-Basques (as identified by their family names) are becoming increasingly active in ETA. My impression, as explained in chapter 6, is that such participation may have increased between the 1960s and the late 1970s; but there is no doubt that ETA remains what it has always been—an ethnically Basque organization. I also see no evidence whatever that ETA has attracted members who have prior criminal records or who have exhibited antisocial behavior outside of a clearly political context.

Some observers have suggested that ETA's command and control net has failed and that the organization is basically out of control. I have made much in chapter 5 and elsewhere of ETA's precise control over the actions of its members. There is some evidence that this control is weakening and may even be disintegrating. One piece of evidence is the rise of the Comandos Autónomos, which have taken up their own agenda of political killings. This kind of weakened internal control becomes critical in the negotiation of a cease-fire. There is some evidence that cease-fire agreements have been near to closure, only to be violated by ETA comandos without authorization from the organization's leadership.

Another factor in self-sustaining violence is deep mutual distrust on both sides which prevents a cease-fire. After many years of struggle, both ETA and Spanish law-enforcement bodies have a deep distrust of each other. There are very few if any shared values that would permit the two groups to engage in dialogue, and probably ample evidence on either side of duplicity, treachery, and deceit. It seems to me probable that many ETA members are afraid to lay down their arms and return to civil politics; many of their comrades who have done so have later been killed by unknown assassins, either in Spain or in France. This fear of reprisals freezes or immobilizes many who might otherwise be prone to seek, and to give, concessions.

Furthermore, the insurgents cannot disengage from the struggle, even if they want to do so. Many men remain ETA militants not out of choice but simply because they cannot fashion for themselves an alternate image that would permit them to continue a nonviolent struggle for political goals. We must not forget that many of these men, now in their late twenties or early thirties, have been engaged in violent struggle since they were adolescents. They do not know any other way of life. They define themselves in terms of armed struggle; other roles (politician, student, journalist, artist, etc.) simply do not occur to them. They continue to fight because they do not know what else they can do.

Finally, there are persons who have vested interests in perpetuating the struggle. After so many years of struggle, and so many lost opportunities for a negotiated cease-fire, it now seems clear that there are those on both sides who want the struggle to continue, perhaps because it helps them reach other objectives they regard as important. Within ETA, there are key leaders who have built their reputations within the organization out of a violent and intransigent hatred of the enemy, and they would have to renounce their status to pursue a more conciliatory policy. On the Spanish side, there are no doubt members of the neo-Francoist Right and the armed forces who do not want ETA to fade away, for it is ETA's insurgency that provides them with the rationale they need to promote the interests of neo-Francoism within the Spanish political system.

The combination and interaction of the forces described in these propositions suggests a formidable array of influences that will ensure the perpetuation of ETA violence for some years to come. ETA continues to kill its enemies because revolutionary struggle is the organization's imperative that its members cannot put aside even if the need for the struggle has faded into the past (and it is by no means obvious that such is the case). ETA's members, recruited and trained for their bloody task, cannot lay aside their weapons and return to peaceful pursuits, either because they fear for their lives as the spiral of revenge or feud violence continues unabated, or because they have become so alienated from normal society that they fear what awaits them when a cease-fire is finally called. The long years of the Franco regime have bred a generation of revolutionary youth dedicated to the life of the gun. The confluence of post-Franco forces continues to feed the struggle and to subvert efforts at a truce between the warring parties. If this analysis is correct, it suggests that the threat from ETA will not go away in the near term. What I see is a case of violence begetting violence in a spiral that periodically goes out of control. The situation is likely to remain that way for some time to come, quite apart from developments in the political world that caused ETA to declare war in the first place.

REFERENCE MATTER

APPENDIX 1. Principal ETA Members

Listed below are the names of and some pertinent biographical details about fifty of the best-known members of ETA from its founding in the 1950s to 1980. The names in lower case are given names; those in all capital letters are family names. The names in quotation marks are code names or nicknames used while in ETA.

Jesús ABRISQUETA. One of Burgos 16. Sentenced to 62 years in prison.

José Manuel AGUIRRE. Founder of Ekin and of ETA.

Iciar AIZPURUA. Wife of Jokin Gorostidi. One of the Burgos 16. Sentenced to 15 years in prison.

José Luis ALVAREZ ENPARANZA "Txillardegi." Founder of Ekin and of ETA. Associated with ethnolinguistic or culturalist approach, and with Branka faction. Left ETA voluntarily in 1967. Still active in Basque political and cultural affairs.

Miguel Angel APALATEGUI AYERBE "Apala." Leader of Berezi Comandos of ETA(p-m). Separated in 1977 to join ETA(m). Arrested in France in 1977, but dropped out of sight while free on bail.

Victor ARANA BILBAO. One of the Burgos 16. Sentenced to 60 years in prison.

Eduardo ARREGUI. Member of ETA Executive Committee after Fifth Assembly. Leader of ETA-V after Sixth Assembly split.

Arantxa ARRUTI. Wife of Gregorio Lopez Irásegui. One of the Burgos 16. Was the only accused who was acquitted.

José Miguel BEÑARÁN ORDEÑANA "Argala." Leader of "new ETA" movement in 1970s. Joined the Mendizábal group in 1970. Participated in Zabala kidnaping in 1972. Leader of *comando* that killed Carrero Blanco in 1973. Joined ETA(m) after split. Leader of Political Office of ETA(m). Killed by bomb explosion in car in 1978.

José María BENITO DEL VALLE LARRINAGA. Founder of Ekin and of ETA. Member of Branka faction. Left ETA voluntarily in 1967.

José Antonio CARRERA. One of the Burgos 16. Sentenced to 12 years in prison.

José María DORRONSORO. One of the Burgos 16. Sentenced to death. Commuted.

Juana DORRONSORO. One of the Burgos 16. Sentenced to 50 years in prison.

Juan ECHAVE. One of the Burgos 16. Sentenced to 50 years in prison.

Eugenio ECHEVESTE ARANGUREN "Antxon." Member of Executive Committee of ETA(m) in 1980. Joined ETA(p-m) in 1976, went over to ETA(m) shortly thereafter. Leader of Political Office after Argala's death in 1978. Responsible for ideological training of new members.

Javier ELOSEGUI ALDASORO. Early ETA leader. Went into exile with Txillardegi group in 1961.

Jon ETXABE. Early ETA leader. Went into exile in France in 1963. Leader of *milis* faction. Expelled by Sixth Assembly in 1970. Organized Beihl kidnaping in 1970. Attacked by rightist assassination teams in France several times. Seriously wounded, and wife killed, in attack in 1978.

Francisco Xabier ETXEBARRIETA ORTIZ "Txabi." Early ETA leader. First ETA member killed (June 1968).

José ETXEBARRIETA ORTIZ. Important theoretician in ETA from the 1960s. Economist of maoist orientation. Brother of Txabi Etxebarrieta.

José María EZKUBI. Early ETA leader. Key figure in Fifth Assembly. Principal ETA leader during period 1969–70. Founder of Red Cells faction. Resigned from ETA at Sixth Assembly in 1970.

Isidro María GARALDE BEDIALAUNETA "Mamarru." In 1980, was part of the ETA(m) directorate, responsible for logistical support and training in weapons and explosives.

María Asunción GOENAGA. Wife of José María Ezkubi. Exiled in 1969 with Ezkubi. Member of ETA Executive Committee in 1968.

Jokin GOROSTIDI. One of Burgos 16. Given two death sentences plus 30 years in prison. Commuted.

Enrique GUESALAGA. One of Burgos 16. Sentenced to 50 years in prison.

Javier IMAZ GARAY. Early ETA leader. Member of Branka faction. Left ETA in 1967.

Ignacio IRIGARAY. Early ETA leader. Went into exile with Txillardegi group in 1961. Expelled from France to Belgium in 1964.

Domingo ITURBE ABASOLO "Txomin." Leader of "new ETA" movement, close to Argala and Mendizábal factions in the early 1970s. Participated in numerous major operations, including the Zabala and Beihl kidnapings and the Carrero Blanco assassination. Regarded as "Máximo Dirigente" of ETA(m) in the early 1980s.

Francisco ITURRIOZ "Paco." Early member of ETA. Leader of Political Office in 1960s. Expelled from ETA in 1966. Became leader of ETA-Berri faction.

Francisco Javier IZCO DE LA IGLESIA. One of the Burgos 16. Accused of killing Melitón Manzanas in August 1968. Sentenced to two death sentences plus 27 years. Commuted.

Julen KALZADA. One of Burgos 16. Sentenced to 12 years in prison.

Federico KRUTWIG SAGREDO. Early writer, linguist, and theoretician of ETA. Wrote under pseudonymn Fernando Sarrailh de Ihartza. Author of *Vasconia* and other important works. Joined ETA in 1966. Played important role in Fifth Assembly and in ETA-V. Leading theoretician of third-worldists or revolutionary-war faction. Still active in Basque literary affairs.

Xabier LARENA. One of the Burgos 16. Sentenced to death plus 30 years in prison. Commuted.

Juan Lorenzo Santiago LASA MICHELENA "Txiquierdi." Joined ETA(m) after Berezi Comandos split off from ETA(p-m). Has participated in numerous armed actions, including the killing of seven police or Guardia Civil troops. In 1980, was second in command of ETA(m).

Emilio LOPEZ ADAN "Beltza." Early ETA leader. Active in Fifth Assembly. One of leaders of ETA-V. Co-author of letter attacking Sixth Assembly organizers. Well-known author and historian of Basque political and economic affairs.

Gregorio LOPEZ IRASEGUI. One of the Burgos 16. Sentenced to 30 years in prison.

José Miguel LUJUA GOROSTIOLA "Mikel." Participated in numerous important ETA operations including Zabala kidnaping. Member of ETA(m) directorate in early 1980s, responsible for border operations (moving men and equipment between Spain and France).

Julen MADARIAGA AGUIRRE. Founder of Ekin and of ETA. Author of *La Insurrección en Euskadi*. Member of *mili* faction in 1970. Expelled from ETA at Sixth Assembly. One of leaders of ETA-V.

Eustaquio MENDIZABAL "Txikia." Leader of *mili* faction of ETA from late 1971 to April 1973. Participated in Beihl kidnaping. Leader of Zabala and Huarte kidnapings. Killed by police in Las Arenas in 1973.

Eduardo MORENO BERGARECHE "Pertur." Leader of ETA(p-m) after split. Was principal spokesman for abandoning armed struggle and returning to electoral politics and mass organizing. Disappeared and presumed killed in 1976.

José Ignacio MUGICA ARREGUI. Member of ETA Executive Committee elected by "legitimate" Sixth Assembly in 1973. Arrested in September 1975 and tried and convicted of participating in the Carrero Blanco assassination.

Mario ONAINDIA. One of Burgos 16. Sentenced to death plus 51 years. Commuted. Later returned to electoral politics in Basque provinces as founder, leader of the Basque Revolutionary Party (EIA).

Angel OTAEGI. Rank and file member of ETA(m) who was accused of aiding in killing member of Guardia Civil. Tried and convicted in 1975. His execution caused mass demonstrations in protest throughout Basque region.

José Manuel PAGOAGA GALLASTEGUI. Member of ETA Executive Committee elected by "legitimate" Sixth Assembly in 1973. Killed in France in January 1979.

Jon PAREDES MANOT "Txiki." Member of ETA(p-m). Close to the Apala faction. Arrested in Barcelona, tried and convicted of having participated in killing of member of Guardia Civil. Executed in 1975, in move that caused mass demonstrations in protest throughout Basque region.

Pedro Ignacio PEREZ BEOTEGUI "Wilson." Participated in assassination of Carrero Blanco in 1973. Arrested, tried, and convicted in 1975.

José Martin SAGARDIA ZALDUA "Usurbil." Joined ETA(m) in 1974. Member of Executive Committee in 1976. By late 1970s, had left the organization. Killed in bomb explosion in his car in December 1980.

Iñaki SARASQUETA. ETA member caught in roadblock where Txabi Etxebarrieta killed in 1968. Sentenced to 58 years in prison.

Eduardo URIARTE. One of the Burgos 16. Given two death sentences plus 30 years.

José Luis ZALBIDE. Early ETA leader. Wrote several important works under pseudonym K. de Zunbeltz, the most significant of which was *Hacia una estrategia revolucionaria vasca*. In prison during most of the 1960s.

Benito ZUMALDE "El Cabra." Leader of the Activism Branch after Fourth Assembly, in 1965. Organized mountain guerrilla operations in the period 1966–68.

APPENDIX 2. Political Terms and Organizations

abertzale (patriotic). The Basque label for any group that emphasizes ethnic Basque political and economic interests over Spanish or mixed Basque-Spanish interests. Abertzale groups do not cooperate with or join with Spanish parties, unions, etc., even if their class or programmatic interests may be similar. Thus, abertzale socialist (or Basque Left) parties are those that represent ethnic Basques of the working class. After the transition of Spain to constitutional democracy provided for the legalization of political parties and unions, many new such organizations appeared on the scene in differing combinations, alliances, and coalitions.

action-repression-action spiral theory. ETA ideological principle adopted by the Fourth Assembly in 1965. Based on the principle that ETA would stimulate popular support by provoking the Spanish government into damaging counterinsurgent measures by means of constantly increasing levels of violence.

Assembly. Since 1962 the supreme policy-making body of ETA. This gathering of the senior leaders of the organization has usually been filled with tension and conflict, and significant changes in ideology and strategy have frequently emerged from their debates. (*See also* Biltzar Nagusia and Biltzar Txikia).

Berezi Comandos. Special armed units created by ETA(p-m) in 1975 to conduct violent assaults or attacks of great importance or hazard. Group later split off from ETA (p-m) in 1977 to join briefly with ETA(m).

Biltzar Nagusia (National Assembly) and Biltzar Txikia (Little Assembly). Two principal policy-making bodies of ETA. Biltzar Txikia was the interim executive body while the National Assembly was unable to meet. In practice, the BT became the focal point for much ETA conflict.

Branka. Magazine published from 1966 through 1971. Used in the 1966–67 period to advance the interests of the "culturalist" faction within ETA. After their withdrawal from ETA in 1967, the faction became known as the "Branka group."

Burgos 16. The members of ETA accused of conspiring to kill Melitón Manzanas in 1968, brought to trial in Burgos in December 1970.

buzón. ETA members who serve as drop points for messages, supplies, weapons, explosives, money, or other items that must be transported among members but cannot be entrusted to the mails.

Celulas Rojas (Red Cells). Marxist-Leninist faction within ETA in 1969–70. Advocated primacy of class struggle over ethnicity. After succeeding in expelling milis faction at Sixth Assembly in 1970, they subsequently withdrew from ETA and later became the Partido Comunista de España (Spanish Communist Party). Because they used the magazine *Saioak* as their medium of communication, they were referred to as the "Saioak group."

comando. The basic operating unit, or cell, of ETA. Composed of three to five members, based in or near their home town. May be used for armed actions, or for other support services such as transportation, intelligence, etc.

Comandos Autónomos (Autonomous Comandos). Small faction that split off from ETA in 1977 and 1978. Composed of former Berezi group members, ETA(m) dissidents, and independents. Especially violent and unpredictable.

culturalists. The faction in ETA in the 1960s that advocated giving primacy to Basque ethnicity, and especially language, over all facets of the struggle.

Ekin (from the Basque verb "to make" or "to do"). The original group from which ETA was formed. Founded in Bilbao in 1952. Ceased to exist after 1956, but founders still referred to as "Ekin group" until the 1960s.

enlace. ETA members who serve as couriers or links between comandos, and between comandos and the Executive Committee.

españolista. Epithet used to label ETA members who placed greater emphasis on the class struggle than on ethnicity and who were therefore disposed to cooperate with working class Spanish parties.

ETA-Berri (New ETA). Faction expelled from ETA in December 1966 at the Fifth Assembly. Advocated primacy of social class over ethnicity. Later changed name to Komunistak (Communists), and then to Movimiento Comunista de España (Spanish Communist Movement).

ETA-V (ETA-Fifth Assembly). One of two major factions in ETA from 1971 to 1973. ETA-V represented many so-called old guard ETA leaders who wanted the organization to return to its ideological principles of the early 1960s. While they began the period as the weaker of the two factions, by 1973 they had become so strong that the other faction had declined to the point of extinction.

ETA-VI (ETA-Sixth Assembly). The other major ETA faction from the early 1970s. Took its name from its links to the allegedly illegal Sixth Assembly held in 1970. Became weaker during early 1970s, and finally merged with the Liga Comunista Revolucionaria (Revolutionary Communist League) and ceased to exist in 1973.

ETA-Zarra (Old ETA). The faction left in control of ETA after the expulsion of ETA-Berri in 1966.

etarra. A member of ETA.

Euzkadi ta Askatasuna (ETA) (Basque Homeland and Freedom). Basque revolutionary separatist group founded in 1959. Parent group of numerous factions and subgroups that split off subsequently.

Euzkadiko Ezkerra (EE) (Basque Left). A coalition of parties, principally EIA, active in electoral contests since 1977. Usually associated in the media with the position of ETA(p-m).

Euskal Iraultzale Alderdia (EIA) (Basque Revolutionary Party). The mass party created by ETA(p-m) in 1976 to contest the 1977 Spanish parliamentary elections.

Executive Committee. The central governing body of ETA, first established in 1962 and still active through 1980. Usually based in southern France. As of 1980, it consisted of seven members.

fichado. An ETA term meaning that a member is known to the police, and there is in police files a card (*ficha*) on him.

front structure. During the 1960s, ETA developed an internal organizational structure based on several fronts, including a Military Front (Frente Militar), Workers' Front (Frente Obrero) and a Cultural Front (Frente Cultural). These fronts developed their own vested interests, and subsequently became the base from which several schisms developed in ETA.

Goma-2. An explosive used by ETA. Usually stolen in large quantities from quarries and construction sites.

herrialdes. "Popular Zones" used as an organizational basis for ETA during the 1960s.

Herri Batasuna (HB) (Popular Unity). A coalition of parties created in 1978 as an answer to what many intransigent Basque Left members regarded as a weakening or betrayal of their position by EE. Principal coalition members were HASI and LAIA, along with Accion Nacional Vasca (ANV) (Basque National Action) and Euskal Sozialista Biltzarrea (ESB) (Basque Socialist Assembly). Since 1978, has become the second strongest Basque political party in the region. Usually associated with the position of ETA(m).

informativo. ETA comandos used to gather and transmit intelligence information.

Koordinadora Abertzale Sozialista (KAS) (Patriotic Socialist Coordinating Council). Formed in 1975 shortly after the executions of Txiki and Otaegi. Later emerged in 1977 as the principal political spokesman for ETA(m). Platform became known as the "KAS Alternative" and consisted of five basic points, including the withdrawal of all Spanish law-enforcement authorities from the Basque provinces, and self-determination for Basques. During the 1975–76 period, the KAS consisted of ETA(p-m) and the following three abertzale socialist groups:

Eusko Herriko Alderdi Sozialista (EHAS) (Basque Popular Socialist Party). A party formed out of the Euskal Alderdi Sozialista (EAS) (Basque Socialist Party), created in 1974 by members of ETA's Frente Cultural who split off from the parent organization, and the Herriko Alderdi Sozialista (HAS) (Popular Socialist Party), created at the same time by the FC counterparts in France.

Langille Abertzale Iraultzalean Alderdia (LAIA) (Patriotic Revolutionary Workers Party) and Langille Abertzale Komiteak (LAK) (Patriotic Workers Committee). In addition to these four coalition partners, the KAS enjoyed the support of ETA(m) and the Langille Abertzalean Batzordea (LAB) (Patriotic Workers Council). In 1977, the EHAS component in the coalition changed its name to Herriko Alderdi Sozialista Iraultzalea (HASI) (Popular Revolutionary Socialist Party).

legales. ETA members who are not known to the police and who follow a normal life, living at home and working at a conventional job.

liberados. ETA members who are known to police, and who have abandoned conventional life to work full time for the organization.

mayos (majority faction) and minos (minority faction). Two factions within ETA-VI. So-called because of their relative strength and status at the second half of the Sixth Assembly held in 1972. Their quarrelling and disputes led to the dissolution of ETA-VI the next year.

milis. Anticommunist faction within ETA that developed in exile in France in 1969 and 1970. Advocated armed struggle, placed greatest emphasis on ethnicity rather than social class. Expelled from ETA at Sixth Assembly in 1970. Declined in strength after death of Mendizábal in 1973. However, a second milis faction developed in the Frente Militar in 1973 and 1974, which later became the base for ETA (militar).

poli-milis. The so-called "political-military" faction that developed within ETA in the early and mid-1970s as an answer to the growing strength of the mili faction. In October and November 1974, after the Cafe Rolando bombing incident, the milis (militar faction) split off from ETA to form ETA (militar), or ETA(m), leaving behind the poli-mili faction to form ETA (político-militar), or ETA(p-m). The two groups differed not only in ideology (the poli-mili faction more oriented toward marxism-leninism) but also in strategic approach (the poli-mili faction was much more oriented toward mass political organizing, especially in the 1976–77 period). The two groups, ETA(m) and ETA(p-m), continued to be the dominant ETA factions through the remainder of the decade and into the 1980s.

revolutionary war thesis. An aspect of ETA ideology that holds that the Basques must wage an unremitting guerrila war, or war of national liberation, against Madrid to force the Spaniards to set them free. Much influenced by the anticolonial wars of the early 1960s, especially in Algeria, Indo-China, and Cuba.

tendencia obrerista. Literally, "workerist tendency," this term referred, pejoratively, to those who believed that the struggle for Basque liberation could be waged only by working class persons and organizations.

tercermundistas. Literally, "Third Worldists," this term refers to persons within ETA who held that Euzkadi was a colony of Spain just like colonial holdings in the Third World, as in Africa and Asia, and that the struggle for Basque independence would have to take the same form as did those struggles in the Third World (closely related to the "revolutionary war" thesis).

zulo. A cache of arms or other supplies.

Zutik. ETA's magazine published in several different versions from the early 1960s. Became the focal point for much conflict within the organization. Factions fighting for control of ETA would first try to secure control over *Zutik* in order to be able to disseminate their views to the membership.

APPENDIX 3. Major Events in the History of Euzkadi ta Askatasuna (ETA)

1936	Spanish Civil War begins.
1937	Bilbao falls to rebel forces. Basque government goes into exile.
1939	Spanish Civil War ends. Basque government moves to Paris.
1940	Basque government leaves Paris with outbreak of World War II.
1945	Basque government returns to Paris after World War II ends. Basques organize Resistance activities in Spain.
1947	Bilbao general strike begins activist or "heroic" phase of the Resistance, characterized by belief in Franco's early downfall.
1951	Bilbao general strike marks end of the activist phase of the Resistance.
1952	Small group of Deusto University (Bilbao) students forms study group named Ekin for its internal newsletter.
1956	Ekin fuses with EGI, the youth wing of the Basque Nationalist Party (PNV).
1959	Ekin members split away from EGI to form ETA.
1961	First wave of arrests and deportations of ETA leaders. Appearance of ETA newsletter *Zutik*. First direct action, an attempted train derailment in Guipúzcoa.
1962	Establishment of ETA Executive Committee in exile. Organization of the four "fronts" structure (political, economic, military, cultural). Publication of first ideological principles.
	First Assembly held. Defines ETA as a "revolutionary Basque movement for national liberation." Old Guard from Ekin remains in control.
1963	Publication of *Vasconia: Estudio dialéctico de una nacionalidad*, by Federico Krutwig Sagredo. Basis for "third world" or revolutionary-war thesis.
	Second Assembly held in March. Approves principles of revolutionary war, organizational structure based on *herrialdes*.
	ETA participates in strikes in October, resulting in second wave of arrests and deportations.
1964	ETA Executive Committee publishes *Insurrección en Euskadi*.
	Third Assembly meets. Defines ETA as anti-imperialist and anti-capitalist. Adopts statements of principles entitled "Carta a los intelectuales," written by José Luis Zalbide.
	Old Guard Ekin leaders expelled from France to Belgium. ETA comes increasingly under the control of the advocates of revolutionary war.
1965	Fourth Assembly held. Statement of principles links national, social liberation for first time. Assembly approves *Bases teoricas de la guerra revolucionaria*, written by José Luis Zalbide. Adopts the action-repression-action spiral theory. "Front" structure replaced with "branches." First paramilitary force created. Political Office becomes focal point of struggle between trotskyites, third-worlders.

First armed action by ETA (robbery of bank courier).

1966   First half of Fifth Assembly held. Alliance of third-worlders and culturalists expel trotskyites from Political Office. Expelled members form ETA-Berri (New ETA), later (1970) changed to Communist Movement of Spain (MCE).

1967   Second half of Fifth Assembly held. ETA coins term "Basque Working People" (PTV) to suggest link of class, ethnicity in struggle. Four "fronts" structure reestablished.

In April, Ekin (culturalist) group voluntarily withdraws from ETA to form Branka.

First bank robberies committed. Considerable violence leading into 1968.

1968   Etarra Txabi Etxebarrieta killed by Guardia Civil near Tolosa. ETA retaliates by killing police inspector Melitón Manzanas in Irun. Mass demonstrations. Franco imposes state of exception. Mass arrests, deportations, torture in prisons.

José Luis Zalbide writes *Hacia una estrategia revolucionaria vasca*.

1969   Mass arrests through spring, but especially in April, destroy leadership infrastructure of ETA. José Ezkubi goes into exile.

Emergence of various exile factions, including Red Cells (José Ezkubi), *milis* (Jon Etxabe), and Old Guard (Krutwig, Emilio Lopez Adan "Beltza").

1970   Sixth Assembly held. *Milis* expelled, followed by resignation of Red Cells.

Old Guard (later to be called ETA-V) tries to take back control of the organization.

Burgos 16 tried and convicted. Eugen Beihl kidnaped by *milis* faction, released later unharmed. Death sentences commuted.

1971   ETA splits into two factions: ETA-V (followers of the Old Guard), and ETA-VI (those who had dominated the Sixth Assembly). ETA-VI begins as the stronger of the two factions, but declines in strength during the year. Many members of ETA-VI defect to ETA-V during the year.

"Era Txikia" phase of ETA. Dominant leader of ETA-V is Eustaquio Mendizábal "Txikia."

1972   Zabala kidnaping. First time armed action directed against ethnic Basque.

ETA-V fuses with EGI-Batasuna to form new ETA.

Beginning of conflict between Frente Militar and Frente Obrero within ETA-V.

1973   Huarte kidnaping ends after ransom paid and Huarte released. "Txikia" killed in Las Arenas. ETA holds first half of the "legitimate" Sixth Assembly.

ETA-VI fuses with Revolutionary Communist League (LCR).

ETA *comando* assassinates Spanish Prime Minister Luis Carrero Blanco.

1974   ETA splits once again. Frente Obrero leaves ETA to form the Patriotic Revolutionary Workers Party (LAIA), and the Frente Cultural splits off to form the Basque Popular Socialist Party (EHAS).

After the Cafe Rolando bombing in September, the *milis* and the *poli-milis* split to form ETA (militar), or ETA(m), and ETA (político-militar), or ETA(p-m).

1975   ETA(p-m) holds second half of the Sixth Assembly. Creates the Berezi Comandos for special armed actions.

Upsurge of ETA violence in April and May causes Franco to decree state of exception for Vizcaya and Guipúzcoa.

In September, etarras Txiki and Otaegi are executed, creating mass protests. Franco decrees second state of exception. Leads to creation of the Patriotic Socialist Coordinating Committee (KAS).

In November, Franco dies. Struggle over amnesty for imprisoned etarras begins.

1976   Transition to democracy begins in Spain. First Suárez cabinet appointed. Parties legalized. Parliament approves transition to constitutional democracy. Popular referendum approves transition in December.

Struggle over amnesty intensifies with mass demonstrations and police repression. Second amnesty decree in July.

Large scale street violence in Basque region in March and September.

Berezi Comandos kidnap and kill Berazadi, touching off power struggle within ETA(p-m) between Apala and Pertur. In July, Pertur disappears, presumed killed. ETA now split three ways between advocates of abandoning armed struggle (Pertur faction of ETA(p-m)), and two armed factions (Apala faction of p-m and Argala faction of ETA(m)).

ETA(m) assassinates president of Guipúzcoa provincial assembly.

ETA(p-m) holds first half of Seventh Assembly. Creates Basque Revolutionary Party (EIA).

ETA kills 17 during the year.

1977   First post-Franco Cortes, or parliament, chosen. Begins drafting new democratic constitution. In elections, Basque Nationalist Party emerges as most powerful Basque party. KAS urges followers to boycott elections, but another faction of Basque Left, Euzkadiko Ezkerra (EE) contests the elections anyway. All Basque Left parties combined win 11 percent of vote; EE wins 5 percent.

At end of the year, Basque region given "pre-autonomy" status.

Struggle over amnesty intensifies. After elections, nearly all "historical" ETA prisoners are released to go into exile.

Berezi Comandos launch spring offensive designed to sabotage efforts of followers of Pertur to return to conventional politics. In May, Berezi group kidnaps Basque industrialist Ybarra and kills him. Berezi group separates from ETA(p-m) to joint ETA(m) for brief time. Apala is arrested in France, but extradition is refused. While free on bail, he disappears.

ETA(m) attacks Lemóniz nuclear power plant for first time.

ETA(m) assassinates President of Vizcaya provincial assembly.

During year, ETA kills 9, wounds 7, kidnaps 1.

1978   New Spanish constitution approved and submitted to referendum. Majority of Basque voters abstain. Constitution gives legal status to autonomous regions. Constitution promulgated in December. Basques submit proposed Autonomy Statute for consideration.

EIA is legalized as a political party. A new and more radical electoral coalition appears in the Basque Left: Herri Batasuna (HB).

ETA(m) launches major new offensive in spring, directed especially against police and Guardia Civil. During spring and summer, Spanish Interior Minister Martín Villa attempts to negotiate with ETA but fails. Bilbao newspaper publisher Portell assassinated in June. Spanish government responds with new anti-terrorist Law.

In April, new ETA faction, Comandos Autónomos, appears and makes first armed assault.

In December, ETA(m) leader Argala is killed in bombing of his car in France.

Late in year, nearly 100 ETA prisoners moved out of Basque prisons to Soria. Region erupts in street violence.

In 1978, ETA kills 67, wounds 91, and kidnaps 4.

1979   Second Cortes elections held in March. Basque Left parties win 21 percent of the vote, with EE winning 6.3 percent and HB, 13 percent. HB deputies to Cortes refuse to take seats.

Municipal and provincial assembly elections held in April. Basque Left wins 25.4 percent, with EE winning 5 percent and HB 15.1 percent.

Basque referendum approves Autonomy Statute in October. Spanish parliament subsequently approves.

ETA(p-m) launches bombing campaign in Spain's tourist areas to force Madrid to move prisoners back to regional prisons. First dozen or so bombs explode without killing anyone, but in July three bombs explode in Madrid airport, two train stations, killing 6 and wounding about 100. ETA(p-m) suspends bombing campaign after accusing Madrid police of not removing bombs.

In November, ETA(p-m) kidnaps UCD leader Rupérez and demands amnesty, return of prisoners. Rupérez released in December. Madrid promises to return, release some prisoners, but says there was no deal.

Toll of ETA violence for the year: 72 killed, 141 wounded, 8 kidnaped.

1980   In March, first Basque parliament elected and begins its work. Basque Left parties win 28 percent of vote, with EE winning 10.4 percent and HB 18.3 percent. HB, the second strongest party in Basque region, refuses to take its seats in parliament.

Three-month period from September through November one of bloodiest in ETA history. ETA kills 36 persons during this period.

In all, during the year, ETA kills 88, wounds 81, kidnaps 7.

Notes

A Note on Sources

As I mentioned in the preface, the great bulk of this book is drawn from public, open sources. These are of such variety, and in all probability are unfamiliar enough to an American audience, however, that a brief note on sources might be appropriate here, in addition to the chapter notes below. The principal sources on which I have drawn fall into five categories: original documents; first-person accounts and historical works written by participants; secondary analyses, mostly by American or American-based scholars and appearing in scholarly papers or articles; Basque and Spanish newspapers and magazines; and interviews.

Without doubt, the greatest single source of documentary information on ETA is a massive eighteen-volume set of books carrying the simple title *Documentos* (San Sebastián: Hordago, 1979–81). *Documentos* claims to be a compilation of virtually everything written by ETA, including newsletters, ideological statements, and magazines. In addition, most of its volumes carry brief historical accounts of the relevant periods to help the reader understand the documents in context. The documents cover the period from ETA's beginnings, in 1952, to mid-1977, when the celebration of Spain's first post-Franco parliamentary elections supposedly changed the nature of the Basque political struggle. Because of the size and cost of this set of documents, not many complete sets are available, but the interested scholar should know that there is at least one complete set in the United States, in the library of the Basque Studies Program at the University of Nevada, Reno. The program's coordinator, Dr. William Douglass, was most generous in giving me access to *Documentos* for use in this study.

Documentos is not the only source of documentary information concerning ETA. Two other works carry much useful information on the ideological themes in ETA's writings. The first of these is a two-volume general history of ETA written by José Mari Garmendia, *Historia de ETA* (San Sebastián: L. Haranburu, 1980), containing several hundred pages of documentary material as appendixes. The second is a more interpretive work by Gurutz Jáuregui Bereciartu, *Ideología y estrategia política de ETA: Análisis de su evolución entre 1959 y 1968* (Madrid: Siglo Veintiuno, 1981).

Another important source of information about ETA is a collection of accounts written by actual participants in the ETA drama. In a few cases the authors were members of ETA, either when they wrote the books in question or earlier. In other cases the authors, while not actually in ETA, were close to ETA members and can be regarded as authoritative reporters of the events described. In a few instances, the authors' names are code names or pseudonyms. The most significant of these books are the following: Julen Agirre, *Operation Ogro* (New York: Ballantine, 1975); Angel Amigo, *Pertur: ETA 1971–1976* (San Sebastián: Hordago, 1978); Angel Amigo, *"Operación Ponch": Las fugas de Segovia* (San Sebastián: Hordago, 1978); Beltza, *El nacionalismo vasco en el exilio, 1937–1960* (San Sebastián: Editorial Txertoa,

1977); Beltza, *Nacionalismo vasco y clases sociales* (San Sebastián: Editorial Txertoa, 1976); Miguel Castells Arteche, *El mejor defensor el pueblo* (San Sebastián: Ediciones Vascas, 1978); Gisele Halimi, *El proceso de Burgos* (Caracas: Monte Avila, 1972); Mario Onaindia, *La lucha de clases en Euskadi* (San Sebastián: Hordago, 1980); Ortzi, *Historia de Euskadi: El nacionalismo vasco y ETA* (Paris: Ruedo Ibérico, 1975); Ortzi, *Los vascos: Síntesis de su historia* (San Sebastián: Hordago, 1978); José Maria Portell, *Los hombres de ETA* (Barcelona: DOPESA, 1974); Kepa Salaberri, *El proceso de Euskadi en Burgos* (Paris: Ruedo Ibérico, 1971); and Javier Sanchez Erauskin, *Txiki-Otaegi: El viento y las raices* (San Sebastián: Hordago, 1978).

The present work also owes much to a small group of American or American-based scholars who share the results of their research through scholarly journals and professional gatherings. The specific titles of their reports are too numerous to be repeated here, and in any case, they are all included in the notes below. Here I would simply like to acknowledge my debt to the research of Stanley Payne of the University of Wisconsin, Juan Linz of Yale University, Richard Gunther of the Ohio State University, and Peter McDonough of the University of Michigan.

Aside from the opening four chapters, which are primarily historical, most of my book is based on a careful reading of original periodical literature. The most important single source of information is the Basque newspaper *Deia*, published in Bilbao since mid-1977. *Deia* is as close to being a newspaper of record in the Basque country as any periodical published there. In only five years, it has established a fairly good record for journalistic standards. Nevertheless, like nearly all media in Spain and the Basque country, *Deia* is linked to certain political groups and perspectives. In *Deia*'s case, these groups are most closely associated with the moderate, center-right Basque nationalism espoused by the Basque Nationalist Party. Thus, while the newspaper supports Basque nationalism, it opposes ETA. The other principal bilingual (Basque and Spanish) newspaper published in the Basque country is *Egin*, in San Sebastián, a paper that is much more to the left than *Deia* and more supportive of ETA. The more traditional periodicals, like *Diario vasco* of San Sebastián, are generally much more conservative than *Deia* and not as comprehensive in their treatment. I have done some comparative reading of various newspapers from the Basque country, and I believe that there is little material in the others that does not appear in *Deia*. That fact, plus the paper's reputation for reporting honestly, make *Deia* the principal source of daily information about ETA, and I have relied on it heavily, though not exclusively. My reading of the Basque media, including news magazines, has been supplemented with some information from the Madrid press, especially (for newspapers) the highly regarded *El país*, and (for magazines) *Cambio 16*. The strengths of these publications are their journalistic reputation and their reportorial style; their weaknesses are their failure to cover events in the Basque country with the same comprehensiveness that we would expect from Basque publications, and their undisguised opposition to Basque nationalism in most of its manifestations, but particularly as espoused by ETA. This slant is not surprising, since ETA threatens the integrity of the Spanish state as well as, some say, the success of the Spanish democratic experiment. In sum, all these periodical sources reflect a certain political perspective that I have tried to take into account in using the material they present. If we are to use contemporary press information from Spain, we really have no alternative.

This brings me to my last source of information, personal interviews. In two trips to the Basque country, in 1973 and in 1978–79, I was fortunate to be able to speak to many Basque political figures of all persuasions and at all levels. During the 1973 visit, these interviews included several with men who purported to be members of ETA. I say they claimed to be members of ETA, since I really have no way of verifying that fact. The interviews were arranged by intermediaries in such a way that I could not know for sure who the men were or whether their stories were true. Most of the interviews were conducted in a bar in St. Jean-de-Luz, in France; but one was held in our apartment in San Sebastián, and another in the home of a friend in Bilbao. The structure of the interviews reflected my interests at the time, and I concentrated almost solely on these men as individuals, why they had joined ETA, how they lived, how they related to others, including their families, and so forth. At no time did the interviews touch on ETA activities, ideology, or goals. Thus the material gleaned from the interviews appears in the portions of the book that deal with the members of ETA, where they come from, how they are recruited, how they live within the organization, and such matters. The reader of this book who hopes to find "inside" information about a specific ETA attack (the assassination of Prime Minister Carrero Blanco, for instance) will I am afraid be disappointed. In the course of my interviews, I never asked questions of that nature. If I had, they certainly would never have been answered, and in fact, the interviews would probably have been terminated abruptly had I probed in these directions. Thus while the interviews provided me with some sense of the flavor of life in ETA, indispensable to the writing of this book, they should not be relied upon for facts about ETA as an insurgent organization. That was not their purpose.

Chapter One

1 Details are from *Deia* (Bilbao), December 12 and 13, 1980. *Deia* (Bilbao) will hereafter be cited as *Deia*.
2 *Deia*, December 31, 1980.
3 Walter Laqueur, *Terrorism* (Boston: Little, Brown, 1977); Albert Parry, *Terrorism: From Robespierre to Arafat* (New York: Vanguard, 1976); Edward Hyams, *Terrorists and Terrorism* (New York: St. Martin's, 1974); Paul Wilkinson, *Political Terrorism* (New York: Wiley, 1974).
4 Robert P. Clark, *The Basques: The Franco Years and Beyond* (Reno, Nevada: University of Nevada Press, 1980).
5 Cynthia Enloe, *Ethnic Conflict and Political Development* (Boston: Little, Brown, 1973); Joseph Rothschild, *Ethnopolitics: A Conceptual Framework* (New York: Columbia University Press, 1981).
6 Walker Connor, "The Politics of Ethnonationalism," *Journal of International Affairs* 27, no. 1 (1973):1–21; Oriol Pi-Sunyer, "The Maintenance of Ethnic Identity in Catalonia," in Oriol Pi-Sunyer, ed., *The Limits of Integration: Ethnicity and Nationalism in Modern Europe*, Research Reports no. 9, (Amherst: University of Massachusetts, 1971), pp. 111–46.
7 As quoted in Juan Linz and Amando de Miguel, "Within-Nation Differences and Comparisons: The Eight Spains," in Richard L. Merritt and Stein Rokkan, eds., *Comparing Nations: The Uses of Quantitative Data in*

Cross-National Research (New Haven: Yale University Press, 1966), p. 318.

8 One significant exception has been Walker Connor. See his article "Nation-Building or Nation-Destroying?" *World Politics* 24, no. 3 (April 1972):319–55.

9 Milton J. Esman, ed., *Ethnic Conflict in the Western World* (Ithaca: Cornell University Press, 1977); Charles R. Foster, ed., *Nations without a State: Ethnic Minorities in Western Europe* (New York: Praeger, 1980).

10 Brian Jenkins, *International Terrorism: A New Mode of Conflict*, Research Paper no. 48, California Seminar on Arms Control and Foreign Policy (Los Angeles: Crescent Publications, 1975), p. 1; cited in U.S. Central Intelligence Agency, *International and Transnational Terrorism: Diagnosis and Prognosis* (Washington: C.I.A., April 1976), p. 8.

11 Manuel de Terán Alvarez, "País vasco," in Manuel de Terán, Luis Sole Sabaris, and others, *Geografía regional de España* (Barcelona: Ediciones Ariel, 1968), chap. 3.

12 Luis C.-Nuñez Astrain, *Clases sociales en Euskadi* (San Sebastián: Editorial Txertoa, 1977), chap. 1; Talde Euskal Estudio Elkartea, *Euskadi, ante las elecciones municipales* (San Sebastián: Ediciones Vascas, 1978), chap. 1.

13 Beltza, *Nacionalismo vasco y clases sociales* (San Sebastián: Editorial Txertoa, 1976), chap. 5, esp. pp. 155–69.

14 Pedro de Yrizar, "Los dialectos y variedades de la lengua vasca: Estudio linguístico/demográfico," *Separata del boletín de la Real Sociedad Vascongada de los Amigos del País* 29, nos. 1/2/3 (1973).

15 Clark, *The Basques*, p. 147.

16 Robert P. Clark, "Language and Politics in Spain's Basque Provinces," *West European Politics* 4, no. 1 (January 1981):85–103, table 5.

17 Salustiano del Campo, Manuel Navarro, and J. Felix Texanos, *La cuestión regional española* (Madrid: EDICUSA, 1977), p. 125, table 4.7.

18 Richard Gunther, "A Comparative Study of Regionalisms in Spain" (Paper delivered to the Society for Spanish and Portuguese Historical Studies, Toronto, 1981), p. 2.

19 Robert P. Clark, "Recent Voting Trends in Spain's Basque Provinces," *Iberian Studies* 9, no. 2 (Autumn 1980). For 1980 vote totals, see *Deia*, March 11, 1980.

20 For general historical material on the Basques, the reader may consult Stanley Payne, *Basque Nationalism* (Reno: University of Nevada Press, 1975); and Clark, *The Basques*. These two works together cover the period through the end of 1978. Several shorter works are also available in English: Robert P. Clark, "Euzkadi: Basque Nationalism in Spain since the Civil War," in Foster, *Nations without a State*, pp. 75–100; Pedro Gonzalez Blasco, "Modern Nationalism in Old Nations as a Consequence of Earlier State-Building: The Case of Basque-Spain," in Wendell Bell and Walter E. Freeman, eds., *Ethnicity and Nation-Building: Comparative, International and Historical Perspectives* (Beverly Hills and London: Sage, 1974), pp. 341–73; and Juan Linz, "Early State-Building and Late Peripheral Nationalisms against the State: The Case of Spain," in S. N. Eisenstadt and Stein Rokkan, eds., *Building States and Nations: Analyses by Region* (Beverly Hills and London: Sage, 1973), vol. 2, chap. 2. The bibliography in Spanish is extensive, and most works will be cited throughout this book.

21 Lawrence Guy Straus, Geoffrey A. Clark, Jesus Altuna, and Jesus A. Ortea, "Ice-Age Subsistence in Northern Spain," *Scientific American* 242, no. 6 (June 1980):142–52.

22 Glyn Daniel, "Megalithic Monuments," *Scientific American* 243, no. 1 (July 1980):78–90.

23 José Miguel de Azaola, *Vasconia y su destino*, 1, *La regionalización de España* (Madrid: Revista de Occidente, 1972).

24 Charles W. McMillion, "Spain's Rapid Transition to Industrial Democracy: Inter-national Integration and Intra-national Disintegration" (Paper delivered to the American Political Science Association, Washington, 1979).

25 Beltza, *El nacionalismo vasco, 1876–1936* (San Sebastián: Editorial Txertoa, 1976).

26 The following is based on press reports from *Deia*: January 3 and 12 and December 16, 1979; February 17 and August 1, 1980; May 15, 1982.

27 *Deia*, March 3 and 22, September 26, and December 27, 1981; *Diario Vasco* (San Sebastián), September 26, 1981.

28 This material is discussed in greater detail in Clark, *The Basques*, chap. 4.

29 Luis C.-Nuñez Astrain, *La sociedad vasca actual* (San Sebastián: Editorial Txertoa, 1977), p. 126, table 49.

30 Beltza, *El nacionalismo vasco en el exilio, 1937–1960* (San Sebastián: Editorial Txertoa, 1977), pt. 3.

31 Koldo San Sebastián, "Las organizaciones juveniles vascas," *Deia*, June 28, 1981.

32 José Luis Alvarez Enparanza, "Txillardegi," in Eugenio Ibarzabal, ed., *Cincuenta años de nacionalismo vasco: 1928–1978* (San Sebastián: Ediciones Vascas, 1978), p. 362.

33 Gurutz Jáuregui Bereciartu, *Ideología y estrategia política de ETA: Análisis de su evolución entre 1959 y 1968* (Madrid: Siglo Veintiuno, 1981), p. 75; José Mari Garmendia, *Historia de ETA*, 2 vols. (San Sebastián: L. Haranburu, 1979), 1:18; Ibarzabal, *Cincuenta años*, pp. 362–69; interview with José Luis Alvarez Enparanza in *Garaia* 1, no. 1 (September 2–9, 1976):24. See also the historical notes by Patxo Unzueta and Jon Nicolás in *Documentos* (San Sebastián: Hordago, 1979), 1:9–49.

34 Jáuregui Bereciartu, *Ideología*, p. 76.

35 Mercé Ibarz, *Breu historia d'ETA, 1959–1979* (Barcelona: La Magrana, 1981), pp. 44–46.

36 Federico de Arteaga, *ETA y el proceso de Burgos* (Madrid: Editorial E. Aguado, 1971), pp. 212–13.

37 Ortzi, *Los Vascos: Síntesis de su historia* (San Sebastián: Hordago, 1978), p. 178. See also Garmendia, *Historia*, 1:231–38.

Chapter Two

1 This discussion leans heavily on Gurutz Jáuregui Bereciartu, *Ideología y estrategia política de ETA: Análisis de su evolución entre 1959 y 1968* (Madrid: Siglo Veintiuno, 1981), esp. chaps. 11, 12, and 13. See also José Mari Garmendia, *Historia de ETA*, 2 vols. (San Sebastián: L. Haranburu, 1979), esp. the documents contained in the comprehensive appendices to both volumes.

2 Jáuregui, *Ideología*, pp. 10–40.
3 For a review of the entire early period from 1959 to 1964, see an article by Koldo San Sebastián, "El resurgir del movimiento nacionalista," *Deia*, June 20, 1982. Federico de Arteaga, *ETA y el proceso de Burgos* (Madrid: Editorial E. Aguado, 1971), p. 214.
4 Mercé Ibarz, *Breu historia d'ETA, 1959–1979* (Barcelona: La Magrana, 1981), pp. 63–64. See also *Documentos* (San Sebastián: Hordago, 1979), 1:367–79.
5 de Arteaga, *ETA*, p. 215.
6 This first statement of principles is contained in a Spanish version in Beltza, *El nacionalismo vasco en el exilio, 1937–1960* (San Sebastián: Editorial Txertoa, 1977), pp. 96–99. A version in Basque is in Garmendia, *Historia*, 1:238–41. See also *Documentos*, 1:525–28.
7 Ortzi, *Los Vascos: Síntesis de su historia* (San Sebastián: Hordago, 1978), p. 180.
8 F. Sarrailh de Ihartza, *Vasconia: Estudio dialéctico de una nacionalidad* (San Sebastián: Ediciones Vascas, 1979). See also *Documentos*, III:75–126.
9 Jáuregui, *Ideología*, p. 225.
10 *Documentos*, 2:433–36.
11 *Documentos*, 3:127–50.
12 Garmendia, *Historia*, 1:151–61; *Documentos*, 3:507–18.
13 According to Ibarz, *Breu historia*, p. 70, the detention and deportation of these etarras was caused by an old PNV leader and Basque industrialist Ramon de la Sota, who, it is alleged, informed French police of what was going on in Irigaray's export-import office.
14 *Documentos*, 5:55–68.
15 *Documentos*, 5:113–89.
16 Ortzi, *Los Vascos*, p. 192; Garmendia, *Historia*, 1:221.
17 Garmendia, 1:221.
18 *Documentos*, 7:101.
19 The following is based on Garmendia, 2:195–200.
20 The word *bai* means *yes* in Euskera. In the Campaña del BAI, the letters also stood for the three key elements of the Basque National Front movement: *batasuna* (unity), *askatasuna* (freedom), and *indarra* (force).
21 An author writing a second book is fortunate to have the opportunity to correct an error made in his first. In my more general treatment of the subject, *The Basques: The Franco Years and Beyond* (Reno: University of Nevada Press, 1979), p. 169, I stated that Etxebarrieta's death had been the first in the struggle between ETA and the police and Guardia Civil. I now have the chance to set the record straight.
22 For details of the Manzanas killing, see Clark, *The Basques*, p. 182. See also *Documentos*, 7:483–506, 536–41.
23 Luis C.-Nuñez Astrain, *La sociedad vasca actual* (San Sebastián: Editorial Txertoa, 1977), p. 126, table 49.
24 Ortzi, *Los Vascos*, pp. 198, 200.
25 The arrest of Arantxa Arruti and her later acquittal led to some confusion about the number of accused in the Burgos trial. Many newspapers talked of "the Burgos 16," but at the close of the trial only fifteen were convicted and sentenced.
26 Kepa Salaberri, *Sumarísimo 31–69: El proceso de Euskadi en Burgos*

(Paris: Ruedo Ibérico, 1971). See also Gisele Halimi, *El proceso de Burgos* (Caracas: Monte Avila, 1972), trans. Mercedes Rivera.

27 Ortzi, *Los Vascos*, p. 200.
28 Ortzi, p. 199.
29 *Documentos*, 10:137–455.
30 According to Luis C.-Nuñez Astrain, about 55 percent of all industrial workers in the Basque provinces were on strike at one time or another during December 1970 to protest the Burgos trial. See *Clases sociales en Euskadi* (San Sebastián: Editorial Txertoa, 1977), pp. 206–9.
31 For details of the kidnaping see Carol Edler Baumann, *The Diplomatic Kidnappings: A Revolutionary Tactic of Urban Terrorism* (The Hague: Martinus Nijhoff, 1973), pp. 86–88.

Chapter Three

1 The text of the letter is in José Mari Garmendia, *Historia de ETA*, 2 vols. (San Sebastián: L. Haranburu, 1980), 2:114–17. See also *Documentos* (San Sebastián: Hordago, 1979), 10:199–218; Ortzi, *Los Vascos: Síntesis de su historia* (San Sebastián: Hordago, 1978), pp. 217–18; Ortzi, *Historia de Euskadi: El nacionalismo vasco y ETA* (Paris: Ruedo Ibérico, 1975), pp. 383–84.
2 Garmendia, *Historia*, 2:123.
3 Garmendia, 2:127. See also my analysis in chap. 6 below.
4 Ortzi, *Los Vascos*, p. 212; Mercé Ibarz, *Breu historia d'ETA, 1959–1979* (Barcelona: La Magrana, 1981), p. 95.
5 Ortzi, *Los Vascos*, p. 213.
6 "Atlas político sindical de Euzkadi sur," *Garaia* 1, no. 2 (September 9–16, 1976):22–28.
7 José María Portell, *Los hombres de ETA* (Barcelona: DOPESA, 1974), pp. 73–80, 122, 154, 156.
8 Ortzi, *Historia de Euskadi*, pp. 381–83.
9 Ortzi, *Historia de Euskadi*, p. 377.
10 Gurutz Jáuregui Bereciartu, *Ideología y estrategia política de ETA: Análisis de su evolución entre 1959 y 1968* (Madrid: Siglo Veintiuno, 1981), pp. 417–19.
11 Cited in Ortzi, *Historia de Euskadi*, p. 381.
12 Jáuregui, *Ideología*, pp. 419–43.
13 Garmendia, *Historia*, 2:158. See also Portell, *Los hombres*, pp. 168–69.
14 Garmendia, 2:156; Ortzi, *Historia de Euskadi*, p. 379, and *Los Vascos*, p. 214.
15 This account of the Zabala kidnaping is based on the following: Portell, *Los hombres*, pp. 156–64; Garmendia, *Historia*, 2:164; Ortzi, *Los Vascos*, pp. 214–15, and *Historia de Euskadi*, pp. 384–85.
16 Portell, *Los hombres*, pp. 163–64.
17 Portell, pp. 172–73.
18 Ortzi, *Historia de Euskadi*, p. 391.
19 Garmendia, *Historia*, 2:166.
20 Garmendia, 2:171–73.
21 Julen Agirre, *Operation Ogro*, trans. Barbara Probst Solomon (New York:

Ballantine, 1975). See also Rafael Borras Betriu, *El día en que mataron a Carrero Blanco* (Barcelona: Editorial Planeta, 1974).

22 Ortzi, *Historia de Euskadi*, p. 399.

23 Portell, *Los hombres*, pp. 205–14; Ortzi, *Historia de Euskadi*, pp. 398–99, and *Los Vascos*, p. 220.

24 Details of the case are contained in press coverage of the trial, in *Diario vasco* (San Sebastián), June 7 and 8 and July 3, 4, and 5, 1973; and *La voz de España* (San Sebastián), July 4, 1973.

25 For details of the trial, see sources in the note above, and Portell, *Los hombres*, pp. 219–31.

26 Agirre, *Operation Ogro*, photo caption facing p. 91; Portell, *Los hombres*, p. 213.

27 Portell, pp. 215, 218.

28 Portell, pp. 235–39.

29 Portell, pp. 238–39.

30 Portell, pp. 240–49.

31 Ibarz, *Breu historia*, 103–4, 137–38; also "Atlas político sindical de Euzkadi sur."

32 Garmendia, *Historia*, 2:178–79.

33 Ibarz, *Breu historia*, pp. 137–38.

34 *New York Times*, September 14, 1974. See also Ortzi, *Historia de Euskadi*, p. 412, which lists the casualties as eleven killed and seventy-one wounded. In the account of one of the accused, Lidia Falcon, in *Deia*, July 12, 1981, the casualties are listed as thirteen killed and more than eighty wounded.

35 Ortzi, *Los Vascos*, pp. 226–27.

36 Mario Onaindia, *La lucha de clases en Euskadi* (San Sebastián: Hordago, 1981), p. 109.

37 Garmendia, *Historia*, 2:181–84; Onaindia, pp. 108–9.

38 Onaindia, p. 114; Ortzi, *Historia de Euskadi*, p. 415, and *Los Vascos*, p. 229.

39 Ibarz, *Breu historia*, pp. 107–8, 138.

40 Ortzi, *Los Vascos*, p. 228; *Documentos*, 17:301–6.

41 Onaindia, *La lucha*, p. 110; Ortzi, *Los Vascos*, p. 229.

42 Luis C.-Nuñez Astrain, *La sociedad vasca actual* (San Sebastián: Editorial Txertoa, 1977), pp. 121–28.

43 Ortzi, *Los Vascos*, p. 231.

44 *Cambio 16*, June 2, 1975.

45 Onaindia, *La lucha*, p. 118.

46 Javier Sanchez Erauskin, *Txiki-Otaegi: El viento y las raices* (San Sebastián: Hordago, 1978).

47 Luis C.-Nuñez Astrain, *Clases sociales en Euskadi* (San Sebastián: Editorial Txertoa, 1977), p. 209; Ortzi, *Los Vascos*, p. 234.

48 Ortzi, *Los Vascos*, pp. 232–33, 235–36.

49 "Una meta: Euskadi socialista," *Punto y hora*, no. 19 (January 1–15, 1977):30–32; *Documentos*, 17:482–85.

Chapter Four

1 There is a small but growing literature in English on the transformation of the Spanish state after Franco's death. The principal works include

Raymond Carr and Juan Pablo Fusi Aizpurua, *Spain: Dictatorship to Democracy* (London: Allen & Unwin, 1979); and John Coverdale, *The Political Transformation of Spain after Franco* (New York: Praeger, 1979). For a review of the various approaches to the transformation, see Cyrus Ernesto Zirakzadeh, "The Puzzling 'Transformation' of the Spanish State" (Paper delivered to the Conference of Europeanists, Washington, D.C. 1982).

2 For more details on the issue of amnesty, see Robert P. Clark, *The Basques: The Franco Years and Beyond* (Reno: University of Nevada Press, 1979), chap. 10.

3 For details of the institutional transformations leading to the 1977 parliamentary elections, see Clark, chap. 11 and accompanying notes.

4 A survey reported by the Spanish newsmagazine *Cambio 16* in December 1976 showed considerable dissatisfaction with the reforms of the Suárez government in the Basque provinces. In Euzkadi, 35 percent said they were more satisfied with Suárez than they had been several months earlier, compared to 52 percent nationwide. Only 28 percent of the Basque respondents said that they would vote for him, compared to 49 percent across Spain generally. *Cambio 16*, no. 261 (December 12, 1976):9. In the December 1976 referendum to approve the democratic reforms proposed by Suárez, slightly less than 43 percent of all Basques abstained (including 47 percent in Vizcaya and 55 percent in Guipúzcoa), compared to 22.6 percent nationally. See Luis C.-Nuñez Astrain, *La sociedad vasca actual* (San Sebastián: Editorial Txertoa, 1977), p. 51, table 15. Finally, in the 1977 parliamentary elections, Premier Suárez's party, UCD, won only about 16 percent of the votes cast in the Basque provinces, compared to 24 percent for the Basque Nationalist Party and 25 percent for the socialist PSOE. See Clark, *The Basques*, chap. 11, p. 329, table 18.

5 Mercé Ibarz, *Breu historia d'ETA, 1959–1979* (Barcelona: La Magrana, 1981), pp. 115–16.

6 *Deia*, July 15, 1980. Gabilondo, in addition to the Berazadi killing, had taken part in the assassination of a policeman in San Sebastián in 1977 and of two Guardia Civil troops in San Sebastián in 1978. According to Spanish police, he had received advanced training in both Algeria and South Yemen, the latter just several months before his death in July 1980, in an attempted ambush of a Guardia Civil convoy near San Sebastián.

7 Miguel Castells, *El mejor defensor el pueblo* (San Sebastián: Ediciones Vascas, 1978), esp. pp. 48–64.

8 Ibarz, *Breu historia*, pp. 116–17; also *La actualidad española*, no. 1,299 (November 22–28, 1976):44; and Julie Flint, "A Democracy under Threat," *New Statesman*, January 12, 1979.

9 See Angel Amigo, *"Operación Poncho": Las fugas de Segovia* (San Sebastián: Hordago, 1978).

10 *Deia*, January 22, 1982.

11 *La actualidad española*, no. 1,313 (February 28–March 6, 1977):17; no. 1,299 (November 22–28, 1976):44. See also *Documentos* (San Sebastián: Hordago, 1981), 18:49–59.

12 "Historia de EIA," *Arnasa* 6 (1980):33–57; *Congreso EIA: Resoluciones* (1979).

13 Alberto Perez Calvo, *Los partidos políticos en el país vasco* (San Sebastián: L. Haranburu, 1977); Idoia Estornes Zubizarreta, *Que son los parti-*

dos abertzales (Zarauz: Itxaropens, 1977). For a brief description of the Basque party system see Richard Gunther, Giacomo Sani, and Goldie Shabad, "Party Strategies and Mass Cleavages in the 1979 Spanish Election," (Paper delivered to the American Political Science Association, Washington, D.C., 1980), pp. 30–34.

14 Ibarz, *Breu historia,* p. 139; "Una meta: Euzkadi socialista," *Punto y hora,* no. 19 (January 1–15, 1977):30.

15 *Deia,* February 23, 1980.

16 "A por votos etarras, *Cambio 16,* no. 278 (April 10, 1977):22.

17 The debate within EE over its representation on the Basque General Council is covered in *Deia,* February 11, 12, 14, 16, 17, and 21, 1978.

18 Ibarz, *Breu historia,* pp. 138–39.

19 *La actualidad española,* no. 1,313 (February 28–March 6, 1977):18.

20 *La actualidad española,* no. 1,316 (March 21–27, 1977):25.

21 Clark, *The Basques,* p. 195.

22 *Washington Post,* May 21, 1977.

23 *Washington Post,* March 14, 1977.

24 Clark, *The Basques,* p. 291.

25 *Deia,* July 14, 1981.

26 Clark, pp. 296–98; *La actualidad española,* no. 1,330 (June 27–July 3, 1977):8–9; *Blanco y negro,* no. 3,400 (June 29–July 5, 1977):30.

27 Castells, *El mejor defensor,* pp. 82–187.

28 Ibarz, *Breu historia,* p. 122; *Documentos* 18:486.

29 *Washington Post,* October 9, 1977. My figures show ETA responsible for twenty-four killings at the same time.

30 Based on data reviewed in chapter 5 below. A total of 447 attacks were attributed to ETA during 1977. *Informaciones,* September 13, 1978.

31 A useful chronology of key events during the period June 1977–June 1982 is available in a fifth anniversary supplement published by *Deia* on June 1, 1982.

32 Excluding Navarra, of course, which was not included in the regional arrangement.

33 *Cambio 16,* no. 370 (January 7, 1979):28.

34 Based on Ibarz, *Breu historia,* pp. 123–27.

35 *Deia,* March 21, 1978.

36 I am indebted to Dr. Richard Gunther, Department of Political Science, The Ohio State University, for allowing me to use his data on political violence in Spain covering the period 1978–79. His work enabled me to fill major gaps in my own data.

37 See below, chap. 5.

38 *Deia,* October 31 and November 1 and 9, 1979.

39 See articles in *Deia,* January 29 and February 3 and 11, 1978.

40 *Deia,* February 22, 1978.

41 *Deia,* April 4 and 11, 1978.

42 *El país* (Madrid), May 17, 1978.

43 Ibarz, *Breu historia,* pp. 127–32.

44 This was the fourth such attack, according to *Deia,* February 14, 1979.

45 Robert P. Clark, "Recent Voting Trends in Spain's Basque Provinces," *Iberian Studies* 9, no. 2 (Autumn, 1980).

46 *Deia,* January 12, 1979.

47 *Deia*, March 8, 1979.
48 *Deia*, May 1, 1979.
49 *Deia*, May 19, 1979.
50 *Deia*, September 11, 1979.
51 *Deia*, May 2, 1979.
52 *Deia*, January 3 and March 7, 1979.
53 *Deia*, June 15, 1979.
54 *Deia*, June 28, 1979.
55 For a summary of these events, see *Deia*, June 22, 1980.
56 *Deia*, July 14, 1979.
57 *Deia*, August 4, 1979.
58 *Deia*, August 7, 1979.
59 *Deia*, October 31 and November 1 and 9, 1979.
60 *Deia*, November 17 and December 4, 13, and 14, 1979. The twenty-six etarras in question were all released by January 10, 1980. See *Deia*, January 11, 1980.
61 *Deia*, January 22, 1980.
62 *Deia*, February 13 and 24, 1980.
63 Vote data are taken from *Euzkadi*, no. 171 (March 13, 1980).
64 *Cambio 16*, July 20, 1980.
65 *Deia*, June 22, 1980.
66 *Deia*, July 4, 1980.
67 *Deia*, August 2, 1980.
68 *Deia*, November 1, 2, and 4, 1980.

Chapter Five

1 The primary sources for the ETA attack data set include *Deia* (Bilbao) (cited throughout as *Deia*), the *Washington Post, La actualidad española* (Madrid), *El país* (Madrid), *Cambio 16* (Madrid), *Diario vasco* (San Sebastían) (cited hereafter as *Diario vasco*), *Punto y hora* (San Sebastián), the *New York Times*, and *The Times* (London). The secondary sources include the data base developed by Richard Gunther, Department of Political Science, The Ohio State University (covering 1978 and 1979), and these books: Edward F. Mickolus, *Transnational Terrorism: A Chronology of Events, 1968–1979* (Westport, Conn.: Greenwood Press, 1980); Ortzi, *Los vascos: Síntesis de su historia* (San Sebastián: Hordago, 1978); José María Portell, *Los hombres de ETA* (Barcelona: DOPESA, 1974); Equipo Cinco, *Las víctimas del post franquismo* (Madrid: Sedmay, 1977); Javier Sanchez Erauskin, *Txiki-Otaegi: El viento y las raices* (San Sebastián: Hordago, 1978); and Miguel Castells Arteche, *El mejor defensor el pueblo* (San Sebastián: Ediciones Vascas, 1978).
2 *Diario vasco*, January 4, 1979.
3 *Washington Post*, January 3, 1981.
4 *Deia*, October 14, 1980.
5 See *Deia*, November 28, 1980, for a list of police chiefs killed.
6 For lists of armed forces personnel killed at various times by ETA, see the following: *Diario vasco*, January 4, 1979; *Deia*, May 26, 1979, and September 20, 1979.

7 A report by the deputy chief of staff of the Guardia Civil in June 1982 presented the following pattern of ETA victims from June 7, 1968, to May 1, 1982:

	Killed		Wounded		Total	
	No.	%	No.	%	No.	%
Civilians	152	43.5	273	55.5	425	50.5
Guardia Civil	103	29.5	121	24.6	224	26.6
Police	62	17.8	91	18.5	153	18.2
Military	32	9.2	7	1.4	39	4.6
Total	349		492		841	

Source: *Deia*, June 13, 1982.

The report also estimates that during the same period, 64 members of ETA died violently, including 41 killed in gun battles with police or Guardia Civil, 2 executed, 12 killed by rightist counterterrorist groups, and 9 killed in accidents of their own making (e.g., premature bomb explosions).

Chapter Six

1 As examples, see the following: Konrad Kellen, "Terrorists—What Are They Like? How Some Terrorists Describe Their World and Actions," RAND Publication N-1300-SL (Santa Monica: RAND, 1979); Herbert Hendin, "A Psychoanalyst Looks at Student Revolutionaries," *New York Times Magazine*, January 17, 1971; Bruce Mazlish, *The Revolutionary Ascetic* (New York: Basic Books, 1976); Walter Laqueur, *Terrorism* (Boston: Little, Brown, 1977); and Albert Parry, *Terrorism: From Robespierre to Arafat* (New York: Vanguard, 1976).
2 The entire list is found in Julen Agirre, *Operation Ogro*, trans. Barbara Probst Solomon (New York: Ballantine, 1975), pp. 150–58.
3 *Deia*, December 6, 1979.
4 *Deia*, July 19, 1980.
5 One methodological note on the age data: In many cases, I have the actual ages of joining ETA. In a majority, however, the age on record is that of the person at first arrest. Since most etarras have been arrested soon after joining the organization (a fact referred to in the text), there will not be much difference, if any, between the age of joining and age of first arrest. Hence my decision to use one datum as a surrogate for the other.
6 Charles A. Russell and Bowman H. Miller, "Profile of a Terrorist" (Washington: Headquarters, Office of Special Investigations, United States Air Force, August, 1977), p. 3.
7 Russell and Miller, "Profile," p. 14.
8 Beltza, *Nacionalismo vasco y clases sociales* (San Sebastián: Editorial Txertoa, 1976), p. 153.
9 José María Portell, *Los hombres de ETA* (Barcelona: DOPESA, 1974), p. 64.
10 José Mari Garmendia, *Historia de ETA*, 2 vols. (San Sebastián: L. Haranburu, 1980), 2:142.

11 This is especially unusual, given the high rate of unemployment that wracked the Basque economy during the late 1970s. From a base of almost total employment, the unemployment rate climbed to 5 percent in 1977, 11.2 percent in 1978, and 17 percent in 1979. The estimated rate on March 31, 1980, was 14.8 percent, compared with an official rate of about 10 percent throughout Spain. Guipúzcoa (with a rate of 18.6 percent in late 1979) and Vizcaya (17.2 percent) were the provinces hardest hit by the economic crisis. See, for sources, *Deia*, December 16, 1979, and February 17 and August 1, 1980.

12 The authoritative source on this subject, consulted in this analysis, is Luis Michelena, *Appelidos vascos*, 2d ed. (San Sebastián: Biblioteca Vasconga-da de los Amigos del País, 1955). In cases of doubt, I have consulted my wife, who as a Basque herself, was able to identify questionable names as Basque or non-Basque.

13 See, for example, Charlotte Crawford, "The Position of Women in a Basque Fishing Community," in William A. Douglass, Richard W. Etulain, and William H. Jacobsen, Jr., eds., *Anglo-American Contributions to Basque Studies: Essays in Honor of Jon Bilbao*, Desert Research Institute Publications on the Social Sciences no. 13 (1977), pp. 145–52.

14 Miguel Castells, *El mejor defensor el pueblo* (San Sebastián: Ediciones Vascas, 1978), p. 49.

15 Castells, *El mejor defensor*, p. 57.

16 Portell, *Los hombres*, p. 66.

17 Erik H. Erikson, *Gandhi's Truth: On the Origins of Militant Nonviolence* (New York: Norton, 1969), p. 259.

18 Castells, *El mejor defensor*, p. 50.

19 Portell, *Los hombres*, pp. 147–48.

20 *La actualidad española*, no. 1,326 (May 30–June 5, 1977):34.

21 Castells, *El mejor defensor*, p. 63.

22 Javier Sanchez Erauskin, *Txiki-Otaegi: El viento y las raices*, p. 50.

23 Much of the following is drawn from the interesting account of ETA recruiting contained in Portell, *Los hombres*, pp. 39–45.

24 The story of one such meeting is told in detail in Portell, pp. 47–61.

25 *Deia*, May 20, 1980.

26 *Deia*, November 29, 1980.

27 *Deia*, November 9, 1980.

28 *Deia*, May 1, 1979.

29 I am told reliably that in small Basque villages everyone knows who the etarras are among the young men—everyone, that is, except the Guardia Civil. As soon as a youth joins, most of his friends "know" it, at least in the limited sense that they know something important has happened to him and can guess most of the rest.

30 In contrast to members of the Basque Nationalist Party, who, even though they were active in the anti-Franco underground, still kept a family together in remarkably good order. See my treatment of this in *The Basques: The Franco Years and Beyond* (Reno, Nevada: University of Nevada Press, 1980), pp. 121–24.

31 Sanchez Erauskin, *Txiki-Otaegi*, p. 220.

Chapter Seven

1 *Cambio 16*, no. 502 (July 13, 1981):20.
2 Comparable figures in the United States, Great Britain, and Germany are typically below 5 percent. See Joseph LaPalombara, "Italy: Fragmentation, Isolation, Alienation," in Lucian W. Pye and Sidney Verba, eds., *Political Culture and Political Development* (Princeton: Princeton University Press, 1965), p. 290, n. 13.
3 Peter McDonough, with Samuel H. Barnes and Antonio Lopez Pina, "The Spanish Public and the Transition to Democracy," (Paper delivered at the American Political Science Association, Washington, D.C. 1979), p. 6, n. 8.
4 Nathan S. Caplan and Jeffrey M. Paige, "A Study of Ghetto Rioters," *Scientific American* 219, no. 2 (August 1968):15–21.
5 For a description of this matter, see *Cambio 16*, no. 502 (July 13, 1981). See also *Deia*, July 7 and 12, 1981.
6 Salustiano del Campo, Manuel Navarro, and J. Felix Tezanos, *La cuestión regional española* (Madrid: Editorial Cuadernos para el Diálogo, 1977). See esp. pp. 139, table 5.3; 175, tables 6.7, 6.8; and 174–76. The data that interest us here have been reprinted in altered form in Luis C.-Nuñez Astrain, *La sociedad vasca actual* (San Sebastián: Editorial Txertoa, 1977), pp. 180, 186. The del Campo study was based on a sample of 2,512 respondents, of whom 349 came from the Basque provinces, defined to exclude Navarra. About one-third of the sample had been born outside the province in which they were living at the time of the survey. In other words, at least one-third of the sample (and very likely more) were non-Basque.
7 *Clases sociales y aspiraciones vascas* (Bilbao: Cámara de Comercio, Industria y Navegación de Bilbao, 1979), chap. 9. For press reports of the study, see *Deia*, October 24 and 25, 1979, and March 7, 1980.
8 The two Basque government surveys, for April–May 1979 and December–January 1981–82, although unpublished, were supplied to me by Dr. Andoni Cayero of the Department of Sociology of Deusto University in Bilbao. I want to thank Dr. Cayero for his assistance.
9 This calculation and those that follow are based on the following assumptions: (1) that the total population of the Basque region in 1976 was 2,557,000; and (2) that in terms of age, the Basque population is distributed approximately as described by Amando de Miguel in *Manual de estructura social de España* (Madrid: Editorial Tecnos, 1974), p. 90, table 7, which would indicate that 63.6 percent of the population of the Basque region is above the age of nineteen. From these figures, it is relatively easy to estimate the number of persons in the general Basque population who to one degree or another support ETA.
10 del Campo and others, *La cuestión*, p. 139, table 5.3.
11 Center for Sociological Research (CIS), as reported in *Cambio 16*, no. 502 (July 13, 1981):20.
12 These data come from Juan Linz, as reported in Richard Gunther, "A Comparative Study of Regionalisms in Spain" (Paper delivered to the Society for Spanish and Portuguese Historical Studies, Toronto, Canada, 1981), p. 26. See also Richard Gunther, Giacomo Sani, and Goldie Shabad, "Party Strategies and Mass Cleavages in the 1979 Spanish Election" (Paper delivered to the American Political Science Association, Washington,

DC., 1980), p. 40; *Cambio 16*, no. 502 (July 13, 1981):20; and the Bilbao Chamber of Commerce report cited in note 7 above.

13 The Linz data, from the 1978 study as well as that of 1979 to be discussed below, are all presented in narrative form in Juan J. Linz, "The Basques in Spain: Nationalism and Political Conflict in a New Democracy," in W. Phillips Davison and Leon Gordenker, eds., *Resolving Nationality Conflicts: The Role of Public Opinion Research* (New York: Praeger, 1980), pp. 11–52, esp. 46–49.

14 See note 7 above.

15 Gunther and others, "Party Strategies," p. 45, table 10.

16 This analysis is drawn from Robert P. Clark, "Recent Voting Trends in Spain's Basque Provinces," *Iberian Studies* 9, no. 2 (Autumn, 1980). See also Robert P. Clark, "Basque Socialism at the Polls: An Analysis of Four Post-Franco Elections," (Washington, D.C.: Conference on European Studies, October, 1980); and Ramiro Cibrian, "El sistema electoral y de partidos en Euzkadi," *Papers: Revista de sociología* 14 (1980):71–97.

17 *Cambio 16*, no. 502 (July 13, 1981):20. See also Gunther and others, "Party Strategies," p. 40.

18 Linz, in Davison and Gordenker, *Nationality Conflicts*, p. 47.

19 Gunther and others, "Party Strategies," pp. 44, 45.

20 Linz, in Davison and Gordenker, *Nationality Conflicts*, pp. 47–48.

21 Goldie Shabad and Richard Gunther, "Language, Nationalism and Political Conflict in Spain" (Paper delivered to the Conference of Europeanists, Council for European Studies, Washington, D.C., 1980). p. 12, table 2.

22 Linz, in Davison and Gordenker, *Nationality Conflicts*, pp. 32, 33, tables 2.3 and 2.4.

23 del Campo and others, *La cuestión*, pp. 174–75.

24 *Deia*, October 25, 1979.

25 Gunther, "Comparative Study of Regionalisms," pp. 17, 19.

26 Gunther and others, "Party Strategies," p. 21, table 4.

27 Linz, in Davison and Gordenker, *Nationality Conflicts*, p. 38, table 2.6.

Chapter Eight

1 See, for example, Robert W. McColl, "The Insurgent State: Territorial Bases of Revolution," *Annals of the Association of American Geographers* 59, no. 4 (December 1969):613–31; Robert W. McColl, "A Political Geography of Revolution: China, Vietnam and Thailand," *Journal of Conflict Resolution* 11 no. 2 (June 1967):153–67; James K. Mitchell, "Social Violence in Northern Ireland," *Geographical Review* 69, no. 2 (April 1979):179–201; David A. Preston, "The Revolutionary Landscape of Highland Bolivia," *The Geographical Journal* 135, no. 1 (March 1969):1–16; Andrew W. Orridge and Colin H. Williams, "Autonomist Nationalism: A Theoretical Framework for Spatial Variations in Its Genesis and Development," *Political Geography Quarterly* 1, no. 1 (January 1982):19–39. See also the debate on the role of territory in the Vietnam conflict carried on in the pages of *World Politics* in these articles: E. J. Mitchell, "Inequality and Insurgency: A Statistical Study of South Vietnam," 20, no. 3 (April 1968):421–38; and Jeffrey Paige, "Inequality and Insurgency in Vietnam: A Reanalysis," 23, no. 1 (October, 1970):24–37; and the rejoinder by

Anthony J. Russo, "Economic and Social Correlates of Government Control in South Vietnam," in Ivo K. Feierabend, Rosalind L. Feierabend, and Ted Robert Gurr, eds., *Anger, Violence, and Politics: Theories and Research* (Englewood Cliffs, N.J.: Prentice-Hall, 1972), pp. 314–34.

2 For a discussion of the data base from which this analysis was drawn, see above, chap. 5, n. 1 and accompanying text.

3 For a discussion of that data base and analysis, see notes to chap. 6, and accompanying text.

4 These calculations were based on data in José Miguel de Azaola, *Vasconia y su destino, 2, Los Vascos ayer y hoy* (Madrid: Ediciones de la Revista de Occidente, 1976), esp. pp. 431, 432, 524, 572–73, 583, and 674–75.

5 For a discussion of this data base and analysis, see chap. 7, nn. 16–27 and accompanying text.

6 The region's name is also spelled Goiherri or Goyerri. It is an amalgam of two Basque words, *goi* meaning "high," "up," or "heights," and *erri* meaning "people." Rendered into English it would be, roughly, "the highlands," and the people who live there would be "highlanders." The name is obviously derived from the mountainous terrain of the area.

7 José María Portell, *Los hombres de ETA* (Barcelona: DOPESA, 1974), p. 47.

8 José Mari Garmendia, *Historia de ETA*, 2 vols. (San Sebastián: L. Haranburu, 1979), 2:142.

9 Manuel de Terán Alvarez, "País vasco," in Manuel de Terán Alvarez, Luis Sole Sabaris, and others, *Geografía regional de España* (Barcelona: Ediciones Ariel, 1968), p. 97.

10 de Terán Alvarez, p. 97.

11 de Azaola, *Los Vascos*, p. 697.

12 de Azaola, p. 720.

13 José Miguel de Azaola has pointed to this as one of the central features of the industrialization of southern and central Guipúzcoa province. See de Azaola, p. 681.

14 Miguel Castells, *El mejor defensor el pueblo* (San Sebastián: Ediciones Vascas, 1978), pp. 48–51.

15 Javier Sanchez Erauskin, *Txiki-Otaegi: El viento y las raices* (San Sebastián: Hordago, 1978), p. 201.

16 ETA is not the only social structure found in the Goierri that reflects a union of industrial and traditional values. A second such social invention is the flourishing industrial cooperative movement, which by 1980 had grown to include 87 cooperatives with more than 18,000 members. This movement is a product of Basque social and ethnic forms as they mix with the modes of industrial production. It is highly significant that the movement is concentrated in southern and central Guipúzcoa province, in the Goierri region. For additional details, see Iñaki Gorroño Areitio-Aurtena, *Experiencia cooperativa en el país vasco* (Durango: Leopoldo Zugaza, 1975), esp. pp. 43–116. See also Luis C.-Nuñez Astrain, *Clases sociales en Euskadi* (San Sebastián: Editorial Txertoa, 1977), chap. 5. For an interesting comment on the Mondragón industrial cooperative movement, see William Foote Whyte, "Social Inventions for Solving Human Problems" (the 1981 Presidential Address of the American Sociological Association). See also, Koldo San Sebastián, "La experiencia cooperativa de Mondragón," *Deia*, May 23, 1982.

Chapter Nine

1 José María Portell, *Los hombres de ETA* (Barcelona: DOPESA, 1974), p. 93.
2 Ortzi, *Historia de Euskadi: El nacionalismo vasco y ETA* (Paris: Ruedo Ibérico, 1975), p. 323. See also Portell, *Los hombres*, p. 89.
3 The following discussion is based on several contemporary news reports, including "Así es la organización interna de ETA(m) y sus dirigentes," *Deia*, May 5, 1981; "La gran redada," *Cambio 16*, no. 370 (January 7, 1979); and "Todos contra ETA," *Cambio 16*, no. 487 (March 30, 1981).
4 The following is based on an article in *Deia*, November 9, 1980, detailing the capture, composition, and operations of Comando "Besaide." Details about other comandos are found in the following issues of the newspaper: July 4, 1980 (twelve arrested in Navarra and accused of belonging to four ETA cells); May 1, 1979 (arrested, two members of a four-member cell named "Urola" that operated in the Ezquioga-Azcoitia-Legazpia area of the Goierri); November 29, 1980 (five persons arrested in Amorebieta, Vizcaya, and charged with belonging to the Comando "Kioto," which had operated in the Guernica area); and February 10, 1979 (six persons arrested in San Sebastián and Rentería, accused of belonging to two ETA cells operating in the zone between San Sebastián and the French border).
5 "La gran redada," *Cambio 16*, no. 370 (January 7, 1979):20.
6 It must be emphasized here that this account is based on several contemporary press reports (see above, n. 3), which in turn are based on Spanish police information. Many Basques believe, however, that this kind of information is essentially false or exaggerated. They believe that there are some in the Spanish government and media who have a vested interest in portraying ETA as stronger, tougher, better organized, etc., than it really is. In chapter 10, I will discuss why there should be such an interest and how it affects attempts to reach a ceasefire with ETA. Here I can only report the information I have available, with appropriate disclaimers. Without direct access to ETA I have no way to check its accuracy. *Caveat lector.*
7 It would go beyond the scope of this study to deal with major changes in ETA structure after 1981. The reader should know, however, that there were several minor changes in organizational structure, particularly in the composition of the Executive Committee, in late 1981 and early 1982. These changes do not alter in any significant way the structure that is described in these pages or that is depicted in figure 9.1. For a description of the structure of the Executive Committee in early 1982, see *ABC internacional*, February 3–9, 1982, pp. 18–19.
8 "Txomin Iturbe herido por tres policías franceses de paisano en Biarritiz," *Deia*, February 8, 1980.
9 "Refugiados: Derechos restingidos," *Punto y hora*, January 1–15, 1977, pp. 34–35.
10 "Yeu, cada vez peor," *Punto y hora*, January 1–15, 1977, pp. 33–34. See also "Porquerolles, la nueva Yeu," *La actualidad española*, no. 1,326, (May 30–June 5, 1977):35.
11 *Deia*, December 15 and 18, 1981.
12 The following is based on these press accounts: *Deia*, January 18 and 31, February 1, 2, 3, 13, 15, and 16, 1979.

13 *Deia*, June 4, 1981.
14 Miguel Castells, *El mejor defensor el pueblo* (San Sebastián: Ediciones Vascas, 1978).
15 *Blanco y negro*, no. 3,494 (April 18–24, 1979):18–19; *Deia*, May 3, 10, and 17, 1979.
16 *Deia*, February 8, 9, and 10, March 5 and 6, 1980.
17 *ABC internacional*, February 3–9, 1982, p. 18.
18 Portell, *Los hombres*, p. 96.
19 Ortzi, *Historia*, p. 353.
20 Based on press reports, including "Todos contra ETA," *Cambio 16*, no. 487 (March 30, 1981).
21 Frederick Forsyth's novel *The Dogs of War* (New York: Bantam, 1974) describes in great detail the workings of this arms traffic, and has much information about the flow of weapons into and through Spain. Although it is fictional, the book is reputed to be based on fact.
22 "El tráfico de armas para ETA(m) pasa por Bélgica," *Deia*, May 17, 1981. See also "Altos functionarios de aduanas franceses implicados en el tráfico de armas para ETA militar," *Deia*, September 30, 1981.
23 *Deia*, January 21 and 22, 1982.
24 "'Marietta,' la asesina de acero," *La actualidad española*, no. 1,310, February 7–13, 1977, pp. 20–22. Se also "A 'marietta' limpia," *Cambio 16*, February 20, 1977, p. 5.
25 For details on the operating characteristics of these weapons, see *Brassey's Infantry Weapons of the World, 1975* (London: Brassey's, 1975); and Joseph H. Smith, *Amall Arms of the World*, 10th rev. ed. (Harrisburg, Pa.: Stackpole, 1973).
26 *Deia*, February 23, April 18, and September 12, 1980.
27 *Diario vasco* (San Sebastián), May 8, 1973.
28 Julen Agirre, *Operation Ogro*, trans. Barbara Probst Solomon (New York: Ballantine, 1975), pp. 108–9. See also Portell, *Los hombres*, pp. 213–14.
29 See press reports in *Deia*, February 7 and 20, 1981.
30 These three sources of funds are only the most significant and best known. ETA has many ways of obtaining funds, including counterfeiting. We have at least one press report of such a plan, which involved ETA(m) with a criminal syndicate in a scheme to steal large quantities of the special paper used to make bank notes in order to produce counterfeit bills. The group got far enough with the plan to actually steal enough paper to make 150 to 200 million pesetas in false money, but the two groups fell out over the payment, and the criminals ended by throwing the paper in a river before ETA could get its hands on it. See "ETA(m) y delincuentes comunes, mezclados en una falsificación de doscientos millones," *Deia*, November 11, 1979.
31 Robert P. Clark, *The Basques: The Franco Years and Beyond* (Reno, Nevada: University of Nevada Press, 1980), p. 159. See also, Portell, *Los hombres*, pp. 109–10.
32 *Deia*, January 5, 1979.
33 Risks International, *Regional Risk Assessment: Europe* (Alexandria, Va.: Risks International, February, 1979), p. 39.
34 *El país*, May 13, 1978.
35 Julie Flint, "A Democracy under Threat," *New Statesman*, January 12, 1979.

36 See press reports in *Deia*, April 30 and May 1, 1980.
37 "Euzkadi: Treinta y dos secuestros 'momentáneos,'" *Deia*, February 9, 1978.
38 *Deia*, April 2, 1981.
39 *El país*, October 30, 1981.
40 "Los últimos detenidos en Vizcaya acusados de 'buzones' de ETA(m)," *Deia*, June 3, 1979.
41 Agirre, *Operation Ogro*, p. 1.
42 Portell, *Los hombres*, pp. 156–57.
43 For an interesting discussion of the structure that exists to support kidnapings, see the articles about the kidnap attempt of a UCD political leader from Galicia, Eulogio Gomez, in June 1980: "ETA(p-m) quería canjear a Eulogio Gomez por los presos de mayor condena," *Deia*, June 12, 1980; and "Descubierta una 'cárcel del pueblo' de ETA(p-m) en Vigo," *Deia*, June 13, 1980.
44 Claire Sterling, *The Terror Network* (New York: Holt, Rinehart and Winston, 1981), chap. 10. The reader of this work, incidentally, is put on notice at the very opening of the chapter of Sterling's orientation, since the chapter is titled "Terror in Basqueland." Her avoidance of the real name of the Basque homeland, Euzkadi, and her substitution of a word never used to describe the Basque country, seem to trivialize the Basque struggle, almost as if the chapter had been titled "Terror in Disneyland."
45 Portell, *Los hombres*, p. 88.
46 "ETA no está relacionada con otros grupos armados europeos," *Deia*, April 8, 1980.
47 *Deia*, May 29, 1980.
48 Sterling, *Terror Network*, p. 195. See also *Cambio 16*, no. 494 (May 18, 1981), which reports the number trained in Algeria as 144.
49 "Todos contra ETA," *Cambio 16*, no. 487 (March 30, 1981).
50 *Deia*, May 27, 1980; *Cambio 16*, no. 519 (September 11, 1981).
51 *Deia*, June 6, 1980.
52 *Deia*, January 4, 1981.
53 Gurutz Jáuregui Bereciartu, *Ideología y estrategia política de ETA: Análisis de su evolución entre 1959 y 1968* (Madrid: Siglo XXI, 1981), p. 89.
54 *Deia*, June 13, 1982; *Washington Post*, November 10, 1982.

Chapter Ten

1 This section leans heavily on Kepa Salaberri, *El proceso de Euzkadi en Burgos: El sumarísimo 31/69* (Paris: Ruedo Ibéricio, 1971), pt. 1. See also Ortzi, *Historia de Euskadi: El nacionalismo vasco y ETA* (Paris: Ruedo Ibérico, 1975), pp. 341–48; and Robert P. Clark, *The Basques: The Franco Years and Beyond* (Reno: University of Nevada Press, 1980), pp. 170–87.
2 A reference to the French underground group active during World War II, from which many of the anti-Franco underground leaders had come in the 1940s after the war was over.
3 For a discussion of the flaws in procedure permitted by military courts, see the following accounts of the more famous Burgos trials: Gisele Halimi, *El proceso de Burgos*, trans. Mercedes Rivera (Caracas: Monte Avila Editores, 1972), pp. 131–66; Salaberri, *El proceso*, pp. 134–52; and Javier

Sanchez Erauskin, *Txiki-Otaegi: El viento y las raices* (San Sebastián: Hordago, 1978), pp. 270–73.

4 Salaberri, *El proceso*, p. 254, citing a Paris newspaper.
5 José María Portell, "E.T.A.: Objetivo, la insurrección de Euzkadi," *Blanco y negro*, June 29–July 5, 1977, p. 28.
6 Portell, "E.T.A.," p. 28.
7 Mercé Ibarz, *Breu historia d'ETA* (Barcelona: La Magrana, 1980), p. 64.
8 Gurutz Jáuregui Bereciartu, *Ideología y estrategia política de ETA: Análisis de su evolución entre 1959 y 1968* (Madrid: Siglo XXI, 1981), p. 225.
9 Ortzi, *Historia*, p. 343.
10 Ortzi, p. 348.
11 Iñaki de Zabala, "Informe sobre Euzkadi" (1972, Mimeographed).
12 Julen Agirre, *Operation Ogro*, trans. Barbara Probst Solomon (New York: Ballantine, 1975), pp. 150–58.
13 José María Portell, *Los hombres de ETA* (Barcelona: DOPESA, 1974), p. 280.
14 Ibarz, *Breu historia*, p. 119.
15 *Cambio 16*, June 2, 1975.
16 *Cambio 16*, May 26, 1975.
17 The Amnesty International findings are contained in its publication *Report of an Amnesty International Mission to Spain* (London: Amnesty International, 1975).
18 Amnesty International, *Report*, p. 7. Emphasis in original.
19 Amnesty International, p. 7.
20 Clark, *The Basques*, p. 269.
21 *Washington Post*, December 31, 1976; *La actualidad española*, no. 1,304 (December 27, 1976–January 2, 1977), p. 15; and no. 1,305 (January 3–9, 1977), p. 9.
22 In November 1978, some two years after the Public Order Tribunals were abolished, ETA finally exacted its revenge on the court. An ETA assassination team shot and killed the judge who had presided over the tribunal until its abolishment in 1976. The attack was carried out on a Madrid street by two young men who escaped on motorcycles. Police later alleged that the leader of the attack against José Mateu Canovas was Juan Lorenzo Santiago Lasa Michelena "Txiquierdi," who had risen in ETA by 1981 to become the man in charge of its *comandos especiales*. See the *Washington Post*, November 17, 1978; *Cambio 16*, no. 487 (March 30, 1981).
23 Clark, *The Basques*, pp. 282–83.
24 *Washington Post*, January 27, 1977.
25 *El país*, May 21, 1978.
26 *El país*, June 29, 1978.
27 The quotations in this paragraph are from *El país*, July 1, 1978.
28 The first eleven times are listed in table 10.1. The twelfth time must refer to the steps taken in January 1977 during the Oriol and Villaescuesa kidnaping episode.
29 The following discussion is adapted from my more detailed treatment of the amnesty question in *The Basques*, chap. 10. For full documentation, the reader should consult that source.
30 *Deia*, October 19, 1979.
31 For an example of such a statement, see *Deia*, October 23, 1979.
32 *La actualidad española*, no. 1,313 (February 28–March 6, 1977), p. 18.

33 *Deia*, February 1, 1978.
34 *Deia*, February 5, 1978.
35 *Deia*, March 8, 1978.
36 *Deia*, March 23 and throughout April, 1978.
37 *El país*, June 28, 1978.
38 *El país*, June 29, 1978.
39 *Deia*, December 22, 1978.
40 *El país*, July 2, 1978.
41 *Diario vasco*, December 28, 1978.
42 *El país*, July 6, 1978.
43 *Deia*, February 14, 1979.
44 *Deia*, March 3, 1979. Martín Villa's trip to Switzerland is confirmed in an article by Mario Onaindia, "Historia de EIA," *Arnasa*, no. 6 (1980):52.
45 Ibarz, *Breu historia*, p. 113.
46 The statistical material presented in this account has been drawn from a list of all the attacks perpetrated by extreme rightists from April 1975 through mid-September 1980. The list appeared in *Deia*, September 16, 1980. It has been supplemented by my review of daily press accounts from mid-September through December 31, 1980. Thus it should be a complete listing and account of all the attacks committed by rightist groups in the Basque regions of both Spain and France.
47 *Deia*, January 22, 1982.
48 The text of these two laws can be found in Amnesty International, *Report of an Amnesty International Mission to Spain, 3–28 October 1979* (London: Amnesty International, November 1980), pp. 55–61.
49 *Deia*, October 19 and 23, 1980.
50 For details on the 1980 antiterrorist law see the following press reports: *Deia*, October 26, 30, and 31, 1980; and *Washington Post*, October 31, 1980.
51 *Deia*, January 15 and 30, 1982.
52 *Deia*, March 3, 1981.
53 *Deia*, December 18, 1981.
54 For press accounts of the removal and succeeding events, see *Diario Vasco*, December 28, 1978, and through the following two weeks. For a description of the measures taken to strengthen the prison at Nanclares de Oca, Alava, to bring the Basque prisoners back to a jail in the Basque country, see "Nanclares, la cárcel de ETA, espera la llegada de los 'polimilis,'" *Diario 16*, October 30, 1981. See also "Todos los presos de ETA(p-m) trasladados a Nanclares para finales de febrero," *Deia*, January 16, 1982.
55 *Deia*, January 8, 1982.
56 Amnesty International, *Report*. See also *Deia*, December 10, 1981. In February 1982 the Spanish Government officially rejected the Amnesty International report, saying that it was based on statements and testimony of convicted terrorists. See "El Gobierno Español rechaza el informe de Amnistía Internacional sobre torturas," *Deia*, February 13, 1982.
57 Amnesty International, *Report*, p. 20.
58 See, for details, *Deia*, November 3, 4, 6, 7, and 8, 1979.
59 See, for details, the following issues of *Deia*: December 29, 1979; February 12, March 1, March 27, April 10, May 1, June 18, June 22, June 27, July 18, and July 20, 1980.

60 International Institute for Strategic Studies, *The Military Balance, 1981–1982* (London: IISS, 1981), p. 44; *Deia*, April 17, 1980.
61 *Deia*, October 14, 1980.
62 "118 etarras a la calle," *Cambio 16*, no. 519 (November 9, 1981):40. A June 1982 report from the deputy chief of the Guardia Civil estimated the number of ETA members arrested up until May 1, 1982, at more than 3,500. See *Deia*, June 13, 1982.
63 *Deia*, March 22 and 31, 1978.
64 *El país*, July 6, 1978; *El Alcazar*, July 5, 1978.
65 *Deia*, December 27, 1978; "La gran redada," *Cambio 16*, no. 370 (January 7, 1979):18–21.
66 For details on this affair see the following press accounts in *Deia:* December 20, 1978; June 15, 1979; and June 4 and 7, 1980.
67 *Deia*, November 16, 1980.
68 *Deia*, December 21, 1978; *Cambio 16*, no. 370 (January 7, 1979).
69 See press accounts in *Deia:* January 18 and February 10 and 11, 1979.
70 See these press accounts from *Deia:* February 2, 3, 6, and 18; April 2; and May 9, 1980.
71 *Deia*, September 25, 1980.
72 *Deia*, August 3 and October 23, 1979; *Egin* (San Sebastián), October 26, 1979.
73 *Deia*, November 17 and December 4, 13, and 14, 1979.
74 *Deia*, February 24, 1980.
75 *Deia*, March 16 and 18, 1980.
76 *Deia*, March 21, 1980.
77 *Deia*, May 18 and 24, 1980.
78 *Deia*, July 4, 1980.
79 *Deia*, September 30, 1980.
80 *Deia*, September 26, 1980.
81 *Deia*, February 8, 1980.
82 *Deia*, March 5, 1981.
83 *Deia*, September 4, 1981.
84 *Deia*, March 5, 1981.
85 *Deia*, February 15, 1980.
86 *Deia*, December 31, 1980; February 13, 1981.

Index

DESIGNED BY ED FRANK PRODUCTIONS
COMPOSED BY THE NORTH CENTRAL PUBLISHING COMPANY
ST. PAUL, MINNESOTA
MANUFACTURED BY THOMSON-SHORE, INC.
DEXTER, MICHIGAN
TEXT AND DISPLAY LINES ARE SET IN CALEDONIA

Library of Congress Cataloging in Publication Data
Clark, Robert P.
The Basque insurgents.
Includes bibliographical references and index.
1. ETA—History.   2. País Vasco (Spain)—Politics and
government—20th century.   3. Insurgency—Spain—History
—20th century.   I. Title.
DP302.B53C54   1984   946'.6   83-40259
ISBN 0-299-09650-5